INDUSTRIAL RELATIONS IN INDIA

INDUSTRIAL RELATIONS
IN INDIA

CHARLES A. MYERS
SUBBIAH KANNAPPAN

ASIA PUBLISHING HOUSE

NEW YORK

First published 1958
Reprinted 1960
Second revised and enlarged Edition 1970

SBN 210. 33680.3

PRINTED IN INDIA

BY A.K. MUKERJI AT THOMSON PRESS (INDIA) LTD., FARIDABAD, HARYANA, AND PUBLISHED BY P.S. JAYASINGHE, ASIA PUBLISHING HOUSE, INC., 118 EAST 59 STREET, NEW YORK, N.Y. 10022

PREFACE TO FIRST EDITION

THE problems facing labour, management, and government in the industrial development of the Indian economy are the central concern of this book. Possibly the most significant changes in India during the next decade will be in the rural sector, where the vast majority of the Indian people still live. However, the Second Five-Year Plan which is now under way is based on the premise that *industrialization* is the keystone of any successful effort to raise living standards and achieve national stature in the twentieth century. Therefore, I make no apology for concentrating in this volume on *industrial* labour, defined broadly enough to include all types of manpower resources—including supervisory and managerial.

This is one of the "country" studies of the Inter-University Study on Labour Problems in Economic Development, financed in part by a grant from the Ford Foundation. In this larger project, the Industrial Relations Section at Massachusetts Institute of Technology has been associated with similar groups at the University of California, the University of Chicago, Harvard University and Princeton University. The broad framework developed for this project has been used in the present study.* M.I.T. has had the responsibility for the research on Indian labour problems, and this has been related to a broader study of Indian economic development and Indian elites undertaken by the Center for International Studies at M.I.T.

Initial exploratory work began on the present study in September, 1952, when Subbiah Kannappan joined me as Research Associate. Several memoranda were subsequently prepared, based on materials and data available in the United States and on interviews with a number of Indian labour, management and government officials who visited this country during 1952-54. Two M.S. theses

*See Clark Kerr, Frederick H. Harbison, John T. Dunlop and Charles A. Myers, "The Labour Problem in Economic Development," *International Labour Review,* Vol. LXXI, No. 3, March, 1955, pp. 3-15.

were completed by Indian graduate students in Industrial Management at M.I.T. under our direction : P. R. Ramakrishnan, Sloan Fellow and manager of a number of Indian companies, who wrote on "Labor legislation in India" and J.I. Mehta, now with the National Carbon Company in Calcutta, whose thesis was entitled, "Industrial Relations in Ahmedabad Textile Industry." Professor George Baldwin, then in the Industrial Relations Section at M.I.T. and also with the Center for International Studies, went to India during the last half of 1953 to study the growth of industry in Bangalore; and John C. Eddison, graduate student in Industrial Economics, was also in India on a Ford Foundation fellowship to study the development of the paper industry. Both have contributed ideas to the present volume.

In September 1954, I went to India for an intensive field study to test some of our initial tentative conclusions put forth in the earlier exploratory memorandum. Mr. Kannappan came to India at the same time, remaining for more than a year to study at first hand the Indian trade union movement through extensive interviews in the major industrial centres. My own interviews were centred largely on the management side, although I did talk with trade union leaders and government officials also. Altogether, during the five months I was in India, I had interviews (lasting from one to several hours) with 125 officials in forty-nine firms—private and public enterprises (thirteen were European or American firms)—fifteen employer association officials; twenty-four national and local union officers; twenty-five government officials in New Delhi and in state governments; fifteen college and university professors concerned with labour problems; seven members of the I.L.O. and United States government technical assistance missions; and six others. In addition, I had sixteen group discussions with mill technicians, labour officers, union leaders and management groups; and gave nearly forty speeches, largely to management and university audiences, following which there was an opportunity for discussion and exchange of ideas. Among the industrial and governmental centres I visited were Bombay, Ahmedabad, New Delhi, Calcutta, Sindri, Jamshedpur, Burnpur, Madras, Bangalore, and Coimbatore.

I am most grateful to all of these people in management, labour and government who gave unselfishly of their time to answer my questions and to give me an insight into India's industrial relations problems. This is a debt which can never be adequately acknowledged or repaid.

The first draft of this study was completed in December, 1956, long after I had returned from India; and it would not have been finished then without the help of Subbiah Kannappan, who continued as my Research Associate until he returned to India to join the staff of the Xavier Institute of Labour Relations in Jamshedpur in August, 1956. Fred Munson, formerly with Standard-Vacuum Oil Company in India, and Philip Kotler were also very helpful. Kotler completed a doctoral dissertation in Industrial Economics at M.I.T. on "Industrial Wage Policy in India" after two years of research culminating in a six months' field trip to India during 1955-56.

I am greatly indebted to some twenty persons, in India and in the United States, who were kind enough to read the first draft of the manuscript and give me the benefit of their comments and criticisms. While I am wholly responsible for errors of fact and interpretation, these have been minimized by the comments from the following, in particular : Vishnu Sahay, formerly Secretary, Ministry of Labour, Government of India; V. K. R. Menon, Director, Indian Branch of the International Labour Organization; P. C. Rao, Secretary, All-India Organization of Industrial Employers; Kamla Chowdhry, Chief, Human Relations Division, Ahmedabad Textile Industry's Research Institute; S. D. Punekar, Tata Institute of Social Sciences, Bombay; M. R. Masani and Daniel Thorner of Bombay; David Burgess, Labor Attache, American Embassy, New Delhi; Cornelius Miller, Industrial Relations Adviser, United States Technical Cooperation Mission, New Delhi; R. G. Wagenet, formerly Industrial Relations Adviser, former United States Technical Cooperation Mission, New Delhi; Van Dusen Kennedy, Institute of Industrial Relations, University of California (Berkeley); Paul Fisher, International Cooperation Administration, Washington; Jorma Kaukaunen, Office of International Labor Affairs, United States Department of Labor; Ralph James, formerly Research Associate, New York State School of Industrial and Labor Relations, Cornell University and now on the staff of the Industrial

Relations Section, M.I.T.; Hy Fish, formerly Chief of the I.L.O. Productivity Mission in India; and Wilfred Malenbaum, Helen Lamb, and George Rosen—all of the Center for International Studies at M.I.T. Subbiah and Nancy Kannappan were particularly helpful with their comments and in furnishing further data after they had returned to India in September, 1956.

This study is not intended to cover developments in detail after January 1, 1957. Although some references are made to recent developments.

During my visit in India and subsequently, Dr. Douglas Ensminger, representative of the Ford Foundation in India, gave welcome assistance and encouragement to this study. I am deeply grateful to the Ford Foundation for making the study possible, as part of the Inter-University Study; Dr Thomas H. Carroll, Vice-President of the Foundation, was especially helpful. My colleagues in the project—Clark Kerr, Frederick H. Harbison and John T. Dunlop—have made this effort one of the most stimulating that I have undertaken. John Dunlop has given me the benefit of his detailed comments on the manuscript and encouragement in its publication.

Beatrice Rogers, Rhoda Abrams and Inez Chase Zimmerman have seen the manuscript through several drafts; but most of all, my wife has borne the brunt of this effort, both in the manuscript stage and earlier when she remained behind in Geneve with the children while I was in India on the field interviews.

Cambridge, Massachusetts CHARLES A. MYERS
June 1957

FOREWORD TO SECOND IMPRESSION

BEFORE Asia Publishing House notified me in March 1959 that the first printing of the Indian edition of this book was exhausted, I had hoped that I might be able to make some revisions before the second printing. However, this is now impossible in the light of my own commitments for the next six months, and with apologies to my many friends in India, I offer this Foreword with a few comments on developments since May 1958 when the book was first published, both in India and in the United States. In fact, as I have noted in the Preface to the first printing, most of the content of the book applied to the period before January 1, 1957, although there were some references to later developments.

The reception of the book in India, indicated both by its sales and by the large number of favourable reviews in newspapers and periodicals, is a source of gratification to an author who tried to understand, as best as an outsider could, the significance of the tremendous developments which have occurred in India since Independence. The world has been watching with growing interest and increasing material support, the effort of the people of India to achieve the revised goals of the Second Five Year Plan. Present discussions of the magnitude of the Third Five Year Plan, which will determine whether India can really become a modern industrial nation, indicate that the role of industrial labour and industrial management (private or public) with which this book is concerned, will continue to grow in importance. The rate of economic growth, the level of capital formation, the level of employment and unemployment, are all closely related to problems of industrial labour and management.[1]

During two subsequent trips to India, after the main field work

1 For a careful analysis of the dimensions and problems of the Second and Third Five Year Plans, see the article by my M.I.T. colleague, Wilfred Malenbaum, "How Large the Public Sector, 1961-66?" in *Economic Weekly Tenth Annual Number* (Bombay), January 1959, pp. 199-202. See also K.N. Raj, "Resources for the Third Plan," *ibid.*, pp. 203-8.

for this book was completed, I had an opportunity to observe briefly some later developments affecting management and labour in India. At the invitation of the Ford Foundation, I spent about a month in India in January and February, 1958, in order to discuss with several Indian universities their current and prospective research in industrial relations. Then, in January 1959, I came again for a shorter period in connection with a series of seminars in seven countries with my colleagues on the Inter-University Study of Labour Problems in Industrialization (Dr. Clark Kerr, President of the University of California; Professor John T. Dunlop of Harvard University; Professor Frederick H. Harbison of Princeton University; and Dr. Thomas H. Carroll, Vice-President of the Ford Foundation). We participated in a notable three-day seminar at the Delhi University, under the sponsorship of Dr. V. K. R. V. Rao, Vice-Chancellor of the University, and had an opportunity to exchange views with distinguished Indian economists.

On both trips I was struck by the growing interest in the development of better management in Indian private and public industry. The growth of local management associations, the formation of the Indian Management Association, the establishment of the Administrative Staff College in Hyderabad, the management conferences and the research at the Ahmedabad Textile Industry's Research Association, the work of the Indian Institute of Personnel Management, and the post-graduate management courses at a number of Indian universities and technical institutes, all testify to this growing interest.[2] More recently, Prime Minister Nehru has stressed the importance of technical training in India's further economic development and of the need for training management personnel in India's public enterprises.[3] This certainly coincides with the experience of other advanced industrial nations which require all types of high-level manpower.

The Workers Education Movement, under the guidance of the Ministry of Labour and the Planning Commission, has also grown since I was first in India in 1954-55. This developed in part out of

---

[2] These developments have been summarized and evaluated in my article, "Recent Trends in Management Training," *The Indian Journal of Public Administration* (New Delhi), Vol. IV, No. 2, April-June, 1958, pp. 154-64.

[3] *The Hindu Weekly Review*, December 7, 1959, p. 2.

a visit of a Workers Education Team (composed of American, British and Swedish members) which came to India in 1957 under Ford Foundation auspices, to join with an Indian team for study of the problem and recommendations for action. The team's report has been implemented through establishment of a Workers Education Training Centre in Bombay which trains teacher-administrators for local worker education schemes to be established in a number of centres. The success of this effort will be watched with great interest, for many of the problems of Indian trade unionism which I discussed in the book spring from the lack of "inside" leadership and the illiteracy of the majority of Indian industrial workers. The teacher-administrators are, for the most part "outsiders," but it will be their challenge to help develop more and better inside leadership among Indian workers.

This challenge is great, especially among the INTUC and HMS unions, for the Communist-dominated unions in AITUC have been making inroads on the membership of the other unions. While evidence on this is difficult to document, it is widely believed in India that the Communist organizers and trade union leaders have frequently done a better job of meeting the day-to-day problems of workers than those trade union leaders who sit in offices and engage in non-trade union activities. The earlier example of the Textile Labour Association in Ahmedabad in meeting workers' problems is still not followed by most INTUC unions in other industrial centres, for a variety of reasons. The role of the Communists in one of the most important recent strikes (Tata Iron and Steel Company in Jamshedpur in May 1958) was clear, although there were apparently many reasons why this strike took place—not all attributable to Communist influence.[4]

4 For a perceptive analysis, see Morris David Morris, "Order and Disorder in the Labour Force: The Jamshedpur Crisis of 1958," *The Economic Weekly* (Bombay), November 1, 1958, pp. 1387-95. My former research associate, Dr. Subbiah Kannappan, who spent some time in Jamshedpur as Director of Research at the Xavier Labour Relations Institute, has also analysed the significance of this strike in an article "The Tata Steel Strike: Some Dilemmas of Industrial Relations in a Developing Economy," *Journal of Political Economy*, Vol. LXVII, No. 5, October 1959, pp. 489-507. While at Jamshedpur, Dr. Kannappan wrote a notable case study of the union-management relationship at the Belur works of the Indian Aluminium Company, published by the Ministry of Labour, Government of India, as *The Belur Report*, in 1958.

Another development for which there are great hopes in India is "worker participation in management." I discussed the earlier experience with works committees in Chapter VII, but the new effort developed subsequent to this writing should be noted. The Ministry of Labour sponsored a Seminar on Labour-Management Cooperation in New Delhi from January 31 to February 1, 1958, which I had the privilege of attending as a guest. There were over 100 participants representing a number of public and private enterprises which had indicated a willingness to inaugurate a new type of worker participation scheme. While I have not been able to follow this experience closely, I am hopeful that some enlightened managements and trade union leaders have made a real effort to broaden the involvement of workers in the success of the enterprise. There is danger, however, that worker expectations may be too great, that their representatives may feel that "joint management" is possible before there has been a lot more experience in joint consultation on matters of common concern at the level of welfare activities, working conditions, and production problems on the shop floor. Management is still, and always will be, an art or a skill, which can be developed by experience and by professional training on and off the job. If worker participation in management widens the knowledge and understanding of the role of management in any enterprise, whether private or public, it will be beneficial; if it hampers the efficient functioning of enlightened management (which India badly needs), it may well do more harm than good.[5]

Finally, the role of government in labour-management relations, which I discussed in Chapters VIII and IX, continues to grow. This seems inevitable in any industrially developing country which, like India, hopes to achieve a rapid rate of economic development. Should government continue to intervene in labour-dispute settlement through the compulsory adjudication system? With some

5 For a discussion of different management philosophies and attitudes, including democratic-participative management, in the context of economic development, see Frederick H. Harbison and Charles A. Myers, *Management in the Industrial World: An International Analysis*, McGraw-Hill Book Company, New York, 1959. This study is also a part of the Inter-University Project, and includes comparisons of management in a number of countries, including India.

reluctance, I concluded that it should, for the reasons discussed in the book, but I am aware that such a distinguished student of Indian labour problems as Mr. V. V. Giri, the former Central Labour Minister and author of the notable *Labour Problems in Indian Industry*, continues to argue that collective bargaining would develop on a healthier basis if compulsory adjudication could be gradually eliminated. He may well be right, and his view is shared in part by my fellow countryman and student of Indian industrial relations, Professor Van Dusen Kennedy of the University of California.[6] Nevertheless, the prospect that this will occur in the near future seems slight, especially since the issue was debated by Mr. G. L. Nanda, Minister of Labour and Minister of Planning, and Mr. Giri, at meetings of the Indian Institute of Personnel Management in New Delhi in February 1958 and later at the annual meeting of the State Labour Ministers in Nainital. On both occasions, there was apparently uniform opposition to the suggested experimentation with suspension of compulsory adjudication in a few regions.[7]

This matter is so important to industrial peace and to the development of collective bargaining on a sound basis in India that it deserves continued study and discussion, and Mr. Giri has certainly made an important contribution in continuing to keep this issue alive. My own view has not yet changed, for I believe that some government control of industrial relations is necessary in present-day India, with a divided and still relatively weak labour movement. Furthermore, a few more managements and unions are

6 See his article, "The Conceptual and Legislative Framework of Labour Relations in India," *Industrial and Labour Relations Review* (New York State School of Industrial and Labour Relations, Cornell University, Ithaca, New York), Vol. 11, No. 4, July 1958, pp. 487-505. Professor Kennedy was in India during 1959-60 as a Ford Foundation Specialist on research programmes in Industrial Relations.

7 See "Nanda-Giri Clash at Symposium on Industrial Peace," *Times of India*, February, 9, 1958, for a report of the 2 p.m. meeting. Mr. Nanda agreed to present the Giri proposal before the next Labour Ministers Conference, and it was rejected at that Conference. However, at the 17th session of the Indian Labour Conference held in Madras in July, 1959, Mr. Nanda urged labour and management to settle more disputes "without outside intervention," and the Conference subsequently favoured more recourse to mediation and voluntary arbitration and less to compulsory adjudication. *The Hindu Weekly Review*, August 3, 1959, p. 2.

learning that direct negotiations are possible and even desirable, despite the availability of compulsory adjudication. I agree that compulsory adjudication does tend to discourage the kind of collective bargaining that might emerge from a series of strikes and work stoppages that advanced industrial countries have experienced in their history, but I am not persuaded that Indian workers or the Indian nation can yet afford this type of experimentation. And a number of Indian managements with whom I have talked on recent trips, when pressed for a definite view, still believe that compulsory adjudication is the better present alternative.

These observations point to the need in India for continuing study and research on Indian Industrial Relations. It is encouraging to note that the Ministry of Labour and the Planning Commission have sponsored case studies of good industrial relations, and that a number of Indian universities have undertaken empirical studies of labour and management problems. There is need, both in the universities and in the research institutes, for further specific studies of particular problems. Research is the only sound basis for realistic public policy recommendations, and this needs to be done by Indians in India.

I would be remiss in concluding this Foreword to the second printing of my book if I did not acknowledge my indebtedness to Harvard University Press, which has published the American edition under the title *Labor Problems in the Industrialization of India* and which kindly permitted Asia Publishing House to publish a separate edition in India; to the Ford Foundation and particularly Dr. Douglas Ensminger, the Representative in India, for continued interest and support for work in industrial relations in India; and to my Indian publishers, Asia Publishing House, for their part in making my book so widely available in India. It has been a pleasure to work with them.

Cambridge, Massachusetts   CHARLES A. MYERS
January 1, 1960

PREFACE TO THE SECOND EDITION

THE exhaustion of the second printing of the first edition of this book, and the continuing interest in it in India, led the publishers to request the preparation of this second edition. The original author invited his friend and colleague, Dr. Subbiah Kannappan, now Associate Professor of Economics in the Department of Economics and Research Associate of the School of Labor and Industrial Relations at Michigan State University, to collaborate as co-author in this edition.

This revision is, by necessity, less thorough than we would have liked it to be. Neither of the authors was able to repeat the phase of extended field interviews conducted in 1954-55 for the first edition published in 1958. However, we have been materially aided on many points by the increasing number of research studies focusing on the labour problems of Indian industrialization. We have also kept in touch with developments in India through Indian newspapers, books, documents, and correspondence with friends and associates, both Indian and American. Indian visitors to the United States have also given us the benefit of their comments and impressions. Finally, we have been able to draw on our Indian experience as follows: the senior author has returned to India three times since 1954-55, for a total of perhaps three months; and the junior author was in India in 1956-58, and the summers of 1959 and 1962, on teaching and research assignments. The last of these visits was devoted to field interviews on industrial relations in the principal industrial centres and was made possible by a grant from the Dean of International Programs, Michigan State University.

In preparing this revision, we have had the assistance of two graduate students in economics at M.I.T., Malcolm Cohen and David B. Lipsky; and two graduate students at Michigan State University, V. N. Krishnan and I.C. Shah. The initial revisions of Chapters I, II, III, and VI, were under the direction of the senior author, and Mr. Cohen assisted in the preparation of the first

xv

drafts of the first three chapters. The junior author prepared, with the help of Mr. Krishnan, the drafts of Chapters IV, V, VII, VIII and IX. In the preparation of the final drafts, we have had the benefit of each other's comments as well as the valuable assistance of Mr. Krishnan. There is little change in the tone or content of the concluding chapter which, as we re-read it in the first edition, seemed, rather surprisingly, to require little revision.

We have attempted to add new material which seemed relevant, and there are a number of new sections in most of the chapters. Also, where necessary, the analysis of particular topics has been refined to incorporate the results of the most recent research. We have omitted from this edition the appendix containing labour agreements, since this was originally included in the American edition, published by the Harvard University Press. It may be assumed that Indian students are more familiar with the content of collective bargaining agreements in India, which are more readily available there.

Finally, we should like to acknowledge the competent assistance of our secretaries, Linda Thompson and Patricia Macpherson of M.I.T., and Vicky Mail and Elizabeth May at Michigan State University, in re-typing the drafts for this edition. At the Michigan State University, Eugene de Benko, International Affairs Librarian, and Martha Jane Soltow, Librarian for the School of Labour and Industrial Relations, were particularly helpful by ensuring early availability of material from the University's rapidly expanding Indian collection. Our indebtedness also extends to the publishers of the first edition, Harvard University Press, for permission to republish the book in India at that time, and to Asia Publishing House for their part in making it so widely available in India and elsewhere. The junior author's work at the Michigan State University was supported by the Dean of International Programs, School of Labor and Industrial Relations and the Department of Economics. This revision, like the first edition, has had financial support from the Inter-University Study of Labor Problems in Economic Development, under a grant from the Ford Foundation.

CHARLES A. MYERS
SUBBIAH KANNAPPAN

CONTENTS

CHAPTER I

THE DIMENSIONS OF THE PROBLEM

INDIA is in the midst of an ambitious and critically important effort to raise the living standards of her people by an integrated economic development programme. The First and the Second Five Year Plans (1951–56 and 1956–61) have already achieved many of their goals. The Third Five Year Plan (1961–66) has been formulated with long-term goals in mind extending to 1977 through the Fifth Plan. As the *Economist* has so aptly put it as long ago as 1955:

> The Indian economy today is the subject of what is, without doubt, the world's most fateful experiment. Its problems may be expressed in economic terms—in so many millions of investment, in such-and-such percentage of the national income—but the outcome is nothing less than the demonstration that under-developed economies can, or cannot, achieve progress by Western and liberal means.[1]

Economic development in India might be better described as proceeding under a "mixed" economy, for the role of the state in planning and in public investment is necessarily larger than in many Western countries in earlier periods. But there is still a place for private enterprise under the Plan, and for labour organizations and individual freedom in the labour market. The "socialistic pattern of society" approved by the Indian National Congress at its 1955 conference is, in the late Prime Minister Nehru's words, not a "doctrinaire" or "dogmatic" pattern, but one in which all sectors of the economy and society are expected to pull together to achieve more rapid economic development. As Nehru later put it, "for the first time in the history of mankind an experiment in combining rapid social and economic progress with democracy and freedom of the individual" is now being carried out in India.[2] Outstanding recent studies have commented similarly on the significance of India's development efforts.[3]

1

It is the purpose of this chapter to outline briefly the dimensions of the three Five Year Plans which are the heart of the Indian effort, and to emphasize the crucial role of industrial labour in the Plans. As we shall see, the industrial force in India is small, probably not more than 11–14 million in a total working population of about 188 million. But these 11–14 million people are very articulate through labour organizations and political parties. Urban unemployment, low wages, and industrial conditions are the sources of its unrest. Further industrialization is the challenge; additional labour problems may be the response. The interaction of industrialization on labour will concern us throughout this book.

The First Five Year Plan

When Indian independence was achieved in 1947 and a new nation was born, the tasks facing the Congress Party which had the responsibility of organizing the government were enormous. Political integration of the former "independent" princely states with the Indian Union, accomplished without bloodshed, was a major one. But the partition of India and the formation of Pakistan brought Hindu-Muslim riots, costing a million lives and uprooting 12,000,000 people, to add to the economic problems facing the new nation. Food production failed to keep pace with the rising population, prices rose steeply, and industrial disputes plagued the country. In this gloomy context, the First Five Year Plan was launched in 1951, with the major objective of raising the national income of India from Rs. 90 billion a year to Rs. 100 billion a year by 1956.[4]

About half of the total anticipated investment of Rs. 36 billion over the five years was to be in the public sector. The major programmes included (1) agriculture and community development,[5] (2) land reform, (3) irrigation and power projects, (4) industrial production, (5) transport and communication, and (6) social services. Public investment for industrial production was to be Rs. 1 billion, with Rs. 3.8 billion expected to be in the private industrial sector.[6] Government investment was rightly in those sectors which provide the basis for a more highly developed agricultural and industrial economy in the future.

The results achieved were substantial. In overall terms, the actual increase (18.6 per cent) in India's national income exceeded the goal of an 11 to 12 per cent increase over the Plan period (1951–56), as Table I indicates. Per capita income rose by only 8.2 per cent during the Plan period owing to a rapid population increase.

TABLE I

INDEX NUMBERS OF INDIA'S NATIONAL AND PER CAPITA INCOMES
IN 1948-49 PRICES

Year	Total income (1948-49 = 100)	Per capita income (1948-49 = 100)
1948-49	100.0	100.0
1949-50	102.0	100.4
1950-51	102.3	99.2
1951-52	105.2	100.3
1952-53	109.4	102.4
1953-54	116.0	106.7
1954-55	118.8	107.3
1955-56	121.2	107.3
1956-57	127.2	110.4
1957-58	125.9	107.1
1958-59	134.7	112.2
1959-60	137.1	111.9
1960-61	147.4	117.7
1961-62*	150.5	117.5
1962-63**	154.3	117.8

*Preliminary estimates.   **Quick estimates

SOURCE: *Economic Survey* 1963-64, Government of India (New Delhi, February 1964), Table 1.1.

Industrial production increased by 22 per cent between 1951 and 1955–56,[7] but the most striking gain was in food grains, with production up by 20 per cent over the Plan period as contrasted with the Plan goal of 14 per cent.[8] Agricultural production recorded a substantial increase largely due to the impact of favourable monsoon and weather conditions. Other favourable factors included the community development programmes, irrigation projects, better seeds and fertilizers, and improvements in methods of cultivation. Food imports were cut, food controls ended, and there was a slight fall in food prices until early 1956 when they began to rise again.[9]

The community development scheme deserves special mention because it is not simply a means of raising food production; it aims at a transformation of rural life in India's villages in which approximately 82 per cent of her 439 million people live. By 1963, over 5,100 development blocks covering almost the entire rural area of India had been set up.[10] Education, health and sanitation, cottage industries, housing, road building, and social welfare are included in the programme. Land reforms are related, and have involved the abolition of zamindaris and revision of tenancy regulations in order to encourage the independent cultivator.

Related schemes include multipurpose river valley projects to provide power, irrigation, flood control, and canals. Rehabilitation of the railways and domestic production of locomotives and rolling stock, as well as the construction of new national roads and repair of existing ones, were also undertaken. Social services included health schemes to control disease, expansion of elementary education, subsidized industrial housing, and resettlement of refugees from Pakistan.

Relatively speaking, the major emphasis was not put on industrial production. However, the capacity and production targets set for most of the newer industries (such as electric cables, motors and transformers, bicycles, sewing machines, drugs, and so on) and for many of the older industries (heavy chemicals, electric fans, cement, paper, matches, cotton textiles, and footwear) had already been reached by the end of the third or fourth year of the Plan. Despite the feeling of the business community that the government's attitude to private business had not been very encouraging, the index of industrial production rose at an increasing rate since the beginning of the First Five Year Plan in 1951, partly because unutilized capacity was brought into production. (See Table IX.) However, this rapid expansion in industrial production left its legacy of economic problems. Most importantly, at the end of the First Five Year Plan, prosperity in private industry as well as increased state activity resulted apparently in greatly increased imports of capital equipment, which served as a major factor precipitating the foreign exchange crisis of 1957.[11]

This expansion, however, was not sufficient to reduce the level of urban unemployment, which increased substantially during the period of the First Five Year Plan.[12] The Planning Commission estimated that, in 1956, unemployment in urban areas was 2.5 million and in rural areas 2.8 million. Originally the Planning Commission estimated a net increase in the labour force of about 2 million per year, as a result of growth in population. Thus, some 15 million jobs were estimated to be needed before 1961 to meet this problem fully. However, 11.7 million workers entered the labour force during 1956–61, 1.7 million more than the Commission's earlier estimate, placing an added burden on the already ambitious plans.[13] Yet even if 17 million new jobs were found, this would not have been a complete answer; for, in addition to unemployment, there is in India today a severe problem of underemployment.

Underemployment occurs in two situations: first, if workers are not applying themselves to their utmost capabilities; secondly, if workers are not employed full time. The first type is nearly impossible to measure, but the magnitude of the second type has been estimated. Statistics are available for the percentage of gainfully employed persons in India, reporting availability for additional work. The Planning Commission estimates this figure at 15–18 million workers.[14] The National Sample Survey reports that, in 1956–57, 15 per cent of rural, gainfully employed persons in India were underemployed in this second sense, while 11 per cent of urban, gainfully employed persons were underemployed. Over half of the underemployed persons were available for 29 or more hours of work a week.[15] The four largest cities of Calcutta, Bombay, Madras, and New Delhi had an estimated 38 per cent of their workforce unemployed or severely underemployed in the early fifties.

The First Five Year Plan thus fell far short of dealing with this central problem of employment. The Second Five Year Plan stepped up industrial production, construction, and small-scale industries and was successful in providing 8 million additional jobs, 6·5 million outside of agriculture, by 1961.[16]

The Second Five Year Plan

Most of the new jobs envisioned in the Plan were in manufacturing,

mining, construction, trade and commerce, and services, both in
the urban and in the rural areas. While there has been considerable
controversy in India over the wisdom of industrial development
as opposed to small-scale cottage or handicraft industries which
employ some 12 million people largely in rural areas, the shapers
of the Plan have decided to emphasize heavy industry as a way of
generating a dynamic industrial expansion. Some emphasis,
however, is still placed on expanding the small-scale industries
for the production of consumer goods and to provide more
employment.[17]

The changes in employment by industrial category from the
beginning of the First Plan to the end of the Second Plan are shown
in Table VIII. The biggest nonagricultural expansion in employment came in the category "other services." Factory employment
increased from 2.45 million in 1951 to 3.91 million in 1961. Employment in the basic metal industries, metal products and machinery
including electrical increased from 303,000 in 1951 to 552,000 in
1960.[18] The increase in employment in several selected industries
is shown in Table II.

TABLE II
EMPLOYMENT IN SELECTED INDUSTRIES, 1951-60

(in thousands)

Industry	1951	1956	1960
Paper and paper products	27	31	40
Printing, publishing	79	89	105
Leather, leather products	18	21	20
Rubber, rubber products	24	30	38
Chemicals, chemical products	90	104	139
Petroleum refineries	9	14	13
Cement	26	22	26
Basic metal	102	113	158
Metal industries	62	78	123
Machinery including electrical	139	176	271
Railway workshops	112	144	155
Motor vehicle manufacture	6	8	11

SOURCE: Tata Industries Private Limited, *Statistical Outline of India* 1963
(Bombay, 1963), p. 53.

Investment during the first two Plans exceeded Rs. 101 billion. Rs. 52 billion were spent in the public sector while Rs. 49 billion were spent in the private sector. Half of the outlays in the public sector were for agriculture and irrigation. A more detailed break-up of the outlays under the two Plans is contained in Tables III and IV.

TABLE III

INVESTMENT AND FINANCING OF THREE PLANS

(Rs. crores)

	First Plan actuals	Second Plan estimates	Third Plan targets
Total investment	3.360	6.750	10.400
Public sector	1.560	3.650	6.300
As percentage of total	46	54	61
Private sector	1.800	3.100*	4.100*
As percentage of total	54	46	39
Public sector outlay	1.960	4.600	7.500†
Financed by internal resources	1.772	3.510	5.300
As percentage of total	90	76	71
External assistance	188	1.090	2.200
As percentage of total	10	24	29

*Excluding transfer of Rs. 200 crores from public to private sector.
†Financial provision.

SOURCE: Tata Industries Private Limited. *Statistical Outline of India* 1963 (Bombay, 1963), p. 53.

Table IV contains a break-up of the financing of the first two Plans. To meet the needs of internal financing for the Second Plan, additional taxes (both direct and indirect) were introduced. Deficit financing was also increased to about Rs. 9.5 billion. During the First and the Second Plans, national income increased by 42 per cent while per capita income rose by about 16 per cent. The less rapid increase in per capita income was due to a decennial population growth of 21.5 per cent—one of the largest in the twentieth century. Industrial production rose by 94 per cent during the decade of the first two Plans, as measured by the index

TABLE IV
OUTLAYS UNDER THREE PLANS

(Rs. crores)

	First Plan	Second Plan		Third Plan targets	
	Actuals	Targets	Estimates	Programme outlay	Financial provision
Agriculture and community development	291	568	529 (47)	1,090 (125)	1,068 (125)
Irrigation	310	460	420 (75)	661 (18)	650 (18)
Power	260	400	445 (18)	1,020 (113)	1,012 (109)
Village and small industries	43	200	176 (103)	264 (123)	264 (123)
Organized industries and mining	74	880	900 (871)	1,882 (1,802)	1,520 (1,450)
Transport and communications	523	1,345	1,300 (1,118)	1,655 (1,370)	1,486 (1,225)
Social services and miscellaneous	459	947	830 (325)	1,527 (525)	1,300 (350)
Inventories	—	—	—	200 (200)	200 (200)
Total	1,960	4,800	4,600 (2,557)	8,299 (4,276)	7,500 (3,600)

NOTE: Combined figures of outlay by the Centre and the States (including Union Territories); the Centre's outlay also shown separately within brackets.

SOURCE: Tata Industries Private Limited, *Statistical Outline of India* 1963 (Bombay, 1963), p. 89.

of industrial production. But this index has a downward bias, owing to its exclusion of quality changes, new products and new industries.[19]

To judge the effectiveness of the Plans, one can compare the original goals with the actual results.

The initial proposals for the Second Five Year Plan included a doubling of installed power capacity during 1956–61, an increase in coal production from 38 million to 60 million tons, an increase in steel capacity from 1.3 to 4.3 million tons, a more than threefold increase in aluminium production, nearly a trebling of heavy chemicals production, an expansion of textile mill production, the building of machinery-fabricating shops, the development of a heavy electrical industry, a doubling of cement production and a fourfold increase in fertilizer output in the period 1956–61.[20]

The Third Five Year Plan

Despite the progress made by the Second Five Year Plan, national income did not grow as fast as had been hoped. The growth rate was impeded essentially by four factors: (*a*) a foreign exchange crisis, (*b*) administrative inadequacies, (*c*) a lagging export programme, and (*d*) an inadequate agricultural growth rate.[21]

The Third Five Year Plan was an attempt to correct these factors as well as to continue the long-term objectives laid down in the first two Plans. The principal targets laid down in the Third Plan to be achieved by 1975–76 were:

(*a*) attaining a cumulative rate of growth approaching six per cent per annum;
(*b*) creating nonagricultural employment for 46 million persons, of whom 10.5 million will obtain new jobs, and reducing the proportion of the population dependent on agriculture from 70 to 60 per cent;
(*c*) providing universal education up to age 14.[22]

The Third Plan was guided by the following objectives:

1. to secure an increase in national income of over 5 per cent per annum, the pattern of investment being designed also to sustain this rate of growth during subsequent Plan periods;
2. to achieve self-sufficiency in food grains and increase agricultural production to meet the requirements of industry and exports;

3. to expand basic industries like steel, chemicals industries, fuel and power and establish machine-building capacity, so that the requirements of further industrialization can be met within a period of ten years or so, mainly from the country's own resources;

4. to utilize to the fullest possible extent the manpower resources of the country and to ensure a substantial expansion in employment opportunities;

5. to establish progressively greater equality of opportunity and to bring about reduction in disparities in income and wealth and a more even distribution of economic power. [22a]

This follows the language employed in the Second Plan, the notable exception being the second objective of self-sufficiency in food which was inspired mainly by the growing adversity of the relationship between population and food production. [22b]

It is now possible to summarize the progress of the Indian economy under planning. Table V presents a statistical summary of the main achievements during the First and Second Plan periods, as well as projected targets for the Third Plan. As can be seen from the last two items in the table, the Indian economy at this stage of its development is limited in its ability to distribute the gains in output in the form of higher immediate real incomes, except for those who benefit through increased employment. The difficulty in meeting planned targets may maintain this limitation in the years ahead.

Thus, for the Third Plan, Table VI provides a progress report of how well the Plan has fared in accomplishing its principal goals. The percentage of the target goal reached is shown for each of the first three Plan years and an estimate is given for the fifth year (1965–66) from an assessment made by the Planning Commission in November 1963.

The Third Five Year Plan, as can be seen from Table VI, is not likely to achieve many of its goals. National income was expected to rise by over 5 per cent per annum for the first two years of the Plan, but the rate of growth was less than half of this goal. Industrial production was expected to grow by 11 per cent per annum, instead it actually grew by 6.5 per cent, 8.0 per cent and 10.0 per cent (estimated) for the first three years of the Plan.

TABLE V
ACHIEVEMENTS OF FIRST TWO PLANS AND PRINCIPAL TARGETS OF
THIRD PLAN

		Achievements		Targets	Percentage increase in 1965-66 over
	1950-51	1955-56	1960-61	1965-66	1960-61
Index number of agricultural production (1949-50=100)	96	117	135	176	30
Food grain production (lakh tons)	5.22	6.58	7.93	10.00	26
Nitrogenous fertilizers consumed (thousand tons of nitrogen)	55	1.05	2.30	10.00	335
Area irrigated (net total) (lakh acres)	5.15	5.62	7.00	9.00	29
Cooperative movement: advances to farmers (Rs. crores)	22.9	49.6	200	530	165
Index number of industrial production (1950-51=100)	100	139	194	329	70
PRODUCTION OF:					
Steel ingots (lakh tons)	14	17	35	92	163
Aluminium (thousand tons)	3.7	7.3	18.5	80	332
Machine tools (graded) (value in Rs. crores)	0.34	0.78	5.5	30.0	445
Sulphuric acid (thousand tons)	99	1.64	3.63	15.00	313
Petroleum products (lakh tons)	—	36	57	99	70
Mill-made (lakh yards)	372.00	510.20	512.70	580.00	13
Handloom, powerloom and khadi (lakh yards)	89.70	177.30	234.90	350.00	49
Total (lakh yards)	461.70	687.50	747.60	930.00	24
Iron ore (lakh tons)	32	43	1.07	3.00	180
Coal (lakh tons)	3.23	3.84	5.46	9.70	76
Exports (Rs. crores)	624	609	645	850	32

TABLE V (*Contd.*)

	1950-51	Achievements		Targets 1965-66	Percentage increase in 1965-66 over 1960-61
		1955-56	1960-61		
Power: installed capacity (lakh kw)	23*	34*	57	1,27	123
Railways: freight carried (lakh tons)	9,15	11,40	15,40	24,50	59
Road transport: commercial vehicles on road (thousand)	1,16	1,66	2,10	3,65	74
Shipping tonnage (lakh grt)	3.9	4.8	9.0	10.9	21
General education: students in schools (lakh)	2,35	3,13	4,35	6,39	47
Technical education: engineering and technology—degree level—intake (thousand)	4.1	5.9	13.9	19.1	37
Doctors (practising) (thousand)	56	65	70	81	16
Hospital beds (thousand)	1.13	1.25	1,86	2,40	29
Consumption level: Food (calories per capita per day)	1.800	1.950	2,100	2,300	10
Cloth (yards per capita per annum)	9.2	15.5	15.5	17.2	11

SOURCE: Adapted from *India, A Reference Annual,* 1963, Research and Reference Division, Ministry of Information and Broadcasting, Government of India (New Delhi, 1963), pp. 161-62.

There were three principal reasons for the failure of the Plan to meet its stated objectives in addition to the obvious reason that the Planning Commission was overly ambitious in its goals:

1. bad weather, which caused large setbacks in agriculture, which in turn contributed to a major slowdown in the growth of national income;

2. shortages in raw materials (power, coal, transport);
3. organizational and administrative difficulties, especially in agriculture.

The Plan did well in other areas, however. Its performance in the railroad, road development, shipping, power, education and health is now ahead of schedule.[23]

A major problem facing the Indian-planners is how to increase production in the agricultural sectors, especially food grains, to feed an exploding population. As the *New York Times* put it, "Fears are that, if something concrete is not done quickly to break the age-old pattern of recurring food shortages, India may face catastrophe."[24]

As of writing this, it is learnt that the Fourth Plan will involve a considerably enlarged outlay of Rs. 225 billion with higher allocation for agriculture and lesser for power, transport, and organized industry.[25] It has been reported that the allocation for agriculture will increase from 13.3 per cent in the Third Plan to 15.4 per cent. The distribution of expenditures has been set at Rs. 70 billion for the private and Rs. 155 billion for the public sector. The planners appear to be counting on external assistance to the tune of Rs. 25 billion. A larger public sector, greater role for the central as opposed to the state governments, and more active participation of the public

TABLE VI

ACCOMPLISHMENTS OF THE THIRD FIVE YEAR PLAN

Accomplishment	Percentage of (1965-66) *target goal reached by year*			
	1961-62	1962-63	1963-64	1965-66**
Index of agricultural production	3	—10	—	—
Food grain production	0	—8	0	—
Nitrogenous fertilizers consumed	10	19	31*	75
Major irrigation (utilization)	6	15	32*	70
Cooperative movement: advances to farmers	9	21	39*	—
Index of industrial production	10	21	36	—
Steel ingots	16	36	44	82
Aluminium (virgin metal)	2	39	54	80
Machine tools	5	19	32	78
Sulphuric acid	7	11	21	75

TABLE VI *(Contd.)*

Accomplishment	Percentage of (1965-66) target goal reached by year			
	1961-62	1962-63	1963-64	1965-66**
Petroleum products	3	19	40	—
Cloth	13	—12	100*	—
Iron ore	10	13	21	74
Coal	2	22	29	83
Exports	6	19	59	75
Power: installed capacity	6	16	30*	97
Railways: freight carried	5	23	41*	95
Road transport: commercial vehicles on the roads	—	39	—	77
Shipping tonnage	85	—	—	316
HEALTH AND EDUCATION				
Hospital beds	14	31	52	100
Doctors (practising)	38	69	88	131
General education: students in school	27	50	72*	120
Technical education: engineering and technology—degree level— admissions annually	38	64	123*	100

*Indicates figures are 1963-64 targets; other 1963-64 data (nonasterik data) are realized production, but data are still provisional.
**Indicates likely achievement as determined by the Planning Commission in November 1963.
SOURCES: Interpolated from the *Third Plan Mid-Term Appraisal,* Planning Commission, Government of India (New Delhi, November 1963); *New York Times* 2, August 1964, p. 4E; *Economic Survey* 1963-64, Government of India (New Delhi, February 1964); *Reserve Bank of India Bulletin,* Reserve Bank of India, vol. XVIII, no. 6 (June 1964); *India, A Reference Annual* 1963, Publications Division, Ministry of Information and Broadcasting, Government of India (New Delhi, 1963), pp. 159-68.

sector in producing consumer goods with a view to stabilizing prices of essentials, appear to be part of the strategy currently in favour. The key question will continue to be the effectiveness of the Plans in generating employment which we shall briefly discuss now.

Unemployment and the Population Problem

The employment goals in the Second and the Third Plans are substantially affected by the continual growth of population in India. If the rate of economic development fails to exceed the rate of population growth, unemployment will rise still further. Except for occasional famines and epidemics, there has been a steady increase since 1871, with the increase since 1921 serving as the most consistent and rapid throughout the period. Table VII gives the population growth since 1901 and the projections to 1976.

TABLE VII
INDIA'S POPULATION GROWTH

Year	Population (millions)	Average annual growth (per cent)
1901	236	
1911	252	.6
1921	251	—.03
1931	279	1.1
1941	319	1.4
1951	369	1.3
1961	439	2.1
1966*	492	2.4
1971*	555	2.6
1976*	625	2.5

*Estimates used in Third Five Year Plan. The growth rates refer to the preceding decennial or five-year period.

SOURCE: Tata Industries Private Limited. *Statistical Outline of India* 1963, pp. 10, 88.

Since 1951, population has been growing at an average annual rate between 2.0 and 2.5 per cent. Each year over 2 million new persons enter the labour force. The death rate has been falling steadily for the past three decades.[26] In the period 1941–51, the rate was 27.4/1000. During 1951–61 the rate was 18.0/1000.[27] The death rate may be expected to decline still further as incomes increase and standards of public health and sanitation improve.

It has been suggested that a rise to the "biological maximum" of 3 per cent is possible in any industrially developed country as economic development proceeds.[28] Coale and Hoover point out that a rapid increase in the number of consumers (mostly children), with the condition of unchanged fertility, would increase the amount of investment necessary in schools, housing, and so on, yet decrease the amount of funds available for investment by increasing consumption requirements. Both changes would reduce the size of the development programme. Moreover, the small per capita consumption would make the labour force less productive because of malnutrition, and because a rising consumption level is needed to combat apathy.

Rapid population growth will thus worsen the Indian dilemma so well expressed by the following contrasting statements in the tentative framework for the Second Five Year Plan. Emphasizing the need for austerity, the statement observes:

In an underdeveloped economy, where there are idle resources, increased investment need not imply reduction in current consumption. It would, however, imply austerity, that is, preparedness to hold down consumption, especially of luxuries, in the face of rising incomes.[29]

Yet the draft states earlier:

In formulating the Second Plan, emphasis must be placed on . . . bridging the gap between the haves and the have-nots and on the protection and enhancement of the well-being of the weak and unorganized sections of society. Men do not give of their best in the absence of a secure and fair share in the fruits of their labour; and achievement of social justice is a necessary condition for releasing the productive energies of the people.[30]

The cumulative effect will thus be to limit employment increase, while adding to the numbers employed. For the next fifteen years, the labour force will continue to expand rapidly regardless of the change in birth rates, but lowering of the birth-rate would permit much more expansion of the type of investment which can provide industrial employment. In a sense, the choice lies between additional factories, mines, and hydroelectric projects, or additional food, clothing, and primary schools. Reduced fertility would not reduce the supply of labour immediately, but it would increase the demand for it. The conclusion is obvious that an industrially underdeveloped and highly populous country like India needs to devote more resources to the spread of birth control measures with a view to accelerating her economic progress.[31] Some efforts at family planning were made during the First Five Year Plan, but the results were not striking. This remains a serious problem for Indian economic development, and a solution probably awaits the discovery and widespread dissemination of methods which can be adopted cheaply and simply. The Third Five Year Plan provides Rs. 270 million for family planning, a 150-fold increase since the First Five Year Plan. During the First Five Year Plan, 147 family planning clinics had been set up. At the end of January 1963, there were 8,441. Since 1956, over 1.5 million persons have been reported to have been sterilized.[32] There appear to be no basic religious or cultural objections to the use of birth control methods. The task is largely an educational one, to be undertaken on a vast scale—when inexpensive methods become available.

The Significance of the Industrial Labour Force

Industrialization and more employment in secondary and tertiary industries are, as we have seen, major goals of the Second Five Year Plan and subsequent planning. The magnitude of the task is seen in the distribution of Indian population according to working status (Table VIII). Seventy per cent of the total workers were engaged in agricultural work in 1951 (categories I and II of Table VIII). This proportion fell only slightly in 1961.

The nonagricultural labour force, however, is not exclusively, or even primarily, industrial in the modern industry sense. The other employment categories for total workers are also shown in Table VIII. The relative importance of commerce and services is clearly evident, since they accounted for over half of the total nonagricultural employment.

To obtain a realistic figure for the industrial labour force in India in 1961 (the latest census year), we must make some adjustments in the data presented in Table VIII. If we accept the total

TABLE VIII
WORKERS AND NONWORKERS OF INDIA BY BROAD INDUSTRIAL
CATEGORY

(in millions)

Category	1901	1921	1931	1951	1961
Nonworkers	128	133	158	217	250
Total workers	111	118	121	140	188
I. As cultivators	56	64	54	70	100
II. As agricultural labourers	19	21	30	28	31
III. In mining, quarrying, livestock, forestry, fishing, hunting, plantations, orchards and allied activities	5	5	6	4	5
IV. At household industry	—	—	—	—	12
V. In manufacturing other than household	13	11	11	13	8
VI. In construction	1	1	1	1	2
VII. In trade and commerce	7	7	7	7	8
VIII. In transport, storage and communications	1	1	1	2	3
IX. In other services	9	8	10	15	20

NOTE: Persons working in household industry category (IV) were included in industrial categories III and V prior to 1961, thus explaining the decrease in category V in 1961.

SOURCE: *Census of India 1961—Final Population Totals,* Paper No. 1 of 1962, Registrar General (New Delhi, 1962), p. 395.

for manufacturing other than household as 8 million, and add 600,000 employed in mines (in 1959), 1.3 million in the plantation industries (tea, coffee and rubber—1959),[33] 2 million in construction, and 3 million in transport, storage and communications (including railways, road transport, post and telegraph, etc.), the total is 14.9 million. Probably this figure is too high for the actual number employed in modern industry, since some construction, transport and storage industries are small-scale ones. Offsetting this is the fact that modern banking, insurance and trading (in the trade and commerce category) are not included, and should be We can conclude tentatively that the total is somewhere between 11 and 14 million, which represents an upward revision over the 1951 estimate made in the first edition of this book (7 million of between 57 and 100 per cent. But it should be noted that this higher total is only 7.5 per cent of the total working force, which is still predominantly agricultural, and about 25 per cent of the non-agricultural labour force. India's industrial development still has a long way to go, notwithstanding the substantial progress in modern industry over the decade 1951–61.

How can so small a proportion of the labour force of India be a crucial area for investigation and analysis? Here is where economic expansion occurs; it is the growth part of the economy. In the words of the late Prime Minister Nehru: "The alternative [to industrialization] is to remain a backward, underdeveloped, poverty-stricken and weak country. We cannot even retain our freedom without industrial growth...."[34] Furthermore, here is where discontents and dissatisfactions arising from industrialization tend to be centred. The rural agricultural labour force, and even much of the nonagricultural group, are scattered and diffuse; the urban industrial labour force is concentrated and easier to organize. Trade union activity, the focus of the protest against the consequences of industrialization for the urban worker, is centred on the industrial labour force, and especially on key industries such as coal, transportation, docks, textiles, and engineering. In 1959-60, 3.9 million members belonged to unions submitting returns under the Indian Trade Unions Act.[35] These members are highly vocal and bring pressures both on employers and on government. It is also important to note that the industrial worker reflects a more selective segment of the Indian labour force—in terms of literacy, training and skills. Also, since industrial workers in the modern wage-earning sector are typically the main bread-winners for their families, the population dependent on them is several times the 11 to 14 million employees. Taking into account their dependants, the 50 to 60 millions involved obviously constitute an important segment of the population and the electorate.

The government, in turn, has devoted considerable attention through labour legislation and dispute settlement machinery to the aspirations and grievances of industrial workers. The labour and personnel policies of private and public enterprises are designed (with varying success) to develop a stable industrial work force and to deal with the agencies which seek to represent it. Division within the labour movement is at once a source of weakness which employers can exploit, and a cause of many problems which plague both the employers and the government.

Finally, unemployment in the urban labour force is more visible and more threatening, because of the agencies of protest. This was well expressed by T.T. Krishnamachari (a key minister in several Indian cabinets), commenting on the problem of urban unemployment:

> We have a legacy of the past. We were functioning under a social structure where unemployment never came to the surface in villages. In a joint family system nobody knew who was unemployed.
>
> Unemployment is an industrial concept and a concept of urban civilization. Educated unemployment and industrial unemployment come to the surface. It is difficult to evaluate disguised unemployment. Unless the country is fully industrialized there cannot be full employment.[36]

Trends in Industrial Wage Levels [37]

Unemployment and low wages are two of the most important sources of discontent and protest in the Indian industrial labour force. The demand for a "living wage" is, as we shall see, a principal objective of the trade unions; and the pressure for increases in existing wage levels constitutes a problem for economic development planning. How much of the increase in national income should go to industrial wage earners in the form of higher wages, and how much to agriculturists, businessmen and other claimants? Will money-wage increases come at the expense of industrial profits, and, if so, will this curtail the capital formation necessary for economic development according to the Plan?

The answers to these questions are enormously difficult, and the Planning Commission has suggested only general guidelines in the several Five Year Plans.[38] The First Plan maintained that wage increases should be avoided if they threatened to lead to price increases, since price stability was a paramount objective following a period of wartime and postwar inflation. But, subject to this condition, wage increases might be granted under the following conditions:[39]

1. to remove anomalies or the existing rates which were abnormally low;
2. to restore the prewar real wage, as a first step towards the living wage,[40] through increased productivity resulting from rationalization and the renewal or modernization of the plant.

The Second Plan sounded more positive, favouring rising real wages to the extent that they were accompanied by increased productivity. The employment consequences of wage increases are mentioned, but discussed inconclusively. Apart from the general nature of these pronouncements which have been interpreted in varying ways by wage-fixing authorities at the different levels of the economy, a number of independent factors have been at work in practice. These are, apart from the increasing numbers seeking wage employment in the cities, the availability of wage goods (mainly food), and the rate and direction of industrial development as well as the associated increases in urban employment. In overall terms, the index of real earnings has remained stable except for the war years and towards the end of the First Five Year Plan when food prices went down sharply. This is consistent with the general predictions derived from the "unlimited labour supply" hypothesis. However, there have been sharp increases in particular industries and the relative ranking of industry wage levels have changed. The overall stability is also consistent with increases in real terms for all workers employed in industry. Pending a more definitive analysis of wage trends in the Indian economy (and, one may add, the availability of more refined data), we can only summarize the major features of wage movements.

The prewar real wage level declined sharply during the Second World War. Table IX compares the trends in cost of living, money and real earnings, employment, production, and productivity.

During the war, the level of prices took a sharp upward turn as a result of pronounced shortages in goods aggravated by hoarding and large increases in the money supply. Profits also rose to peak

levels. Both of these developments led to widespread industrial
unrest. Although wage increases were granted, they barely kept
pace with the rise in prices. By 1954, workers' real earnings had
fallen to 67 per cent of the prewar level. In 1945, approximately
4.1 million man-days were reported lost as a result of industrial
disputes, and this rose sharply to 12.7 million in 1946 and 16.6
million in 1947.[41] This latter figure is well below one per cent of the
man-days worked in industries from which reports were received.[42]
During the period 1946–49, the industrial tribunals granted large
wage increases to industrial workers involved in labour disputes.
Money earnings rose faster than the cost of living. Productivity, on
the other hand, showed no signs of improving.

With the start of the Korean War in June 1950, prices and profits
both rose, and productivity began a steady upward climb. Money
earnings continued to rise faster than the cost of living. By 1952,
real earnings had recovered, on an all-India basis, to their prewar
level.[43] Since then they have been marked by only minor fluctuations.

TABLE IX

ALL-INDIA INDEX NUMBERS OF COST OF LIVING, MONEY AND REAL
EARNINGS, EMPLOYMENT, PRODUCTION AND PRODUCTIVITY, 1939-64
(1939 = 100)

Year	Cost of living	Money earnings[1]	Real earnings[2]	Employ- ment[3]	Produc- tion[3]	Produc- tivity[4]
1939	100	100	100	100	100	100
1940	97	105	109	104	108	104
1941	107	111	104	121	114	95
1942	145	129	89	125	107	85
1943	268	180	67	133	112	84
1944	269	202	75	134	116	86
1945	269	201	75	141	112	79
1946	285	209	73	138	103	75
1947	323	253	78	137	99	72
1948	360	304	84	141	112	79
1949	371	340	92	143	108	76
1950	371	334	90	136	107	79
1951	387	357	92	136	120	89

TABLE IX *(Contd.)*

Year	Cost of living	Money earnings[1]	Real earnings[2]	Employ- ment[3]	Produc- tion[3]	Produc tivity
1952	379	386	102	137	133	97
1953	385	385	100	133	141	106
1954	371	381	103	136	156	113
1955	352	403	114	138	168	123
1956	387	411	106	151	184	122
1957	408	431	106	156	184	121
1958	427	424	99	158	193	122
1959	446	434	96	160	210	131
1960	456	464	102	166	235	141
1961	464	468	101	172	250	145
1962	481	—	—	—	269	—
1963	485	—	—	—	295	—
1964	—	—	—	—	315*	—

*Based on first two months of 1964 seasonally adjusted.

1 "Trend in the Index of Real Earnings of Factory Workers in India," *Indian Labour Gazette,* vol. XIII, no. 4 (October 1955), p. 249, up to 1954. *Indian Labour Statistics* 1963, Labour Bureau, Ministry of Labour and Employment, Government of India (Delhi, 1963), p. 17 and *International Labour Office Yearbook of Labour Statistics* 1963, International Labour Office (Geneva, 1963), p. 458, up to 1963.

2 The index of real earnings is the index of money earnings divided by the index of the cost of living.

3 "Trend in the Index of Productivity of Factory Workers in India," *Indian Labour Gazette,* vol. XIII, no. 5 (November 1955), p. 325, up to 1954. Later employment data come from *Statistical Abstracts of the Indian Union,* 1961, Central Statistical Organisation, Department of Statistics, Government of India (New Delhi, 1961), p. 515; *Indian Labour Statistics,* 1963, p. 26. Later production data from *Reserve Bank of India Bulletin,* vol. X, p. 319, vol. XI, p. 391, vol. XVIII, pp. 691, 807; *Indian Labour Statistics* 1963, p. 171.

4 The index of productivity is the production index divided by the employment index.

NOTE : The reader is cautioned to check original sources for limitation of data. The time series were derived by combining, in some cases, several different indices · and therefore the series are subject to error.

The actual improvement in real earnings since the low point of 1943 has varied markedly among states and occupational groups. Table V shows how real earnings have progressed in various states between 1939 and 1954. Only the workers in Bihar had not recovered their prewar real earnings by 1954. The workers in other states, particularly Assam, Orissa, West Bengal, and Madras, were earning substantially higher wages, in real terms, than before the war. Both real and money earnings have tended to show the greatest improvement in those states paying the lowest wages in 1939, such as Madras, Orissa, and West Bengal; the higher-paying states, like Bihar and Bombay, lagged behind. As a result, the differentials in money earnings between the highest and the lowest paying states tended to narrow between 1939 and 1954.[44] Even then, the actual level of money earnings was still very low: converted into dollars, the highest figure for any state (Bihar) was about $ 25.50 per month in 1954.[45]

Since 1954, there have been substantial differences in the index of money earnings by states (Table X) in factories and in consumer prices for working class families by cities (Table XI). Money earnings in Orissa increased by 70 per cent from 1951 to 1961, contrasted with only about a 20 per cent increase in Uttar Pradesh and Delhi. The consumer price index increased by as much as 44 per cent in Madras City between 1951 and 1961, while it declined in Gauhati during the same period.

TABLE X

INDEX NUMBER OF MONEY EARNINGS OF PERSONS EMPLOYED IN FACTORIES EARNING LESS THAN RS. 200 PER MONTH BY STATES. 1952-61 ON BASE 1951=100

State	1952	1954	1956	1958	1960	1961
Assam	109.8	118.2	153.2	142.4	156.3	132.4
Bihar	118.5	120.0	104.8	110.8	125.2	131.5
Bombay*	104.8	99.9	111.4	115.4	130.6	131.5
Madhya Pradesh	95.1	106.7	111.0	129.8	—	—
Madras**	132.1	128.4	137.7	—	—	—
Orissa	112.4	106.5	114.8	126.1	156.8	169.8
Punjab	105.3	118.3	129.7	153.7	126.6	130.5
Uttar Pradesh	103.4	100.1	101.1	112.3	119.3	120.7
West Bengal	102.5	111.8	120.4	125.1	133.2	134.0
Delhi	100.0	99.8	112.2	106.2	123.3	121.4

*Includes Maharashtra and Gujarat.   **Includes Andhra Pradesh.

Source: *Indian Labour Statistics*. 1963, Labour Bureau. Ministry of Labour and Employment. Government of India. p. 40.

TABLE XI
CONSUMER PRICE INDEX FOR WORKING CLASS FAMILIES FOR
1950-61 ON BASE SHIFTED TO 1951=100 BY CITIES

State—City	1952	1954	1956	1958	1960	1961
Assam-Gauhati	101	90	87	94	94	96
Bihar-Jamshedpur	97	88	91	106	103	103
Bombay*-Bombay	102	108	106	119	127	130
Madhya Pradesh Bhopal	101	91	98	111	111	113
Madras**-Madras City	99	103	107	120	139	144
Orissa-Cuttack	89	81	86	94	103	106
Punjab-Ludhiana	90	88	90	94	100	103
Uttar Pradesh-Kanpur	98	90	95	104	105	108
West Bengal-Calcutta	98	90	95	104	105	109
Delhi-Delhi	100	97	101	105	111	118

*Includes Maharashtra and Gujarat. **Includes Andhra Pradesh.
SOURCE: *Indian Labour Statistics,* 1963, pp. 84-5.

Another characteristic of wage trends since 1939 is that the lower-paid workers received larger wage increases, in percentage terms than the higher-paid workers. "Dearness allowance" payments, to compensate for increases in the cost of living, and revisions in the "basic" wage rates ordered by government-appointed tribunals, were generally weighted in favour of the lowest-income workers. As a result, the gap between the earnings of skilled and unskilled workers narrowed. For example, fitters in the Tata Iron and Steel Company at Jamshedput had earned 3.73 times as much as the least skilled workers in 1939; by 1952, the fitters earned only 2.76 times as much.[46] For all categories of workers, the index of real earnings approached the 1939 level only in 1952.[47]

Since 1951, there have been differences in money earnings by industry as shown in Table XII. In the personal services and furniture-fixtures industries, money wages rose by less than 20 per cent while in the chemical, petroleum, coal, transport, water and sanitary service industries money wages rose by over 50 per cent.

Although the position of the industrial worker had certainly improved from the wartime low point, there was still a gap between actual money wages and the amount said to be necessary for a

TABLE XII

INDEX OF NUMBERS OF AVERAGE ANNUAL MONEY EARNINGS OF
PERSONS EMPLOYED IN FACTORIES EARNING LESS THAN RS. 200
PER MONTH BY SELECTED INDUSTRIES
1952-61 (1951=100)

Industry	1952	1954	1956	1958	1960	1961
Textiles	107.1	103.9	116.2	118.0	133.6	139.3
Furniture, fixtures	86.4	102.4	90.9	121.5	131.4	114.8
Printing, publishing	109.0	115.0	111.2	115.4	114.7	123.6
Chemicals	112.3	120.4	118.1	136.3	146.9	155.6
Petroleum cost	102.3	118.9	146.9	171.9	178.9	151.9
Basic metal	113.6	117.7	113.2	114.3	124.1	126.4
Machinery	98.9	107.5	113.8	120.1	120.2	131.3
Transport	141.6	119.0	124.6	115.0	116.7	153.5
Electricity, gas, steam	101.6	107.0	118.2	131.8	124.0	125.8
Water, sanitary services	108.5	119.8	152.4	134.8	95.7	152.0
Personal services	92.2	94.2	94.5	99.8	104.7	117.8

SOURCE: *Indian Labour Statistics*, 1963, p. 51. The source contains a more complete listing.

"living wage" or even, in many cases, for a "subsistence wage" in 1954. The Rau Court of Inquiry estimated that Rs. 35 would have supported, in 1939, a Bombay city industrial worker, his wife, and two children in their minimum requirements for food, clothing and shelter.[48] The Bombay city cost of living had risen 3.32 times by 1954, and therefore the minimum subsistence wage in 1954 prices amounted to Rs. 116 per month. While average monthly earnings of cotton textile workers probably exceeded this slightly,[49] the least skilled workers in the Bombay city cotton textile industry were earning Rs. 96.12.[50] These workers were therefore receiving only 79 per cent of what was considered a subsistence wage (or probably a little better, assuming some change in consumption patterns). In view of the fact that the Bombay city cotton textile industry pays relatively high wages, the plight of unskilled workers in other industries is even more acute.

In 1956, factory workers earning less than Rs. 200 per month earned on the average less than Rs. 50 per month in Andhra Pradesh and as high as Rs. 130 in Assam. In 1961, average wages in Andhra Pradesh rose to Rs. 90 while they declined to about Rs. 100 in

Assam. They were as high as Rs. 135 in Maharashtra in 1961. In 1956, the average factory worker earning less than Rs. 200 per month received as little as Rs. 40 in the personal services industries and as much as Rs. 140 in petroleum and coal. In 1961, these averages were Rs. 80 and Rs. 155 respectively.[51]

What is the gap between actual wages and the "living wage"? The living wage should provide the family with a certain measure of frugal comfort and security, over and above the bare essentials of food, clothing, and shelter. The "living wage" has been variously estimated; the figure of Rs. 600 per year (in 1939 prices) has often been cited.[52] In 1954 prices, the living wage would have amounted to Rs. 2000. Thus the lowest-paid cotton textile workers in Bombay city earned in 2954 only 58 per cent of this "living wage."[53] Of course, in multi-worker families, the total family income would be closer to this level. In 1958–59 prices, this would amount to Rs. 2200 (see Table XI). About 20 per cent of Bombay families had a monthly income less than this.[54]

Over 30 budget enquiries have been conducted by the Labour Bureau and state governments since 1944-45. The average size family ranged from 1.89 to 6.69 with median size of about 5.0. The number of earners per family ranged from 1.16 to 2.84; the median number was about 1.6.[55] The living standards of larger families suffer, for there can be no presumption that total family earnings increase in proportion to the number of dependants or even the number of earners.

As Palekar points out:

Increasing the per capita earnings in proportion to the average number of earners in the family assumes that the extra earners are employed in factories paying about the same wage as received by the principal earner. This may not be so in the case of many working class families. For instance, the worker may be employed in a textile factory but his wife may be working in a low-wage unorganised industry like the bidi industry or domestic service. A study of the relevant figures given in the family budget reports reveals ... as the family income increases, the number of dependants also increases, and sometimes increases in greater proportion.

A more reliable idea of the relationship between family income and needs is derived directly from the budget studies. The average income per family ranges from a low of Rs. 240 per year to a high of Rs. 1675. The median is about Rs. 840. The expenditure on food in the various studies was always greater than 50 per cent of total expenditures and always less than 80 per cent.

So long as the gap between actual earnings and a subsistence level persists in many states, there will be continued agitation for increases in money wages;[57] and this may be expected to continue afterwards with the "living wage" as the goal. These are the relevant comparisons for industrial workers and their representatives—not the "remoter" comparison between industrial wages and earnings in agriculture. The Second Enquiry on Agricultural Labour estimated the 1957 income of agricultural labour families to be about Rs. 437, with a range from Rs. 319 in Orissa to Rs. 755 in Assam.[58] Superficial considerations of equity may suggest raising the agricultural labour income relatively, or increasing industrial and agricultural employment before raising the already higher industrial wages still further. But it would be hazardous to conclude from "straight" comparisons of agricultural and industrial incomes that the latter is unduly high.[59] Further, the methods of wage determination in India are not likely to permit this type of decision. We shall examine these methods, and the role of government in wage determination, in Chapter IX.

It is widely believed that many Indian workers are in debt due mainly to inadequate incomes. Adequate data are not available, especially relating workers' assets to their debts. A helpful recent contribution is provided by Julius Rezler's case study of indebtedness among workers at the Tata Engineering and Locomotive Company, Limited (TELCO), in Jamshedpur.[60] About 70 per cent of the sample of TELCO workers were indebted. The amount of debt went as high as Rs. 3000 for one worker. One-third of the workers had debts under Rs. 400. Fifty per cent were indebted to the tune of between Rs. 400 and Rs. 2400. Nearly 2.5 per cent were indebted to an amount more than Rs. 2400. The causes of indebtedness were primarily "ceremonial." Thirty-five per cent of the debts were incurred for births, weddings and festivals. Eleven per cent were incurred to visit relatives. Illness was responsible for 20 per cent, while burials accounted for another four per cent. Domestic maintenance accounted for eleven per cent. Only one per cent of the debts were undertaken for educational purposes. Eleven per cent of them were for investment.

The median length of debt was about two years. The principal source of credit was the TELCO cooperative which lent money at 6 per cent per annum. The second source was the moneylender or *kabuli* who charged an average interest rate of 99 per cent per annum. Fellow-workers, friends, relatives and others provided the remainder of the loans.

We have stressed the numerically small but strategically critical role of industrial labour in India's economic development plans. We have seen how the First Five Year Plan concentrated on the agricultural sector and succeeded in raising food production. But urban unemployment remains a central problem. So the Third Five Year Plan is designed to step up industrialization and to provide new jobs for 14 million unemployed and new market entrants by 1966.

Several key questions suggest themselves. Will the Indian entrepreneurial and managerial system respond adequately to the accelerated industrial programmes? How have they responded to similar tasks in the past? Will industrialization proceed at such a pace and with such rapid adjustments that a stable industrial labour force will develop, fully committed to industrial discipline and an industrial way of life? To what extent has a committed industrial labour force already developed, and what part have management practices played in this development?

As industrialization imposes its requirements and disciplines more extensively, will protest against some of the harsher aspects continue—and in what direction? Or will protest take the form of seeking more of the immediate gains from industrialization? What has been the role of the organized labour movement in developing and redirecting this protest, and what has been the managerial response, both in the private and in the public sectors? Does this experience suggest anything about future trends as India enters her Fourth Five Year Plan? Finally, and perhaps most importantly, what role has the government played in managing and redirecting the protests arising from the industrial labour force?

What may it be expected to do in the future?

These are the questions to which our attention will be directed in the subsequent chapters as we consider the labour problems arising from the industrial development of India.

NOTES

1 Supplement on *India—Progress and Plan,* vol. CLXXIV, no. 5813 (22 January 1955), p. 2.

2 Speech to students at Lucknow University, 7 February 1957, reported in *Hindu Weekly Review* (11 February 1957), p. 2.

3 See John P. Lewis, *Quiet Crisis in India,* Washington, D. C., Brookings Institution, 1962, especially pp. 8-11; see also Wilfred Malenbaum, *Prospects for Indian Development,* Free Press of Glencoe, 1962, especially p. 53. Additional insights are given by Norman D. Palmer, *The Indian Political System,* Boston, Houghton Mifflin Company, 1961, pp. 168-81.

4 *First Five Year Plan,* Planning Commission, Government of India (New Delhi, 1952), p. 84. The predevaluation par value of one rupee was 21 cents.

5 Initially, American aid through the Point 4 Programme was concentrated largely on agricultural and community development programmes. See Jonathan B. Bingham, *Shri Sleeve Diplomacy : Point 4 in Action* (New York, 1953), Appendix B. pp. 244 and 257-58. See Malenbaum, *op. cit.,* for subsequent development of the community development programme. While noting the difficulties and the need for improved machinery, he observes (p. 225): "It is the most courageous programme and effort yet launched for this purpose by a poor nation under a system of popular government."

6 *First Five Year Plan,* p. 436.

7 The revised Index of Industrial Production (1951 = 100) was 121.9 for 1955. This is a more broadly based index than the Interim Index of Industrial Production (1946 = 100), but is not so helpful as the latter for considering growth since the war. The revised index is used for all interpolations since 1955. A source which gives both of these indices is *Monthly Statistics of the Production of Selected Industries of India for October* 1955, vol. VII, no. 10, Ministry of Commerce and Industry, Directorate of Industrial Statistics (Calcutta), pp. 1-27. See also *Reserve Bank of India Bulletin* (Bombay), published monthly.

8 *Second Five Year Plan,* pp. 2, 255.

9 The All India Food Index (1949 = 100) was 95 in February 1956, and 106 in June, more than an 11 per cent rise in five months. *Indian Labour Gazette,* vol. XIV, no. 2 (August 1956), p. 162. Further price rises were avoided by the agreement signed in August 1956, between the Governments of India and the United States, providing for the use of United States agricultural surpluses. *New York Times* (30 August 1956), p. 1. Commenting on the agreement, *Reserve Bank of India Bulletin* notes that "the imports envisaged under the agreement will enable the Government

to build up a sizable reserve of food grains which will assist considerably in controlling food grain and other prices during a period when large-scale development expenditure and deficit financing are contemplated." *Reserve Bank of India Bulletin,* vol. IX, no. 9 (September 1956), p. 941. The Food Index has risen steadily to about 135 in 1963. *Indian Labour Journal,* superseding *Indian Labour Gazette,* vol. V, no. 3 (March 1964), p. 261.

10 *The Third Plan Mid-Term Appraisal,* Planning Commission, Government of India (New Delhi, November 1963), p. 85.

11 SOURCE: Reserve Bank of India, *Reserve Bank of India Bulletin* (issued monthly, Bombay), vol. X, p. 319, and vol. XI, p. 391, except for 1957 which is taken from *Indiagram* (issued weekly by the Information Service of India, Washington, D.C.), 19 July 1957. p. 2. Goals for private sector investment in industry during the First Plan period were Rs. 4.63 billion gross investment, including replacement and modernization, of which Rs. 2.33 billion were to be net new investment. Actual gross investment is reported as Rs. 3.4 billion, of which 2.32 billion are net new investment. In short, the private sector met the Plan goals of growth, but not of modernization (pp. 389-90). Businessmen have felt that government actions have caused this shortfall of gross investment. A prevalent business view of the problem is summarized in these words: "It is felt that fiscal policies have been based on inadequate appreciation of the needs of private investment and have been designed to meet the demands of ever-hungry Government departments. In the fixation of price-ceilings or the bonus and other remuneration payable to labour, the Government and the Industrial Tribunals appear to have assumed an unreasonably low return on capital as fair. Ideologically based labour policies seem to have placed an undue burden on industry and/or created practical difficulties in the handling of labour relations. It is felt that the general atmosphere for industrial operations has become less and less favourable as Government control over industry became more and more detailed and nationalization of one industry after the other came to be proposed as the inevitable remedy for certain assumed evils. In view of these trends it has been commonly felt that Government actions in practice reflected a lack of sympathy for and appreciation of business operations." Decline in the number of new companies registered, and rising unemployment, suggest, however, that "the overall rate of industrial expansion has not been satisfactory. Although the Plan targets have been mostly reached, industrial expansion has not acquired momentum of a kind in which expansion in one sphere stimulates expansion in other fields." *Tata Quarterly* (April-July 1955), pp. 33, 46.

12 The average number of applicants (in thousands) on live register of the employment exchanges was as follows:

1950	331	1960	1,606
1955	692	1961	1,833
1956	759	1962	2,380
1958	1,183	1963	2,518

SOURCE: *Economic Survey* 1963-64, Government of India (New Delhi, February 1964), Table 3.1.

Employment exchange statistics measure only urban unemployment, and understate even this, since employment offices are located in large cities and, through ignorance of the service or lack of faith in it, many unemployed do not register. Passage of the Compulsory Notification of Vacancies Act, 1959, makes the bare statistics look worse since 1959 as a result of more reporting. See *Third Plan Mid-Term Appraisal*, p. 53.

13 *Third Five Year Plan*, Planning Commission, Government of India (New Delhi, 1961), p. 156.

14 *Ibid.*

15 Institute of Applied Manpower Research, *Fact Book on Manpower* (New Delhi, 1963), p. 49. Data were for 1956-57.

16 *Third Five Year Plan*, p. 156.

17 *Second Five Year Plan*, p. 115.

18 *Fact Book on Manpower*, p. 57; and Tata Industries Private Limited, *Statistical Outline of India* 1963 (Bombay, 1963), pp. 52-3.

19 *India, A Reference Annual* 1963, pp. 159-60.

20 "The basic strategy would be to increase purchasing power through investments in heavy industries in the public sector and through expenditure on health, education, and social services: and to meet the increasing demand for consumer goods by a planned supply of such goods so that there would be no undesirable inflationary pressures." The demand for consumer goods "must be met by increasing the supply of such goods as much as possible through the expansion of household or hand production. This would also quickly generate a large volume of work all over the country." *Second Five Year Plan: The Framework*, Government of India, Publications Division (New Delhi, July 1955), pp. 14-5. The final version of the Second Plan placed somewhat less emphasis on the employment-creating potential of the small scale industries. *Second Five Year Plan*, p. 59.

21 *India, A Reference Annual* 1963, p. 160.

22 *Ibid.*, p. 159; and *Third Five Year Plan*, p. 159.

22a *Third Five Year Plan*, p. 48.

22b Cf. *Second Five Year Plan*, p. 24.

23 Most of the material in the last few pages on the Third Five Year Plan comes from *Third Five Year Plan Mid-Term Appraisal*, pp. 8-10. Data for 1964 are from *Reserve Bank of India Bulletin*, vol. XVIII, no. 6 (June 1964), p. 807, and are provisional.

24 *New York Times*, 2 August 1964, p. 4E.

25 "Rs. 21,500-Crore IV Plan Approved by Cabinet," *Economic Times*, 15 October 1964; and "Public Sector Must Enter Consumer Goods Industry," *Economic Times*, 28 October 1964.

26 See N. K. Choudhry, "A Note on the Dilemma of Planning Population in India," *Economic Development and Cultural Change*, vol. IV, no. 1 (November 1955), pp. 69-71.

27 *Statistical Outline of India* 1963, p. 7.

28 Ansley J. Coale and Edgar M. Hoover, *Population Growth and Economic Development in Low-Income Countries — A Case Study of India's Prospects* (Princeton, 1958), p. 62.

29 *Second Five Year Plan: The Framework*, p. 106.

30 *Ibid.*, p. 54.

31 This applies, of course, to all industrially underdeveloped countries with large populations. A group of United Nations experts stated: "Countries cannot afford to wait on the slow cultural effects of modernization to bring their fertility and mortality rates into balance, since in the meantime their population will increase with disastrous consequences. It is therefore important that thought be given to discovering ways and means, which are consistent with the values and culture of each of the peoples concerned, of speeding up the reduction of fertility rates." United Nations, *Measures for the Economic Development of Underdeveloped Countries* (New York, 1951), p. 48.

32 *Third Five Year Plan Mid-Term Appraisal*, p. 164; The Times Publishing Co., Ltd., *India—A Survey Compiled from the Times* (London, January 1962), p. 42; *India, A Reference Annual* 1963, p. 104.

33 Data for mining and plantations are contained in *Indian Labour Statistics* 1963, Labour Bureau, Ministry of Labour and Employment, Government of India (New Delhi, 1963), p. 29, and *Statistical Abstract of the Indian Union*, 1961, Central Statistical Organization, Department of Statistics, Government of India (New Delhi, 1961), p. 564.

34 *Report to the All-India Congress Committee at Avadi* (January 1955)..

35 For a fuller discussion of trade union membership, see Chapter IV.

36 Reply to debate in Lok Sabha, as reported in *Hindustan Times* (15 and 16 April 1955).

37 Much of the following is based on the study, completed after seven months in India during 1955-56, by Philip Kotler, *Problems of Industrial Wage Policy in India* (unpublished doctoral dissertation), Department of Economics and Social Science, Massachusetts Institute of Technology, Cambridge (September 1956).

38 For a scathing criticism of the official approach, see S. A. Palekar, *Problems of Wage Policy for Economic Development*, New York, Asia Publishing House, 1962. See also Subbiah Kannappan, "Wage Policy in Economic Development," *Economic Weekly*, February 1964, pp. 287-96, which discusses some of the issues raised by Dr. Palekar.

39 *First Five Year Plan*, p. 583.

40 The concept of a "living wage" has meaning at two levels of generality. It is a part of the "socialist pattern of society," an ultimate aim of organized labour, and a rallying cry with the same degree of quantification as "a fair day's pay for a fair day's work" or other slogans of the American labour movement. But it also has been given a more precise definition in rupee figures. Such estimates necessarily differ according to the calculation of an adequate living standard.

41 *Indian Labour Gazette*, vol. XIII, no. 12 (June 1956), p. 976.

42 Reports of industrial disputes are received in general from those industries in which the labour force was estimated at about 6 to 8 million. Statistics depend in part on voluntary reports of disputes. Since both the employment base and the dispute statistics are either incomplete or rough approximations, combining them in a percentage estimate provides nothing but a very general estimate of man-days lost to man-days worked. This problem is discussed briefly in *Indian Labour Year Book*, 1953-54, p. 159.

43 A different conclusion was reached by Shreekant Palekar in his excellent study, *An Analysis of Real Wages in India*, 1939-50 (doctoral dissertation, Department of Economics, Harvard University, Cambridge, 1954, published by International Book House, Bombay, in 1958). Palekar used the wage data collected under the Payment of Wages Act, but employed a statistical method which differed in important respects from that of the Labour Bureau. His index indicated that real wages recovered to the prewar level as early as 1949. A discussion of the principal weaknesses and differences between the indices prepared by the Labour Bureau and Palekar can be found in Chapter IX of Philip Kotler, *op. cit.*

44 For further discussion, see Kotler, *op. cit.*, Chapter VI, "Inter-Regional Wage Differentials," pp. 247-60.

45 *Indian Labour Gazette*, vol. XIV, no. 2 (August 1956), p. 154.

46 Kotler, *op. cit.*, p. 284.

47 The official figures should be interpreted with some caution. For a discussion of some of the limitations of the data and implications for trend analysis, see Subbiah Kannappan, "Unions, Adjudication and Wages," *Economic Weekly*, February 1962, Annual Number, pp. 223-33.

48 *Report of the Court of Inquiry (Rau Court) Constituted under the Trade Disputes Act, 1929, to Investigate the Question of Dearness Allowance for Railway Employees*, vol. 1, *Report* (Delhi, 1941). We should note here, however, that minimum wages have seldom equalled estimated minimum family budgets in any country. .

49 Although 1954 figures are not available at the time of writing, the average monthly earnings of cotton textile workers in Bombay Province were Rs. 119, with the cost of living little different from two years later. *Indian Labour Gazette*, vol. XIII, no. 2 (August 1955), p. 85.

50 *Indian Labour Year Book*, 1953-54, p. 176. Figures are for September 1954.

51 *Indian Labour Statistics* 1963, pp. 35-7, 41-2. The Payment of Wages Act, 1936, provides that factories shall report employee earnings, but only employees earning less than Rs. 200 per month are covered by the Act. In 1958, the Act was amended to cover employees earning less than Rs. 400, hence data on factory workers earning less than Rs. 400 are available since 1958. The average annual earnings of factory workers earning less than Rs. 400 per month in 1961 ranged from a low of Rs. 760 in Rajasthan to a high of Rs. 1852 in Bihar. Workers in "processes allied to agriculture" in Assam earned an average of Rs. 191 per year while workers in products of petroleum and coal in Assam earned an average of Rs. 2734.

52 This estimate was prepared by the Bombay Textile Labour Enquiry Committee in 1940. See its *Final Report*, vol. II (Bombay, 27 July 1940; reprint, 1953).

53 For detailed estimates of the gap, as of 1950, between actual wages and subsistence wages or living wages, see Palekar, *op. cit.*, pp. 506, 525.

54 *India: A Reference Annual* 1963, p. 150. The distribution of middle class families by income (1958-59) by actual income in Bombay is :

Annual income in Rs.	Percentage of families in group
0— 900	0.2
900— 1,200	1.2
1,200— 1,800	10.8
1,800— 2,400	16.0
2,400— 3,600	27.5
3,600— 6,000	26.4
6,000— 9,000	9.5
9,000—12,000	4.0
12,000—18,000	3.2
18,000 and above	1.3

55 See *Indian Labour Statistics* 1963, pp. 80-1, for a summary of 30 budget enquiries. In 1960, budget enquiries were conducted in 50 industrial centres, but these enquiries were not available at the time of publication.

56 Shreekant A. Palekar, *Problems of Wage Policy for Economic Development* (Bombay, 1962), pp. 39-41.

57 For example, the Working Committee of the Indian National Trade Union Congress called on all affiliated unions to demand at least a 25 per cent general increase. *Indian Worker,* 26 November 1956, p. 3.

58 *Report of the Second All-India Agricultural Enquiry,* Labour Bureau, Government of India (Simla, 1960).

59 First, such differences exist in rural-urban comparisons in which the role of the government or the unions is slight. There are also differences between the rural and the urban sectors in terms of the number of earners per family, the unit of maximization, cost of living and, especially for industry, the skills and capacities of the work force. See Dipak L. Mazumdar, "Underemployment in Agriculture and the Industrial Wage Rate," *Economica,* November 1959, pp. 328-40, and Jacob Viner, *International Trade and Economic Development,* London: Oxford University Press, 1953, pp. 46-53. These points have been discussed more fully in Subbiah Kannappan, "Industry-Agriculture Wage Differentials in India: An Exploratory Memorandum," 1961, and "Labour Force Commitment in Early Stages of Industrialization," unpublished paper presented at the December 1964 meeting of the American Association for the Advancement of Science.

60 Julius Rezler, *Indebtedness Among TELCO Workers: A Case Study in Indian Labour Problems* (Jamshedpur, 1964).

CHAPTER II

THE DEVELOPMENT OF ENTREPRENEURSHIP AND INDUSTRY

INDIA'S development plans offer hope that industrial development will raise per capita real incomes from the poverty level in India and at the same time provide more employment in an economy burdened with serious unemployment and underemployment of its human resources. The success of these efforts depends not only upon the planning process and the energies which are brought to bear upon it, but also upon the present industrial capacity of India and its businessmen.

This chapter summarizes briefly the background of industrial development in India, the growth of industrial employment and capacity, and the development of the managing agency system which has given a particular slant to the way in which Indian industry has developed and is controlled.[1] Finally, we shall consider the climate for industrial development in India today, including the impact of religious and cultural factors. All of this is the necessary background for an understanding of the labour problems involved in the industrial development of India.

The Beginnings of Modern Industry

The decade 1850–60 stands out sharply in the industrial development of India as one in which the first successful jute and cotton mills were established, the coal fields were connected by rail to the port city of Calcutta, and the beginning of a rapid expansion of rail lines throughout India took place. Unlike countries moving into an industrial revolution, however, this was not the beginning of a diversified industrial growth, but both a beginning and an ending; for, not until a century later, with the coming of independence, did India again move toward an active broadening of her industrial base.[2] For a half-century following 1860, the history of industrial growth in India is the history of the growth in these four sectors. Only in 1911, with the completion of the Tata Iron and Steel Works, was there an important addition to the established industries of jute, cotton, coal, and rails.[3]

A brief review of these early developments will help to place India's current position in historical perspective. In 1854, a rail line connecting the Raniganj coal-fields with Calcutta was opened, providing for the first time economical and reliable transport from the coal-fields. Coal production rose from less than 100,000 tons annually in the 1840's to 300,000 in 1860 and 1,000,000 in 1880. Growth levelled off sharply after World War I at about 20,000,000 tons, and did not go above 25,000,000 for twenty years. The coal industry was developed initially by British capital and managerial talent, with the largest units remaining in British hands; but, by 1920, there was a noticeable shift, particularly in the smaller units, to Indian ownership and management. The managing agency method of control has been used extensively, and this has been blamed for the lack of efficiency and generally loose organization which have been typical of many units in the industry.[4]

Like coal mining, jute manufacture has been a direct result of European (in this case, Scottish) initiative. In 1854, the first factory was established and, by the end of 1862, four were in operation. Between 1869 and 1877, the number of looms had quadrupled to slightly less than 4,000. In the next twenty years, only about 6,000 new looms were added, but thereafter progress was more rapid, increasing from 15,000 looms in 1900 to 40,000 in 1920.

Jute mill owners established the Indian Jute Mills' Association in 1884 in a successful effort to regulate production already overtaking demand; and this was facilitated by the managing agency form of control described later. The jute mills have been recognized in the past as among the best and most efficiently operated factory units in the country.[5]

Alone among major developments in the industrialized sector, railroads grew as a direct result of governmental encouragement. In 1853, the first short lines out of Calcutta and Bombay were built; and Lord Dalhousie, Viceroy of India, recommended in that same year that Madras, Calcutta, Bombay and the North-East Frontier Province be connected by rail. Action was not taken until later however and, by 1900, track mileage had reached only 25,000. This rose to 40,000 miles in 1928 but has not increased since. India also lost some mileage due to the partition of the subcontinent in 1947.[6]

The railroads, in addition to serving the needs of the articulate and politically important English trading firms, both in India and in England, were planned and operated to facilitate the prompt movement of troops and military supplies to trouble spots, and food grains and other assistance to famine areas. These requirements led in some cases to commercially uneconomic trackage; and such were the costs of construction and operation that by 1900 losses to the government were over $250,000,000.[7] Daniel Thorner summarizes railboards' impact in India in the following paragraph :

> In the economic sphere the railways fostered a measure of regional specialization in both agricultural and industrial production and encouraged the bringing of more land under cultivation. The railways appear also to have helped raise the level of wages and prices and to have helped make them more nearly uniform in the subcontinent as a whole. Yet when we consider the fact that the railways have been the largest and most important enterprise of a truly modern character in India, involving heavy machinery, precision techniques, and advanced communications, we have to conclude that they have had surprisingly few *constructive* results. They helped spread a veneer of modernization over the countryside while doing little to initiate a process of genuine modernization.[8]

Advances in the cotton textile industry in the latter half of the nineteenth century were the only industrial advances which were basically the results of indigenous entrepreneurship in that period. The first mill was established in 1854 by a member of the Parsi community, already successful as a cotton merchant—a transition from cotton trading to cotton manufacture which appears to have been the most typical form of entry into the industry. Most of the early mills were built by Parsi yarn and cloth merchants already concerned with supplying the Chinese and African markets.[9] The growth of the industry was rapid, the number of mills rising from 8 in 1861 to 193 in 1900 and 271 in 1914.

Early mills were at least as interested in producing yarn for the handlooms of India and China as for their own power looms. From a ratio of approximately 100 spindles to 1 loom in the years before 1900, however, there was a rapid decline to about 50 to 1 in 1920; and the ratio has remained approximately constant since then. Even in the 1930's, handloom output accounted for 25 to 30 per cent of total cloth production, using in large part mill-produced yarn.[10] As late as 1950, this figure was 15 to 20 per cent.

The experience of the First World War provides considerable indirect evidence of the state of Indian industry during that period. With no merchant marine of her own, India was cut off in large part from European imports. As a result, there was a sharp levelling off in growth in cotton textile industry capacity (an actual decrease in spindles), in jute capacity, and in railway maintenance. This latter aggravated an already difficult situation; for prewar railway depreciation policy had been a shortsighted one. The result was an acute shortage of transport and a near breakdown of railway service. The almost complete lack of organized industry in light engineering meant a trickle of inferior replacements to industries subject to heavy wartime strains. British prewar policy in India, particularly the refusal to protect infant industry and the government policy of buying all government stores in England, had helped to create the situation.[11] But the needs of total war initiated a reversal of this trend and were in part responsible for the rapid growth of the newly formed Tata Iron and Steel Company. Yet India's World War II experience shows that surprisingly little growth in light engineering had taken place between the two world wars. Not until the outbreak of World War II were factories started for the manufacture of spinning ring frames and looms or even such simple items as pickers, bobbins, and starch, all of which were required by an industry which had been in operation since 1854.[12]

Growth of Industrial Capacity and Employment

One measure of the growth of industry is the number of joint stock companies and their paid-up capital. From Table XIII, it can be seen that the number of joint stock companies has increased more than 18-fold since the beginning of the century, while their paid-up capital has increased more than 50-fold. The increase in paid-up capital in recent years has been considerable and reflects obviously the government's policy of encouraging public and

TABLE XIII

NUMBER OF COMPANIES AT WORK AND THEIR PAID-UP CAPITAL
(1900-62)

(Paid-up capital in crores of Rs.)

Year ended the _31st March_	_Number of_ _companies_ _at work_	_Paid-up_ _capital_
1900	1,340	34.7
1920	3,668	123.2
1930	6,919	286.3
1940	11,372	303.7
1948	22,675	569.6
1950	27,558	723.9
1951	28,532	775.4
1952	29,223	855.8
1953	29,312	897.6
1954	29,492	941.2
1955	29,625	969.6
1956	29,874	1,024.2
1957	29,357	1,077.6
1958	28,280	1,306.3
1959	27,403	1,516.0
1960*	26,921	1,593.1
1961	26,108	1,725.0
1962	24,757	1,879.0

*Provisional.

SOURCE: Raj K. Nigam and N. C. Chaudhuri, _The Corporate Sector in India_, Research and Statistics Division, Department of Company Law Administration, Ministry of Commerce and Industry, Government of India (New Delhi, 1960), pp. 8-9; and _Statistical Outline of India_ 1963, Tata Industries Private Limited (Bombay, 1963), p. 57.

private, including foreign, investment. Some of these, for instance the Hindusthan Steel Company Limited, are exceptional in their size in relation to other companies in India. The recent fall in the number of companies is an attempt, in the words of the Department of the Company Law Administration, "to weed out the moribund or inactive companies from the official records."[13] Table XIV compares paid-up capital and the number of firms by selected important industrial groups.

The industrial base in India during the beginning of the twentieth

TABLE XIV

PAID-UP CAPITAL AND NUMBER OF COMPANIES BY IMPORTANT
INDUSTRIAL GROUPS

(Paid-up capital in crores of Rs.)

Important Industrial group	Number		Paid-up capital		
	1899-1900*	1955-56**	1899-1900	1955-56	1960-61 (Est.)
Tea plantations	129	600	3.3	28.5	34
Rubber plantations	24†	71	.7	4.2	5
Coal mining	34	498	1.3	28.8	29
Sugar industries	11	211	.4	31.3	40
Cotton mills	152	759	11.7	123.0	141
Jute mills	21	100	2.9	30.6	33
Paper mills	7	120	.5	16.1	23
Total	388	2,359	20.8	262.5	305
Total: All industries	1,340	29,874	34.7	1,024.2	1,725

*Figures relate to British India.
**Figures relate to Indian Union.
†Figures relate to the year 1920-21.

SOURCES: Raj K. Nigam and N. C. Chaudhuri. *The Corporate Sector in India*, Research and Statistics Division, Department of Company Law Administration, Ministry of Commerce and Industry, Government of India (New Delhi, 1963), p. 17. The 1960-61 estimates are made by applying the 1955-60 growth rates of the paid-up capital in selected industries to the 1955-56 data. The 1955-60 growth rate was computed from a survey of the paid-up capital of 1,001 companies in *Reserve Bank of India Bulletin*, vol. XVI, no. 7 (July, 1962), pp. 1160-79.

century was quite narrow as seen in the distribution of her industrial work force. Table XV presents the essential facts.

Several striking conclusions emerge from an analysis of these data. From 1850 to 1940, the construction, maintenance, and operation of the railways employed at least one man for every two employed in all branches of modern industry. And within organized industry itself, the operations of spinning and weaving in the jute and cotton sectors employed over one-third of all factory employees. Not until World War II and independence was there a substantial broadening of India's industrial base.

TABLE XV

THE GROWTH OF INDUSTRIAL EMPLOYMENT IN INDIA[a]

(in thousands)

	1899	1909	1919	1929	1939	1949	1954[c]	1961[e]
Railways	309	510	713	818[d]	709	901[d]	966	1,162
Coal mines[b]	83[f]	129[g]	190	180	227[b]	345	341	411
All mining			249	364	413[h]	519	594	671
FACTORY EMPLOYMENT (SELECTED INDUSTRIES)								
Cotton textiles	163[d]	237	280	338	499	653	661	831
Jute textiles	102[d]	204[d]	276	347	299	322	272	215
General and electrical Engineering			30	53	58	136	150	na
Railway workshops	52[i]	93	134	136	104	108	118	151
Ordnance	13[i]	15	24	22	31	84	67	na
Iron and steel	17[j]	24[j]	21	32	41	60	77	148
Chemicals			2.8	3.5	4.8	18	23	45
Total factory employment	452	786	1,171	1,553	1,751	2,434	2,590	3,912

na Not available.

a Because the definition of "factory" and the degree of coverage (both in detail and geographic area) have changed over time, the figures are only generally comparable. Figures for 1939 and before are for British India, excluding native states; 1949 and 1954 are for the Indian Union (thus excluding Pakistan). Data, unless otherwise noted, are taken from the annual *Statistical Abstracts,* relating to British India (pre-1947), and the *Statistical Abstract,* India (post-1947): no. 35, 1889-91 to 1899-1900 (1901); no. 52, 1907-08 to 1916-17 (1919); no. 56, 1911-12 to 1920-21 (1924); no. 65, 1930-31 (1933); no. 72, 1939-40 (1943); New Series, no. 1, 1949, vol. II (1950); New Series, no. 2, 1950 (1952).

b Employment in Mines: For 1890, see D. R. Gadgil, *Industrial Evolution of India* (Madras, 1924); for 1899 and 1909, see *Report of the Royal Commission on Labour in India* (June 1931), pp. 7, 8, 9, 514; for 1919, see *Indian Year Book,* 1921, Stanley Reed, ed. (Bombay, 1929), pp. 187, 354.

c Employment statistics for 1954 are published on a different basis than that used for years up to 1949, and in certain cases, particularly engineering and chemicals, the comparability of figures provided is open to doubt. Factory employment statistics are from *Indian Labour Gazette,* vol. XIII, no. 8 (February 1956), pp. 616-46; railway and mining employment from the *Indian Labour Year Book* 1953-54, pp. 5, 8; mining employment statistics are for the year 1953.

d Accounting year.　　e *Indian Labour Statistics,* 1963, Labour Bureau, Ministry of Labour and Employment, Government of India (New Delhi, 1963), pp. 14-30. f 1901-05 annual average.　　　g 1911-15 annual average.　　　h 1938. i 1905.　　　j includes brass foundries.

The war period (1939–45) was on the whole beneficial to India's industrial growth. A shortage of ocean transport, as in the earlier World War, forced a drastic reduction of imports; and India's proximity to an active theatre of war placed heavy demands on her productive capacity. Again, however, a shortage of machine-making capacity and internal transport, this time aggravated by considerable political unrest, left a disappointing record of output. Industrial production increased by only 16 per cent over the six-year war period. But with the establishment of independence at the end of the war in contrast to the experience of World War I, when war-born light engineering industry was allowed (and even encouraged) to die after the crisis passed, the new government offered substantial tariff protection and assistance to the new producers.[14] Thus the beginnings of a more diversified industrial base made during the war were nurtured in the years following it.

The contrast in the rate of growth of the older industries with those more recently established is indicative of the change taking place. From 1950 to 1961, capacity increased by less than 100 per cent in tyres, storage batteries, ball bearings, matches, soap, and sugar. Capacity doubled or tripled in electric fans, radio receivers, sewing-machines, power-driven pumps, calico looms, cement, paper and paper board, sulphuric acid and super phosphates. Finally, capacity more than quadrupled in electric motors, ring frames, bleaching powder, aluminium, caustic soda and soda ash, and viscose yarn, while capacity increased 10-fold in the manufacture of bicycles.[15]

From 1951 to 1963, the index of industrial production increased by 125 per cent. The output of jute and cotton textiles increased by less than 50 per cent. Coal production nearly doubled, while production of cement, paper, electricity, iron and basic steel tripled. Production of chemicals, sewing machines and bicycles increased by no less than 600 per cent.[16]

The changing composition of India's industrial production over the years required revision of the index of industrial production in 1951 and again in 1956. The index with the base year of 1946 had nearly 80 per cent of its weight in value added by cotton textile, jute textile, coal and steel industries, contrasted with 61 and 52 per cent in 1951 and 1956.[17]

Growth of the Public Sector

We have referred above to the change taking place within industry, the movement toward a more diversified industrial structure. Even more important are the developments of basic services which the government is undertaking directly, and without which industry could not expand. These developments, the river valley projects, railway expansion, industrial investment corporations, are all part of the "public sector," a term of growing importance in India today.

In 1947, the year of Independence, the public sector already included substantially all railroads, the post-office and telegraph system, and all ordnance factories.[18] The only government-owned factories of importance were the rail workshops (producing freight cars), Hindustan Aircraft Limited (producing trainers, bus bodies, and railway coaches), and the ordnance factories (which after the war were used to produce nonmilitary goods).

Between 1947 and 1951, the Reserve Bank of India was nationalized (formalizing the existing government control), the telephone system was centralized under a single government department, and other projects were undertaken.[19] The most important of these were the river valley power and irrigation developments, the Chittaranjan Locomotive Works, and the Sindri Fertilizers and Chemicals, Limited. Work was also begun on factories for producing machine tools, penicillin, D.D.T. (post-1951), and telephones and cables.[20] Gross assets of the central and state enterprises in 1951 were estimated at Rs. 12.4 billion (approximately $2,500,000,000). This was nearly equal to the Rs. 14.7 billion estimated as the gross assets of the private sector. However Rs. 10.7 billion of the Rs. 12.4 billion were gross assets in railways and irrigation-power projects; and of the Rs. 2 billion balance remaining, only Rs. 0.44 billion (something less than $100 million) were in publicly owned industry.[21] This was about the same as the gross assets of the Tata Iron and Steel Company at that time.[22]

Since 1951, three important units—the airlines, the Imperial Bank of India and various "state" banks, and the life insurance companies—have been nationalized, and the government has become the only builder of ocean-going ships. A railway coach factory, new units in the iron and steel industry, and several smaller projects have all been initiated since 1950. In electric supply and coal mining, there has been some movement towards nationalization, and collieries formerly run by the railroads have been placed under a separate coal authority also responsible for enforcing the governmental controls over the rest of the industry.[23]

The names of but a few government companies coming into operation since 1951 are Bharat Electronics, Indian Rare Earths, Travancore Minerals, Indian Refineries, Neyveli Lignite Corporation, National Instruments, Heavy Electricals, National Coal Development, National Mineral Development and a number of Hindustan companies such as Hindustan Machine Tools, Hindustan Steel, Hindustan Antibiotics, Hindustan Insecticides, Hindustan Housing Factory and Hindustan Shipyard.[24]

Gross fixed assets in the public sector, excluding railroads, increased by over 85 per cent from 1951 to 1958–59.[25]

Other measures are available to determine the growth of the public sector since 1951. One of these measures is total investment in organized industry by private and public sectors in three Plans.[26] The increase from Rs. .59 billion in the First Plan to Rs. 13.3 billion in the Third Plan represents better than a 22-fold increase.

TABLE XVI

(Rs. billions)

	First Plan	*Second Plan*	*Third Plan (Targets)*
Public sector	.59	7.7	13.3
Private sector	3.39	8.5	12.75

A third measure of the growth of the public sector is the position of government companies in the total corporate group, shown in Table XVIa.

A final measure of the growth of the public sector is the total investment by public and private sectors for the Second and Third Plans. Total investment in the Second Plan was Rs. 67.5 billion,

TABLE XVIa

THE POSITION OF GOVERNMENT COMPANIES IN THE CORPORATE SECTOR

(paid-up capital in billions of rupees)

Year ended the 31st of March	Total companies		Government companies		
	Number	Paid-up capital	Number	Paid-up capital	Per cent of total paid-up capital
1956	29,874	10.2	61	.7	6.8
1957	29,357	10.8	74	.7	6.4
1958	28,280	13.1	91	2.6	19.8
1959 (provisional)	27,479	15.1	103	4.2	27.8
1960 (provisional)	26,921	15.9	125	4.7	29.6

SOURCE: Raj K. Nigam and N.C. Chaudhuri, *The Corporate Sector in India,* Research and Statistics Division, Department of Company Law Administration, Ministry of Commerce and Industry, Government of India (New Delhi, 1961), p. 89.

54 per cent of which was in the public sector. The Third Plan targets project investment of Rs. 104 billion; Rs. 75 billion, or 65 per cent of this, is to be in the public sector.[27] This implies 80 per cent of expenditure in 1965–66, or by the end of the Third Five Year Plan, which John P. Lewis calls unreasonable.[28] During 1961–64, the Centre and the states made a total outlay of Rs. 42 billion. The cost of the Third Plan has been boosted due to increases in desired outlays in transport and communication, and power, requiring total government expenditure of Rs. 80 billion instead of Rs. 75 billion. This implies a boost in expected expenditures during 1964-66 of Rs. 38 billion. This is a difficult target to reach. These are the words of the Planning Commission:

It is obvious that the ability to undertake outlays of this order will depend on a variety of factors, including the performance of the economy and specifically the growth of agricultural and industrial production, rise in domestic savings, effective coordination and implementation at various levels and the extent to which external assistance becomes available. Inevitably, *there are many uncertain factors, and the tasks immediately ahead are considerably more difficult and call for greater efficiency, speed and concentration of effort than has been realized so far.*[29]

This comment was undoubtedly occasioned by some of the shortcomings of the management of public enterprises. There has not only been a "civil service mentality" in the management of such enterprises, but even able managers are handicapped by the detailed auditing and control procedures which different government ministries exercise over public enterprises. We shall consider these special problems of public enterprise management in greater detail in Chapter VI.

Role of the Managing Agency System

While we have briefly summarized above the growth of Indian industry, equally important for an understanding of industry in India today is the distinctive form of control which has developed with it—the managing agency.

As we have seen, managing agencies have been prominent in Indian industry from the beginning. Technically, they are firms which, for a fixed fee, or more commonly a percentage of profit or sales, operate the business of one or more firms for the owners. In practice, the managing agents typically dominate the firms they manage, normally through substantial ownership or control of voting rights, and thus dominate the board of directors with whom they make the agency contract. The origin of this form of business control appears to have been a severe shortage of managerial ability and venture capital in India, combined with the absence of owners in England who saw the managing agency as the best means of utilizing these scarce resources for the maximum profits. Time did not materially change the situation and, by the end of the nineteenth century, a managing agent had become a near necessity for securing loans and for general business respectability.

As in the case of the railroads, the managing agency system was useful in preserving British control and supremacy. Indian investors often preferred to put their money into firms controlled by British managing agencies; they had the advantages of business experience and competence, international connections, and the support of a generally friendly government. Table XVII shows how pervasive this control was as late as 1915.

The clearest picture of this form of business control is obtained by regarding the agency as the "firm" and the companies it controls as so many operating divisions.[30] Certainly it is true that the managing agencies have been primarily responsible for whatever

TABLE XVII
EUROPEAN CONTROL OF INDUSTRY IN 1915

Industry	Total employment (thousands)	No. of units	Total employment in European-controlled firms (thousands)	No. of units
Cotton spinning and weaving	273.5	278	56.4	34
Sugar	7.8	30	3.5	8
Jute mills	250.8	72	250.8	72
Woollen mills and carpets, etc.	11.9	23	5.2	2
Dockyards and other port trust works	12.4	9	12.4	9
Railways and tramway workshops	79.6	83	a	a
Engineering workshops and iron and brass foundries	39.4	94	22.8	b
Tile and brick	28.2	205	8.9	27
Jute presses	26.3	122	c	c
Paper	4.7	7	3.6	2
Printing presses	16.7	102	4.6	17
Rice mills	10.5	158	d	
Oil mills	4.1	152	d	
TOTAL	772.6	1,335	460 (approximate)	

a. Overwhelmingly foreign   b. Indians predominate in iron and brass foundries
c. More than half of the units were foreign   d. Negligible
SOURCE: Gokhale Institute of Politics and Economics, *Notes on the Rise of Business Communities in India,* preliminary study by staff members of Gokhale Institute. International Secretariat, Institute of Pacific Relations (New York, 1951), pp. 4-5. The study does not indicate the source from which the statistics are drawn.

industrial growth and business initiative occurred after 1850. [31] Nor is there any question that managing agencies are still the dominant form of business control wherever they are permitted to operate. Excluding banks and insurance companies (which are not permitted to have managing agencies, but are in some cases tied to agents through other means), over 95 per cent of the gross assets of public stock companies operating in Bombay in 1948 were controlled by managing agents.[32] Each major Indian industry was, to the extent of at least 70 per cent, controlled by managing agencies; and coal, cotton, and jute were over 90 per cent under agency control.[33]

The Rise of Indian Business Communities

While British control was still dominant in 1915, there was a gradual growth of Indian entrepreneurship. Perhaps an additional reason for the slowness of this growth, besides English economic and political control, was the apparent difficulty for Indians in making the move from one field of endeavour to another. Without question, the strong ties of caste and family, and the security which both provided, made a plunge into business more difficult than in the West. The first successful efforts were indeed made by the Parsis, a community which was outside the Hindu caste system, and had no traditionally fixed occupation.[34] Their contacts with Western enterprise were undoubtedly an important advantage.[35]

These early Parsi entrepreneurs were originally cotton merchants, and the transition from merchant to manufacturer was repeated by the first Hindus who moved into the cotton spinning and weaving business.[36] These were members of the Gujerati trading caste, from the region north of Bombay City. Historically, the second transition, but one equal in importance, has been that from the moneylending to the industrial enterprise; and it is in the moneylending castes in Marwar that the important business community, the Marwaris, have their roots. Helen Lamb describes their growth as follows:[37]

> The most spectacular rise was that of the Marwaris, the foremost Indian business community today. Though there had been a few wealthy Marwari merchants in Bombay in the 1850's, it

was not until 1920 that several families of this community opened textile and other industrial plants in a number of cities, particularly in Calcutta. Today, eight Marwari families, some of them related by marriage, hold 565 directorships in Indian industry, banking, and insurance. One of these families, the Birlas, sparked by G. D. Birla's talent and zeal, has been an innovator in textile machinery, bicycle, and automobile production since 1939.

The growth in business leadership is reflected not so much in the companies owned—which, under the managing agency system, signify no particular managerial competence—as in managing agencies controlled. One study classified a selected sample of firms in Bombay province by the community affiliation of their managing agents (or by the community of the chairman, if the company was independent). While the sample understates Marwari strength, which is greatest in Calcutta and up-country centres, the changing relative position in business control is clearly evident in Table XVIII.

TABLE XVIII

PERCENTAGE OF PAID-UP CAPITAL AND OF GROSS ASSETS CONTROLLED BY VARIOUS COMMUNITIES IN BOMBAY PROVINCE (1912, 1935, 1948)

Community	1912		1935		1948	
	Paid-up capital	Gross assets[a]	Paid-up capital	Gross assets	Paid-up capital	Gross assets
British	30.8	43.0	21.6	10.0	8.9	3.6
Parsis	49.7	31.4	47.6	41.3	36.0	46.5
Gujeratis	11.5	21.8	12.5	18.3	24.5	18.5
Marwaris	0	0	0.8	2.4	14.3	7.3
All others	8.0	3.8	17.2	27.9	16.3	24.6

a For approximately 40 per cent of the companies in the 1912 sample, the gross assets are for 1913.

SOURCE: Andrew Brimmer, "Some Aspects of the Rise and Behavior of the Business Communities in Bombay," unpublished research paper, M.I.T., Centre for International Studies (August 1953), adapted from appendix II, Table I. Brimmer used a sampling technique. For each year analyzed, the sample contains from 4 per cent to 10 per cent of public registered companies in Bombay representing over 50 per cent of total paid-up capital.

Role of Foreign Private Investment

Since 1948, there has been a net inflow of foreign business capital. The Reserve Bank of India estimates that, between July 1948 and December 1960, it has exceeded Rs. 4.35 billion. This is seen by examining the outstanding foreign investment in the private sector at different points in time.[38]

(Rs. billions)

End of		Total	End of		Total
June	1948	2.56	Dec.	1957	5.43
Dec.	1953	3.92		1958	5.73
	1955	4.56		1959	6.11
	1956	4.93		1960	6.91

Of the total outstanding stock of foreign investment of Rs. 6.95 billion in 1960, Rs. 2.89 billion (41.6 per cent) was invested in manufacturing and Rs. 1.52 billion was invested in petroleum. From 1956 to 1960, gross investment amounted to Rs. 3.04 billion. Rs. 1.75 billion (57.6 per cent) was invested in manufacturing. The United Kingdom was responsible for Rs. 1.22 billion of the total gross investment from 1956 to 1960, and the United States accounted for another .8 billion.[39] Thus the United Kingdom and the United States accounted for two-thirds of the foreign gross investment made in India during the period. Yet, even with this substantial inflow of foreign capital, the contrast with the situation in 1915 is very marked indeed. It is estimated that, in January 1955, the percentage of capital in Indian industry controlled by foreign interests was not greater than 16 per cent.[40] compared with approximately 60 per cent controlled in 1915.[41]

Concentration of Control

In April 1964, a Monopolies Commission was appointed by the Government of India to inquire into monopolies and the concentration of economic power. When the findings and recommendations of this committee are made public, new legislation may affect the present concentration of economic power in Indian industry.[42] The Mahalanobis Committee appointed to inquire into the matter of income distribution did not arrive at any definite conclusion. One contributor, H. Venkatasubbiah, has argued, with the use of income-tax data, that the rich are not getting richer, and possibly the poor are losing in real terms due to inflation, leaving the middle groups among the gainers. The income-tax data related to incomes of Rs. 5,001 and above per annum and covered both salary and nonsalary incomes. The data are reported to have revealed that the lower 70 per cent and the middle 20 per cent of all individuals increased their share of the total income in 1961–62 over 1953–54. The share of the top 10 per cent went down. The pattern of the shift was broadly the same for both salary earners and nonsalary earners.[43] Again a recent assessment indicates that income inequality (based on income before taxes) is probably not worse in India compared to other developed countries, but that, in the latter, the egalitarian impact of taxes is probably stronger.[44]

One measure of the concentration of economic power is the total net assets and paid-up capital of the 100 largest companies in India. Excluding banking and insurance in 1957–58, the 100 largest companies (approximately 0.5 per cent of all joint-stock

TABLE XIX

THE TEN LARGEST JOINT STOCK COMPANIES IN INDIA RANKED ACCORDING TO PAID-UP CAPITAL (1956-57)

(Rs. millions)

Name of company	Paid-up capital	Total gross sales	Net profit	Total net assets
Tata Iron and Steel	235	517	63	983
Sindri Fertilizers and Chemicals	170	321	55	540
Associated Cement	158	306	44	406
Imperial Tobacco	152	278	19	378
Burmah-Shell Refineries	138	278	16	364
Scindia Steam Navigation	94	261	13	327
Ahmedabad Electricity	87	243	11	272
Indian Iron and Steel	79	226	10	272
Tata Locomotive and Engineering	70	215	9	269
Hindustan Aircraft	68	181	9	185

SOURCE: Raj K. Nigam and N. C. Chaudhuri, *The Corporate Sector in India,* Research and Statistics Division, Department of Company Law Administration, Ministry of Commerce and Industry, Government of India (New Delhi, 1961), pp. 49-50.

companies in India) had about one-third of the net assets and total paid-up capital of the entire corporate sector.[45] By contrast, in the United States, the largest 200 corporations (approximately .05 per cent of all corporations) hold between a fifth and a fourth of income-producing national wealth, and own 40 per cent of the total assets of all nonfinancial corporations.[46] Some interesting statistics on the 10 largest joint-stock companies in India are contained in Table XIX.

Many of the managing agencies individually manage several of the largest corporations, further concentrating the control of industry in India. In 1954–55, the largest 17 managing agencies managed 359 companies having paid-up capital of Rs. 1.14 billion. Table XX lists the paid-up capital by various industrial groups and the paid-up capital of managing agencies in these groups. Approximately a sixth of the companies belong to the managing agency category, but control nearly half the total paid-up capital. The largest 17 of the managing agents account for less than 10 per cent of the companies in this group, but control nearly 25 per cent of the paid-up capital.

To get some idea of the industrial interests of the managing agencies, one can examine the holdings of some of the large managing agencies. Data relating to 11 of the 17 largest managing agencies in 1954–55 were available for 1959. Except for Martin Burn, whose interests include railway transport, generation of electrical energy, brass, bridge contracting, castings, shipbuilding, wagons, public works contracting, engineering, pig iron, steel, pottery and firebrick manufacturing, the other ten are mainly interested in tea, coal and jute industries.[47]

The Mahalanobis Committee which was recently appointed to report on the trends in the distribution of income and wealth and the concentration of economic power has submitted the first part of its report.[48] The major conclusion reported to have been reached in the report is that statistics do not show any significant and definite trends in concentration ratios during the first ten years of planning. The data do, however, show the presence of concentration of economic power in terms of income, property, and especially of control over the nongovernmental sector. Concentration has increased significantly between 1951 and 1958. According to the committee, in the Indian context, it is the concentration of control in the industrial sector as a whole rather than in any one or other particular industry that presents the "more menacing aspect" of

TABLE XX

NUMBER AND PAID-UP CAPITAL (IN MILLIONS OF RUPEES) OF THE COMPANIES MANAGED BY MANAGING AGENCIES (ALL AND THE 17 TOP MANAGING AGENCIES) IN CERTAIN PRINCIPAL INDUSTRIAL GROUPS, (1954-55)

Industrial groups	Total companies at work in the industrial group		Total managed companies in the industrial group		Total Companies managed by 17 top managing agencies* in the industrial group	
	No.	Paid-up capital	No.	Paid-up capital	No.	Paid-up capital
Tea plantations	591	27.9	266	16.1	117	7.8
Coal mining	495	22.7	204	18.3	52	6.7
Cotton textiles	760	118.7	438	101.1	14	9.3
Jute textiles	101	30.1	78	27.6	38	16.0
Iron and steel and engineering	318	34.2	85	30.0	9	27.0
Cement	30	24.0	13	21.2	1	0.8
Paper	117	14.8	50	12.4	7	6.2
Electricity supply	354	34.5	209	30.5	22	3.7
Wholesale and retail trade	7,149	103.8	371	11.1	10	3.8
Total (including all other groups).	29,625	969.6	5,055	465.4	359	114.0

*The 17 top managing agencies to which the data in the table relate are Bird & Co., Andrew Yule & Co., McLeod & Co., Duncan Bros. & Co., Macneill & Barry Co., Karam Chand Thapar & Bros., Octavious Steel & Co., Gillanders Arbuthnot & Co., Birla Bros., Martin Burn, H. V. Low & Co., Kilburn & Co., Shaw Wallace & Co., Jardine Henderson, Tata Industries, Williamson Magor and Co., and Begg Sutherland & Co. Since 1954-55, position of these agencies has undergone considerable change.

SOURCE: Raj K. Nigam and N. C. Chaudhuri, *The Corporate Sector in India,* Research and Statistics Division, Department of Company Law Administration, Ministry of Commerce and Industry, Government of India (New Delhi, 1961), p. 57.

concentration of economic power. Twenty selected groups have increased their share of all corporate private capital, including both public and private companies, from 29.2 per cent to 32.4 per cent during the eight years ending with 1958. The committee also is reported to have come to the conclusion that concentration of economic power in the private sector is more than what could be justified as necessary on functional grounds.

What is the reason for this concentration of control? Traditionally the explanations have focused on the scarcity of Indian entrepreneurial talent as a central cause. As M.M. Mehta explains:[49]

It was natural that the development of [the managing agency] form of industrial organization should have led to the concentration of ownership and control in fewer hands. This tendency was greatly accentuated by the great dearth of entrepreneurial ability and industrial leadership in the country.

He also points to a group of 25 agencies controlling more than 600 firms in 1951 as a reflection of continuing shortage in Indian managerial ability.[50]

Business confidence was also a scarce commodity as indeed one would expect in early stages of development. Thus British managing agents were initially preferred by British and Indian investors, and the latter tended to funnel their capital—to the extent that Indian managing agents were employed—through agents belonging to the same community. Even in the public enterprises of the most recent period, there is evidence of such exclusiveness. The Indian government, for instance, has been reluctant to accept private equity participation in its ventures despite some public pressure reflected in the demands made in the Estimates Committees of the Lok Sabha. Further the government has been unwilling to go outside the ranks of the senior civil service to meet its needs for top managerial personnel and reluctant to relinquish the authority over individual enterprises. Some of the secretaries and high officials of the Indian and state governments thus are directors or top officials of several firms, and exercise substantial control over the economic enterprises of the government.

The role of the managing agents was thus critical. They played a key role in the efforts to obtain short- and long-term capital. They also commanded the access routes to the technology and skills of the industrialized West.

The increase in the number of companies from 15,000 to almost 30,000 between 1945 and 1955 suggests a broad expansion at the base of the business pyramid.[51] Thus the rapid growth in the number of firms since the end of the war, and the accompanying promise of independence, would suggest that, prior to this time, the lack may have been one of entrepreneurial opportunity rather than of entrepreneurial ability. There is no evidence that this rapid rise in the number of firms has diminished the relative economic power of the large agencies in the last decade, but it may suggest that some new blood is moving into commercial and industrial channels. Various steps taken by the Indian government to expand the sources of industrial finance, the encouragement of small industry, and the vast increase in the provision for training, both in India and abroad, have all undoubtedly stimulated industrial enterprise.[52] At least one recent scholarly study of Indian economic development concludes that entrepreneurial shortages are no longer a major restraint on economic growth in India.[53] Fr. Berna's study of small-scale entrepreneurship indicates the emergence of new, dynamic, entrepreneurial elements in Madras state as do other studies for Delhi and other parts of India.[54] The limiting factors now appear to be the expensiveness of credit, the nonavailability of equipment and spare parts, raw materials, or foreign exchange, and uncertainties caused by administrative policies rather than the lack of entrepreneurship.[55]

The Indian joint family has facilitated the concentration of industrial control. Unlike American experience, where the Ford family empire was a long-noted exception to the more familiar separation of ownership and control, substantially all Indian agencies, large and small, are family concerns. Typically partnerships rather than joint-stock companies, the partners are commonly related by blood or marriage, and even the managerial ranks are filled from within the family or sub-caste whenever possible.[56] The Hindu joint family views cousins, nieces and nephews, the same way as the Westerners view brothers, sisters, sons and daughters; and the responsibility for and to a family thus broadly defined is far more inclusive than in Western countries.[57] The result is often to make any business venture a family venture, for the cost of hiring a brother is something like paying one's wife a salary. Obviously, this attitude could have a paralysing effect on initiative. Pandit Nehru, noting that a family's joint property was used to support productive and nonproductive family members alike, has said :[58]

> Inevitably this meant a guaranteed minimum for all of them, rather than high rewards for some. It was a kind of insurance for all, including even the subnormal and the physically or mentally deficient.

The ties of family, caste or region reflect the strength of ascriptive attributes characteristic of early stages of growth and overall low mobility of the population. Such particularistic affiliations also serve as sources of strength where a number of professional and business opportunities are rationed out on a nonprice basis. The increasing strength and cogency of caste associations and community-based business associations reflect these trends.[59] The family tie is still of considerable importance in choosing personnel for top positions in Indian firms.[60] This point will be discussed further in Chapter VI. Nevertheless most observers agree that the influence of the joint family, caste, etc. in India is declining. Symbolic of this decline is the growing significance of a professional managerial class, particularly in recent years, and the growth of employer organizations which tend to cut across traditional parochial divisions.

Growth of Employer Federations

Commercial organizations as such have a long history in India. British business interests organized the Calcutta, Bombay and Madras Chambers of Commerce in the 1830's, and the first industry associations in the 1870's and 1880's.[61] But the divergent political aims of British and Indian business led to the establishment of separate Chambers of Commerce in all the major business centres and, in the 1920's, two India-wide organizations were formed : the Associated Chambers of Commerce of India, representing foreign interests, and the Federation of Indian Chambers of Commerce and Industry, representing Indian business.[62] The latter normally aligned itself with the nationalist movement before Independence.[63]

The most common businessmen's organizations in India are the industrial federations such as the Millowners' Association, both at Bombay and Ahmedabad, the Indian Jute Mills' Association, Indian Tea Planters' Association, Indian Mining Association, and so on. They have been active in establishing standards, providing industrial representation in official and unofficial bodies, and in the case of the Indian Jute Mills' Association in limiting industrial output. Their number has increased rapidly from the beginning of World War II, and the planning of balanced industrial development in the Five Year Plans has made such associations useful channels through which the intentions of government and the requirement of industry could be exchanged and discussed. Some of them have accepted an important role in handling labour relations for member firms in the post-war period, providing in some cases advice and services, similar to those offered by the central personnel office of a multiplant firm.

In some of these cases, the industrial federations have taken an even more active role, in effect handling the settlement of collective disputes before the industrial tribunal and the union, the determination of general service conditions (standing orders, leave, dearness allowance adjustments, and even plant-level grievances). Outstanding examples are provided by the United Planters' Association of South India, the Bombay and Ahmedabad Millowners' Associations, the Northern India Employers' Federation (Kanpur) and the Indian Jute Mills' Association in Calcutta.

After the turn of the century, a formal organization of business groups on sectional and community lines also emerged, among them the Marwari Chamber (now Bharat Chamber) and Muslim Chamber of Commerce, Calcutta, the Marwari Chamber (now Western India Chamber) and Maharashtra Chamber, Bombay.[64] This communal bias has moderated in recent years, and a publication of the Federation, to which the majority of them belong, indicates that membership restriction has in most cases been removed.[65]

One of the more important businessmen's organizations born during the war period was the All-India Manufacturers' Organization, established in 1941, and active particularly in manufacturing enterprise. Problems of labour relations and labour legislation are touched only generally by this body, and its basic emphasis has been on shaping industrial policy through publications, membership in commissions, organizing local manufacturers' associations and generally urging on government the private manufacturers' point of view.[66] The organization lays great stress on technical education and training and includes in its ranks several of the more prominent and active entrepreneurs outside of the large business houses. Their ranks have been fortified in recent years by the emergence of several associations of small-scale industrialists in the different urban centres.

The two most important employer associations concerned solely with employer-employee problems were both established in 1933. The Federation of Indian Chambers of Commerce started the All-India Organization of Industrial Employers. The Employers Federation of India was originally established under the auspices of the Bombay Millowners' Association and represented not only the British business interests, but generally the group of Indian businessmen who were not members of the Federation of Indian Chambers of Commerce.[67]

The stresses of war, Independence, and Partition, and more recently of an avowedly socialist-oriented government, have encouraged further cooperative action by business; and in so doing have helped to weaken the ties of family, caste, and community which have traditionally determined business associations. Since the goal of Swaraj (Independence) has been reached, the Indian businessmen of the 1960's find they have many problems in common with foreign business groups.

The two employers' federations mentioned above have been very active in recent years in influencing the formulation and implementation of the labour policy of the Indian government. Their activities have also been greatly stepped up with a view to gaining greater support for private employers and improving business practices. Government-sponsored training and research institutions, industrial development councils, tripartite bodies such as the Indian Labour Conference, and management journals, seminars, and conferences have all witnessed an increasing measure of busi-

ness participation. Notable beginnings have been made in shaping
a business ideology which would emphasize the scope for the private
sector in a mixed economy. An example is provided by the Code
of Conduct adopted by the Forum for Free Enterprise, an organization of influential businessmen.

The Climate for Industrial Development

One of the major problems still facing Indian business is the negative and sometimes hostile attitude towards it held by other segments
of the community, and even by government. The Code of Conduct
makes it clear that the Indian businessman must bear some responsibility for this situation.

Until 1947, Indian businessmen operated along with British
business interests, which had the support of a friendly government.
They tended to retain the psychology of a trader and speculator
interested in quick profits rather than in long-term investments
in the building of a business.[68] Even today, many members of the
business community of India have a background of industrial
management as limited as the industrial empire-builders of America
during the latter part of nineteenth century; and it is not surprising
that parallels can be drawn between the watering of railroad stock
and Spanish-American war profiteering, and some recent Indian
business practices.

No section of Indian. opinion recognizes this problem more
clearly than some of the leading businessmen themselves. Writing
in 1952 in a publication primarily for businessmen, an ex-president
of the Federation of Indian Chambers of Commerce and Industry
cautioned his colleagues as follows:[69]

For the fact must be recognised, however unpalatable it may
appear to be, that businessmen are now under suspicion everywhere. We are fast losing goodwill. This is no doubt sad, but
nevertheless true. In a condition where social forces are bringing in new thought-currents and new complexes, businessmen
should learn to move with the times and so guide their policy
and change their perspective that social conscience may not
react against them.... So, we must develop a new perspective

and a new approach so that mere money-making and profit-grabbing may no longer remain the main urge of our existence as businessmen. If we do so, we may have to pay a bitter price in the future.

Government itself has expressed its opinion of private enterprise in several notable policy declarations and in statements by its leaders. A 1949 speech by Prime Minister Nehru to the Federation is exceptionally sharp in some of its criticisms:[70]

> This is a fundamental fact—the capitalists, industrialists, etc. in India are not big enough to face the problems of the day or not quite big enough, and generally the idea is spreading that their stature is rather small and that they get frightened at the slightest upset and start complaining and retiring into their shells and asking others to help them.
>
> With all respect, I should like to inform you that if your demands come in the way of the good of the masses, your demands will be completely ignored. Of course, they need not and should not, because your interests are really tied up with their interests. Whatever the rights and wrongs of things may be, the industrialists and the commercial classes in India have become unpopular with the general mass of people. They have become unpopular because some people among them have not behaved rightly, have taken advantage of situations to obtain profit for themselves at an inordinate rate to the disadvantage of the community at large. . . .
>
> But I say to you, make every effort to improve your reputation because ultimately it is not through legislation or through Government protection that we can go very far in the production of goods, but through the goodwill of the various parties concerned in that undertaking.

The tone and content of this talk offer distressing evidence of how far apart government and business were in the immediate postwar period.

The 1947–55 period has been characterized as one in which "the Indian state and private enterprise have fought an undercover war ...."[71] While this was an extreme characterization, it did show the gulf between them. Some of this friction is understandable, and was perhaps even inevitable. Nehru and the Indian government were concerned primarily with assuaging the pent-up frustrations of post-Independence India and tended to regard the businessmen and their complaints as lacking in a sense of perspective. Nehru is reported to have related an anecdote involving a personal business friend, with several houses and estates, who complained that taxes were making it difficult to maintain all his property. Nehru commented:

> What makes the story so ironic is that here I am, fighting back
> legislation to confiscate luxurious property, and this chap wants
> me to give him a tax refund. I suppose each man has to have his
> own dream world.[72]

Some of the difficulty stems from the fact that business has not had a vital impact on other parts of the Indian social system, with the consequence that key segments of Indian opinion have little sympathy for the average businessman, and little respect for that system of values which considers the pursuit of wealth an honourable calling. Leadership in the civil services, the professions, the universities, the Congress party and even the trade unions comes largely from the intellectual class, whose traditions place the government functionary, the lawyer, the teacher and the social worker well above the typical small businessman.[73] Also the colonial heritage, including its educational system, exalted the role of the civil servant and the political elite while business pursuits and skills were relegated to an inferior status of grubby profit-seeking. A fairly common current view of the profit motive is well illustrated by the following anecdote used in an editorial published in an official organ of the Congress party:[74]

> [Rajarshi Tandonji, President of the All-Indian Congress Com-
> mittee] ... had just been released after a long incarceration
> following the August, 1942, Quit India movement. A rich man,
> his dear friend, came to see him. Tandonji asked him how much
> he had earned during the war. He mentioned many lakhs, certainly

not inconsiderable. And this is what Tandonji said: "Whenever I see a rich man, I can't help feeling that either he, or his father, or someone else among his near and dear ones had adopted questionable means to amass wealth. *Wealth cannot be amassed by following methods which are above board.*"

This view of businessmen is changing in a climate of fairly rapid economic, social and cultural change. What the status system is may be less important than the direction and speed of its change. As the government increases its participation in economic activity, the role of the technician, the economist, the statistician, and professional manager has become increasingly important. Attitudes towards profit have undergone a subtle change. "Profiteering" is still looked down upon, but there has been an increasing recognition of "profitability" of an enterprise as an indication of its efficiency. A national seminar of prominent statesmen and economists convened in 1959 by the All-India Congress Committee to discuss the proposed Third Five Year Plan supported this principle as conforming to "socialistic" standards of efficiency for public sector enterprises. Business and entrepreneurial skills have also been increasingly valued due to the achievements of the businessmen themselves. They have played a valuable role in developing India's commercial contacts abroad and expanding trade. As the government enterprises have been handicapped by management problems, the State has turned towards the business sector for needed skills. The Air India International thus has at its helm J. R. D. Tata, a private industrialist of world stature; the Life Insurance Corporation, the State Bank of India, and other financial corporations, have drawn on the talents of high-level businessmen to advise them; more recently, the entire top management of the Hindusthan Steel Company, Limited, was replaced by a new Board which included several prominent business leaders. There are also many "lesser" instances of business leadership involvement, notably in planning committees for industrial development. The direction of change is thus favourable to business, or at least management skills, although the older tradition continues to cast its shadow. The belief that an unfavourable climate for private enterprise exists is still evident in many business circles.[75]

Another difficulty facing the private businessman was the decision of the government to work towards a "socialist pattern of society." While within this pattern private and government enterprise were to work side by side, apprehensions were entertained as to which industries would escape nationalization, and for how long. The numerous and sometimes irritating controls which accompany the planned economic development of a nation were a source of many complaints, and foremost among these were the controls included in the Industries Development and Regulation Act of 1951.[76] As its title suggests, the law provided certain assistance by way of advice and coordinating activity, and also regulation which required government approval before a broad range of business decisions could be carried out. The most prominent feature of the Act provided for complete takeover of the management of a business, if, in the opinion of the government, the quality of the product or the consumer's interest suffered under the existing management. Continued uncertainty of ultimate government intentions led to an increasing sense of isolation and mistreatment on the part of business.[77] The constitutional amendment in 1955 which made the legislature the final authority for setting the compensation for nationalized firms deprived business of redress through the courts. In fairness to the Indian government, it should be noted that the 1955 amendment was necessary if land reforms, a quite separate problem, were to proceed without endless litigation between the government and landowners. While business opinion did not fear immediate and outright seizure of privately owned industry with only token payments, there was distress at the loss of judicial review over what in the future they feared might be a largely political decision.[78]

Perhaps, of all the causes of concern, the Company Law reform was the one which appeared to threaten the businessmen's security more than any other.

The Company Law Reform

Hearings on the proposal for the Company Law reform had been in progress for several years prior to its enactment in 1956, and generally moderate changes suggested by a commission studying the subject met with only minor criticism by business. But the final result was a complex and sweeping Act which, among other things, provided for strict licensing of managing agents by government by 15 August 1960, a 10-company limit for any one agent or his close associates, a fixed maximum agency commission, and the right to prohibit managing agents in any industry by governmental decree. The Act also prohibited managing agencies in banking and insurance. The increased authority for government to intervene in business affairs was so broad that, in the opinion of the business publication *Eastern Economist,* it made such intervention almost purely discretionary.[79]

However, the government of India had no immediate intention of ending the managing agency system. Between 1 April 1956 and 15 August 1960, the Government gave their approval to 1,345 applicant companies for appointments or reemployment of managing agencies. A comparison of the number of managing agencies and the number of companies managed by them is shown for 1954–55 and 16 August 1960.[80]

Number of companies managed	1954-55	16 *August* 1960
1	3,526	776
2-10	402	532
11 and more	16	0
Total	3,944	1,308

The Role of the Private Sector

What the future holds for Indian business has been a question which has troubled many in government as well as in industry. In 1948, the Industrial Policy Resolution was published, specifically reserving government's right to undertake new development in six basic industries with private enterprise assisting only as the state found necessary. These were coal, iron and steel, aircraft and shipbuilding, telephone and telegraph equipment, manufacturers and mineral oil production.[81] Furthermore, arms and ammunition, atomic energy and rail transport were to be state monopolies.

The First Five Year Plan, with its emphasis on the development of agriculture and multi-purpose river valley projects, drew heavily on the resources of the state, and not until 1954 was there any official revision of the government's economic policy. But, in December that year, in an economic policy debate already concerned with the investment programme for the Second Five Year Plan, Parliament passed a resolution which, in the words of a later government publication, "accepted the socialist pattern of society as the objective of social and economic policy."[82] *Capital,* a leading Calcutta financial journal with British interests, defined it somewhat differently.[83]

"Nehruism" would seem to be Capitalism without the confidence of inalienable property rights, Socialism with a private sector, and Communism without revolution or ruthlessness. It is a strange hybrid policy with which to face the future.

One month later, at the Avadi Congress, the "strange hybrid policy" was given added weight by the Congress party in the Economic Policy Resolution.[84] Two elements of the Avadi declaration stand out in importance: the increased role of government in developing heavy industry, and the positive role assigned to private enterprise. Both stemmed from the belief that India had to industrialize at a more rapid pace than called for in the First Five Year Plan, then within eighteen months of completion. An excerpt from the address by Prime Minister Nehru to the Avadi Congress suggests both of these points.[85]

Land ... will remain essentially in the private sector. Small-scale and cottage industries will also remain ... so also most of the lighter industries. It may be advantageous to allow some heavier industries to be organized by private enterprise, if the state is not prepared to assume the burden.

If this is so, then we must adopt a healthy attitude toward the private sector, keeping always in view the main objective of achieving a socialist pattern and preventing the growth of any tendency which might come in our way later.

The term "socialist pattern of society" was distinguished from "socialism" in the debates. This, Maulana Azad, a Cabinet Minister[86] and mover of the resolution, explained :[87]

I would like to draw your attention, especially at this time, to the deliberate use of the phrase socialist pattern of society. This is most important, as we want to have a socialist pattern and not Socialism.

The socialist pattern meant control of industry for the common good, and did not always require State ownership.

In April 1956, a new Industrial Policy Resolution replacing the 1948 resolutions was published, reflecting the changed economic policy.[88] It declared :

It is essential to accelerate the rate of economic growth and to speed up industrialization and, in particular, to develop heavy industries and machine-making industries, to expand the public sector, and to build up a large and growing cooperative sector.

The confusion of an earlier period was sought to be averted by dividing industry into three categories, the first being reserved to the State, the second to be progressively State-owned, and the third category left to private enterprise. The three categories are given below :

Category A	Category B	Category C
Arms and ammunition	Some mining	All other industry
Atomic energy	Aluminium	
Iron and steel	Machine tools	
Heavy electrical plant	Ferro alloys	
Most mining, including coal, iron, copper, lead	Chemicals, including drugs, dyestuffs, plastics, fertilizers,	
Basic machine-making capacity		
Aircraft and ship industry	synthetic rubber	
Air and rail transport	Road and sea transport	
Communications and communications equipment, excluding radios		
Electric power		

Although the public sector was to be substantially enlarged, the private sector found within the resolution much that was encouraging. For example, in the first category, existing private enterprise could continue and even expand present units. The resolution also promised government encouragement to private enterprise by the development of transport and power and other essential services, by appropriate fiscal policy, by fostering institutions to provide financial aid, and on occasions by supplying direct financial aid. When state and private enterprise worked side by side, the government committed itself to a fair and impartial treatment. In one of the sentences most encouraging to business in the whole resolution, this promise was made:

> The Government of India . . . recognizes that it would, in general, be desirable to allow such [private] undertakings to develop with as much freedom as possible consistent with the targets and objectives of the national plan.[89]

The moderate tone and the appreciation of the role that private enterprise would have to play in rapid industrial development was in marked contrast to earlier statements, and was greeted with restrained approval by the private sector.[90] This was all the more remarkable, because the attitudes of the business community which find their way into print are typically not balanced appraisals of the actions of government, nor even entirely accurate indicators of the feelings businessmen act upon. But there has been increasing recognition that, for example, additional steel plants are badly needed, and the important thing is not who owns them, but that they are built promptly. This belief that the public and private sectors supplement and serve each other, and are not antagonistic may be gaining ground in both business and government thinking. In an analysis of the 1956 Resolution, an American economist working, with the Ministry of Commerce and Industry has noted that "with the possible exception of one or two industries dealing with public utilities and national resources, India has abandoned the overall programme to nationalize private industry falling within the public sector."[91] Government has in no way given up its "socialistic pattern of society," but the emphasis appears to have shifted towards the maximum speed in industrialization, and this means utilizing the private sector to the full.[92] .The Indian government is not willing to spend its limited supply of capital and managerial resources where independent businessmen are already doing an adequate job.

This attitude of reasonableness and accommodation by both government and private enterprise reflects a growing recognition of the immensity of the job ahead and awareness that there is room enough for both to function in an expanding economy. This has been particularly striking in the performance of the industrial sector during the First, Second, and Third Five Year Plans.[93] No one would suggest that mistrust and bad feeling between government and private enterprise are now a past history.[94] But the changes since Independence have brought in a more flexible and positive government attitude towards business which has been described by John P. Lewis as a "new pragmatism in the private sector."[95] In 1963, for instance, just before the proposal for an American-financed steel mill at Bokaro was dropped, an influential spokesman for this public sector venture was J. R. D. Tata, India's top steel man in the private sector. Earlier, G. D. Birla similarly led a leading group of Indian industrialists to the United States to explain the basis of Indian "socialism" and pointed out that there had been an expanding scope for private industry.

Over the years, government and business leaders have thus shown an increasing appreciation of their respective contributions to Indian economic development. In part, this is due to the strains of growth and the promise provided by expanding opportunities. In the words of an influential international bankers' mission which visited India in 1960 on behalf of the World Bank:

> If the issue of public *versus* private enterprise has lost some of its sharpness, it is because it has become more widely recognized that both sectors of the economy have their contribution to make.[96]

It may not be premature to conclude that the first and most difficult phase of the adjustment between a business group, with a tradition of private enterprise, and a new government, dedicated to a socialistic pattern of society, is coming to an end. Observers have noted the widespread consensus on the role of the government and the need for a planned framework to guide the activities of the several groups in the economic community.[97]

The Impact of Social and Cultural Factors

The national commitment to economic development and purposive public action to advance this goal is thus an impressive achievement since Independence. There can be no doubt that India is heading towards development and modernization of her economy. However, the speed or ease with which these goals are accomplished will at least in part be determined by deep-seated social, cultural and religious factors. This is as yet an imponderable issue and we can do no more than suggest the different directions in which their impact may be felt.

The opposition of Mahatma Gandhi and his followers to the "evils" of industrialization has been interpreted by some to reflect elements in the Hindu ethics, and therefore in Indian society and culture, which may be discouraging to the kind of initiative and enterprise necessary for a dynamic industrial society. A brief summary of Mahatma Gandhi's philosophy is appropriate at this point.[98]

From his value system based on the reduction, rather than on the satisfaction of wants, Gandhi posited two closely related requirements for solving India's economic problem: the development of self-sufficient Indian villages and the elimination of modern industrial machinery. He believed that industrialism was responsible for a host of evils; among the gravest were unemployment, destruction of the village unit, and concentration of wealth in the hands of a few. Admittedly, some machinery would, as a practical matter, have to stay, but these machines must be subordinated to men and his requirements, instead of what Gandhi considered to be the usual state of "enslavement" of man by machine.

The manufacture of this limited machinery should be in the hands of the state, which would avoid in its factory organization and its distributive policy the evils associated with industrialization. But, until the state accepted this responsibility, the owners of capital—the fortunate few—should be trustees for the masses. Service, rather than gain, should guide their conduct.

Among the Indian merchants and industrialists, the "fortunate few" whom Gandhi had in mind, one of the foremost exponents of this view today is G. D. Birla, India's leading Marwari industrialist and close associate of Gandhi, who seeks to convince businessmen that they *must* not think of profit alone, and that they *need* not think of service alone.

> The profit reward is the greatest incentive to a businessman. But it is not realized that profits come automatically if the business is based on service. Those who talk of doing business with the service motive alone forget that the two are intermixed and indivisible. There is no such thing as a purely profit motive, nor can there be business with an undiluted service motive. But profit, in the ultimate analysis, is a secondary thing in a business because, if the business is really useful and renders service to society, then profit is inevitable and automatic. On the other hand, there can be no lasting profit without service. This is a point which we have not fully realized and on which we have to educate our fellow travellers.[99]

Nevertheless few students of recent Indian developments will agree that, however admirable the precept, the practice of Indian business today is noticeably affected by the basic Gandhian tenets.[100] The late Prime Minister Nehru, the principal architect of free India's economic policies, was also forthright in his rejection of the concept of trusteeship to the extent that it seemed to imply that self-regulation by businessmen could be a sufficient substitute for government for the common good.[101]

The Gandhian opposition to industrialization has also been equally clearly rejected by the Indian government. Industrialization—not the village handicraft economy—is the primary goal of India's present government. It is also evident that the philosophy of "wantlessness" has no part in present concern with national income statistics and the rapid growth of heavy industry—what W. W. Rostow calls the age of the compound interest. When a Gandhian at the Avadi Congress suggested that the phrase "socialistic pattern of society" be replaced with the word "sarvodaya," a purely Gandhian concept of which at least one connotation can be described as gaining by giving, Maulana Azad said that this beautiful word suggested the dawning of a new era, but that Gandhiji did not mean to place an economic programme before the country.[102]

There are nevertheless many parallels between some of the policies and exhortations currently advocated in India and the views which Gandhi advanced. The planning of the Indian government has much more than rapid industrialization as its goal: the encouragement to cottage and small-scale industry, for instance, follows a pattern which accords well with Gandhian thinking.[103] Perhaps the clearest example is the encouragement to hand-spinning and handloom output, even artificial restrictions on Indian mills weaving their own production of yarn. The development of large-scale enterprises in the public sector also accords well with Gandhi's "less-than-ideal" compromise which would accord such ventures to public rather than private enterprise. Perhaps the best illustration of Gandhi's influence is India's renowned community development projects. The government's interest in exploiting the potential for development inherent in India's labour surpluses (and rationing the use of scarce capital) thus echoes Gandhi's ethical concern with self-reliance as a vehicle of development.

Related to this is Gandhi's emphasis on the dignity of labour. The attitude towards manual labour is of some importance in India, for many educated Indians consider it socially beneath them to work with their hands. The Second Five Year Plan tactfully noted that "there is a general disinclination among the educated to look for employments other than office jobs," and recommended that orientation camps be established to help remove the problem.[104] Also, although Gandhi expressed reservations about industrialism, he stressed the need for proper work habits, including the care of the machine, the provider. In many workshops and factories, a common occurrence is the *Vishwakarma Puja,* a religious celebration doing honour to the product of manual labour and to the tools and equipment used. This practice predates Gandhi, and illustrates the extent to which he sought to "rediscover" elements in traditional Indian culture which will enable his countrymen to prepare for the responsibilities of Independence and growth. It is interesting to note that the Bharatiya Mazdoor Sangh, one of the competing groups in the Indian labour movement, exhorts its members to celebrate the *Vishwakarma Puja* day rather than the "May Day" commonly celebrated by trade unionists.

Some aspects of the Indian social system may, however, be less favourable towards industrialization. The compartmentalization and the ordering of occupations by caste lines have declined in significance in recent years (a decline aided by the teachings of Gandhi). In its pure form, however, the caste system may be expected to dampen mobility, the acquisition or dissemination of skills, and returns on capital employed. Even today, there is evidence of the pervasive, although diminished, influence of caste and the hindrances it poses in the way of the efficient utilization of the country's manpower. Even if the caste system, with its particularistic, ascriptive features, is held to stand in the way of industrialization, one unanswered question is the extent to which it adjusts to changing economic conditions. Scholars disagree on the answer, the resolution being made more difficult by the confusion over nomenclatures, the enormous diversity of reported experience, the changes taking place in India, and the varying perspectives of the investigators themselves.[105] About the only thing that can be said now is that, other things being equal, the caste system would be a negative influence, but that such factors as education, income, and expanding product and factor markets tend to undermine the role of caste. On the other hand, scarcity of jobs or opportunities, or nonprice rationing of these opportunities by, say, the government, and the prevailing conditions in India would emphasize the value of caste and similar parochial associations.

There are other carry-overs from the essentially static, rural society which characterized pre-British as well as colonial India. The opposition to cow-slaughter places an economic burden on the country which already must spend scarce resources on raising agricultural productivity. Less easily defined but possibly also a problem is the willingness with which peasants, employees, and the governed generally accept a "dependent" attitude, expecting that things will be done for them without more effort on their part than to request it.[106] This attitude may also be encouraged by the concept of a welfare state. Improved education, higher standards of living, increased job opportunities—in short most of the factors which will change this attitude—may themselves be delayed by its existence.[107]

Given the total impact of a social system adapted to a static rural village economy, modified by Gandhian teachings and admittedly eroded by Western and nationalistic influences, how much will it affect the future industrialization of India? Serious students of the subject offer differing conclusions, and one must beware of simple answers.[108] The dynamics of the Indian situation is best understood by a recognition of the immense variety of social and cultural attitudes throughout India and the immeasurability of forces which are acting on and reacting with them. Moreover, the factors aiding industrialization are not always separate from those hindering it. Gandhi consistently opposed mechanization, but with equal consistency championed the dignity of manual labour. Joint families may have smothered initiative, but were a natural vehicle for adapting the managing agency system to Indian conditions, and currently do much to lessen the sharp and politically difficult problem of unemployment. Finally, important as the hindrances to industrialization may be, their measurement or the drawing up of a definite balance-sheet is still beyond the skill of the social scientist.

It is clear, however, that the articulate and influential elements of Indian leadership are committed to change and have drawn on the traditions of the Indian nationalist movement, the rich heritage left by the long years of British rule, and the positive aspects of India's own culture to achieve their goals. The contribution of Gandhi, dubbed the "peaceful revolutionary," has been notable in this respect. Equally important have been the efforts of Nehru and his colleagues in encouraging change within a framework of continuity towards a "consensual" society. A perceptive English civil servant and businessman with long experience in India draws out the balance in these terms:[109]

India has been fortunate . . . in national leaders who have known how to lead instead of driving their people, how to push and pull them into change instead of shooting them into it. India is abolishing untouchability with the consent of the touchables, making women equal with the help of the men, getting rid of landlords with their own resigned acceptance, emphasising physics and economics rather than Sanskrit with hardly a murmur from the Pandits. Indian planning still shows an inadequate respect for business and the consumer, the Indian peasant still too often saves in order to spend on ceremonies rather than on investment. But, on the whole, Indian society has changed and is changing enough to make it probable that it can achieve development by its own bootstraps, that the Indian people are now interested enough in planning to raise their incomes to make the many sacrifices of habits as well as of money, which will be needed.

From 1850 to 1940, the industrial history of India is essentially the story of cotton textiles, jute textiles, coal mining, and railroads. The British rule tended to make India a buyer, and not a supplier, of industrial products; and this was aided by the social and economic conditions prevailing in India. Not until the Second World War and Independence was there both a desire and an opportunity for substantial industrial development.

A unique development in the growth of Indian industry has been the use of managing agents to control several companies through a single group of managers. It facilitated British dominance for a long period, and it was equally useful to Indian entrepreneurs in extending family empires over wide fields of commerce and industry. The large majority of these "captains of industry" have come from three relatively small communities: the Parsees in Bombay city, and the trading castes from Gujerat and Marwar. More recently, the dominant position in Indian industry, which over the last century has moved from the British to these three business communities, seems to be moving to the government. Already the largest operator in several important fields, the state plans to expand its participation in every basic industry, transport, communications, and mining, and in numerous smaller segments of the industrial sector of the economy.

This rapidly expanding role of the state has been a source of much concern to private enterprise. On the other hand, the democratically elected government of India has been concerned with the needs of planned development and the obvious limitations of private enterprise to undertake some of the required investment. Several factors complicate the situation in which private businessmen find themselves. Influential intellectuals have been distrustful of the profit motive, and their views have had a powerful impact on the people of India and its ruling political party, the Congress. Questionable business practices, and businessmen's dislike of regulations designed to integrate them with the "socialistic pattern of society," have fostered this distrust.

However the years during which business and government have dealt with each other since Independence have helped government to see that entrepreneurial and managerial skills are not easily developed and should not lightly be discarded. Businessmen have also modified their ideas on the role of government in a free nation, and there is reason to believe that the working relationship between the two will improve with the passage of time. The present economic system is best described as a "mixed economy" in which the government plays a key, but by no means exclusive, role whose success is dependent upon a mixture of public authority and economic incentives to secure cooperation and coordination among the constituent units.[110]

Are Indian social and cultural conditions inhospitable to industrialization? This is a question which has no precise answer. While there is no doubt that the low level of education, the many different languages, and the large and growing population pressing down on an already low standard of living are very real restraints, the effect of less tangible considerations such as the caste system or the joint family, sometimes, hinders and, sometimes, helps industrialization. If we look at the prospects for the successful industrial development of India from the vantage point of 1965, the factual statistics of progress during the eighteen years since Independence are more impressive than any catalogue of cultural or social impediments to progress.

A critical and favourable factor has been the quality of India's leadership. Its achievements in effecting many important changes within a framework of consent constitute a striking augury for the future.

NOTES

1 Much of the initial work for this chapter in the first edition was done by Fred Munson, Research Assistant in the Industrial Relations Section, MIT, at that time. Malcolm Cohen, Research Assistant in 1964, and V. N. Krishnan, Research Assistant in the Department of Economics, Michigan State University, also worked on the draft for the second edition.

2 In 1946, the industrial index of production still allotted over 70 per cent of its weight to three industries: cotton textiles, jute textiles, and coal. All other mining and manufacturing industries, including iron and steel (7.16 per cent), and some not included in index construction, accounted for perhaps one-third of total value added by manufacture in India in 1946. Data are taken from *Statistical Abstract, India,* 1950, Government of India Central Statistics Organization, Cabinet Secretariat (1952), Table 160, pp. 552 et seq.; explanation of 1946 index, p. 627; Table 174, pp. 636-37.

3 D. R. Gadgil, *The Industrial Evolution of India in Recent Times* (Madras, 1924), p. 136.

4 Daniel H. Buchanan, *The Development of Capitalist Enterprise in India* (New York, 1934), p. 269.

5 "The jute mills are a great monument to Scottish enterprise and Indian labour. While Indians have furnished the land and labour for growing, and the labour for manufacturing, Scotland has furnished the brains and the careful oversight." Buchanan, *op. cit.,* p. 243. See also Vera Anstey, *The Economic Development of India* (London, 1942), p. 280.

6 As of March 1962, railway mileage was 35,473 miles. *Statistical Outline of India* 1963, Tata Industries Private Limited (Bombay, 1963), p. 33.

7 Buchanan, *op. cit.,* p. 184.

8 Daniel Thorner, "Great Britain and the Development of India's Railways," *Journal of Economic History,* vol. XI, no. 4 (Fall 1951), pp. 399-400.

9 Buchanan, *op. cit.,* p. 201.

10 B. V. N. Naidu, "Handloom Industry in India," *Indian Cotton Textile Industry Centenary Volume* (1851-1950), M. P. Gandhi, ed. (Bombay, 1950), p. 128. See also S. D. Mehta, *The Indian Cotton Textile Industry: An Economic Analysis* (Bombay, 1953), pp. 123, 127.

11 For a more detailed discussion of these points, see East India (Industrial) Commission, *Report of the Indian Industrial Commission* 1916-18, His Majesty's Stationery Office, Cmd 51, London, 1932, pp. 45-6, 126. The report stressed the imbalance in Indian industrial development, with insufficient local manufacture, and concluded that "the manufacturing capacity of the country has been far from sufficiently utilized by Government departments."

12 G. L. Mehta, "Development of Cotton Textile Machinery Industry and Textile Accessory Industries," *Indian Cotton Textile Industry Centenary Volume* (1851-1950), pp. 81-2. Mehta, a former president of the Federation of Indian Chambers of Commerce and Industry, was, at the time of writing this article, a member of the Planning Commission, and was later Ambassador to the United States.

13 Raj K. Nigam and N. C. Chaudhuri, *The Corporate Sector in India,* Research and Statistics Division, Department of Company Law Administration, Ministry of Commerce and Industry, Government of India (New Delhi, 1961), p. 9.

14 "Indian Industry," *Eastern Economist,* Annual Number, vol. xiii, no. 24, New Delhi, 30 December 1949, p. 1000.

15 *Statistical Outline of India* 1963, pp. 25-31.

16 These figures are based on production data contained in *Reserve Bank of India Bulletin,* vol. XVIII, pp. 691, 806-07; *Economic Survey* 1963-64, Government of India (New Delhi, 1964), Table 1.5; *India, A Reference Annual* 1963, Publications Division, Ministry of Information and Broadcasting, Government of India (New Delhi, 1963), pp. 262-82. The latest available data for paper and electricity generation were for a terminal year, 1961. All other industrial data cover increases from 1951 to 1963.

17 Index weights for the four industries were :

Industry	1946 *Index*	1951 *Index*	1956 *Index*
Cotton textiles	43.49	36.10	32.10
Jute textiles	16.53	11.91	5.62
Coal	11.95	6.69	7.09
Steel	7.16	5.92	7.48
Total	79.13	60.62	52.29

18 N. Das, *The Public Sector,* Eastern Economist Pamphlets, no. 32, E. P. W. da Costa, general editor (New Delhi, September 1955), p. 1.

19 *Ibid.,* pp. 22-4.

20 *First Five Year Plan,* p. 444, Appendix: "Industrial Projects in the Public Sector."

21 Das, *op. cit.,* p. 28.

22 *49th Annual Report* 1955-56, Tata Iron and Steel Company Limited, p. 19.

23 "The New Coal Policy," *Eastern Economist,* vol. XXV, no. 22, November 1955, p. 13.

24 See the revised edition of the Das volume, *The Public Sector in India,* Asia Publishing House (Bombay, 1961).

25 This estimate is based on data contained in Nigam and Chaudhuri, p. 4, and *Statistical Abstracts of the Indian Union* 1961, pp. 316-21, and the source cited in foot-note 20 of this chapter. The estimate is arrived at by comparing the amount of gross fixed assets in the public sector in 1958-59 with the estimate available for 1951. Since the 1951 estimates include government railroads while the 1958-59 estimates do not, the value of government railroads must be subtracted from the 1951 figure. In 1950-51, the capital-at-charge to the end of the year in all railroads was Rs. 8.38 billion. In 1951-52, government railroads carried over 98 per cent of all passengers and goods. If we assume that the capital-at-charge of government railroads is in proportion to the number of passengers and goods carried, we would

estimate the capital-at-charge of government railroads at Rs. 8.2 billion. Subtracting Rs. 8.2 billion from the total reported assets of all government enterprises of Rs. 12.4 billion in 1951, we can say that gross assets in the public sector excluding railroads was Rs. 4.2 billion as compared with Rs. 7.8 billion in 1958-59.

26 *Statistical Outline of India* 1963, p. 95.

27 *Third Five Year Plan,* p. 59.

28 John P. Lewis, *Quiet Crisis in India,* The Brookings Institution (Washington, 1962), p. 89.

29 *The Third plan Mid-Term Appraisal,* Planning Commission, Government of India (New Delhi, November 1963), p. 21.

30 Andrew F. Brimmer, "The Setting of Entrepreneurship in India," *Quarterly Journal of Economics,* vol. LXIX, November 1955, p. 555.

31 M. M. Mehta, *Structure of Indian Industries* (Bombay, 1955), p. 247.

32 Andrew F. Brimmer, *Some Aspects of the Rise and Behavior of Business Communities in Bombay,* unpublished research paper, Massachusetts Institute of Technology, Center for International Studies, August 1953, Table XL. This conclusion was based on a sample of Bombay firms.

33 Brimmer, *The Setting of Entrepreneurship in India,* 1953, pp. 564-65.

34 Buchanan, *op. cit.,* p. 144.

35 Helen B. Lamb, "The Rise of Indian Business Communities," *Pacific Affairs* vol. XXVIII, no. 2 (June 1955), p. 104.

36 Foreign firms have also followed this pattern; it is one which, after all, accords well with the perfectly sound business principle of finding a market before producing the product. For a study of this trader-to-manufacturer transition by foreign firms, see K. K. Das, *Management of American Enterprise in India,* unpublished doctoral thesis, Harvard University, Graduate School of Business Administration, July 1956, Parts III and IV.

37 Lamb, *op. cit.,* pp. 105-06.

38 "Foreign Investments in India: 1960 and 1961 (Preliminary Trends)," *Reserve Bank of India Bulletin,* vol. XVI, no. 10 (October 1962), p. 1531.

39 *Ibid.,* pp. 1534-35.

40 "India, Progress and Plan," Supplement to *Economist* (London), vol. CLXXIV, no. 5813, (22 January 1955), p. 18 of supplement. *Economist* does not state its source. An identical figure was calculated in 1951 by an Indian employer group interested in showing the predominance of Indian ownership and control ("Role of Private Enterprise in India—in Retrospect and Prospect," Employers' Association, 15, Park Street, Calcutta, March 1951, p. 16).

41 See Table IV.

42 The Commission has been asked to submit its report by October 1965. For further details, see *Keesing's Contemporary Archives,* 2-9 May 1964.

43 "Are the Rich Really Getting Richer," *Hindu,* 25 January 1964.

44 P. D. Ojha and V. V. Bhatt, "Pattern of Income Distribution in an Underdeveloped Economy: A Case Study of India," *American Economic Review,* vol. LIV, no. 5 (September 1964), p. 719.

45 Nigam and Chaudhuri, *op. cit.,* p. 48.

46 George L. Bach, *Economics,* Third Edition, Prentice-Hall, Inc. (Englewood Cliffs, 1960), p. 311. Paul A. Samuelson, *Economics,* Sixth Edition, McGraw Hill Book Co., (New York, 1964), p. 90.

47 Nigam and Chaudhuri, *op. cit.,* pp. 136-50.

48 *Economic Times,* 30 April 1964.

49 M. M. Mehta, *op. cit.,* p. 248.

50 *Ibid.,* p. 249.

51 *Statistical Abstract, India,* 1952-53, p. 399. These figures include mills, plantations, banks, trading companies, etc. as well as manufacturing firms. Part of this growth may be due to the incorporation of existing companies to the fake advantage of certain tax benefits and the general benefit of limited liability. There has been little expansion in number since 1952, however.

52 For details on financial assistance for Indian industry, see S. L. N. Simha, *The Capital Market of India,* Bombay, Vora and Co., 1960, pp. 197-207, and Government of India, Ministry of Information and Broadcasting, *India: A Reference Annual* 1963, pp. 253-55.

53 See Ranjit Singh Bhambri, "Myth and Reality about Private Enterprise in India," *World Politics,* vol. XII, no. 2 (January 1960), pp. 194-200; and John P. Lewis, *Quiet Crisis in India* (Washington, 1962), p. 36.

54 J. J. Berna, S. J., *Industrial Entrepreneurship in Madras State,* Asia Publishing House, Bombay, 1960.

55 See among others P. N. Dhar and H. F. Lydall, *The Role of Small Enterprise in Indian Economic Development,* Bombay, Asia Publishing House, 1961, p. 88; J. J. Berna, *op. cit.,* pp. 101-06; James T. McCrory, *Small Industry in a North Indian Town: Case Studies in Latent Industrial Potential,* New Delhi, Government of India, Ministry of Commerce and Industry, 1956.

56 M. M. Mehta, *op. cit.,* pp. 260, 288.

57 Vera Anstey, *The Economic Development of India,* pp. 56-7.

58 Jawaharlal Nehru, *The Discovery of India* (London, 1951), p. 233.

59 Lloyd I. Rudolph, "The Political Role of India's Caste Association," *Pacific Affairs,* vol. 33, 1960, pp. 1-22.

60 M. M. Mehta, *op. cit.,* p. 260.

61 International Labour Office, *Industrial Labour in India* (London, 1938), p. 117.

62 Geoffrey W. Tyson, *The Bengal Chamber of Commerce and Industry* 1853-1953: *A Centenary Survey,* Calcutta, 1952, p. 123.

63 *Silver Jubilee Souvenir* 1927-51, Federation of Indian Chambers of Commerce and Industry, New Delhi, 1952, pp. 13-4.

64 *Silver Jubilee Souvenir,* 1927-51, pp. 22-31.

65 *Ibid.,* p. 31.

66 *Ibid.,* p. 42. See also address by Sir M. Visvesvaraya, AIMO president, at 13th annual conference of AIMO, Nagpur, 14 March 1953. AIMO *Journal,* vol. VII, no. 3 (March 1953), p. 2.

67 I. L. O., *Industrial Labour in India,* p. 119.

68 Helen Lamb, "The 'State' and the Economic Development in India," *Economic Growth: Brazil, India, Japan,* Simon Kuznets and others, eds. (Durham, N. C.), 1955, p. 487.

69 Nalini R. Sarkar, "My Days in the Federation," *Silver Jubilee Souvenir* 1927-51. pp. 197-98. Sarkar was Federation President in 1933.

70 Jawaharlal Nehru, *Independence and After,* 1950, pp. 189, 191, 193.

71 *Christian Science Monitor,* 5 June 1956, p. 1.

72 Norman Cousins, "Nehru, Man and Symbol: A Fragmentary Appreciation," *Saturday Review,* 20 June 1964, p. 18.

73 Helen Lamb, "The Indian Business Communities and the Evolution of an Industrial Class," *Pacific Affairs,* vol. XXVIII, no. 2 (June 1955), p. 113.

74 "A Capitalist in Rage," *A.I.C.C. Economic Review,* vol. VII, no. 23 (1 April 1956), H.D. Malaviya, ed., p. 15; see also Nehru, *The Discovery of India,* p. 391.

75 Even such a distinguished and enlightened industrialist as J.R.D. Tata has expressed this feeling. In his annual chairman's speech to the shareholders of Tata Iron and Steel Company, Limited, he said, "I feel that the charge that free enterprise has shown no initiative in recent years is particularly hard to take. I, for one, am in fact surprised at the amount of initiative displayed considering the discouragement and disincentives to which it has been subjected." Reprinted in *Economic Weekly,* vol. VIII, no. 35 (1 September 1956), p. 1048. For an interesting discussion of businessmen's attitudes towards the private sector, see Myron Weiner, *The Politics of Scarcity* (Chicago, 1962), pp. 124-9.

76 "The Industries Development and Regulation Act, 1951," *Reserve Bank of India Monthly Bulletin,* Bombay, February 1952, pp. 121-23.

77 Jerome B. Cohen, *The Role of the Government in Economic Development in India,* unpublished paper, Massachusetts Institute of Technology, Centre for International Studies, October 1953. See especially Chapters III and V. A review of statements by the business community and its spokesmen in the commercial and industrial journals suggests that this attitude reached its peak in late 1954 and 1955, though it is still much in evidence.

78 See, for example, the speech by Sir Jehangir Ghandy, Director-in-Charge, Tata Iron and Steel Co., Ltd., 23 January 1955. Reported in *Hindustan Times,* 24 January 1955, p. 2.

79 "Company Law," *Eastern Economist,* July 29, 1955, Supplement follows, p. 168, vol. XXV, no. 5.

80 Nigam and Chaudhuri, pp. 55, 151. The managing agency system has only been briefly sketched here. Additional sources available for further reference include: Raj K. Nigam, *Managing Agencies in India (First Round—Basic Facts),* Research and Statistics Division, Department of Company Law Administration, Ministry of Commerce and Industry, Government of India (New Delhi, 1957); and National Council of Applied Economic Research, New Delhi, *The Managing Agency System. A Review of Its Working and Prospects of Its Future,* Asia Publishing House (Bombay, 1959).

81 Das, *The Public Sector,* 1955, p. 7.

82 "The Debate on Industrial Policy," *Capital,* vol. CXXXIII, no. 3339, 23 December 1954, p. 837; Industrial Policy Resolution, New Delhi, Government of India, 30 April 1956. A balanced summary of the main current of socialist thought in India is provided in *Indian Approaches to a Socialist Society,* Margaret W. Gisher

and Joan V. Bondurant, editors, Indian Press Digests—Monograph Series, no. 2, July 1956, Berkeley, Institute of International Studies, University of California.

83 *Capital, loc. cit.*

84 *Statesman* (New Delhi), 21 January 1955, p. 1. Technically, this resolution was one plank of the published Congress party platform. But, in India, where Congress is in complete control of the Central government and every important state government, the Congress party platform is essentially a statement of forthcoming government policy.

85 "The Prime Minister's Report to the Avadi Congress," (January 1955, reported in "The State of the Nation," *Eastern Economist,* vol. XXIV, no. 3.21 January 1955). p. 83.

86 Minister of Education and Natural Resources and Scientific Research, until his death in 1958.

87 *Statesman* (New Delhi), 20 January 1955, p. 9.

88 The following material unless otherwise cited, is from *Industrial Policy Resolution* (New Delhi, 30 April 1956).

89 *Ibid.,* p. 4.

90 *Capital,* vol. CXXXVI, no. 3408 (10 May 1956), p. 678. Seven industrialists commented on the new resolution, five of them favourably. See also *Economic Weekly,* vol. III, no. 19 (12 May 1956), p. 562. Reporting on the Industrial Policy Resolution's effect on the market, the article states: "The absence of any rigidity in implementing this policy within a given time limit and scope given to the private sector to contribute its quota to the development of the country seems to have tipped the scales in favour of the investors." *Capital* headlined its weekly review of the Calcutta stock market with this phrase: "Stock Market Welcomes the Industrial Policy Statement," vol. CXXVI, no. 3407 (3 May 1956), p. 633. Even the Federation of Indian Chambers offered surprisingly moderate criticism (*Hindustan Times,* 7 May 1956, p. 1). The chairman of the All-India Manufacturers' Organization was, on balance, favourably impressed with the resolution (*Capital,* vol. CXXXVI, no. 3408, 10 May 1956, p. 678).

91 Harry Robinson, signed article appearing in *Commerce,* 17 November 1956. Robinson is a research economist, Stanford Research Institute, then working with the Ministry of Commerce and Industry in analyzing private investment needs and opportunities.

92 *Ibid.* Robinson, writing in a businessmen's weekly journal, concludes his article with the following statement: "In India's new concept of the industrial development, nationalization does not become a programme, and the socialistic State does not become a totalitarian State. The 1956 Resolution charts a fresh course, permitting a freedom of development in the private sector, but with checks and balances to prevent a detrimental concentration of economic power and wealth. Private enterprise has been given a new opportunity to justify its existence in a socialistic State. It is now up to the industrialists to prove by action that the Government's re-appraisal of the worthwhileness of private enterprise has not been misconceived. Private industry's future position in India's socialistic State will depend upon good behaviour during the years ahead."

93 The following indices provide some measure of this growth. They have been recomputed to a base year of 1947 or 1946-47.

	Index of industrial Production[a]	Labour productivity[a]
1947	100	100
1949	109	106
1951	121	124
1953	139	147
1955	167	171
1957	189	168
1959	212	182
1961	252	201
1963	297	

	Capital's index of industrial activity[b]		Index number of wholesale prices[c]
1946-47	100	1947	100
1948-49	94	1949	128
1950-51	96	1951	148
1952-53	115	1953	132
1955	129	1955	120
1957	146	1957	142
1959	156	1959	151
1961	183	1961	164
1962	200	1963	173

a See, for source, Chapter I, Table IX.

b *Capital,* vol. CXXXVI, no. 3401, 22 March 1956, p. 416, and vol. CLI, no. 3790, 19 December 1963, p. 920.

c *Monthly Abstract of Statistics,* vol. 8, no. 10 (October 1955), p. 81; *Reserve Bank of India Bulletin,* vol. X, no. 10 (October 1956), p. 116; *Economic Survey* 1963-64, Table 5.1; *Reserve Bank of India Bulletin,* vol. XVIII, no. 6 (June 1964), p. 825.

94 A. M. Rosenthal, *New York Times* correspondent in India, reported: "This reporter has met a variety of businessmen who say about Prime Minister Nehru what New Dealers said about FDR when he was under attack in the early 1930's. They say he is saving the private enterprise system." *New York Times,* 3 January 1957, p. 56.

95 Lewis, *op. cit.,* pp. 208 ff.

96 *Report of the Bankers' Mission to Pakistan and India,* February-March 1960, Government of Pakistan, Ministry of Finance, 1960, p. 16.

97 Malenbaum and Lewis.

98 For an able review of this phase of Gandhi's thinking, see D. P. Mukerji,

"Mahatma Gandhi's Views on Machines and Technology," *International Social Science Bulletin,* vol. VI, no. 3 (1954), pp. 411-24. The following information has been drawn from this article.

99 *Silver Jubilee Souvenir* 1927-51, p. 187.

100 A distinguished Indian economist has commented: "Gandhism was little more than revivalism. Its useful work lay in fields where it combated evils, such as untouchability, within the older framework. But it made no attempt to deal with the major problems of coming to terms with the machine techniques and the new materialist economic ends. Therefore, with all of its supposed influence among the Indian merchant and capitalist classes, it induced no moral restraints in their economic behaviour and left them as among the most predatory types in the world today. . . . Gandhism failed, in addition, because it would not frankly acknowledge the need for adopting machine technology." D. R. Gadgil, "Some Requirements for Technical Progress in Asia," *Pacific Affairs,* vol. XXIV, no. 2, June 1951, reprinted in *Economic Policy and Development,* Gokhale Institute of Politics and Economics, Pub. No. 30 (Poona 1955), p. 150.

101 *Congress Presidential Addresses,* Madras, G. A. Natesan, 1934, p. 896.

102 "Report on the Avadi Congress," *Statesman,* 20 January 1955, p. 5.

103 Milton Singer, "Cultural Values in India's Economic Development," *Annals,* vol. 305 (May 1956), pp. 87-8.

104 *Second Five Year Plan,* pp. 121, 123.

105 A sample of recent writings may be cited in this connection. D. R. Gadgil "Some Requirements for Technical Progress in Asia," *Pacific Affairs,* vol. XXIV, no. 2 (June 1951). Noting that the caste system has broken down or is fast doing so, Dr. Gadgil continues: "Though caste no longer functions effectively in most spheres, caste loyalties still obtrude in all fields and prevent the building of a homogeneous society. Their harmful effects linger, while their potentiality for good has been largely lost: members of old caste or family groups have been found to act under considerable moral restraint while within the orbit of these institutions though becoming almost amoral outside it. The breakdown of the old institutions has thus dualistic behaviour. The situation cannot be remedied so long as new social codes and new foci of loyalty do not appear." (p. 149.) Two recent accounts based on field impressions in India suggest the presence of forces favouring change, but raise doubts about the extent or effectiveness of this change. Thus, in mid-1964, Selig S. Harrison reports that, in the village Janglapur, 74 households were segregated in the untouchable quarter, and had to share one well as the higher castes combined to prevent the use of the other wells. Only 15 untouchable boys attended school as, although tuition was free, few could afford the other expenses for books, etc. "The grand total of University graduates in the history of the village is three—all from landlord families." "Poverty Scars Life of Indian Untouchables; Foreigners' Visits Rare in Remote Villages; Schools, Roads, Gradually Broaden Horizon," in *Los Angeles Times,* 20 July 1964, Part I, pp. 17-8. A more comprehensive report is in Harold R. Isaacs, "The Ex-Untouchables," *New Yorker,* 12 and 19 December 1964. India's official policy of ending untouchability, including selective discrimination

in favour of untouchables in such matters as schooling and government employment. still has to overcome deep-seated social practices while giving rise to new
problems. There may also be resentment at these privileges although Isaacs reports
that "the danger of the caste Hindu's losing his top-dog status is nil, and the ex-
untouchable remains a man who has the burdens of the centuries to shed." (p. 104,
19 December 1964.) The main problem remains one of integrating the untouchables
as *Indians* in a situation characterized by pressures for change encouraged by official
policy conflicting with deep-seated economic and social conditions of poverty and
prejudice.

106 Kingsley Davis, "Social and Demographic Aspects of Economic Development
in India," *Economic Growth: Brazil, India, Japan*, p. 307. "Among the peasantry . . .
there is toward government an exaggerated dependency attitude called 'ma-bap-ism'
or mother-and-fater dependency.... The peasants expect miracles to be per-
formed *for* them without their doing anything."

107 Or they may not be delayed. The difficulty of making even the most elementary
judgments on social and cultural implications is well illustrated by comparing the
statement by Kingsley Davis above with the following statement by D. R. Gadgil,
reporting on the success of a cooperative sugar factory: "The success of the [coopera-
tive]. Society depends essentially on the loyal support of its members, a primary
requirement of all cooperative organizations. From the inception of the Society,
the origin of the idea and its successful development have been due to the imaginative foresight of certain local leaders, their persistence in and devotion to the idea,
and the great loyalty of members and *the faith shown by them in their leaders.* The
greatest test came in the last quarter of 1950.... At this time the vast bulk of members
. . . (did not sell outside the cooperative at the relatively high price then obtaining) and
showed the most remarkable restraint and patience, even though it meant definite
monetary loss to many, which amounted in the case of some to substantial sums."
(Italics supplied.) Clearly, this is the positive side of "ma-bap-ism."

108 G. B. Jather and S. G. Beri conclude their chapter on "Social and Religious
Institutions" with this optimistic comment: "A similar change in outlook (that
man can control his own destiny) has already begun in India, and with the spread
of general education and enlightenment, with the progress of practical science and
the steady pursuit of a policy of national economic development, the existing causes
of Indian pessimism will surely be removed and it will cease to be regarded as one
of the principal hindrances to economic development." *Indian Economics* (Madras,
1949), p. 97.

Kingsley Davis, in summarizing his position, is much less sanguine: "When all
of the social impediments . . . are added together, they mount up to a rather impressive
amount of obstruction. Although the evidence suggests that even though the social
structure will not actually stop economic growth, it must be granted that this structure
will probably slow the change. If so, then we must recall the other difficulty from
which India is suffering—overpopulation in relation to resources. The two together
(a partially archaic society and overpopulation) may well constitute such a barrier
to steady economic progress that the present programme under a democratic government will bog down completely." *Economic Growth*, p. 315.

Milton Singer suggests that, within the present cultural framework, there are sufficiently appreciated values which will themselves motivate economic development in India. "Is it necessary to seek new spiritual incentives to make the Indian people work hard and bear the austerities added by their struggle to modernize their economy? In their indigenous 'materialism,' as well as in their philosophy of renunciation, interpreted by Gandhi as a discipline of action in the service of others, and in their quest for spiritual salvation under the guidance of *gurus* who have already achieved self-realization, may reside the psychological and moral motive forces needed for a democratic and nonviolent industrial development of India." "Cultural Values in India's Economic Development," *Annals*, vol. 305 (May 1956), p. 91.

109 Maurice Zinkin, "Colonialism," *Development for Free Asia* (New Jersey, 1956), pp. 112-30.

110 For a competent recent account of the Indian economic framework, see P. S. Lokanathan, "The Indian Economic System," in Calvin B. Hoover, *Economic Systems of the Commonwealth,* Duke University Press, 1962, pp. 262-328. See also *Economic Review* (All India Congress Committee Publication), July 22, 1959 (esp. the article by V.K.R.V. Rao, "Implications of Socialist Pattern of Society"), and August 22, 1960. These two are special issues comprising the proceedings of symposiums on the Third Plan which included a number of distinguished participants.

CHAPTER III

THE EMERGENCE AND COMMITMENT OF AN INDUSTRIAL LABOUR FORCE

INDUSTRIALIZATION requires not only the recruitment and training of an industrial labour force, but also its commitment to an industrial as opposed to an agricultural way of life. As an underdeveloped economy moves toward industrialization, some part of the rural labour force is either pushed or pulled toward the growing industrial cities. The ties with the village and the land may remain strong. The development of a labour force which accepts the discipline of factory work and the conditions of urban living is much slower than the initial recruitment of enough workers to man the mills and factories.

We can say that a "committed" industrial labour force has developed, when workers no longer look on their industrial employment. as temporary, when they understand and accept the requirement of working as part of a group in a factory or other industrial enterprise, and when they find in the industrial environment a more adequate fulfilment of personal satisfactions than they enjoyed in the village or rural society. Commitment in this sense also involves the "structuring" of the labour force;[1] and management, unions and government may each play a role in the development of a "web of rules" which leads to a stable and committed industrial labour force.

Of course, there are several stages of commitment. Four types of workers can be so identified: (1) the uncommitted worker, (2) the semi-committed worker, (3) the committed worker, and (4) the overcommitted worker.[2] A country's entire labour force does not have similar characteristics for all of its members. Some sectors of the labour force can be uncommitted, others semi-committed or committed, while still others can be overcommitted, all at the same time in the same country.

As we have seen, the industrial labour force in India today is probably somewhere around 11-14 million; India is still predominantly an agricultural country. But the rise of the cotton and jute textile industries in Bombay and Calcutta during the latter part of the last century, and their continued growth along with the newer industries like steel, engineering, cement, paper, etc. brought an increase in factory employment from around 300,000 in 1892 to 3.9 million in 1961.[3] Similar gains were registered in the other sectors of the industrial labour force: primarily mining, plantations, railways and other transport, and municipal and public works. During the same period, the migration of people to the cities was proceeding. In 1881, only 9.3 per cent of the Indian population lived in urban areas (over 5,000), while, by 1941, the total was 12.8 per cent and, by 1961, it was 18 per cent.[4]

Where did these workers come from? Why did they migrate to the industrial cities? To what extent do they now represent a stable and committed industrial labour force? These are the questions we shall attempt to answer in this chapter. Management's role in recruiting and developing the labour force will be brought into the discussion, and some reference will also be made here to the part played by unions and by government to show the interrelationship between the structuring of the labour force and the institutions which are concerned with it.

The Push from the Land

An understanding of the changes which have occurred in Indian agriculture and which have given rise to a large group of agricultural labourers willing to move to urban industrial employment is necessary to an understanding of the growth of the industrial labour force. In the pre-British period, the Indian economy was characterized by more or less independent, self-sustaining villages. Plots of land surrounding the village were owned and cultivated by individual peasants who lived in the village, although there were also various types of semi-free and unfree agricultural labourers. Nonagricultural needs were met by local artisans.[5]

In some areas such as Bengal and Bihar, the British encouraged a class of landowners known as "zamindars," who were assigned the responsibility of collecting land taxes for British revenues. When a peasant could not pay his taxes, his lands could be confiscated by the zamindar; and he would be forced to work for hire on the latter's holdings to provide for himself and his family. This increased the number of semi-free or unfree agricultural labourers. The process was further accelerated as some agricultural production began which was oriented to a cash market, as in the case of cotton and jute. The demands of the tax collectors encouraged the growth of cash crops, and moneylenders financed the peasant until his crops were sold. A poor harvest, however, could put the peasant at the mercy of the moneylender, who could also appropriate land when loans were defaulted, or, at least, keep the peasant permanently in debt.[6]

The plight of the small landowner was further accentuated by the subdivision of existing holdings among all sons. Many landholdings became so small as to be uneconomical. The rapid increase in population, especially after 1921, added to the rural impoverishment. The number of agricultural labourers increased and, by 1961, it is estimated that there were 47.3 million working agricultural labourers and 23.3 million agricultural families.[7] This number is still large, but it is clear that considerable surplus labour earlier left the land and migrated into the expanding industrial cities. One study of an Indian village, for example, reported:

A near doubling of population (in thirty years) has stimulated more extensive and intensive use of Kishen Garhi's land for agriculture.... Increased pressure on local lands has brought about an increase in the number of groups in the village whose members have dispersed to the outside urban world. One or two persons of almost every clan have joined with outsiders to earn a living instead of staying to work with kinsmen and neighbours.[8]

In many cases undoubtedly those who migrated to the cities were not only impoverished agricultural labourers; they were also from the lower castes, and had less to lose by leaving the security of the village. This point has been stressed by many early accounts. The character of India's industrial labour force is graphically indicated by a distinguished student of Indian labour problems:

The mass of workers still represents the superfluous elements of

India's rural population whom an impoverished land ... is incapable of supporting. Socially and economically they represent the most backward sections of the population.[9]

But there were also migrants among the better educated and the restless villagers. A study of migrants in Greater Bombay undertaken by the Demographic Centre at Chembur found that the migrants to Greater Bombay "have very much higher levels of educational attainment than the general population of the states from which they are drawn. Thus the cityward migration in India deprived the villages of the best of its population."[10]

These points are best understood against the background of a brief discussion of the caste and joint-family structure of the Indian village.

The Restraining Pull of the Village

Despite the poverty which the average villager faced, the socio-economic structure frequently held him and even today attracts him back from the city. The typical Indian village family is a joint family, including brothers, sons, grandsons, and even cousins, and their wives and children. Often this group may live under one roof; in any case, it is an integrated unit. Each member who works contributes to the support of the joint family, not just to his immediate dependants. Elderly, incompetent, or unemployed members of the family are taken care of by the others; the family thus represents a social security system.

This feeling of security is reinforced by the effect of the caste system on occupational choice and social intercourse. The four major castes in Hindu culture are subdivided into numerous sub-castes, to which many individuals are affiliated. Below these are the millions without caste—the "untouchables." The pervasive influence of caste is underscored in the following statement (which refers to an earlier period):

Hindu society ... is communal; it is the caste and not the individual that counts. A man's social position is that of the caste of which he is a member. The caste chooses his occupation for him, and if he disregards its decision, then it can take away his social position altogether by outcasting him. Secondly, the caste-system is rather a socio-economic than a social organization. Almost every caste is closely associated with a particular occupation.[11]

Today, the impact of caste on occupational choice is less important, but still influential in certain occupations, such as weaving, spinning, sweeping, and so on. To the extent that the broad caste classifications correspond to income classes, low caste members may also be among the least educated, especially in the villages. Caste or sub-caste may also dictate to the tradition-bound villager his choice of a wife, how his food should be cooked and by whom, the clothes he may wear, and the people with whom he associates. If he moves to another village or area, he tries to find members of his sub-caste, and the fear that he will be unable to do so is inhibiting on mobility. Language differences, which are reflected in the fact that there are some 17 distinct linguistic groups and many more dialects, reinforce the villager's attachment to his local area.

The sharp break represented by migration to the impersonal city is well stated in a recent study of 523 working-class families in one section of Bombay:

> The industrial worker comes from a close, familiar, well-knit environment of a village. Born and bred amidst the affections of his parents, brothers and sisters, and in fact the whole village, the industrial worker coming to the city for the first time suddenly gets lost in the tempo of the city life with its accompanying traits of individualism, materialism, indirect contacts and impersonal ways and indifferences. He feels cut off for the greater part of his existence from the family which to him was affectionate and protective.[12]

Yet this family and caste structure may also push certain individuals away from the village. Another survey of the communal composition of a sample of 550 families of Bombay textile workers in 1937 found that 43 per cent were from the "depressed" (untouchable) classes, and most of these were Mahars, whose hereditary occupation was serving as village menials, performing such services as guarding crops, scavenging, carrying messages, cutting fire-wood, carrying cowdung cakes, and so on. "The development of industries in the city has, however, opened a new channel for them for the betterment of their economic condition and for emancipation from the economic and social dependence on the caste Hindus."[13]

The depressed classes were not the only ones who migrated from the villages after the turn of the century: agricultural labourers, more or less regardless of caste, moved in great numbers as pressure on the land increased and inducements were offered to come to the cities. The magnitude of this rural-urban migration is illustrated by the fact that while India's population increased by roughly 50 per cent between 1901 and 1951, Bombay, Calcutta, Delhi and Madras populations expanded by more than 235 per cent. Table XXI shows the differential migration status between the large cities and the largest cities, classified by the employed and the unemployed in 1955. About 40 per cent of the labour force in urban India was migrant in 1955. By industrial status, 50 per cent of the employees were migrants, compared to only about 15 per cent of the unpaid family workers.

Strong as family, caste and language ties were in the past, these began to weaken under the pressure of economic forces. Better alternative job opportunities in the expanding urban industrial centres, as well as growing population pressure, attracted even higher caste villagers. A survey of 38,000 Bombay textile mill workers in 1940, for example, revealed that nearly 60 per cent of the Hindus were Marathas and Kunbis, members of respectable cultivating castes from regions relatively near Bombay, and only 15 per cent were "Harijans" (the so-called "untouchables" or members of "depressed classes").[14] However, this is consistent with continued stratification within the factory.

The significance of weakening village ties and the rush to the cities is summarized in the report of the Labour Investigation Committee in 1946:

In recent years ... there has been a greater concentration of the working class population in industrial areas and this had led to

TABLE XXI

PERCENTAGE DISTRIBUTION OF PERSONS IN THE LABOUR FORCE
BY INDUSTRIAL STATUS AND PLACE FROM WHERE MIGRATED,
MAY-NOVEMBER 1955, URBAN ALL-INDIA

| Place from where migrated | Industrial status | | | | | |
	Employees	Employers	Unpaid family workers	Gainfully employed persons	Unemployed persons	Persons in labour force
Nonmigrants	47%	68%	80%	58%	47%	57%
Migrants from rural areas of same						
state	22	12	7	17	12	17
of other states	12	5	3	9	5	9
Migrants from urban areas						
of same state	5	2	1	4	3	3
of other states	4	5	1	3	2	3
Migrants from Pakistan	5	5	2	5	13	6
Migrants from other countries	1	*	*	*	*	*
Not recorded	4	3	7	4	19	5
Total	100	100	100	100	100**	100
Number of Sample Persons	25,820	863	3,696	46,003	15,328	61,331

*Less than 1%.

**Does not add to 100 because of rounding base: Persons of each industrial status.
Base: Persons of each industrial status.

SOURCE: *The National Sample Survey Ninth Round: Supplementary to Report No.*
16, May-November 1955, Number 62, *Report on Employment and Unemployment*,
Cabinet Secretariat: Government of India (New Delhi, 1962), p. 204.

the rise of an urban proletariat in most cities, which is prepared
to stick to the town to a greater extent than before.... A steady
increase in the ranks of landless labourers moreover has compelled many to remain and settle in the town and to regard it as
their home. Even today, no doubt, large masses of labour do
migrate to the urban areas but it is an unmistakable fact that
the labour force in principal industrial cities like Bombay,

Calcutta, Cawnpore [Kanpur], etc., is getting more and more
stabilized. This stabilization has been a matter of necessity
rather than of choice. The village, the joint family, the caste,
and several other institutions of old, which were the bulwark of
social security for the toiling masses are, unfortunately, steadily
crumbling down. At the same time, the urban areas have not
yet begun to provide for them the degree of social security which
may be considered as necessary.[15]

As we shall see later, the industrial labour force still has important
ties with the village. But the old links were crumbling, and the
process of migration was hastened by the recruiting methods used
by industrial employers.

A more recent study by an American sociologist, Richard D.
Lambert, throws some additional light on the process of recruitment and commitment of an industrial labour force in Poona.
While Poona may not be typical of the larger industrial centres
in India, it has a variety of industries which were able to recruit
industrial workers largely within the city from other occupations.
The process of migration from the villages preceded this recruitment, and the new factory workers had already broken their ties
with the rural village. Commitment in the sense of willingness to
work in factories was not much of a problem, although there was
some variation among types of industries. Furthermore "on the
key social placement variables—caste, literacy, and educational
achievement—the factory workers were not very different from a
cross section of the Poona population."[16] While Lambert concluded that these factory workers were committed to industrial
employment, it is rather significant that nearly one-third wanted to
round off their lives in a village.

The influence of caste, extended family, traditional village ties,
etc. deserve further serious study. One problem arises from the
paucity and incompleteness of the historical record; related to this
is the confusion arising from the fact that traditional social patterns
are in a state of flux and the failure to keep in mind that generaliza-
tions based on past experience need to be qualified before applying
them to the present and *vice versa*. Further, terms like "caste"
have been indiscriminately used.[17] More importantly, there has

been little systematic analysis of the economic implications of prevailing caste or family systems. For instance, it has not often been realized that close family ties may just as likely encourage urbanward migration at low "subsistence" wage rates as at higher "subsistence" levels corresponding to the average rural product.[18] Caste ties may facilitate migration but they also set up non-competing groups and add to rigidities within the factory or the trade union. Nor is the problem of commitment predominantly or even mainly one of resistance to the discipline of industrialism as opposed to the changes ushered in by urbanization.[19] Industry has generally paid more but has also imposed special requirements in the form of discipline, attendance, performance, or skills which may explain its relatively superior rewards. When all of these considerations are kept in mind, the problem of securing a "committed" labour force becomes more than one of merely securing adequate response to economic incentives or confining oneself to a general assertion that, with unlimited supplies of labour, industry should face no special problems in recruitment.

The historical record suggests clearly that, in newly industrializing areas, employers had to invest considerable effort and expenditure to locate and obtain available labour "surpluses."[20] This appears to be true even today, except for established urban settlements.

It is commonplace to observe that the supply of unskilled labour is infinitely elastic, but not that of skilled labour. This is true but something of an oversimplification. Terms like "skill" are relative to the "state of the arts" prevailing in an economic system and, depending upon the previous history of industrialization, shortages may become apparent even at a level of performance which may be classified on an *a priori* basis as requiring only low skills. The "skill" requirements may even extend to an insistence on prior work experience, indicative of socialization in industry. It has also been suggested that employers had a preference for migrants accompanied by their entire families and, of this category, there was historically a shortage.[21] Also, in an imperfect labour market, characterized by substantial gaps in information, knowledge of jobs as well as aptitudes may be limited.[22] Employers under these circumstances develop rules of thumb to determine who may turn out to be satisfactory workers. Parochial preferences may be expressed indicative of prior experience as well as of prevailing value systems. Finally, even in a large labour "surplus" country like India, there may not always be a correspondence between demand and supply as crystallized in specific localities; as there are also costs and uncertainties associated with migration, free market forces may not entirely be effective.

It is perhaps these circumstances which explain the emergence of a class of professional recruiters as a major force in the earlier record of Indian industrialization. These men were partly straw-bosses and in that sense quasi-managerial personnel; in part, they were entrepreneurs who mediated between the supply and demand for labour services in the labour market. As they played a considerable role in the earlier efforts to recruit labour, in overseeing their performance and in enforcing discipline, their role may be discussed briefly now.

Recruitment Through Jobbers

Growing labour requirements in cotton textiles, jute textiles, mining and plantations were filled by employers largely through the use of labour jobbers or contractors, known variously as *sardars, mistries, mukadams* and *jamedars*. These men frequently recruited friends, relatives and fellow members of the sub-caste from their own villages. In some cases, they were risk-takers in their own right and advanced the costs of migration or other expenses before pay-day. Generally, they were paid a commission by the employer for the number they recruited; the worker also had to pay a "commission" to the jobber to keep his job, get promoted, obtain leave, or be re-employed.

There is reason to believe that the jobber served as an important communication link in the earlier stages of industrialization. This included responsibilities in the field of recruitment, discipline, and "translation" of the requirements of industrial work. This last included an ability to communicate the technical requirements of the job as well as to fill, partially at any rate, the communication gap arising from the linguistic barriers between management and workers. The jobber's crucial role is well described by the following graphic account of his activities in the coal mining industry :

> It is he who visits the villages of miners and loaders, offers advances to them and brings them to the colliery, maintaining an adequate labour force from day to day. It is he who keeps the labour in village and family gangs, which adds to the amenities of their toil in an uncongenial environment. He is a man of higher intelligence and ability than ordinary miners. He keeps watch over them, sees that they go to the pits regularly and reports if they do not obtain proper facilities for work, i.e., suitable working faces, and an adequate supply of tubs. He is also responsible for all tools and plant issued to miners and loaders, keeps them under discipline at their work and also remains present when the payment is made to them. He acts in fact as the middleman between the management or the rising contractors and the miners.[23]

In other industries and plants, jobbers also acted as first-line supervisors. They had recruited the workers, knew them personally, and usually spoke their language: further the managers depended on them to get the work done. The supervisory role of the erstwhile labour recruiter persisted even after the recruitment functions were supplanted in many factories much later by the growth of centralized hiring departments.[24]

It became apparent however in course of time, that the jobber was not an unmixed blessing. In a real sense, problems arose because his interests diverged from the interests of both employers and workers. Employers found it costly to depend upon him for continued labour supply and performance, although he was important at one stage in bringing workers. The rising pressure for labour reform and legislation, with a tendency to place upon the employer the responsibility for the treatment of his workforce, also detracted from the contribution of these middlemen. Other factors which contributed to the undermining of their role were the gradual improvement in the supply of labour and emergence of a class of trained supervisors with better knowledge of local conditions. Workers also became increasingly resentful of the authority of the jobber. The added pressure for jobs better knowledge of labour

market conditions, and a growing class consciousness were among
the factors responsible for this development. The jobber himself
did not help the situation for he continued until quite late to resist
all efforts at unionization; his authority was often arbitrary, and
his exactions extreme. This was recognized by the Royal Commission on Labour in India in 1931 in the following words:

> The temptations of the jobbers' positions are manifold and it
> would be surprising if these men failed to take advantage of
> their opportunities. There are few factories where a worker's
> security is not, to some extent, in the hands of the jobber; in
> a number of factories, the latter has in practice the power to
> engage and dismiss the worker. We are satisfied that it is a
> fairly general practice for the jobber to profit financially from the
> exercise of this power.[25]

Management Policies

With labour costs low, relative to that of other inputs and recruitment and even day-to-day supervision in the hands of jobbers,
management failed in most instances to show systematic and
sustained interest in labour problems. The speculative character
of much of early Indian and European management was partly
responsible for this. We shall consider later the extent to which
this is still true of Indian management; here we are concerned with
the management pattern which coincided with the initial development of an industrial labour force. Given relative factor costs, it is
at least arguable that employers were following their own economic
self-interest.

The case of the Bombay textile industry is instructive on this
point. The labour force in the mills before 1934 has been described
by one investigator as "little more than a vast seething mob, with
few loyalties and even less discipline."[26] Yet, in the eighty years
preceding the 1934 intervention by the State to bring order into the
labour force, employers took no effective steps to change this
situation. One reason was that capital equipment was expensive
and labour was relatively cheap, so the "efficiency with which

labour was utilized and the discipline under which it worked were matters of small concern."[27]

Later, in the 1920's, when employers tried to reduce wages and rationalize in the face of increasing competition, they reaped the whirlwind of labour protest, strikes, and unionization in which the Communists played an important role. The labour force was structured and disciplined only through intervention of the Bombay State Government in a series of legislative enactments beginning in 1934.[28] Subsequently, the Millowners' Association established a Labour Office and many mills appointed labour officers before this was required by the Factories Act of 1948. Since the end of World War II, a dominant union, affiliated with the INTUC, has attempted to give stability and direction to workers' aspirations.

With some exceptions, little was done in the developing urban centres to meet the needs of migrants for adequate housing, sanitary facilities, and other amenities which might help the recent migrant from the village to accept industrial employment as a permanent way of life. The evidence suggests that both employers and civic organizations were, by and large, inactive in these respects. The situation, however, became seriously aggravated as two World Wars accelerated population growth heightened urban tensions. An incipient change in the attitude of the government was reflected by the Labour Investigation Committee (1946), which called for greatly increased public (government) initiative, while at the same time criticizing the employers. It said:

On the whole, it may be stated that employers, who take a most indifferent and nonchalant attitude towards welfare work and say that no rest shelters are provided as the whole premises belong to the workers themselves, no latrines are provided because workers prefer the open spaces, no canteens and sports are necessary because they are not likely to make use of such facilities, and so on, constitute the majority. It is apparent that, unless the precise responsibilities of employers in regard to welfare work are defined *by law*, such employers are not likely to fall in line with their more enlightened and farsighted confreres.[29]

Workers' housing was characterized by serious overcrowding. Of 5,000 dwellings in 14 industrial cities, surveyed before 1946 by the Labour Investigation Committee, 73 per cent were one-room huts, with occupancy rates as high as 4.8 persons per room.[30] Only one-third of this housing was provided by employers. A 1948 census of occupancy of the Worli Chawls (tenements) in the textile district of Bombay showed as many as 10 persons to a room, and a later private survey reported: "In a large number of chawls, it is found that ten to twenty persons occupy a single room" (with a floor space of 160 square feet).[31] Furthermore, occupants of a room were not usually members of a single family. Sometimes as many as three or four separate families or individuals shared a room. Single men were frequently accepted as boarders or lodgers, and this accounted for some of the overcrowding. But it was also the result of the attempt of people from the same villages or sub-castes to band together against the inhospitable city.

The Push from the City: Partial Commitment

Crowded housing, lack of privacy and other physical disadvantages of city living were not however so much different from the worst conditions in the villages from which the migrants came. There was less "open space" in the cities, of course; and this difference was often stressed by writers who also emphasized the intolerable working conditions in the factories. The initial lure of higher wages in the industrial city proved, in the view of these commentators, enough to attract workers in great numbers, but at great social cost:

The factories [in the Bombay textile industry] had no difficulty in attracting ... numbers of people, skilled and unskilled, who found the prospects of earning high wages at mechanical tasks more attractive than the hard work and poor returns of their depleted native regions; often it was poverty that drove them to the mills. Mostly leaving their families behind in their village homes, they made their way to the city, to pack for long hours into hot, close, crowded and noisy factories. Thereafter, they huddled fifteen to twenty and more together under any roof they could find, in stifling tenements and sheds where there was no sunshine, no clean air to breathe, not enough water to wash in, no sanitary conveniences, no room for comfortable sleeping and decent living. Lakhs [hundreds of thousands] of human beings were driven by the unthinking greed of what was termed progressive enterprise to such straits that, after hours of devitalizing work, they even lacked a home to turn to for relaxation, gardens and clean open spaces for revitalization.[32]

There is some idealization of village life in this comment, but it helps to explain much of the push that city living exerts on the industrial worker to return to his village, or at the very least, to keep his village ties for periodic visits. Conditions such as these, which are still visible in most Indian industrial cities, also underscore the strong preference which many Indian leaders, following Gandhi, have for village industries as opposed to urban industrialization. Earlier, in 1931, the Royal Commission on Labour observed that "the village is an infinitely better place than the city for the young and the aged, the sick, the maimed and the exhausted, the unemployed and the unemployable."[33]

To some extent, the impersonality of the city was also hostile to the recent migrant from the villages. If he came alone, as nearly four-fifths of those interviewed in the Bombay study did, he faced a new and strange environment. In some cases, he stayed with other members of his family who preceded him to the city. But more frequently he sought out distant relatives and friends from his village, and moved in with them for extended periods. Nearly half of the Bombay workers interviewed could not bring wives, children or other members of the family to the city to live with them, so their close family ties with the village remained.[34] The Chembur study of Greater Bombay estimated that at least 4 out of every 10 married migrant men in Bombay might have been living without their wives at the time of the last census.[35]

The 1961 census includes tables showing the number of females per 1000 males by cities in India. These tables also provide data which allow ready computations of the ratio of female workers per 1000 male workers. These ratios are summarized for a few Indian cities in Table XXII.

TABLE XXII
FEMALES PER 1000 MALES IN SELECTED CITIES AND TOWNS, 1961

City	Females per 1000 males	Female workers per 1000 male workers
Greater Bombay	663	95
Poona	884	195
Jamshedpur	791	126
Ahmedabad	805	86
Delhi Town Group	788	66
Calcutta	612	16
Cuttack	722	82
Madras	901	109

SOURCE: *Census of India Paper No.* 1 of 1961, Registrar General, Government of India (New Delhi, 1961), Sections IV, V.

The data in Table XXII are indicative of sources of tension in urban life which may affect performance in the factory and the ease with which the industrial workforce is stabilized. As mentioned earlier, one account stresses that employers preferred to hire migrants accompanied by their families, in view of their greater stability, and that there was a relative shortage of this category at prevailing real rates of remuneration. Investment in housing might be expected to increase the attractiveness of migration, but this would add to the employers' costs; opportunities for wage income for secondary earners—for example, women—might also increase the attractiveness of urban employment. Unfavourable conditions in these respects reflect the economic constraints limiting the development of a committed labour force.[36]

Even with some family and friends around him, the former villager may still feel somewhat adrift in the new life of the city and the factory. As Hoselitz has suggested, "the comforting security of a known and accustomed environment is lost. The number of face-to-face relationships with persons whom one does not know is increased; the loneliness of the individual becomes, in some cases, almost absolute."[37] This psychological isolation, perhaps as much as the inhospitable physical conditions of work and living, drives the worker to return periodically to his village or "native place," which he still considers as his home. He is pulled also by a number of obligations which his village ties place on him.

Forty-seven per cent of the Bombay textile workers surveyed in 1953-54 visited their villages once a year, 18 per cent twice a year, and 6 per cent three times a year or more—or a total of 71 per cent once a year or oftener.[38] The reasons given for these visits by the 523 workers mentioned are revealing (many respondents gave more than one reason):

	Per cent
Change of climate	84
To pay homage to the Deity	31
To see people at home	24
To recoup health (after illness)	15
To help at harvest season	13
Religious festivals	9
Marriage celebrations	7
Court and litigation business	2

"Change of climate" may mean many things: a chance to escape the heat of the city and factory during the summer months (although it is also hot in the villages), a change of scenery and a chance to be with one's kinsfolk and friends, and an escape from the routine of factory work (this may be a "residual category" in the interviews). The emphasis on "homage to the Deity" and "religious festivals" may reflect the connection between religious practices and the family obligations which the migrant worker has in his native village. Religious obligations are taken seriously by many Hindus and, in the words of one factory manager, "the worker would be considered an outcaste in his village if he did not return to observe these obligations and ceremonies."

These reasons for returning to the village partially account for the high rates of absenteeism, which we shall examine in the next section. But it is important to note that the same workers who gave these reasons also stated that they liked their present mill jobs. Only 21 per cent positively disliked industrial employment because it was "troublesome or involved hard work," and 5 per cent because the income was "insufficient". The investigator reported:

It is quite apparent that an overwhelming majority of migrants are generally content with their job situations or are adjusting themselves to their work in the mills and factories. However, we cannot gainsay the fact that their present position is economically better than what it was in the village.[39]

There have been no similar surveys of other industrial cities in India,[40] but the results of this Bombay study corroborate the impressions of labour officers and employment managers who reported in interviews that workers on leave in their villages will use every device to fight suspension by the employer if they overstay their leave. Telegrams, pleading letters written by hired letter-writers, and even appeals to the union are resorted to by workers who want to hang on to their factory jobs at all costs, even though they also want extended leave in their villages. In a sense, these Indian workers want to have their cake and eat it too: they are partially committed to factory jobs in that they regard them as more or less permanent jobs which can be interrupted (but not lost) by periodic visits to the village.[41] The insufficiency of urban incomes is, of course, an important explanation of this phenomenon. In some cases, this may involve a substantial multiple-livelihood status: the factory worker may own a share in the family plot and till it with the aid of relatives.[42]

Rates of Absenteeism

The general nature of the resulting problems is indicated by available data on rates of absenteeism which are much higher than in more advanced industrial countries. Data on Indian industries are regularly reported in *Indian Labour Journal,* and show that, in 1963, the rate varied from 2.4 per cent to 24.8 per cent in the Mysore engineering industry and from 9.9 per cent to 15.7 per cent in Bombay Cotton Mills. Yearly averages of monthly rates of absenteeism are shown by industry and city in Table XXIII. In 1961–62, the rates of absenteeism were the highest in the Mysore plantations (over 20 per cent) and the lowest in the Madras Cotton Mills (less than 8 per cent).

A measure of the causes of absenteeism in Indian factories was computed from *Indian Labour Journal* and is contained in

TABLE XXIII

AVERAGE ANNUAL MONTHLY RATES OF ABSENTEEISM BY INDUSTRIES AND CENTRES, 1951-62

Year	Cotton mill industry								Woollen industry		Engineering industry			Leather Industry	Gold mining	Plantations	Coal mines
	Bombay	Ahmedabad	Sholapur	Madras	Madurai	Coimbatore	Kanpur	Mysore	Kanpur	Dhariwal	Bombay	West Bengal	Mysore	Kanpur	Mysore	Mysore	All India
1	2	3	4	5	6	7	8	9	10	11	12	13	14	15	16	17	18
1951	12.7	8.3	18.7	8.9	11.3	10.3	12.0	11.8	13.2	10.6	13.9	10.1	9.7	7.8	10.2	18.3	13.3
1952	12.7	8.8	20.2	9.7	10.5	10.3	11.7	11.2	9.4	6.3	13.4	10.3	10.6	9.2	11.5	18.6	13.2
1953	12.6	9.4	20.5	9.3	10.9	8.2	12.3	11.4	11.0	5.0	13.7	10.8	11.4	9.2	11.6	16.4	13.5
1954	10.8	8.7	17.4	9.1	11.0	8.8	12.4	12.1	10.7	5.2	14.9	11.7	11.2	9.8	10.6	15.3	13.3
1955	8.2	6.8	18.0	6.6	12.2	9.9	12.8	11.5	10.6	5.0	15.6	12.8	10.6	10.1	13.5	16.9	14.0
1956	8.3	6.5	18.4	6.2	13.0	11.4	11.1	12.2	7.3	5.2	14.6	12.5	11.8	11.2	10.0	18.2	13.8
1957	7.1	6.8	16.0	7.0	13.2	11.3	13.0	16.3	8.5	4.8	14.6	12.5	11.9	10.0	12.2	20.5	13.7
1958	7.0	7.1	13.6	7.4	18.5	12.3	13.1	17.9	8.5	6.1	14.5	12.2	9.7	9.4	9.7	20.5	13.2
1959	7.3	6.6	13.4	7.7	13.4	11.3	13.7	19.4	8.0	7.8	14.5	12.3	11.4	8.9	10.0	19.5	13.1
1960	10.4	7.3*	16.9	8.2	13.0	11.9	14.2	19.2	10.1	9.2	13.7	11.5	9.3	9.6	9.7	18.8	13.3
1961	11.9	..	14.7	7.7	13.5	12.0	15.1	20.9	8.6	10.6	12.7	13.3	10.6	..	10.3	20.2	13.5
1962(P)	11.3	8.4**	15.3	7.8	13.8	12.8	na	27.3	na	11.9	13.9	13.2	15.0	na	8.6	21.5	13.0

N.B.—Information reported in columns 2 to 17 relate to the selected units only in the respective centres. Rates are simple annual averages of monthly rates.   * Based on figures up to April 1960 only.   ** Based on figures up to October 1962.

†Based on figures up to May 1960 only. The figures from June 1960 are not available.   na : Not available.

SOURCE: *Indian Labour Statistics 1963*, p. 129.

Table XXIV. The monthly variation in the proportion of total manshifts lost to absenteeism varies from a low of 9.1 per cent in January to 13.7 per cent in May with a 10.8 per cent average. The high averages for March, April and May are probably due to absenteeism for harvesting and sowing of crops, prior to the monsoon period. In 1963, with little monthly variation, sickness or accident accounted for 32.4 per cent of all absenteeism reported, social or religious cases for 14.3 per cent, absenteeism with leave for 38.0 per cent, and absenteeism without leave for 15.3 per cent.

The high percentage of absenteeism without leave forces many employers to keep an equivalent amount of surplus labour on hand to fill vacancies. This practice is frequent in the cotton textile industry, where the surplus is known as the "badi pool" and

TABLE XXIV

LABOUR BUREAU SERIES OF ABSENTEEISM IN CERTAIN MANUFACTURING INDUSTRIES IN INDIA BY MONTHS, 1963

Month	Percentage of absenteeism due to					Percentage of total manshifts lost to absentee-ism
	Sickness or accident	Social or religious causes	Other with leave	Causes without leave	Total(all causes)	
January	32.0	15.8	36.4	15.9	100.0	9.1
February	30.2	15.5	39.4	14.8	100.0	10.6
March	31.2	15.8	35.8	17.2	100.0	11.5
April	30.7	15.8	39.1	14.4	100.0	11.7
May	30.0	13.3	43.3	13.5	100.0	13.7
June	30.1	12.4	42.8	14.7	100.0	13.1
July	34.0	13.0	37.6	15.4	100.0	9.7
August	35.0	13.9	36.1	15.0	100.0	9.5
September	36.0	14.2	34.8	15.0	100.0	9.6
October	32.9	14.8	35.7	16.6	100.0	10.0
November	33.1	13.9	35.1	17.8	100.0	11.1
December	34.8	13.7	37.4	14.2	100.0	10.6
1963 Avg.	32.4	14.3	38.0	15.3	100.0	10.8

SOURCE: *Indian Labour Journal,* computed by weighting each report contained in the journal of the number of manshifts absent by the total number of manshifts scheduled to work.

averages about 20 per cent of total employment, thus offsetting absenteeism in the so-called permanent workforce.

Unauthorized absences are lower in other industries where the labourforce is drawn from greater distances, and authorized leave to home villages is arranged well in advance. In a large Calcutta jute mill, for example, unauthorized absences seldom exceeded 3 per cent in any month during the three years 1952-54, and were frequently below 2 per cent. Total monthly absenteeism, however, averaged between 12 and 33 per cent in these years, largely because of generous provisions for authorized leave and sick leave.[43]

In summary, the high rates of absenteeism found in much of Indian industry are a measure of the accommodation which Indian employers have made to the demands of Indian workers that they have considerable periods of time off work for visits to their home villages for a variety of reasons, including genuine or feigned illness. Absenteeism is costly to the worker in terms of lost earnings, particularly for workers on incentive pay, and the increased possibility of discharge. On the other hand, there has been a more liberal provision for authorized absence in Indian labour legislation.[44] Employers' spokesmen have also charged that some measures, like the Employees State Insurance Scheme, have encouraged absenteeism. The fact remains that there has been no appreciable improvement in absenteeism rates, and in some cases even a worsening of the position as can be seen from Table XXIII.

Labour Turnover

Despite the village ties, Indian industrial workers typically do not leave their factory jobs voluntarily to return to the villages. In an economy still characterized by urban unemployment and vast rural underemployment, the industrial worker holds on to his job at all costs. Consequently, labour turnover in many industries and firms relatively low compared to absenteeism, and is relatively low in comparison with American experience, as Table XXV shows. The data may not be strictly comparable however, because extended absence (counted as part of absenteeism in India) would lead to discharge in the United States (and count as part of labour turnover).

Examples of industrial firms illustrate the relatively low level of labour turnover, as computed in India. In one large cotton textile mill with about 15,000 employees, 275 workers left their jobs during the 12 months between 1 April 1950 and 31 March 1951.[45] Of these, only 32 were voluntary resignations, a yearly rate of slightly over two-tenths of 1 per cent. The same pattern was found in a large government-owned factory in South India. Absenteeism here was around 16 per cent per month in 1954, but labour turnover averaged six-tenths of 1 per cent. A Calcutta engineering firm reported an average labour turnover rate (for all reasons) of 6.4 per cent in 1951, 3.1 per cent in 1952, 1.2 per cent in 1953 and 2.1 per cent in 1954. This compared with an average absenteeism rate of 9 to 10 per cent during 1954.[46] Fragmentary data are also available for other industries. Annual turnover rates for the

TABLE XXV

MONTHLY LABOUR TURNOVER RATES IN COTTON TEXTILE
INDUSTRY, BOMBAY STATE AND UNITED STATES, 1951-62

(per 100 workers)

Year	Bombay		All centres		U.S.A.	
	Accession rate	Separation rate	Accession rate	Separation rate	Accession rate	Separation rate
1951	1.84	1.16	1.65	1.12	—	—
1953	1.57	1.20	1.26	1.03	—	—
1955	1.45	1.11	1.39	0.91	—	—
1956	1.37	1.25	1.35	1.04	—	—
1958	1.64	1.59	1.69	1.45	2.4	2.8
1959	1.72	1.41	1.90	1.25	2.7	2.8
1960	1.55	1.29	1.49	1.22	2.4	2.7
1961	1.96	1.32	2.00	1.26	2.4	2.5
1962	—	—	—	—	2.7	3.1

SOURCE: *Indian Labour Statistics* 1963, pp. 130-31; *Employment and Earnings Statistics for the United States* 1909-62, U.S. Bureau of Labour Statistics, Bulletin 1313-1, (Washington, 1963), p. 365. U.S. rates are for cotton broad-woven fabrics industry. Because of the change in the Standard Industrial classification in 1957, they are not available before 1957 on a comparable basis.

glass industry, which are somewhat higher, are as follows: 1952, 24.9; 1953, 27.2; and 1954, 31.4. The leather and tanning industry indicates a comparable level of turnover at 24.5 for 1954.

Larger firms appear to have lower turnover rates. This is indicated by figures for basic metals, silk, cotton textiles, paper mills, and chemicals. Generally the separation rates are very low for the large firms, and in some cases significantly high for the smaller firms. Table XXVI gives turnover rates for selected industries.

TABLE XXVI

LABOUR TURNOVER IN CERTAIN INDUSTRIES BASED ON SEPARATION RATES ONLY, EXPRESSED AS PERCENTAGES WITH YEARS OF REFERENCE

Industry or occupation (In some cases classified by size, group and state)	Year of reference					
	1951	1952	1953	1954	1955	1956
BASIC METAL INDUSTRY						
Employing less than 500	—	—	—	24.70	—	—
Employing more than 500	—	—	—	13.10	—	—
HYDROGENATED OIL INDUSTRY	—	9.70	8.30	7.00	—	—
MATCH INDUSTRY	—	4.30	3.40	4.00	—	—
MINERAL OIL INDUSTRY	—	6.50	—	—	6.60	—
SILK INDUSTRY						
Employing less than 500	—	—	29.80	24.60	30.70	—
Employing more than 500	—	—	13.50	10.50	13.70	—
TANNERIES AND LEATHER FINISHING INDUSTRY	—	—	—	24.50	—	—
COTTON TEXTILE INDUSTRY (BOMBAY STATE) BY SIZES[a] MONTHLY AVERAGES						
Employing up to 100	5.95	6.73	7.33	5.04	5.11	5.87
Employing 101-500	8.18	4.08	3.05	4.10	2.75	2.37
Employing 501-1000	1.94	1.20	2.04	1.49	0.93	1.40
Employing 1001-2000	1.13	0.90	0.87	0.59	0.71	0.89
Employing over 2000	0.98	1.34	1.00	1.01	1.09	1.03
All establishments	1.12	1.23	1.03	0.98	0.91	1.04

TABLE XXVI (*Contd.*)

Industry or occupation (In some cases classified by size, group and state)	Year of reference					
	1951	1952	1953	1954	1955	1956
PAPER MILL INDUSTRY						
(ALL INDIA)	—	—	5.30	4.40	1.70	—
Group A—up to 400—7 units	—	—	—	—	—	—
Group B—401-1000—4 units	—	—	—	—	—	—
Group C—1001 and above—9 units	—	—	—	—	—	—
CHEMICAL INDUSTRY						
Group I—0-100—33 units	—	—	—	—	—	—
Group II—101-500—19 units						
Group III—501 and above—8 units	—	—	—	—	—	—
DOCKS	—	—	10.80	—	6.10	—

Industry or occupation (In some cases classified by size, group and state)	Year of reference				
	1957	1958	1959	1960	1961
BASIC METAL INDUSTRY					
Employing less than 500	—	—	—	—	—
Employing more than 500	—	—	—	—	—
HYDROGENATED OIL INDUSTRY	—	—	—	—	—
MATCH INDUSTRY	—	—	—	—	—
MINERAL OIL INDUSTRY	—	—	—	—	—
SILK INDUSTRY					
Employing less than 500					
Employing more than 500	—	—	—	—	—
TANNERIES AND LEATHER FINISHING INDUSTRY	—	—	—	—	—
COTTON TEXTILE INDUSTRY (BOMBAY STATE) BY SIZES					

TABLE XXVI (*Contd.*)

Industry or occupation (In some cases classified by size, group and state)	Year of reference				
	1957	1958	1959	1960	1961
MONTHLY AVERAGES					
Employing up to 100	7.09	8.10	6.85	—	—
Employing 101-500	2.93	3.26	3.61	—	—
Employing 501-1000	1.13	1.27	1.59	—	—
Employing 1001-2000	0.85	1.46	1.11	—	—
Employing over 2000	1.46	1.53	1.22	—	—
All establishments	1.39	1.45	1.25	—	—
PAPER MILL INDUSTRY (ALL INDIA)					
Group A—up to 400— 7 units	—	—	—	—	3.67
Group B—401-1000— 4 units	—	—	—	—	0.80
Group C—1001 and above—9 units	—	—	—	—	0.27
CHEMICAL INDUSTRY					
Group I—0-100— 33 units	—	—	—	—	3.37
Group II—101-500— 19 units	—	—	—	—	1.43
Group III—501 and above—8 units	—	—	—	—	0.63
DOCKS	—	—	—	—	—

Name of state	Printing	Iron ore Mining	Glass industry		
	1954	1957	1952	1953	1954
Andhra	6.9	16.9			
Assam	4.3				
Bihar	2.9	6.5	22.1	14.6	30.0
Bombay	3.1		33.4	25.9	32.7
Hyderabad			1.6	35.2	13.2
Madhya Pradesh	9.4		11.5	11.2	14.1
Madras	5.2				
Mysore		11.7			
Orissa	3.9	24.7			
Punjab			14.4	15.5	10.1
Rajasthan	13.7				

TABLE XXVI (*Contd.*)

Name of state	Printing	Iron ore Mining	Glass industry		
	1954	1957	1952	1953	1954
Saurashtra			27.3	34.3	8.0
Travancore-Cochin			6.3	4.5	1.6
Uttar Pradesh	3.0		48.4	48.2	56.4
West Bengal	4.8		13.5	17.7	21.4
Delhi	1.3				
Madhya Bharat	0.8				
All India		27.4	24.9	27.2	31.4

SOURCE : *Indian Labour Journal* (formerly known as *Indian Labour Gazette*), Labour Bureau, Ministry of Labour and Employment, Government of India, Manager of Publication, Delhi (Issues of the journals from December 1956 to November 1962 were consulted to assemble the data). Until 1961, the turnover rate was calculated with reference to separation rates (mainly quits, but also discharge from service, or death). Since then, the data relating to accession rates are also being published.

^aThe data on cotton mills are from *Indian Labour Statistics* 1961, Labour Bureau, Ministry of Labour and Employment, Government of India, Manager of Publications, New Delhi, 1962, p. 153.

It can be seen that the data are scanty, and in most cases the break-ups are not detailed enough to permit refined analysis. The influence of factors like premature aging, changing labour market conditions, unauthorized absence, etc. need to be isolated by more detailed investigation. It seems clear that the situation has improved with the passage of time, but some of the reduction in turnover rates is due to employer efforts to build permanent employment rolls and increasing restrictions on their ability to dismiss or retrench workers.

Indiscipline and Poor Performance

High absenteeism rates are not the only reasons for employer concern. This is reflected by reports of indiscipline and poor performance arising from the experience of a number of Indian and European employers in India.

The visitor to Indian factories, particularly in the cotton textile and jute industries, is struck by the amount of loitering which he sees in the mill yards. Workers have apparently left their machines, frequently without permission, to go outdoors for a smoke, to chat or just to sit. Attempts to discipline them are either resisted by the workers with the help of union representatives, or are ineffective, according to many managements.[47] Not all the employers interviewed complained of this indiscipline, but many did. The difficulty of discharging offending workers, and the lack of pressure to utilize labour effectively, because it is so plentiful, help to explain poor labour discipline.

An extreme type of labour indiscipline is illustrated by physical assaults on managerial staff by workers. In 8 months during 1946, for example, 75 assaults were reported in Bombay cotton textile mills, on managers and other high staff, clerks and timekeepers.[48] Writing in 1953, one authority on the textile industry concluded: "In brief, with the exception of some centres, industry-wide forces of indiscipline and defiance make the maintenance of industrial discipline a difficult proposition. To the extent that this spirit is general, industrial efficiency must rest on an unstable and tenuous basis."[49] Other instances were reported in interviews with Indian management, although most cases of assaults on managerial staff took place during strikes, when workers stormed company offices. However, only one was reported during 1954-55 in the 50 firms interviewed. The developments in subsequent years continue to give room for concern as, in a number of cases, protest has taken an "irrational" and violent form.[50] This form of protest should be distinguished from the highly organized challenges to authority which, after all, may arise at any level of development and are subject to reasonable (although not precise) assessment of costs and benefits. As late as the sixties, Indian authorities were concerned about violence or unruly and abusive behaviour in the coal mines, in the modern Rourkela steel plant, in an automobile plant in Bombay, and other places too numerous to mention.

Apart from indiscipline, poor performance by Indian workers is less generally charged by employers. Among the employers interviewed, the frequent response was that the Indian worker was often just as good as his counterpart in other countries, given the same equipment and the same state of health. Malnutrition and disease, of course, lower the stamina of the Indian worker, and these, coupled with poor training and illiteracy, seem to indicate a lower level of performance. But an appreciative view of the Indian worker is found in many of the better managed firms. For example, a high official of the Bombay plant of an American firm said:

> Our men work pretty well; not as fast as in the United States but then these men live ten to twelve in a room smaller than this office, and they don't get the right food. Many are small of stature, so they can't handle the heavy work. But, taking these differences into account, they are equally as productive as American workers.[51]

The Indian superintendent of a well-managed jute mill in Calcutta explained:

> The philosophy I try to get over to our supervisors is—don't look on everything as a challenge to your authority. There is a lot we can do to encourage more consultation and participation in dealing with Indian workers. The man working in the mill has certain problems which he can explain and understand, regardless of literacy. It's amazing to me in dealing with workers how well they can see your problem. But too often supervisors fail to see the workers' problem, either because of their superior education or class feeling.

This suggests that the response of Indian workers to the productivity requirements of modern industry is also related to managerial attitudes and competence. So obvious a point hardly needs emphasis here; and its full implications will be developed in a later chapter dealing with the nature of current managerial attitudes and practices in Indian industry. But so much emphasis in this chapter has been placed on the "partially committed" Indian industrial worker that we need here to stress that, under favourable employment conditions, his aspirations are not greatly different from workers in other industrial societies, despite cultural differences.[52]

Two studies substantiate this point. The first is a random-sample survey of 308 workers in a large Calcutta plant manufacturing sewing machines and other light engineering products. The firm has been expanding, and is known for its progressive and enlightened management, both technically and in terms of its employee relationships. The investigator found that :

the four most important things that the workers want are sufficient and adequate income, a sense of security, an opportunity for promotion and advancement, and finally, opportunity to learn a more interesting trade.... In these and also in their aspirations and expectations, there does not seem to be any fundamental difference between this group and other groups of factory employees in other countries.[53]

The other study pointed to the importance of the approach used by supervisors in dealing with workers, and the effective approach was similar to that found in other more advanced industrial societies. Workers and supervisors in 8 physically similar sections of a cotton textile mill in Ahmedabad, some with high efficiency and some with low efficiency, were interviewed. The differences found between the sections were these: the high efficiency supervisors got their work done by persuasion; the low efficiency supervisors had to give suspension notices for poor work and believed that fear was the major motivation for work.[54]

These studies and other impressions from interviews with Indian employers cast serious doubt on such blanket statements as:

Indian workers are not interested in factory work: they resist adjustment to the type of life which goes with industrial employment. In the value scheme of the majority of Indians, factory labour does not offer any avenue for the expressions of their individual personalities; wage increases and promotions do not operate as stimulants to greater exertion nor does greater exertion lead to changes in status.[55]

Far more important than "the value scheme of the majority of Indians" are developing managerial attitudes, approaches and policies in dealing with employees.

Employer Welfare Policies and Commitment

The development of a stable committed industrial labour force is therefore more a consequence of "managerial pulls" than of "pushes" from the impoverished rural regions. In fact, the push from the land can create a discontented industrial labour force, if nothing is done to adapt it to factory and urban requirements. Inadequate management policies have been, as we have seen, an important explanation of the slowness with which a disciplined labour force has developed in India. Many managements are equally at fault in not taking necessary steps to reduce excessive absenteeism, and other evidences of noncommitment. Here the question will be raised, however : Is not management acting rationally in an economic sense in ignoring these factors when labour is still so plentiful and so cheap? The answer is partly that labour costs are no longer low in India,[56] and partly that management policies which may have been politically adequate in a similar economic context in the nineteenth century are politically explosive in the mid-twentieth. Industrial labour is now more articulate, has powerful political friends competing for its allegiance, and is ready politically to protest against any short-sighted and selfish managerial practices.

It is interesting in this context to examine the data pertaining to the frequency distribution of industrial workers classified according to length of service. Data for the most recent period for various years since 1951 are shown in Table XXVII. The data for 26 industrial groups (including 5 individual employers) indicate general stability, but there are also clear exceptions. There are six industrial groups in which 50 per cent or more of the employees covered have served 10 or more years. These are basic metal (54.5), mineral oil (56.0), municipalities, Group I (52.1), Group IV (50.7), paper mill industry (54.0) and Bombay Cotton Mills (56.3). By contrast, the cases reporting 50 per cent or more of the employees as having served less than 1 year are relatively few. They are cotton ginning (60.9), iron ore mines (51.5), mica mines (65.9), and shellac (62.2). The number of cases are naturally greater, if we consider the cases

TABLE XXVII A

DISTRIBUTION OF WORKERS BY LENGTH OF SERVICE

(length of service in years)

Industry or occupation (All India)	Reference period		Below 1 (per cent)	1 to 5 (per cent)	6 to 10 (per cent)
Basic metal	Jan.	1, 1955	5.6	14.5	25.4
Ceramics and potteries	Dec. 31, 1959		23.2	28.7	20.6
Chemicals	Apr. 30, 1961		15.1	41.1	20.8
Cotton ginning and baling		1956	60.9	15.1	9.3
Dock yards		1955	8.7	11.9	32.6
Glass			36.3	42.4	13.6
Hydrogenated oil	Jan.	1, 1955	14.2	34.6	35.6
Iron ore mines		1957	51.5	18.0	15.5
Match factories	May	1955	9.5	31.4	32.3
	Dec. 31, 1959		31.4	28.6	13.6
Mica mines		1958	65.9	28.9	3.2
Mineral oil		1952	7.0	24.0	33.0
		1955	5.0	29.0	10.0
Municipalities Group I		1958	5.9	19.3	22.7
Group II		1958	8.2	22.6	28.3
Group III		1958	7.3	23.8	30.4
Group IV		1958	6.3	18.4	24.6
Paper mill industry	Mar. 15, 1955		6.0	29.9	31.4
	Mar. 31, 1961		6.2	20.4	19.4
Printing presses			7.0	22.0	35.0
Shellac			62.2	17.1	20.7
					(5 years and over)
Silk		1953	18.9	39.5	30.5
Tanneries and leather finishing		1955	20.0	27.3	28.6
Tata Iron and Steel Company		1940		29.5	28.5
	Jan.	1948	5.3	15.8	28.4
	Aug.	1955	0.5	9.9	19.1
Bombay Cotton Mills		1940		29.5	28.5
		1955		9.7	34.0
Empress Mills, Nagpur	May	1951		7.7	27.6
K. C. Mills, Calcutta	Apr.	1958		13.9	(less than 10 yr.)
Svadeshi Mills, Bombay	Apr.	1958			
Large textile mill, Madras		1954		39.0	28.0

TABLE XXVII A *(Contd.)*

Industry or occupation (All India)	Over 10 or 11-15 (per cent)	16-20 (per cent)	21-25 (per cent)	26-30 or over 25 (per cent)	30 (per cent)	Employees Covered
Basic metal	54.5	—	—	—	—	61239
Ceramics and potteries	27.5	—	—	—	—	15796
Chemicals	23.0	—	—	—	—	45618
Cotton ginning and baling	12.0	—	—	—	—	2227
Dock yards	46.8	—	—	—	—	32707
Glass	7.7	—	—	—	—	15977
Hydrogenated oil	15.6	—	—	—	—	4838
Iron ore mines	11.5	—	—	—	—	4780
Match factories	26.8	—	—	—	—	9990
	26.4	—	—	—	—	18435
Mica mines	2.0	—	—	—	—	3539
Mineral oil	36.0	—	—	—	—	7799
	56.0	—	—	—	—	7997
Municipalities Group I	52.1	—	—	—	—	5966
Group II	40.9	—	—	—	—	6225
Group III	38.5	—	—	—	—	27341
Group IV	50.7	—	—	—	—	60099
Paper mill industry	32.7	—	—	—	—	21712
	54.0	—	—	—	—	26391
Printing presses	36.0	—	—	—	—	20059
Shellac	—	—	—	—	—	5037
Silk	11.1	—	—	—	—	—
Tanneries and leather finishing	23.1	—	—	—	—	2536
Tata Iron and Steel Co.	42.0	—	—	—	—	—
	50.5	—	—	—	—	—
	70.5	—	—	—	—	—
Bombay Cotton Mills	18.8	12.7	6.0	3.0	1.5	—
	25.6	12.0	8.6	5.1	5.0	—
Empress Mills, Nagpur	28.9	16.1	10.9	6.9	1.9	—
K. C. Mills, Calcutta	49.1	22.4	6.2	8.4	—	—
Svadeshi Mills, Bombay	50.9	26.0	10.3	12.9	—	—
Large textile mill, Madras	6.0	7.0	7.0	12.0	1.0	—

SOURCES:

1. Data for Indian industries from *Indian Labour Journal* (formerly *Gazette*), December 1956 to November 1962.

2. Data re. Tata Iron and Steel Company from Morris D. Morris, *op. cit.,* in Moore and Feldman, *op. cit.,* p. 181.

3. Data for Bombay Cotton Mills from R. G. Gokhale, *The Bombay Cotton Mill Worker,* Millowners' Association, Bombay, 1957, p. 27.

4. K. C. Mills and Svadeshi Mills, from UNESCO, *Social and Cultural Factors Affecting Productivity of Industrial Workers in India,* Delhi, 1960, p. 5, and Report on Social and Cultural Factors Affecting Productivity of Industrial Labour, UNESCO, Calcutta, mimeo, vol. III.

5. Data for Empress Mills, Nagpur, supplied by company.

TABLE XXVII B

LENGTH OF SERVICE DISTRIBUTION IN SELECTED INDUSTRIES BY SIZE CATEGORIES*
(Length of Service in Years)

Industry or occupation (All India)	Reference period	No. of units responding	Below 1 year (Per cent)	1 to 5 years (Per cent)
CERAMICS AND POTTERY	Dec. 1959			
Employing up to 50		10	33.1	39.7
Employing 51-200		17	34.0	36.4
Employing above 200		20	17.5	24.2
Grand total		47	23.2	28.7
CHEMICALS	1961			
Employing up to 100		33	21.6	43.3
Employing 101-500		19	13.9	39.7
Employing 501 and above		8	12.9	41.5
Grand total		60	15.1	41.1
MATCH FACTORIES	1959			
Employing up to 100		16	48.3	51.6
Employing 101-500		14	50.8	43.8
Employing above 500		6	5.9	3.8
Grand total		36	31.4	28.6
PAPER MILLS	1961			
Employing up to 400		7	23.1	36.4
Employing 401-1000		4	8.4	5.6
Employing 1001 and above		9	4.4	23.6
Grand total		20	6.2	20.4
SILK	1953			
Employing 101-500		13	24.0	49.5
Employing 500 and above		12	17.5	36.8
Grand total		25	18.9	39.5

TABLE XXVII B (*Contd.*)

Industry or occupation (All India)	5 *to* 10 years (Per cent)	Over 10 years (Per cent)	Number
CERAMICS AND POTTERY			
Employing up to 50	21.3	2.9	1260
Employing 51-200	16.9	12.6	4237
Employing above 200	21.6	36.7	10299
Grand total	20.6	27.5	15796
CHEMICALS			
Employing up to 100	16.6	18.5	9332
Employing 101-500	21.3	25.1	19237
Employing 501 and above	22.6	22.9	17049
Grand total	20.8	23.0	45618
MATCH FACTORIES			
Employing up to 100	0.1	—	3824
Employing 101-500	4.5	0.9	6861
Employing above 500	28.4	61.9	7750
Grand total	13.6	26.4	18435
PAPER MILL			
Employing up to 400	35.2	4.5	1331
Employing 401-1000	15.2	70.8	5663
Employing 1001 and above	19.5	52.5	19397
Grand total	19.4	54.0	26391
SILK			
Employing 101-500	15.6	10.9	—
Employing 500 and above	34.5	11.2	—
Grand total	30.5	11.1	—

SOURCE: *Indian Labour Journal,* Labour Bureau, Ministry of Labour and Employment, Government of India, Manager of Publications, Delhi (Issues from December 1956 to November 1962 were consulted).
*The row percentages for the industries cumulate to 100%.

where 50 per cent or more of the employees have served less than 5 years. These are: ceramics (51.9), chemicals (56.2), glass (78.7), match factories (60.0), and sink (58.4). Thus, altogether nine categories indicate that the majority of the employees covered have served less than 5 years. The data for the individual employers indicate generally high stability, presumably reflecting the special characteristics of firms chosen by investigators. Thus four of them report that over 50 per cent of the employees covered have served over 10 years : Tata Iron and Steel Company (70.5); Empress Mills, Nagpur (64.7); K. C. Mills, Calcutta (86.1); and Svadeshi Mills, Bombay (100.0). But one well-known firm in this category reports that 33 per cent of the employees covered served over 10 years, while 39 per cent served less than five.

These data indicate apparent stability, generally consistent with the low turnover rates. However, there is need for caution. These data pertain to service with individual employers and therefore may understate industrial affiliation to the extent that the workers migrate from one employer to another within the same industry, or between industries. However, the figures pertain to the most recent periods of considerable urban unemployment. New or rapidly growing industries may also be expected to have a greater proportion of their labour force in the lower age groups, but, on the basis of the limited available information, one cannot rule out the influence of other variables. In the two cases where comparative data are available carrying us back to 1940, for the Tata Iron and Steel Company and the Bombay Cotton Mills, they suggest a definite trend toward an increase in the average length of service. Thus, for the former, nearly 30 per cent had served less than 5 years in 1940, as opposed to 21 per cent in 1948, and 10 per cent in 1955. For the latter, nearly 30 per cent served less than 5 years in 1940, as opposed to slightly under 10 per cent in 1955. The trend is clearly in the opposite direction in the case of the match industry between 1955 and 1959, which may reflect either rapid growth or improved coverage. Mineral oil indicates an increase at both ends of the spectrum between 1952 and 1955, with employment approximately constant. The paper mill industry, on the other hand, indicates an increase in the average length of service, with an approximately 20 per cent increase in the employees covered between 1955 and 1961.

More detailed research is obviously required before one can draw firm conclusions. Yet it is significant that the larger firms tend to have a higher average. Since these also tend to be better managed, and more willing to invest in the training of their labour force, the role of conscious employer policy deserves recognition. This may be investigated further with reference to some outstanding examples chosen from field interviews.

The experience of a large cotton textile mill in a South Indian city is illustrative of the policies adopted by an increasing number of Indian firms, although they still constitute a minority. Data supplied by the mill for the year 1954 showed the following distribution of employees according to length of service:

Years of service	Number of employees	Per cent of total
5 and under	6,000	39
6-10	4,369	28
11-15	880	6
16-20	1,054	7
21-25	1,025	7
26-30	1,842	12
31-35	159	1
Over 35	82	—
TOTAL	15,411	100

Sixty-one per cent had been employed longer than 5 years; and nearly one-third longer than 10 years.[57] Absenteeism averaged around 9 per cent a month, and most of this was "authorized" in the sense that it included the statutory leave with wages, sick leave, or unpaid "casual leave." Less than 1 per cent was due to absence without leave.[58]

How is this stability explained? First, in the cotton mills, all of the workforce are Madrasis who have largely broken their ties with the villages, even though periodic visits continue. But, secondly, this came about in part through the extensive welfare activities which the company adopted in connection with high employee earning levels. Thirdly, alternative employment in textiles in the city was nonexistent. Among the welfare programmes are the following: free medical aid for workers and their families, extensive housing, recreation programmes, nursery classes, maternity and child welfare centres, allowance for sick leave and also for accidents beyond statutory requirement, concessions in purchase of cloth, night shift allowance of 25 per cent of basic wages, Sunday work allowance, canteen (cafeteria) subsidized by company, perfect attendance bonus (except for leave with wages) drawn by between 4,000 and 5,000 people each year, an annual increment of 1 per cent of basic wages paid each year since 1942, and a semi-annual profit-sharing bonus since 1919, averaging 20 per cent of basic wages in 1954. The cost of these welfare programmes and wage increments was estimated at Rs. 2.2 million per year, or nearly Rs. 12 per month per worker. Basic wages and dearness allowance totalled about Rs. 105 per month.

It is worth noting further that this mill had a systematic grievance procedure involving 3 joint committees at different levels, on which there were elected representatives of workers and also (on the top committee) the outside leader of the union with which the company had collective bargaining relationship. The Labour Officer, a high level company official with considerable responsibility, reported that the majority of grievances were settled at the departmental level, 51 cases reached the second level committee in 1953, and 11 the central committee. The union president stated in a separate interview that relationships with this company were much better than average.

The success of this firm, of course, may be the result of the comparative advantage it possesses over other firms in the community in offering such welfare programmes and wage increments to its employees.[59] Some of these are now required by legislation, as we shall see in Chapter VIII, and it is clear that the failure of the majority of Indian firms to provide even the minimum amenities in the past led to action by government to establish standards which would help commit industrial labour to urban employment.

The most striking instances of employer policies which facilitate the commitment of a stable industrial labour force are found in the industrial communities which are largely dominated by one firm, like the company towns of an earlier industrial era in the United States. Some of these firms were located in rural regions to escape the tensions and labour problems of the city; some were established in the founder's home village for personal and sentimental reasons. But location of many others was dictated by the availability of raw materials, as in the cement industry or in the steel industry.

Jamshedpur, the city of 250,000 built on the site of a small jungle village close to iron ore and coal deposits in eastern Bihar, is a prime example of enlightened management's efforts to build a stable workforce.[60] The Tata Iron and Steel Company owns the city and administers it. Most of the labour force had to be brought in when the steel mill was built between 1904 and 1911, and additional labour has been attracted with subsequent expansion. Housing had to be provided, streets built, a water supply developed, schools constructed, municipal services organized, and so on. The consequence is that, according to one report, Jamshedpur has the largest proportion of permanently resident industrial workforce of any city in India.[61] It is clear that the enlightened policies of the Tata management in Jamshedpur resulted in the development of a stable industrial labour force much earlier than in most other industrial cities.

The Tata Iron and Steel Company is the largest employer in the city, with nearly 30,000 employees in 1955–56. Less than 1,700 of these were classified on the company pay-roll as "temporary," and labour turnover among the permanent staff was two-tenths of 1 per cent. Absenteeism (adjusted for leave with pay) was only 5.04 per cent during 1955–56, Yet the composition of the workforce according to "province of origin" shows that only 39 per cent come from the state of Bihar (on the border of which Jamshedpur is located), 13 per cent come from Orissa, 12 per cent from Bengal, 9 per cent from Madhya Pradesh, and the remaining 27 per cent from 6 other Indian states and 4 neighbouring countries.[62]

A stable labour force, which can maintain its ties with the village and yet work steadily in the factory, may also be sought by a conscious managerial policy of locating a new factory near a village which previously knew only handicrafts and agriculture. A dramatic example of this is the case of a new bicycle factory, with mixed British and Indian capital and management, deliberately located 15 miles outside a city and next to a village with underemployed or unemployed labour willing to take factory work. One year after it opened, the plant was operating at a level of efficiency satisfactory to the British plant manager, who said that most of his workers "were twisting cows' tails a year ago." They kept their village homes, walked to work, and cultivated small plots of land in their spare time. Many other instances of this type of industrialization were observed and were cited by others in interviews. This is not a phenomenon confined to India; every industrial country has similar examples. But the process of developing a committed industrial labour force is achieved by a variety of methods, including moving the plant to the sources of labour supply.

We have seen that the development of an industrial labour force in India was possible because pressure on the land forced villagers to seek work in the expanding industrial cities. This exodus, however, was facilitated by recruiters who used various devices to entice people to come to the mines, mills, and factories. Industrial wages were, however, low, and living and working conditions in the cities were, on the whole, extremely bad. Thus, even after workers were brought to the city, a number of rural links were maintained and have even continued to the present day. The continuing family, religious, and economic ties with the village contribute, along with such factors as ill health, to high absenteeism. This "partial" commitment has been institutionalized in the form of leave for visits to the village—mostly authorized by statute or employer policy, but some unauthorized. But labour turnover is, on the whole, low; the Indian worker wants to keep his job in the factory but, to get periodic relief from its pressures, he returns to his village for rest, family visits, festivals, or the harvest season.

Commitment to industrial employment, however, implies more than the presence of workers on the job. It involves also their acceptance of industrial discipline and the performance of tasks under supervision. Here the role of the employer has been stressed, as a crucial factor in shaping the kind of responses which the worker gives to the job. The failure of management to structure and discipline the labour force, as in the Bombay cotton textile industry before the 1920's, has led government to intervene, and the nature of this intervention will be examined in later chapters. But the growth of an industrial labour force also brings the emergence of worker organizations to shape and direct the nature of the labour response to industrialization and to the manner in which workers are treated by employers and by government. We turn in the next chapter to an examination of the development of an organized labour movement in India.

NOTES

1 Cf. Clark Kerr and Abraham Siegel, "The Structuring of the Labor Force in Industrial Society: New Dimensions and New Questions," *Industrial and Labor Relations Review*, vol. 8, no. 2 (January 1955), pp. 151-68. Structuring the labour force "involves the setting and enforcing of rules concerned with the recruitment of a labour force, with the training of that labour force in the myriad skills required by the advanced division of labour, with the locating of workers in some appropriate pattern advanced division of labour, with the locating of workers in some appropriate pattern of geographical, industrial, and occupational dispersion. It involves the setting of rules on times to work and not work, on method and amount of pay, on movement into and out of work and from one position to another. It involves rules pertaining to the maintenance of continuity in the work process . . . the attempted minimization of individual or organized revolt, the provision of view of the world, of ideological orientations, of beliefs, the introduction of some checks on the individual insecurity inherent in an industrial order." (p. 163.)

For a more extended discussion of the development of an industrial workforce in underdeveloped countries, see Wilbert E. Moore, *Industrialization and Labour* (Ithaca, New York, 1951).

2 Clark Kerr in Wilbert E. Moore and Arnold S. Feldman, *Labor Commitment and Social Change in Developing Areas*, Social Science Research Council (New York, 1960), p. 351. The *uncommitted* worker "is in industry but not yet of it." The *semicommitted* worker "is a man on the margins of two civilizations. He works more or less regularly in industry but maintains his connection with the land." The *committed* worker "has severed his connection with the land . . . . He is fully urbanized and never expects to leave industrial employment." The *overcommitted* worker "is committed not only to industrial life but also to his particular occupation or his particular employer . . . ."

3 *Main Report*, Labour Investigation Committee (Rege Committee), Government of India (New Delhi, 1946), p. 13. *Indian Labour Gazette*, vol. XII, no. 10 (April 1955), p. 1150. *Indian Labour Statistics* 1963, p. 19.

4 Kingsley Davis, *The Population of India and Pakistan* (Princeton, 1951), p. 127, and *Statistical Outline of India* 1963, p. 7.

5 For further details, see Vera Anstey, *The Economic Development of India* (London, 3rd ed., 1942) Chapter V. For a later analysis, see Daniel Thorner, *The Agrarian Prospect in India* (Delhi, 1956), Chapter I; and Daniel and Alice Thorner, "Types of Employer-Labourer Relationships in Indian Agriculture" (unpublished study for the Inter-University Project on Labour Problems in Economic Development, 1956).

6 Thorner, *Agrarian Prospect in India*, pp. 9-13. Thorner argues persuasively that many of these features continue to characterize Indian agriculture, despite repeated government attempts at "land reform." Chapter V, esp. pp. 75-9. See also, Thomas W. Shea, Jr., "Barriers to Economic Development in Traditional Societies: Malabar, A Case of Study," *Journal of Economic History*, December 1959, pp. 513-16.

7 The *All-India Report of the Second Agricultural Enquiry*, published in 1960,

estimated the average size of the agricultural labour household to be 4.40 in 1956-57, while the average number of earners was 2.03. The 1961 Census in India places the number of agricultural labourers at 47,274,000 (p. 395, paper no. 1 of 1962). The estimate, 23.3 million agricultural families in 1961, is obtained by dividing 47.274 million by 2.03.

8 McKim Marriott, "Social Change in an Indian Village," *Economic Development and Cultural Change*, vol. 1, no. 2 (June 1952), pp. 145-55.

9 Shiva Rao, "Labour in India," *Annals of the American Academy of Political and Social Science* (1944), p. 128. The general applicability of the push from the land in creating an industrial labour force in underdeveloped countries has been stressed by Wilbert E. Moore: "Industrial wages are likely to be 'high' only in relation to serious poverty, as the new worker is typically unskilled . . . . At least in the shorter or longer transitional period, the shortage of land and the loss of markets for handi-craft products are likely to be as important in motivating the search for new opportu-nities as are more positive incentives." *Industrialization and Labour* (Ithaca, New York, 1951), p. 305.

10 "Bombay's Migrants," *Hindu Weekly Review*, 13 July 1964, p. 7.

11 Sir Edward Blunt, "The Economic Aspect of the Caste System," in Radha-kamal Mukerjee, *Economic Problems of Modern India*, vol. I (London, 1939), p. 63. For further discussion of the significance of the Indian caste system, see J. H. Hutton, *Caste in India* (Bombay, 2nd ed., 1951); N. K. Dutt, *Origin and Growth of Caste in India* (London, 1931); Pandhari-Nath Prabhu, *Hindu Social Organization* (Bombay, rev. ed., 1954); and G. S. Ghurye, *Caste and Class in India* (Bombay, 1950). An observer, who was *New York Times* correspondent in India for seven years, has pointed to the diminishing influence of caste: "In the big cities, caste conscious-ness has been largely squeezed out of the shop, the office, the government bureaus, the educational institutions. In India, as elsewhere, the employment opportunities of the city are attracting more and more youth from the farms, who take modern ideas back to their villages. The blanketing of India by the village community pro-jects program is also having its influence on the generation coming up, however stubbornly the oldsters may resist." Robert Trumbull, *As I See India* (New York, 1956), p. 159, Chapter 14, "The Fight Against Caste."

12 Pandhari-Nath Prabhu, "A Study of the Social Effects of Urbanization on Industrial Workers Migrating from Rural Areas to the City of Bombay," in *The Social Implications of Industrialization and Urbanization: Five Studies in Asia*, UNESCO, Research Centre on the Social Implications of Industrialization in Southern Asia (Calcutta, 1956), p. 79. The study was made by the Tata Institute of Social Sciences, Bombay, and does not purport to be a general study of industrial workers in Bombay.

13 S. B. Chirde, *Industrial Labour in Bombay: A Socio-Economic Analysis* (un-published Ph.D. thesis, University of Bombay, School of Economics and Sociology, 1949), pp. 106-07. In this survey, 48 per cent were caste Hindus, mostly Marathas, who were employed as weavers and other skilled workers, and about 9 per cent were Muslims, also employed as weavers. In a later study of 959 migrant families in 8 cities and towns, including Delhi, Nagpur and Indore, during 1950-53, 79 per cent

were "untouchables" and 64 per cent were landless agricultural labourers. Nearly 65 per cent migrated from the villages because of economic distress and related reasons in the villages. M. B. Deshmukh, "A Study of Floating Migration," *Social Implications,* UNESCO, pp. 172, 175, 181.

14 R. G. Gokhale, *Summary of Workmen's Service Records,* The Millowners' Association (Bombay, July 1941). A re-survey in 1955 substantiated these earlier data.

15 *Main Report,* Government of India (New Delhi, 1946), pp. 8-9.

16 Richard D. Lambert, *Workers, Factories, and Social Change in India,* Princeton University Press (Princeton, 1963), p. 56.

17 See M. D. Morris, "Caste and Evolution of the Industrial Workforce in India," *Proceedings of the American Philosophical Society,* April 1960.

18 Dipak Mazamdar, "Unemployment in Agriculture and the Industrial Wage Rate," *Economica,* November 1959.

19 Bert F. Hoselitz, "The City, the Factory, and Economic Growth," *Papers and Proceedings of the Sixty-seventh Annual Meeting of the American Economic Association,* 1954.

20 The points in this paragraph have been amplified in Subbiah Kannappan, "Labour Force Commitment in Early Stages of Industrialization," paper delivered at the Annual Meeting of the American Association for the Advancement of Science, Montreal, December 1964.

21 Dipak Mazamdar, *op. cit.*

22 Thus, under certain circumstances, it may be logical for employers as well employees to prefer unstable associations with industry. While these may reduce some of the risks arising from imperfect information, the risks themselves are likely to discourage, rather than encourage, investment in mobility.

23 Radhakamal Mukerjee, *The Indian Working Class* (Bombay, 3rd ed., 1951), p. 25.

24 For a discussion of the changing role of the jobber in the cotton textile industry, see S. D. Mehta, *The Indian Cotton Textile Industry: An Economic Analysis,* the Textile Association (India) (Bombay, 1953), pp. 66-91. Mehta says, "The failure to substantially reform the jobber system is one of the many great failures of industrial management in India." (p. 69).

25 *Report,* Government of India (Delhi, 1933), p. 24. By 1946, when the Labour Investigation Committee reported, the situation had not changed materially. *Main Report,* Government of India (New Delhi, 1946), p. 80.

26 Morris D. Morris, "Labour Discipline, Trade Unions, and the State in India," *Journal of Political Economy,* vol. LXIII, no. 4 (August 1955), p. 295. Much of the material in this section is taken from this article.

27 *Ibid.,* p. 296.

28 These were (1) the Bombay Trade Disputes Conciliation Act of 1934, which established a labour office to negotiate with employers about workers grievances and to serve as a conciliator; (2) the Bombay Industrial Disputes Act of 1938, which required employers to publish "Standing Orders" defining working rules in the plant and provided for compulsory conciliation of disputes; (3) the establishment of

an Industrial Court system by order of the Governor of Bombay in 1941; and (4) the Bombay Industrial Relations Act of 1947, which provided for "approved" unions which accepted the principle of compulsory conciliation and arbitration, and "representative" unions, which were supposed to be the dominant unions in each industry. For fuller discussion of the 1947 Act, see Chapter VIII.

29 *Main Report,* Labour Investigation Committee, Government of India (1946).

30 *Ibid.,* p. 313.

31 M. S. H. Medi, *Worli: A Study of City Development* (unpublished ph.D. thesis, University of Bombay, School of Economics and Sociology, 1952). pp. 261-62.

32 *Ibid.,* pp. 187-88.

33 *Report,* p. 15.

34 Prabhu, *A Study of the Social Effects of Urbanization,* UNESCO, p. 80. Twenty-three per cent did not bring anybody to the city even after employment; 44 per cent brought wives and children. A later study of the sex distribution of the urban labour force in 1956 in smaller areas and large cities, as compared to the four larges cities (Bombay, Calcutta, Delhi and Madras) brings out clearly that 93.5 per cent of the employed workers were males in the four largest cities, compared to 82.4 per cent in the others. Malenbaum, "Urban Employment in India," *Pacific Affairs,* Table II.

35 *Hindu Weekly Review,* 13 July 1964, p. 7.

36 For one view, which dismisses the female-male ratio as entirely without relevance, see Morris D. Morris, "The Labour Market in India," in Moore and Feldman, *op. cit.,* p. 179.

37 Hoselitz, *op. cit.,* pp. 180-1 adds: "It is not the noise or the soot in the city which corrodes the nerve of the worker ...but rather the 'absence of neighborhood'– the anonymity and impersonality of life in a big city. These factors go far to explain the high absentee rate, the high rate of turnover, and the low standard of performance of many industrial workers in underdeveloped countries." (p. 181.)

38 Prabhu, *op. cit.,* p. 81. Some of the information is drawn from an earlier, more detailed manuscript, made available in Bombay by Dr. Prabhu. Three-fifths of the sample were from the "depressed classes," and this is a higher proportion than in the total Bombay textile labour force. The data are therefore not necessarily representative of Bombay textile workers or of all Indian industrial workers.

39 Prabhu, *op. cit.,* p. 63. Later Dr. Prabhu concludes that the migrants "have been very much allured by the glamour of the city and it is no surprise that they are often in a mood to prefer city life. But the grounds of corrosion in such cases are the backwardness of the village in matters of education, conveniences, communication, lack of sources of knowledge and lack of employment." p. 84.

40 The survey of 959 migrant families in 8 cities and towns, including Delhi, cited earlier, has some comparable information, but deals largely with the background of these families and their life in the cities and towns. The study concludes: "The typical migrant as described in this report is a 'marginal man,' in whom the conflict of rural and urban culture traits is very active and who is consequently the most obvious sufferer from the cultural shock. He is not quite willing or incapable to break with his rual past nor is he quite accepted in the strange and indifferent urban environ-

ment in which he is now trying to seek a footing." M. B. Deshmukh, "A Study of Floating Migration," *op. cit.*, UNESCO, p. 224.

41 A different view has been advanced by the labour officer of a Calcutta shipping firm. The agricultural background and ties of Indian industrial labour produce an "irresponsible attitude to work and a tendency to throw up a job on the slightest provocation because the worker is not solely dependent on it for his livelihood." Mary Sur, "Indian Industry's Growing Pains," *Industrial Welfare* (London), May-June 1953, p. 77. Domestic reasons and family customs, however, also create problems of absenteeism and wrangling over leave, she reports, and this squares with our interpretation. It may be added that inability to gain a family livelihood even from a combination of rural and urban work may produce a deeper kind of irresponsibility—a protest against this kind of life.

42 Daniel Thorner has suggested this possibility. He further argues that, at least up to 1939, "the cities have 'consumed' rural surplus labour and sent the waste back to the countryside." "Casual Employment of a Factory Labour Force, the Case of India, 1850-1939," *Economic Weekly Annual*, Bombay, January 1957, p. 124. On the indebtedness of Telco workers, see p. 28 of this book.

43 Data supplied by the company. The Indian Jute Mills' Association began, in January 1955, to compile absence records for the jute industry, tabulated by absence with leave due to (1) sickness or accident, (2) social or religious causes, and (3) other causes; and absence without leave in the same categories. "Other causes" in absence with leave totalled as much as the first two groups combined. The total absenteeism rate varied between 8.1 per cent in January and 15.9 per cent in April 1955.

44 The Factories Act (1948) provides for "privilege leave" based on days of previous employment; the state Acts and adjudicators' decisions supplement this with provision for paid "casual" and sick leave. These often total as high as one month of paid leave in a year, and do not include the additional paid holidays the number of which is as high as 20 in some states.

45 P. M. Deshpande, "The Extent and Cause of Labour Turnover in Empress Mills, Nagpur" (unpublished dissertation for diploma in Social Service Administration, Tata Institute of Social Sciences, Bombay, 1953). An additional 526 elderly workers were retired from employment by agreement with the union.

46 Data from the latter firms were secured in interviews.

47 Section 33 of the Industrial Disputes Act (1947) was often blamed by management for indiscipline. Under this Section, management was forbidden to discharge workers when there was a dispute pending before an industrial tribunal, unless the tribunal first gave permission. Approval was slow in coming, and has, according to management, been extended even to action not connected with the dispute. An amendment permitting management to take disciplinary action not connected with a pending dispute was included in the Industrial Disputes (Amendment) Act of 1956, passed in July 1956 and subsequent clarification was included in the Code of Discipline.

48 S. D. Mehta, *The Indian Cotton Textile Industry: An Economic Analysis,* The Textile Association (India) (Bombay, 1953), p. 50.

49 *Ibid.*, p. 50.

50 Some indication of this is provided by scanning the daily headlines in newspapers, which report numerous instances of assaults, mob demonstrations and lack of cohesion.

51 This firm also had a serious indiscipline problem, leading to many strikes and slow-downs before 1953. The management discharged 15 ringleaders in 1953 and the discharges were upheld by an industrial tribunal. Discipline improved and there were few difficulties after then, according to the management.

52 See R. K. Das, *Hindusthani Workers on the Pacific Coast* (Berlin, 1923), a study undertaken originally for the United States Bureau of Labour Statistics to test the efficiency of labour of Indian descent in a non-Indian environment. The author reports that such labour compared favourably with the records of the local labour.

53 H. C. Ganguli, "An Enquiry into Incentives for Workers in an Engineering Factory," *Indian Journal of Social Work,* vol. XV, no. 1 (June 1954; reprinted by Bureau of Research and Publications, Tata Institute of Social Sciences, Bombay), pp. 8, 10.

54 This was done as part of the UNESCO study of human behaviour and social tensions, and was also reported in Gardner Murphy, *In the Minds of Men* (New York, 1953), pp. 211-2. For other supporting evidence, see A. Devasagayam, "Employer-Employee Tension in Industry," *Indian Journal of Social Work,* vol. XII, no. 3 (December 1951; reprinted by Bureau of Research and Publications, Tata Institute of Social Sciences, Bombay), p. 7. Dr. Devasagayam, medical officer of Simpson's Welfare Centre, Madras, interviewed workers in a motor engineering company and printing press and a paint manufacturing company in Madras during the latter part of 1948. He concluded: "The employer's attitude is to create fear in the workers' minds by threatening them with dismissal. This policy gives no incentive for work. A great majority of workers manage to stick to their jobs without putting forth their best. The fear of retrenchment and unemployment only helps to antagonize the worker, and it also increases human tensions and induces the worker to revolt." (p. 7.)

55 Ornati, *Jobs and Workers in India* (Ithaca, New York, 1955), p. 46.

56 Labour in India may be abundant in aggregate, but it is neither "cheap" in relation to production, nor abundant in specific types or areas. In all the industries, far more labour is used in India for an equivalent plant with similar basic processes than in the United States, the United Kingdom or Japan. Compared to the far higher wages per worker in the United States, labour cost in India is probably lower, but the opposite is probably true for Japan, and labour costs in comparison with European plants are approximately equal. This means that, in industries which are competing with foreign products, there is pressure to reduce labour costs. Furthermore industrial labour is not abundant and the costs of creating such a labour force at a plant site are high. George Rosen, "Capital-Output Ratios," *Indian Economic Journal,* vol. IV, no. 2 (October 1956), section III, "Qualitative Analysis," pp. 118-20.

57 The stability of this South Indian mill's labour force is not greater than that of the Bombay textile industry, which is much older and has had a longer time to

stabilize. For example, a 1955 survey by the Bombay Millowners' Association showed that only 10 per cent of the females and 18 per cent of the males had less than 5 years' service, as compared to 39 per cent in the South Indian mill. The comparable figures for less than 10 per cent (cumulative) were 23 and 55 in Bombay and 67 per cent in the South Indian mill. Median years of service in Bombay for males were 9.4, for females 14.3 and for the South Indian mill 7.0. We are indebted to Ralph James, of the New York State School of Industrial and Labour Relations. Cornell University, for providing this comparison.

58 In addition to the 15 days statutory paid leave each year, 15 days casual unpaid leave, and 11 festival holidays with pay, this mill provided from 20 to 72 days sick leave each year, according to length of service, paid at the rate of two-thirds of basic wages and full dearness (cost of living) allowance, when the company doctors recommended it.

59 The value of paternalism as a deliberate employer policy in an industrially underdeveloped country was stressed by George B. Baldwin in his discussion of "Urbanization and Industrialization of the Labour Force in a Developing Economy," *Papers and Proceedings of the Seventy-Seventh Annual Meeting of the American Economic Association,* 1955, pp. 185-88.

60 For a discussion of the experience of M. D. Madan, Deputy Director, Education and Social Services, Tata Iron and Steel Company, see "The Tata Steel Works at Jamshedpur," one of the three case studies in *Factory and Community,* Duke of Edinburgh's Study Conference (Oxford University Press, 1956).

61 The reported figure is 39 per cent, as compared to 20 per cent for the Indian industrial labour force as a whole. A.M. Lorenzo, "Agricultural Labour in India," *Asian Labour,* April 1950, pp. 56-7. No source is given for these data. A "recent survey" of Jamshedpur is also mentioned, to the effect that 23 per cent of the labour do not visit their homes in rural areas at all, and 19 per cent return to their home villages only once in 3 years. This probably refers to the Family Budget Survey conducted by the Labour Bureau, Government of India, in 1948.

62 Data supplied by the company.

CHAPTER IV

THE GROWTH AND DEVELOPMENT OF AN ORGANIZED LABOUR MOVEMENT

OUT of a total gainfully employed of over 180 million persons, only about 4 million are organized in trade unions. However, the Indian labour movement is significant and important far beyond the proportion covered by its numbers. It is centred in the growth sector of the economy; it incorporates much of the stock of the country's skilled manpower; and its support is sought by competing political parties.[1]

As we have seen in Chapter I, Indian industrial labour occupies some of the key sectors of the economy, in modern factory industry, transport, mining, plantations and commercial activity, which are of relatively greater importance in their total contribution to the national product than the biggest occupational group—agriculture.[2] In these critical areas of economic activity, the trade union movement has developed its greatest strength. Some obvious examples are cotton textiles, railways, ports and docks, and the nationally important enterprises in India's growing public sector. Furthermore, the concentration of the industrial labour force in important urban areas like Calcutta, Bombay, Ahmedabad, Kanpur and Jamshedpur renders it one of the few concrete, identifiable forces in the huge, unorganized population mass of India. Because of this concentration, and because of industrial labour's relatively superior economic position,[3] the Indian industrial worker represents an *elite* group within the country. The role of industrial labour has become especially significant in the context of present emphasis on industrialization and economic development within the framework of a democratic political system.

It is for these reasons that political parties and prominent national leaders have, throughout its history, taken a great interest in the Indian labour movement and sought the allegiance of organized labour. Political parties have also sustained the labour movement, although their varying interests have given added force to divisive tendencies within the movement itself. The important role of government in labour-management relations has given added emphasis to the strategic importance of Indian labour.[4] These points will be developed in our survey of the origins and growth of the Indian labour movement.

The Origins of the Labour Movement

The Indian labour movement grew slowly, and it was not until 1877 that we have the first indication of labour protest—a "misunderstanding" over wage rates at the Empress Mills in Nagpur.[5] Several years passed before anything resembling a union was started, largely because of the slowness of industrial development, the backwardness of the industrial worker, and the partial stabilization of labour in industry, as Chapter III has indicated. The Royal Commission reported in 1931, approximately eighty years after the first signs of industrialization:

> Few industrial workers would remain in industry if they could secure sufficient food and clothing in the village; they are pushed, not pulled, to the city.[6]

Public-spirited outsiders with a humanitarian interest in the welfare of labour were among the first to assist industrial workers in publicizing their grievances and in formulating demands. The content of these reports constitutes an adequate commentary on prevalent conditions in industry. The early demands were for regulations of hours of work, for holidays and rest periods during the working day, for full and regular payment of wages due, and against physical ill-treatment.[7]

But there was hardly any realization of the value of combination. Buchanan observes, after a detailed analysis of developments up to 1908:

> There was only sporadic and irregular concerted action among Indian laborers, even on the scale of the individual shop. When occasionally there was united action, it was rather that of a mill mob aroused over a particular, temporary, purely local, and often personal, grievance, than that of a businesslike trade union.[8]

Weaknesses of organization were apparent even in the case of the one or two "unions" formed by outsiders. There was little conception of trade union membership or of regular collection of union subscriptions. Outside leadership was also principally individual and unorganized. These unions were therefore shortlived.

Despite these weaknesses of organization, there was some progress in the direction of protective labour legislation, due to other favourable influences. Important in this respect were Lancashire and other English manufacturing interests, which pressed for Indian labour legislation because they were concerned with cheap competition from Indian manufacturing enterprises. The government appointed successively several factory commissions, which led ultimately to the passing of the Indian Factories Act in 1911. This regulated for the first time working hours of adult male labour in Indian factories to 12 hours per day. However, the British Indian government's political, economic and social objectives were rather limited.[9] It was undoubtedly committed to the orderly progress of India towards dominion status, to nurturing the roots of an Anglo-Saxon democratic and social tradition, in short, to encouraging, in the words of the *Annual Report* of the Viceroy and Crown Representative, the "moral and material progress" of the Indian subcontinent. All this was to be achieved within a liberal economic framework characterized by minimum government intervention.

Although the philosophy of *laissez faire* dominated government thinking, in practice, the facts of social power and prevailing legal concepts worked to the disadvantage of the emerging class of industrial workers.[10] To enable the early entrepreneurs to overcome difficulties in securing an adequate labour supply, legislation was passed to assist emigration (within India and abroad) as well as to penalize breach of contracts.[11] There is also some reason to believe that magisterial and police power favoured the employers. It was nearly fifty or sixty years after the first modern textile factories were established that the first efforts were made to extend the benefits of protective labour legislation (regulating hours of work and providing for compulsory breaks in employment) to adult male labour.[12] However there was no uniform policy governing the settlement of industrial disputes, no machinery of public conciliation, not even an assumption that this constituted a major area of governmental responsibility.

The outside leaders of labour worked generally in cooperation and in sympathy with the government's efforts. Nationalist discontent against British rule had not yet entered the labour field.[13]

The Early Involvement of the Nationalist Movement

The increasing militancy of the nationalist movement and the first World War, with its inevitable hardships, led to an identification of political discontent and leadership with rising labour discontent. The Indian National Congress, the party of independence from British rule, adopted a resolution urging its provincial committees and other affiliated associations to "promote" labour unions throughout the country.[14] The All-India Trade Union Congress (AITUC) was formed in 1918, through the initiative and leadership of prominent Congressmen.[15] Many individual unions were also established by outsiders with nationalist sympathies. For example, the Madras Labour Union, considered one of the earliest successful Indian unions, was founded by patriots who regarded the struggle with employers as secondary to winning "home rule."

Most of these unions were nevertheless weak and poorly organized. Even the AITUC was nothing more than a loosely coordinated body, coming to life only around the time of the annual conference to elect worker representatives to the ILO meetings in Geneva.[16] The unstructured state of unionism and of industrial relations is well indicated by a statement of findings contained in the report of the Industrial Disputes Committee appointed by the Government of Bombay:

(a) The frequency of the strike without notice;

(b) the absence of any clearly defined grievance before striking;

(c) the multiplicity and sometimes the extravagance of the claims put forward after the strike had begun;

(d) the absence of any effective organization (except perhaps at Ahmedabad) to formulate the claims of the operatives and to secure respect for any settlement which might be made;

(e) the ... capacity of the operatives to remain on strike for considerable periods despite the lack of any visible organization.[17]

Gandhi and the Ahmedabad Union

The exception cited in this report was in Ahmedabad, second largest cotton textile centre in India.[18] This was due principally to the unique personality of Mahatma Gandhi, under whose leadership an industrial dispute in 1918 was fought on a high moral plane of "struggle for justice,"[19] and during which an important Indian union—the Ahmedabad Textile Labour Association (TLA) —emerged.

In 1918, the Ahmedabad textile workers demanded a 50 per cent increase in wages as dearness (cost of living) allowance when they heard that the millowners contemplated stopping the "plague" bonus that had been paid in previous years. The millowners resisted the demand. Gandhi's mediatory intervention was sought. His handling of the situation was unusual, if not unique. An inquiry convinced him that only a 35 per cent wage increase could be justified, and he advised the workers accordingly to scale down their demand to 35 per cent. As a condition of his leadership, he further required the workers to take a pledge not to return to work until a 35 per cent wage increase was granted by the millowners. He further laid down the rule that the workers were

not to indulge in mischief, quarrelling, robbing, plundering, or abusive language or cause damage to millowners' property, but to behave peacefully.[20]

When the workers began to falter after a strike which lasted about three weeks, he declared:

I cannot tolerate for a minute that you break your pledge. I shall not take any food nor use a car till you get a 35 per cent increase or all of you die in the fight for it.[21]

Gandhi's fast added to the widespread public concern, and also weakened the millowners' resistance. An interim settlement was worked out by Gandhi which respected the millowners' claim and insisted on fair play from both sides. The issue was finally settled by an arbitral award which granted a 35 per cent increase in wages. Gandhi termed the dispute a "righteous struggle," the results of which were announced in the final strike leaflet as a victory for both.

The 1918 struggle is significant because it revealed the unquestioned personal authority of Mahatma Gandhi and indicated the beginnings of a new ideology, appropriately called the "Gandhian" labour ideology. The essence of the Gandhian approach was its emphasis on "truth and fairness" in the formulation of demands and avoidance of bitterness during the course of the struggle. He was concerned with the need for constructive relationships after the termination of the dispute and strongly recommended that in the future all disputes should be settled amicably by means of arbitration.[22] During the struggle, as well as on other occasions, Gandhi stressed the union's responsibilities as well as the virtue of self-help and internal strength.[23] He did not like the political emphasis given to trade unionism over much of the country, and was also dissatisfied with the quality of labour leadership.[24] It was precisely due to these reasons that the Ahmedabad Textile Labour Association stayed away from the AITUC.[25]

Radicalism, Splits and Crises

As we have already indicated, Ahmedabad was distinctly an exception to the prevailing state of Indian unionism. Observations by contemporary students make it clear that the unions of the day were nothing more than inchoate manifestations of industrial unrest.[26] The government, undoubtedly influenced by the gravity of industrial unrest and the pressures exerted by the International Labour Organization at Geneva, acted to provide legislative protection for labour.[27] Among the more important legislative measures of the period were the Indian Factories Act, 1922, providing for a ten-hour day; the Indian Mines Act, 1923 (the first to regulate mining conditions); the Workmen's Compensation Act (also the first of its kind); and finally the Indian Trade Unions Act, 1926. This Act allowed any seven persons to form a registered trade union. Moreover, it granted immunity from criminal prosecution for any agreement furthering trade union objectives, and from civil suit for actions which would induce workers to break a contract of employment or otherwise interfere with trade, business or employment.[28]

Despite these measures, labour unrest increased towards the end of the twenties.[29] This was not only an economic protest against wage cuts and increases in work loads, but was also a manifestation of political and economic radicalism directed against British rule and the prevalent system of private enterprise, a large part of which was dominated by British capital. Moderate leadership was edged out by a Communist-Nationalist coalition which dominated the AITUC and the labour strikes of the period.

A severe blow· was struck at the Communists in the labour movement when the government arrested several of them on the charge of conspiracy to overthrow the state. The famous Meerut Trial of 1928 led to their conviction and removed their influence from the labour field during the following years. Government followed up these measures by passing the Indian Trade Disputes Act, 1929, the major purpose of which was to prohibit lightning strikes.

The appointment in 1929 of the Royal Commission on Labour in India represented, however, a more fundamental search into the causes of labour unrest. After an exhaustive enquiry, the commission recommended in 1931 that employers should adopt a more liberal policy towards "recognition" of unions,[30] and that government should take the lead in the case of their own industrial employees. It favoured a liberalization of the provision in the Trade Unions Act, 1926, relating to the inclusion of "outsiders" in trade union executives. Further the Commission was particularly critical of the Trade Disputes Act and the prevailing government approach to the settlement of industrial disputes, as being influenced unduly by considerations of public order.[31]

The Commission suggested that these outsiders should endeavour to train future union officials from the rank and file and encourage them to assume greater responsibility. Other recommendations favoured a greater emphasis on conciliation, the establishment of joint committees at the plant level, and a tripartite industrial council on a national scale.[32]

But the climate in the thirties was not very conducive to the implementation of the Royal Commission's recommendations. The militant Nationalist-Communist leadership of the AITUC boycotted the work of the Commission.[33] On this issue, and also on the question of participation in the work of the International Labour Organization, a group of "moderate" labour leaders split from the AITUC and formed a rival federation in 1929. The AITUC suffered a further split when the hard core Communists, thwarted in their attempts to control the AITUC, formed another rival labour federation in 1931. With the exception of the "moderate," all these groups emphasized the role of the union as an organ of class struggle.[34] On other issues, they were agreed on the objectives of the labour movement, which included the establishment of a socialist state in India, the attainment of political freedom from foreign rule, and the abolition of economic privileges.[35]

On the whole, the thirties were a depressing period for Indian unionism. Political rivalries dominated the labour movement, despite various attempts at a political level to effect reconciliation.[36] The politically-minded labour leaders were also heavily involved in the increasing tempo of activities in connection with the struggle for independence. Further Indian industry had to face the depressing impact of world economic conditions, and industrial workers were also affected adversely.

Some of these developments were brought to a head in 1934 with efforts on the part of the employers to effect wage cuts and retrenchment, and labour's resistance under militant labour leadership, strengthened by the release of the Communists, and the formation of a new Congress Socialist group within the Congress party with distinctly Marxist leanings.[37] Unrest was most acute in Bombay. The Bombay Government reacted by passing the Bombay Trade Dispute Conciliation Act, which provided for compulsory conciliation and the appointment of a government Labour Officer with statutory powers to enquire into labour conditions in factories, and to represent labour in the absence of its own representatives.

These experiments were carried a step further during 1937–39, when the Indian National Congress assumed power in 7 of the

11 provinces in British India, following elections held under the Government of India Act, 1935. The Congress had promised in its Election Manifesto that its policy was to secure for industrial workers

> a decent standard of living, hours of work and conditions of labour, in conformity, as far as the economic conditions in the country permit, with international standards, suitable machinery for the settlement of disputes between employers and workmen, protection against the economic consequences of old age, sickness and unemployment and the right of workers to form unions and to strike for the protection of their interest.[38]

The Indian National Congress party, although it came to power only in 1946, was a principal force to be reckoned with even during these days.[39] Its principal role was one of opposition to Britain and this banner provided an umbrella for competing ideological groups active in the labour movement. None of them saw eye to eye with others on the purposes of labour activity. The Communists or Marxist Socialists viewed the trade union mainly as an instrument in the class struggle and rejected collective bargaining or any form of cooperation with the employers. There were others who were mainly interested in trade union activity and still others who were interested only in an occasional expression of humanistic concern. The main interest of the Gandhians was in the trade union as an instrument of personal and moral reform. Finally there were the major national figures who were votaries of particular ideologies but undistinguished by more pedestrian union activity. The official position of the Congress was one of accommodating all the rival groups.

The Congress assumed office under favourable auspices. The distribution of powers under the 1935 Act had enlarged considerably the jurisdiction of the provincial governments. Disunity in the labour movement had also been amicably settled within the framework of the AITUC.[40] Some Congress administrations appointed high-level labour enquiry committees which added to the existing knowledge of labour conditions and recommended several measures for the improvement of labour welfare.[41] New concepts were introduced by the Congress-sponsored Bombay Industrial Disputes Act, 1938[42] and by the National Planning Committee of the Congress. The Bombay Act involved regulation of plant-level relations between labour and management and prohibition of strikes except under certain circumstances. It attempted also to eliminate rivalries in the labour movement by providing for different categories of unions, only one of which could be registered in an industry or occupation. A union with 25 per cent of membership of all those employed in an industry or occupation in a local area was placed in a special category, for the Act empowered the government to direct that an agreement or award applicable to a representative union would be applicable to all other employers and employees in the industry.

The National Planning Committee indicated the outlines of a future labour policy by favouring gains for labour within the framework of a planned economy, governed by a comprehensive system of state-sponsored compulsory arbitration. Some idea of future difficulties in securing an acceptance of this policy was indicated in the opposition of influential labour leaders to the abridgement of the "right to strike" provided in the Bombay legislation and in plans for the economy.[43] Yet all of these early plans were later developments under the Five Year Plans.

The outbreak of World War II interrupted these experiments as Congress ministries resigned in protest against the government's policy of committing India to the war effort without consulting representative Indian opinion.[44] In protest against the AITUC's official policy of neutrality in the war, a rival labour federation was started under the leadership of M. N. Roy, a noted former Communist and leader of an anti-Facist group. The opposition of Congressmen to the war effort landed them in jail, and left control of the AITUC principally in the hands of the Communists.

With a steady growth of employment during the war, trade union membership registered a substantial increase from 399,000 for 1938-39 to 889,000 for 1944-45.[45] Industrial unrest during this period was kept in check by the Defence of India Rule 81(A), which empowered government to prohibit strikes or lockouts and to refer any dispute for conciliation or adjudication. Labour itself suffered heavily, due to the wartime rise in prices and decline in real wages,[46] and the temporary disregard, for wartime purposes, of some of the protection offered by Indian labour legislation.

The Postwar Crisis and Labour Legislation

The immediate postwar period was therefore one of violent industrial unrest, reminiscent of the 1928–29 wave of strikes. Chiefly responsible for fanning this unrest were the wartime lag in earnings, the renewal of political activity in the labour field, and the removal of wartime policy considerations which had moderated Communist labour policy. The Congress assumed control of the Government of India during this period when, despite the prospect of freedom, the outlook was gloomy, because of industrial and economic difficulties and the partition of the country.

Faced with unrest, the government adopted the Industrial Disputes Act, 1947, embodying many of the restrictive features of the wartime Defence of India Rule 81(A). Its continuation aroused bitter opposition from the labour representatives in the Constituent Assembly. N. M. Joshi, the president of the AITUC, emphasized that the government was doing workers great harm by prohibiting the right to strike. Similar views were expressed by Mr. Guruswamy and Miss Maniben Kara, the other labour representatives in the Assembly.[47]

Government also secured the passage of an amendment to the Trade Unions Act, 1926. The amended Act of 1947 provided for compulsory recognition of unions, conferred bargaining rights and ensured protection of the right to organize by the proscription of certain "unfair labour practices." But the Act was not enforced for reasons which have never been made clear.

Further measures contemplated by the government were contained in the Five Year Labour Programme, announced early in 1947.[48] The government promised improvement of the conditions of recruitment and tenure of workers, added benefits of social security, and a better wage structure, including the promotion of "fair-wage" agreements, "having regard to the capacity of the industry to pay." In addition, it was announced that the Mines and Factories Acts would be revised, providing for a 48-hour week, rest periods and holidays with pay. It was also proposed to extend labour legislation so as to include those employed in commercial undertakings, docks, transport services and the municipalities. Further welfare measures envisaged included improved attention to the housing and the health of the industrial workers.

Another development, in tune with the policy of moderating labour protest, must be noted. A conference of labour and management representatives was held in New Delhi in December 1947, under the auspices of the government to discuss the serious deterioration in industrial production because of strikes and to suggest ways of improving the situation.[49] The conference, following the call of Prime Minister Nehru, unanimously adopted a resolution calling upon "labour and management to agree to maintain industrial peace and to avert lockouts, strikes or slowing down of production during the next three years." This became known as the "Industrial Truce Resolution." The conference further recommended

> Mutual discussion of all problems common to both and a determination to settle all disputes without recourse to interruption in or slowing down of production should be the common aim of employers and labour. The system of remuneration to capital as well as labour must be so devised that while in the interests of the consumers and the primary producers excessive profits should be prevented by suitable measures . . . both will share the product of their common effort after making provision for payment of fair wages to labour, a fair return on capital employed in the industry and reasonable reserves for the maintenance and expansion of the undertaking.

Formation of the Indian National Trade Union Congress

While the country was plunged in a wave of industrial unrest after the war, the Working Committee of the Congress expressed its dissatisfaction with the radicalism of the labour leadership, especially as represented by the Communist-led AITUC. A series of developments marked by conferences and talks among Congressmen, including the Hindusthan Mazdoor Sevak Sangh (a labour advisory group sponsored by leaders associated with the Ahmedabad TLA), led to the formation of the Indian National Trade Union Congress in May 1947.[50] Foremost among the INTUC's labour supporters were the active leaders of the TLA, who were also subsequently prominent in the leadership of the INTUC.

G. L. Nanda, the first general secretary of the TLA, and prominent for over a decade in the Central Cabinet of the Indian government, drew attention to the AITUC's "violent campaign against arbitration" and its resolutions condemning the Bombay Industrial Relations Act and the All-India Industrial Disputes Act. He pointed out that these ran "directly counter to the declared policy of the Congress." Nanda undoubtedly expressed the official Congress viewpoint when he declared that

the most urgent need of the moment is to speedily bring into being and develop a central organisation of labour in the country which will strive to secure the highest benefits and the maximum of progress for all categories and classes of labour while preserving a national spirit and outlook, and standards and just conditions in accordance with the principles set out in the statement of the Working Committee dated the 13th August, 1946.[51]

The Conference which established the INTUC made clear beyond doubt the high level official support to this move to establish a new central labour organization. Those present included the late Prime Minister Nehru, Deputy Prime Minister Vallabhbhai Patel, other members of the cabinet, chief ministers of states, and the presidents of the All-India and Bombay Congress parties. In 1948, the Government of India declared that the INTUC, and not the AITUC, was the most representative organization of labour in the country entitled to represent Indian labour. Thus almost overnight, a new labour federation was ushered in as the premier spokesman—in the official view at any rate—of labour interests in the country.

Reactions to Congress Labour Policy

These developments aroused fears of a state-sponsored labour movement. Despite the popular mandate with which the Congress assumed office, Congress labour policies came in for serious criticism by non-Congress labour leaders. Some of this reflected basic difference of opinion with the Congress policy of compulsory arbitration. Yet there were many who welcomed the formation of the INTUC because of the alarming incidence of industrial strife and the disturbed conditions of the period. The Indian labour movement entered upon a new phase of political unionism, with the formation of 2 more central labour organizations.

Naturally, among the earliest to react critically were the leaders of the AITUC. Even before the formation of the INTUC, Mr. Mrinal Kanti Bose, the non-Communist president of the AITUC, had complained:

> There have been numerous instances of firing and arrests of labour leaders on some excuse or other; one curious excuse often put forward being that they are goondas [rowdies] and as such externed from their home provinces! The policy seems to be general and I would seriously ask the ... Governments concerned to consider if they have been well-advised in launching upon a policy which could not but fill the minds of the workers with misgivings as to their lot in the India tomorrow.[52]

When the INTUC was established in May 1947, criticism burst out anew. N. M. Joshi, the non-Communist general secretary of the AITUC, charged that the INTUC was in no sense a nonpolitical labour organization, but only an adjunct of the Indian National Congress.[53] Joshi further deplored the active association of high-ranking members of the government in the formation of the new organization and expressed fears that the labour movement would become practically a department of the government. Joshi denied charges that the AITUC encouraged bogus membership or opposed arbitration, and asserted that they were opposed only to compulsory adjudication. Joshi concluded by saying that the AITUC was not dominated by the Communists, though they were in the majority. He pointed out that all the AITUC resolutions since 1938 had been adopted unanimously, and that no union seeking affiliation was denied entry because of its political views.

As we can see, some of this criticism reflected in part a genuine desire for a labour federation independent in its approach of the political views of the leadership. Developments soon afterwards indicated clearly the slender grounds on which these hopes were based.

The Communist leadership of the AITUC embarked on open pursuit of sectarian policies, disregarding in the process the appearances that were considered necessary to claim for the AITUC the status of an independent labour organization. One by one the prominent "independents" associated with the AITUC resigned in protest in 1948.[54]

The Socialists also expressed their dislike of Congress labour policy. They declared themselves opposed to compulsory arbitration, and indicated their disapproval of government-sponsored trade unionism. But the Socialists were also against the Communists, whom they wanted to drive out of the working class movement. Confronted with this dilemma, the Socialists vacillated for a while, during which period the activities of the Socialist labour leaders were coordinated by the Hind Mazdoor Panchayat, the labour bureau of the Congress Socialist Party. Finally, after breaking away from the Congress, the Socialists decided to sponsor a new central labour federation. Accordingly, as the result of a conference of leaders held at Calcutta in December 1948, a new federation—the Hind Mazdoor Sabha (HMS)—was launched, ostensibly with a view to keeping the trade union movement free from domination by government, employers and political parties. It was announced at the conference that the Indian Federation of Labour (established during the war) was merged in the new body.[55]

In addition to the main objective of socialism, the HMS constitution[56] enumerated the following as the aims of the new organization: the nationalization of key industries, the securing of effective recognition to bargain collectively, worker participation in the control and regulation of industry, and a close working relationship with the Indian cooperative movement. In view of the prevalence of a large number of weak unions, it was announced that the HMS intended to sponsor nationwide industrial unions.

The general approach of HMS to trade unionism was stated as follows.[57] "The Labour Movement hopes to soar high on the two wings of combative and constructive activities. The trade union is viewed at once as the organ of class struggle and the school of democracy." The constitution qualified this statement by pointing out that "the Sabha shall employ all legitimate, peaceful and democratic methods," thus emphasizing the difference between the Socialists and the Communists.

Resentful at the attitude of the Socialist majority in the Calcutta conference, a group of left leaders—ranging in their views between the Communists and the Socialists—took the first steps, simultaneously with the conference, to establish still another labour federation.[58] This was finally launched in April-May 1949, and was called the United Trades Union Congress.[59] The new group also claimed that it had been formed to conduct union activity on the broadest possible basis of trade unity, free from sectarian party politics. Its revolutionary attitude was illustrated by the following opening remarks of Mr. M. K. Bose, former president of AITUC, who was elected general secretary of the new body:

The policy of the Congress Government has been a complete repudiation of the pledge repeatedly given by the Congress while in opposition.... Their Government has adopted policies and measures that are calculated to establish ... a Capitalist Raj. The influence of the capitalists as a class on the Government has increased and has been increasing.... The keeping in abeyance of the nationalization of the industries for ten years with the ill-concealed hint by cabinet ministers that the Capitalists had no reason to worry on account of the time limit is a clear indication that the Government is not moving towards the abolition of classes, but the perpetuation of them. The cordial invitation to foreign capital ... also shows which way the wind has been blowing from New Delhi. The threat to hang cloth millowners for the shameless fleecing of the common people is heard no more. On the contrary, facilities are being given to the profiteers to make more and more profit.... The arbitration and conciliation machinery set up under the Industrial Disputes Act is being boomed as a priceless gift to the workers.... But the fact is that these tribunals have benefited the employers more than the workers ... and have attracted all the evils that have made our civil courts a paradise for the rich and hell for the poor.[60]

Subsequent Developments and Their Impact
on the Labour Movement

The year 1952 marked a turning point in the approach of the government towards industrial relations problems.[61] Planning for economic growth dictated the wisdom of continued efforts to spell out basic principles of state policy and to seek sustained improvements in industrial relations. Many of the measures adopted immediately after the war were *ad hoc* responses to immediately pressing conditions. Responsibility for long-term planning forced on the government a re-evaluation of its own role and the extent to which the objectives of industrial relations policy would need to rest on support from labour and management. The year 1952 also witnessed the first general elections based on universal adult franchise. The subsequent political evolution of India demonstrated that independent political pressures would not only continue but also increase in strength. In the labour field, the continuing involvement of the Socialists, Communists, and others with a commitment to mobilize the grievances and aspirations of the industrial and urban workforce would have to be reckoned with. These led to a greater emphasis by the government on "voluntarism" and the "moral" requirements of industrial relations policies which would command support from labour as well as management. These are discussed in greater detail in Chapter VIII.

The postwar developments, nevertheless, signalled a fundamental shift in the role of the state. This was well indicated by the Second Five Year Plan which stated that, in a community organized under a planned economy, strikes and other forms of disruption of work must be held to a minimum. This has led to a continuing conflict between the segments of the labour movement not affiliated to the ruling Congress party and the Indian Government. The climate of constitutionalism has ensured for these dissident groups a prominent voice in the labour movement. There are continuing charges, it is true, of government favouritism to the INTUC, but it is clear that such support has never been total. Actually the orderly development of the Indian political system has encouraged the growth of political action based on mass appeal. The proliferation of different interest groups, and their search for political expression, has been noted by several political scientists.[62] The trade unions have shared in this development.

Pressures Shaping the Labour Movement

Organizationally and ideologically, the principal wings in the labour movement are examples of "political" unionism. The term may be defined as below:

1. The trade union movement is part of a broader political movement with an implied reconciliation of trade union and political goals under one framework.
2. This framework is supplied by party control over the trade union movement, rather than a looser affiliation, or the give and take of political adjustment by relatively open political processes.
3. Tactical and organizational considerations may suggest some degree of autonomy for labour organizations, but these are subordinate to the central objectives of the party.[63]

Indian unionism is political in the basic sense indicated above, although undoubtedly there are good reasons to indulge in political activity to further trade union goals. Nevertheless, the objectives of political unionism have been handicapped by the presence of the following features in the Indian labour movement:

(a) the insufficient attention to organization as opposed to ideological or policy pronouncements;
(b) the essential indifference, perhaps even hostility, of the rank and file of the labour force to the overall political and ideological issues;
(c) conflicts between political and trade union objectives.

Thus, although political and ideological objectives have been dominant in influencing political parties to undertake trade union work, the political returns have been meagre or disappointing.

Of course, the relative fortunes of the different groups have varied but it is doubtful that these gains have been enduring. Also the more limited trade union calculus of the workforce, rather than their ideological commitments, seems to have played the key role in these developments. It is instructive to contrast the position of the three major federations, the INTUC, the AITUC, and the HMS.

The INTUC

The INTUC is the self-labelled votary of an indigenous trade union ideology founded on Gandhian principles of truth and nonviolence.[64]

The constitution of the INTUC is distinctive in its emphasis that negotiation, conciliation and adjudication of industrial disputes (failing which alone) must precede a union's exercise of its right to strike.[65] The objectives of the INTUC are stated to be the establishment of a society most suited to the development of the human personality, which would go to the utmost extent in the progressive elimination of exploitation and inequality, and also of the profit motive and the anti-social concentration of power in any form; the nationalization of industry, with the above end in view; the increasing association of the workers in the administration of industry; the organization of all categories of workers, including agricultural; the improvement of conditions of work, and the establishment of a just basis of industrial relations; and, finally, redevelopment in the workers of a sense of responsibility towards industry and community. The Gandhian heritage is clearly indicated in the following clause embodied in the constitution :

The means to be adopted for the furtherance of the objects ... shall be peaceful and consistent with truth.[66]

The impact of the Gandhian influence on the INTUC is emphasized by the INTUC itself and by its official publication, the *Indian Worker*. The INTUC has also tried to mould the trade unions in other parts of India on the model of the Ahmedabad Textile Association.[67]

In practice, however, it is difficult to understand its role in Indian industrial relations without reference to its links with the ruling Congress party, an affiliation which has not been an unmixed blessing, given the constraints it imposes and the resultant vulnerability to criticism. When confronted with an opposition government, as in Kerala between 1957 and 1959 under a Communist government, the INTUC adopted militant trade union tactics uninhibited by its ideology or its links with the ruling Congress party.[68] Elsewhere in India, however, the INTUC's appeal has been seriously damaged because of the greater freedom with which rival Communist and Socialist labour leaders have marshalled labour protest. Further, while the INTUC ideology does not assign primacy to any particular group so much as to the general interest, in practice INTUC leaders have had to take second place, as Congressmen, to the more broadbased Congress party leadership. Inevitably, this has added to the strains faced by the INTUC leadership on such occasions as major strikes or negative official decisions on key labour issues. The support to the government on these occasions has been costly in terms of INTUC's appeal to the workers. Without risking an open break, the INTUC has tried to counter this loss by specific criticisms directed at government policy.[69] In some states, INTUC units have acted as pressure groups operating to counter the influence of the established Congress leadership. However, these have not been adequate to still opposition criticism. Perhaps the only exception is the situation in West Bengal. Here the local INTUC leadership has been virtually at loggerheads with the state government, and has further pursued a policy of forcing the government's hands by militant tactics.[70]

The HMS

The Socialist-led HMS attitude has been one of rejection of both the Congress party's and the Communist party's leadership. The dominant group of Socialists also held to the belief that, although class conflict was present, the situation did not necessarily warrant the adoption of violent or insurrectionary tactics.[71] The Socialist party's fortunes were severely undermined when the ruling Congress veered towards a "socialistic" framework in its plan for economic development. Within the Socialist party, there arose a school which advocated trade union support to the national plans for economic development.[72] There were inchoate but unsuccessful attempts at unity between the HMS and the INTUC.[73] A number of Socialist and HMS leaders did not subscribe to these changes and the HMS suffered a decline due to weaknesses and factions in the parent political party. In recent years, in its efforts to consolidate its following in the labour movement, the HMS has collaborated with the AITUC or other left wing and independent labour groups in opposition to the INTUC. The most prominent instances include the joint support to the Central Government Employees Strike in 1960, and the several efforts by the Socialist and Communist opposition, under the banner of a United Maharashtra Movement, to establish the Mumbai Girni Kamgar Union, in opposition to the "representative" INTUC textile union in Bombay, the Rashtriya Mill Mazdoor Sevak Sangh. The present Chairman of the Praja Socialist Party has actually been a leader of these efforts in Bombay and succeeded Asoka Mehta, the advocate of trade union cooperation and moderation, in 1963.[74]

The AITUC

The Communist leadership has always been skeptical of the possibilities for progress within the framework of what they have called a "bourgeois" society. Accordingly the focus of their involvement in trade union activity has been on its revolutionary rather than its bargaining implications. However, the weakening of the Socialist position in the Indian labour movement and the timorous' policies of the INTUC encouraged them to adopt pragmatic tactics, ranging all the way from militant class unionism to businesslike collective bargaining.[75]

The AITUC leadership has freely supported the INTUC leadership where the INTUC leadership took the initiative, as in regard to the affairs of the 200,000-man jute industry in Calcutta. However, where unpopular INTUC unions appeared to be supported by state governments or employers (generally employers' associations), the AITUC has tried to discredit the arrangements in force. In several of the All-India industries where the central government is either the major employer or regulator of working conditions, the AITUC has supported employee-run unions, even though they have not been affiliated with the AITUC. The provisions for compulsory conciliation or adjudication have also been freely used, even though the relevant legislation has been mercilessly excoriated. Finally, despite the lukewarmness towards the more conservative goals represented by collective bargaining, wherever the economic environment appeared favourable, the Communist leadership has encouraged decentralized union leadership, detailed plant-level bargaining, and forms of union-management relationship not very dissimilar from local bargaining efforts in the United States.[76]

However, it has always been clear that the primary goal of Communist union activity has been political. This was emphasized when the Communists assumed power in Kerala in 1957.[77] A number of efforts were initiated to lure industrial capital on the promise of low wages and government support to industrial management. A major agreement with the Birlas, one of India's most prominent private entrepreneurial groups, assured the prospective employer of favourable terms in regard to industrial relations such as no Indian government has dared to do publicly. This reversal of a familiar role was matched by militant opposition to the Communist government by the INTUC, HMS and the UTUC (with considerable influence in this state).[78] They succeeded in forcing the Communists to renege on their promise to refrain from the use of police or military power in labour disputes.

Principal and Emerging Trends in the Labour Movement

The evolution of the Indian labour movement since Independence emphasizes certain features. The main reason for the existence of different labour federations is political. Political considerations have also influenced the tactics pursued. Nevertheless, while political strength has been a necessary condition of success in the ideological battle in the labour movement (as the lack of such strength amply proved in the case of the HMS), it has by no means been a sufficient condition. The INTUC's weaknesses over much of India, and the display on a more limited scale of a similar weakness by Communist unions in Kerala, lead to the inference that rank and file support is dependent on vigorous pursuit of trade union objectives. The situation might have been different if the INTUC had received more substantial and exclusive support from the government in power. However, even where the INTUC unions have enjoyed a privileged position under certain state governments, the rivals have had considerable scope to mobilize labour protest.

There have also been subtle changes within the pattern of political unionism which have led to an increasing recognition of the need for consolidating gains and a diminished interest in purely adventurous manoeuvres. In recent times, these changing attitudes have manifested themselves in three principal ways. First, there has developed something like a distinction between political leaders with a secondary interest in labour union activity and labour leaders with a secondary interest in political leadership. A few labour leaders have come into national prominence mainly because of their success in union activities. The stress on labour as opposed to political leadership has been accompanied by statements deprecating the "old" style techniques of agitation and affirming the need for regular trade union cadres, finances, and training in office administration. Secondly, the national federations have also displayed increased interest in long-term activities designed to build up the personnel and organizational side of trade unions, even while maintaining the pattern of rivalries. Initially trade union trainees were sent to the government-run workers' education programmes, and more recently similar programmes have been sponsored by the trade union federations themselves.[79] Finally, there has been a greater recognition in practice of the need for unions to function as autonomous units rather than simply as appendages of the political parties. Some of these points will be amplified in the next chapter.

These developments must be understood in the context of broader developments affecting the nation as a whole. The relative political stability in India during the last fifteen to twenty years since Independence has contributed to an awareness by political parties of the importance of organization and encouraged a shift from wistful dreams of overnight millennia to hard work aimed at gradual accretion of parochial influence. These attitudes have inevitably spilled over into the field of industrial relations where the political parties provide the chief organizational influence. At the same time, the political developments within India have led to a proliferation of parties and sources of political strength. Thus recent developments have led to the emergence, although as yet only on a limited scale, of new groups active in the labour movement. Thus, in Madras and Coimbatore, the Dravida Munnetra Kazhagam, with significant regional following, has made inroads in the labour movement.[80] The Bharatiya Mazdoor Sangh, affiliated to the conservative-traditionalist Jan Sangh, represents a new trade union federation with pockets of influence in several centres.[81] The Swatantra party, a conservative movement dedicated to progressive private enterprise, has constituted a nucleus of independent trade unions under its leadership although disavowing the intention of forming yet another labour federation.[82]

Summary Remarks on Political Unionism

Thus divergent political pressures continue to be the strongest factor causing disunity among leaders. The pattern of splits and conflicts caused by the presence of the four major groups in the Indian labour movement has continued to this day. The efforts towards HMS–INTUC unity, following the merger of the KMPP and the Socialist Party in 1952, led to limited but shortlived accommodations, notably in railways and defence. Most of the remaining unity moves have been confined to *ad hoc* fronts, or citywide combinations of non-INTUC unions. In the 1958 edition of this book, it was observed that the INTUC and HMS have shown some willingness to cooperate with each other, but the INTUC has not been willing to include the other two groups;[83] the HMS has indicated its readiness to cooperate with the UTUC, but not with the AITUC; the UTUC is willing to cooperate with both the HMS and the AITUC, but not with either one alone;[84] and the AITUC advocated the broadest possible basis of unity, irrespective of party affiliations.[85]

This position has continued, but there have been some changes. These include the active collaboration of the Socialists and Communists in the Bombay cotton textile industry, the implicit support given by the Communists to the INTUC leadership in the large

Indian jute industry in Calcutta, and other instances of cooperation cutting across political boundaries mentioned above. There are also scattered instances of trade unions run by workers themselves which have maintained organizational discipline by sticking to trade union issues for which there is rank and file support. Thus, in some of the middle class unions, for instance banking, the workers are organized in disciplined unions, although the leadership is strongly pro-Communist. In some of the newer industries, the rank and file employees manage their own unions and affiliation to the outside federations appears to be of limited substantive importance. These are, however, exceptions so far as the main body of industrial employees are concerned.

Indian unions and leaders continue to be divided in most of the areas they operate in and have not yet discovered a broad basis of trade union unity.[86] In the following chapter, our discussion of the structure of Indian unionism and of the nature of labour leadership will throw light on this relationship.

NOTES

1 These points are developed more fully in the study by Subbiah Kannappan, *The Indian Trade Union Movement: An Account and an Analysis* (unpublished doctoral dissertation, Fletcher School of Law and Diplomacy, Medford, Mass., 1956). This study, based on field research in India during 1954-55, was part of the Inter-University Project on which the present monograph is based. Much of the material from this chapter is drawn from Dr. Kannappan's manuscript, and he is largely responsible for the first draft of the chapter.

2 Cf. figures given in *Final Report of the National Income Committee* 1954, Government of India (Delhi, 1954), p. 106.

3 *Per capita* income for the total Indian population for 1952-53 was estimated at Rs. 261. *Five Year Plan: Progress Report for* 1953-54, Government of India, Planning Commission (Delhi, 1954), p. 7. Average annual earnings for industrial workers as reported in *The Indian Labour Year Book* 1951-52 are (*a*) cotton textiles, Rs. 705 at Madras, the lowest-paying centre, and Rs. 1,569 at Delhi, the highest-paying centre; (*b*) jute, Rs. 915; and (*c*) steel, for most occupations, between Rs. 100-200 per month (pp. 190, 191, and 197, respectively).

4 Political and economic developments in India, and the government's industrial relations policies have obviously influenced the development of the Indian labour movement. For a more detailed treatment with emphasis on developments since

the beginning of development planning, see Subbiah Kannappan, "The Many Facets of Government Influence on Industrial Relations in India," paper delivered at Research Conference on Industrial Relations and Economic Development, International Institute for Labour Studies, Geneva, Switzerland, 24 August to 4 September 1964, mimeo (to be published as part of conference proceedings).

5 D. H. Buchanan, *The Development of Capitalist Enterprise in India* (New York, 1934), p. 416.

6 *Report,* Royal Commission on Labour in India, 1931, Cmd. 3883.

7 For a good summary of developments during this period up to World War I, see *ibid.,* pp. 416-26; and also R. K. Das, *Labour Movement in India* (Berlin, 1923), esp. pp. 7-20.

8 Buchanan, *op. cit.,* p. 426.

9 Thus Professor Morris D. Morris states: "Government policy during the nineteenth century . . . was in its economic aspects essentially *laissez faire.* The British *raj* saw itself in the passive role of night watchman, providing security, rational administration, and a modicum of social overhead . . . " in "Towards a Reinterpretation of Nineteenth-Century Indian Economic History," *The Journal of Economic History,* December 1963, p. 615.

10 Among the best discussions are: B. Shiva Rao, *Industrial Worker in India,* London, 1939; R.K. Das, *Labour Movement in India,* Berlin, 1923; and P. S. Lokanathan, *Industrial Welfare in India,* Madras, University of Madras, 1929. This appears to have been true in a general sense, too. See Thomas W. Shea, Jr., "Barriers to Economic Development in Traditional Society: Malabar, A Case Study," *Journal of Economic History,* December 1959, pp. 513-16. See also Anandjee, *Community Regulations of Labour Management Relations in India* (1947-1957), unpublished doctoral dissertation, New Haven, Connecticut, Yale University Law School, 1959, especially pp. 159 ff, where he points out how employer-dominated Indian legislatures decried government intervention in labour relations unless it was to protect aggrieved employers. The bias in general legislation and legal concepts is also discussed.

11 Thus Alan Gledhill points out: "What little legislation there existed . . . was confined to making breaches of certain acts of service criminal offences . . ." in *The Republic of India: The Development of Its Law and Constitution,* London, 1951, p. 254. The relevant items of legislation included: Regulation VII of 1819; Workmen's Breach of Contract Act, 1859; Employers' and Workmen's (Disputes) Act, 1860; and the Indian Penal Code, 1860. There were also special Acts to protect employers in particular industries (salt, opium, indigo, etc.) against the following actions by the workers: breach of contract; instigation to commit breach of contract; refusal to accept employment; conspiracy; abetment of offences. On these points, see Anandjee, *ibid.,* and especially the more detailed citations in the foot-notes (pp. 42-3). See also Kannappan's discussion in "The Impact of the I.L.O. on Labour Legislation and Policy in India," in Robert L. Aronson and John P. Windmuller, eds., *Labor Management, and Economic Growth,* Ithaca, Cornell University, 1954 pp. 175-90.

12 The best account of the development of Indian labour legislation is by R. K.

Das, *History of Indian Labour Legislation,* Calcutta, University of Calcutta, 1941. The politics and pressures underlying this development are discussed in detail by B. Shiva Rao, *op. cit.,* and R. K. Das, *op. cit.*

13 It has even been suggested that some nationalist leaders viewed these early efforts towards regulation of working conditions with suspicion and resentment, as motivated by a desire to thwart Indian industrial development. B. Shiva Rao, *Industrial Worker in India* (London, 1939), pp. 24 ff.

14 P.-P. Lakshman, *Congress and Labour Movement,* All-India Congress Committee (Allahabad, 1947), p. 17.

15 See S. D. Punekar, *Trade Unionism in India* (Bombay, 1948), pp. 62, 321-22. Congress leaders continued to take interest in the AITUC during the following years. Among those prominently mentioned as associated with the AITUC are Jawaharlal Nehru, Subhas Chandra Bose, C. F. Andrews, and C. R. Das. See Lakshman, *Congress and Labour,* p. 20.

16 See P. S. Lokanathan, *Industrial Welfare in India,* University of Madras (Madras, 1929), pp. 168-69. Lokanathan says: "For the first four or five years the Trade Union Congress [AITUC] was a mere annual show and very few unions really cared to affiliate themselves to it. Its one purpose was to meet and recommend delegates to the I.L.O. Conferences...."

17 As quoted in R. K. Das, *Labour Movement,* pp. 67-8.

18 For more details on the developments in Ahmedabad, see Subbiah Kannappan, "The Gandhian Model of Unionism in a Developing Economy: The TLA in India," *Industrial and Labor Relations Review,* vol. 16, no. 1, October 1962.

19 See M. H. Desai, *A Righteous Struggle: A Chronicle of the Ahmedabad Textile Labourers' Fight for Justice* (Ahmedabad, 1951).

20 *Ibid.,* p. 10.

21 *Ibid.,* p. 25.

22 M. H. Desai, *ibid.,* p. 67. Gandhi said at the conclusion of the dispute: "Two things have been accomplished by this settlement. First, the honour of the workers is upheld; secondly, if a serious dispute arises between parties it should be settled not by resort to a strike but by arbitration. It is not one of the terms of the settlement that in future the parties settle their differences by arbitration; but since the settlement has come about through arbitration it is presumed that on a similar occasion in future also an arbitrator will be appointed."

23 *Ibid.,* pp. 4-5, 7, 10-11, 13, 18, 23, 36, 40-2, 59-60, 64-6, and 71-82; see also *Speeches and Writings of Mahatma Gandhi* (Madras, 4th ed., 1933), p. 1050.

24 *Ibid.,* p. 1047 where he criticizes "labour leaders who consider that strikes may be engineered for political purposes." Later, in 1941, Gandhi wrote in his "Constructive Programme": "If I had my way, I would regulate all the labour organisations of India after the Ahmedabad model. It has never sought to intrude itself upon the All-India Trade Union Congress and has been uninfluenced by that Congress. A time, I hope, will come when it will be possible for the Trade Union Congress to accept the Ahmedabad method and have the Ahmedabad organisation as part of the All-India Union. But I am in no hurry. It will come in its own time." As quoted in R. N. Bose, "The Gandhian Way in Industrial Relations," in *Labour*

Review West Bengal), September-October 1955, p. 17.

25 See Punekar, *Trade Unionism*, p. 322; Lokanathan, *Industrial Welfare*, pp. 167 ff. Gandhi clearly held to the view that the establishment of the AITUC was premature.

26 Cf. the following comments : Das concludes that Indian unions had not yet "come down to the business methods which have already been achieved in Europe and America" (*op, cit.,* p. 68). P.P. Pillai observes : "The organisation and management of these Unions leave much to be desired : they possess no clear-cut features or well-defined duties; most of them have no permanent offices or staffs; and the men themselves are lukewarm in their loyalty to their Union, demurring to Union discipline and to Union contributions" (*Economic Conditions in India,* London, 1925, p. 259). Another contemporary student, Lokanathan, observes : "A number of the so-called unions had sprung up which were no better than strike committees and had grown up like mushrooms and most of them decayed, leaving no permanent marks behind... Little wonder then that before the year 1921 was out, most of the unions all over India had perished...." (*Industrial Welfare,* p. 167).

27 For a discussion of the influence of the ILO, see Subbiah Kannappan, "The Impact of the I.L.O. on Labour Legislation and Policy in India." in Robert L. Aronson and John P. Windmuller, eds., *Labour, Management, and Economic Growth* (Ithaca, 1954), pp. 175-90; and V. K. R. Menon, "The Influence of International Labour Conventions on Indian Labour Legislation," *International Labour Review,* vol. LXXIII, no. 6 (June 1956), pp. 551-71.

28 For the text of the Act, see R. Mathrubutham and R. Srinivasan, *Indian Factories and Labour Manual,* Madras, Madras Law Journal, 1952, pp. 607-17, for a brief background on efforts to secure this legal protection, see Lokanathan, *Industrial Welfare,* pp. 183-91.

29 In the year 1928 alone, the man-days lost due to industrial disputes were of the order of 31,647,404, the highest recorded so far; industrial strife was most acute in Bombay and in the textile industry, railways, and steel industry in Jamshedpur. The following refer to the radicalism of this period : Minoo R. Masani, *The Communist Party of India* (London, 1954), esp. Chapter II; Lester Hutchinson, *Conspiracy at Meerut* (London, 1935); H.N. Brailsford, *Rebel India* (New York, 1931); and Punekar, *Trade Unionism,* pp. 86-95.

30 According to the Royal Commission, this meant that "a union has the right to negotiate with the employer in respect of matters affecting either the common or individual interests of its members...." (*Report,* p. 518).

31 The Commission observed : "At present, even some officers dealing with labour in the provinces, lacking encouragement (and even permission) to interest themselves directly in disputes, tend to depend on police reports for their information. The attention of the authorities is thus apt to be concentrated too exclusively on the effects which a dispute is likely to have on the public peace...." (*Report,* p. 348).

32 For a full list of the recommendations on this subject, see *ibid.,* pp. 518-19 and 527-28.

33 See B. Shiva Rao, *Industrial Welfare in India* (London, 1939), pp. 151-54, and S.D. Punekar, *Trade Unionism,* pp. 92-3, 326.

34 Punekar, *Trade Unionism,* pp. 330-31.

35 *Ibid.,* p. 179.

36 For a survey, see Punekar, *ibid.*, pp. 326-34.

37 *Ibid.*, pp. 98-9; and Masani, *The Communist Party of India*, pp. 52-5.

38 Indian National Congress, *Resolutions on Economic Policy and Programme*, 1924-54, All-India Congress Committee (New Delhi, 1954), p. 14.

39 The following accounts discuss the evolution of the Congress party's labour policies: Margaret Heath Martin, *Indian National Congress and the Labour Unions* (Philadelphia, University of Pennsylvania), 1951, unpublished M.A. thesis; and P. P. Lakshman, *Congress and Labour Movement in India* (Allahabad, All-India Congress Committee, 1947). Minoo R. Masani, *The Communist Party of India*, London, Derek Verschyle, 1954, includes valuable information on the functioning of socialist and communist groups within the framework of the Congress party. A detailed account of inter-group rivalries, and efforts to seek their unity, is provided by S. D. Punekar, *Trade Unionism in India: A Study in Industrial Democracy*, Bombay, New Book Company, 1948.

40 For details, see Punekar, *Trade Unionism*, pp. 333-34.

41 For details, see *ibid.*, pp. 103-06.

42 For text of the Act, see International Labour Office, *Legislative Series*, 1939 (Montreal, 1942); for a brief discussion, see N. S. Pardasani, "Labour Conciliation and Arbitration in India," in A. N. Agarwala, ed., *Indian Labour Problems* (Allahabad, 1947), pp. 80-98. See also *Handbook of the National Planning Committee*, compiled by K. T. Shah (Bombay, 1946), esp. pp. 89-92.

43 Both Mr. N. M. Joshi and Professor R. K. Mukerji opposed the provision for compulsory arbitration of disputes. The former stated that he would "like to see the future State before he could commit himself to the principle underlying this resolution" (*ibid.*, p. 92).

44 For a review of the war period, see International Labour Office, *Wartime Labour Conditions and Reconstruction Planning in India* (Montreal, 1946).

45 *Indian Labour Year Book* 1949-50, p. 156.

46 As noted in Chapter I, the index of real earnings for industrial workers dropped from 100 in 1939 to 70 in 1943.

47 SOURCE: Summaries of newspaper reports at the ILO Branch Office in New Delhi.

48 *The Indian Labour Year Book* 1946, pp. 267-70.

49 *The Indian Labour Year Book* 1947-48, pp. 119-20. Working days lost from labour disputes in 1946 were 12,717,762; and 16,562,666 in 1947, as compared to 4,054,499 in 1945. See Table 1, p. 279 infra.

50 For a more detailed account, see the earlier edition, pp. 112-15.

51 Indian National Trade Union Congress, *Proceedings of the Inaugural Conference* (New Delhi, 3-4 May 1947), p. 12.

52 *Presidential Address of M. K. Bose*, 16 February 1947 (published by Indu Bhusan Sarkar, Calcutta). Bose further criticized the Five Year Labour Programme for having been formulated without prior consultation with representatives of labour.

53 SOURCE: Summaries of newspaper reports at the ILO Branch Office in New Delhi.

54 For a review of this phase of Communist policy, see Masani, *The Communist Party of India,* pp. 87-98. Information supplemented by interviews with N. M. Joshi and M. K. Bose, January and February 1955, respectively. See also M. K. Bose, *Parties and Paradoxes: Plan of a Labour Party,* United Trades Union Congress (Calcutta, 1953), pp. 1-2. Bose says that, after 1947, "a complete change in the attitude and policy of the Communist Party in the All-India Trade Union Congress took place. The spirit of cooperation was gone and a new one of party domination took its place. The Communist Party began to use its majority in the AITUC to advance the political purposes of the party. A split occurred ... N. M. Joshi ... resigned the general secretaryship.... He was followed by several nonparty trade union leaders. The AITUC thus became devoid very largely of its non-Communist elements."

55 See, for a report on this conference, Hind Mazdoor Sabha, *Report of the Calcutta Conference,* 1948 (Bombay, 1948).

56 Hind Mazdoor Sabha, *Constitution* (Bombay, 1948).

57 *Report of the Calcutta Conference,* p. 3.

58 Interviews, Calcutta, February 1955.

59 For a summary report on the conference, see International Labour Organization. *Industry and Labour,* vol. 1 (July-December, 1949), p. 377.

60 United Trades Union Congress, *United Trades Union Conference, Address by Mrinal Kanti Bose,* 30 April 1949 (Calcutta, 1949).

61 See Subbiah Kannappan, "Industrial Relations Problems in the Developing Indian Economy: The Task Posed by Competing Objectives," *Proceedings of the Industrial Relations Research Association,* May 1964. The treatment in this section largely follows the material presented in "The Many Facets of Government Influence . . . . " *op. cit.,* 1964.

62 An excellent analysis, devoted to political pressures in the context of economic scarcity and enhanced expectations, is to be found in Myron Weiner, *The Politics of Scarcity,* University of Chicago, 1962. There is a chapter on the labour movement. See also Lloyd and Susanne Hoeber Rudolph, "Political Role of India's Caste Association," *Pacific Affairs,* March 1960, pp. 5-22.

63 This definition of "political" unionism is intended to distinguish between the political objectives underlying the labour movement and the adoption, by trade unions, of political tactics, See the related discussion in Bruce H. Millen, *The Political Role of Labor in the Developing Countries,* Washington D. C., Brookings, 1963.

64 Among the relevant references to the role of the INTUC, one may mention Ralph James, "Politics and Trade Unions in India," *Far Eastern Survey,* March 1948, and Weiner, *op. cit.*

65 Indian National Trade Union Congress, *Proceedings of the Inaugural Conference* (New Delhi, 3-4 May 1947), pp. 31-8, for full text of the constitution adopted.

66 *Ibid.,* Article 4.

67 See, for example, "Need for Introspection," *Indian Worker,* vol. 5, no. 1 (2 October 1956), p. 3.

68 See the INTUC publication, *Truth about Kerala on the Labour Front,* no date.

69 See INTUC, *Labour Policy in Third Five Year Plan,* New Delhi, 1960, esp. pp. 7-8. A similar indictment was presented on the occasion of the formulation of

the Second Five Year Plan.

70 A scathing criticism of government policy, including details of militant action organized under the auspices of the West Bengal INTUC, is to be found in *Twelfth Annual Conference of West Bengal Pradesh National Trade Union Congress* 1960-61.

71 The development of Socialist politics, including its repercussions on the labour movement, is discussed in Myron Weiner, *Party Politics in India: The Development of a Multi-Party System,* Princeton, 1957.

72 The leader of this school was Asoka Mehta. See his article, "The Mediating Role of the Trade Union in Underdeveloped Countries," *Economic Development and Cultural Change,* October 1957.

73 These are briefly reviewed by V.B. Karnik, *Indian Trade Unions: A Survey,* published by B. K. Desai, Labour Education Service, 127, Mahatma Gandhi Road, Bombay 1, 1960, especially Chapter XIII: 1952 to 1958.

74 On the implications of the change in leadership, see Balraj Puri, "PSP in Search of a New Image," *Economic Weekly,* 29 June 1963, pp. 1033-34.

75 An extreme position was taken in the late forties denouncing leaders belonging to the INTUC and the HMS as well as respected individuals like N.M. Joshi. See especially the account of the 23rd AITUC session in 1949 in V.B. Karnik, *op. cit.,* pp. 135 and ff. By 1954, at the next annual session, the AITUC's views had undergone considerable revision; for one thing, they became ardent advocates of unity with the other federations. See *Report and Resolutions of the Twenty-Fourth Session,* Calcutta, 1954.

76 See the discussion by Myron Weiner, *The Politics of Scarcity, op. cit.,* pp. 88 and ff.

77 See Indian Commission of Jurists, *Report of The Kerala Enquiry Committee,* 1960; V. B. Karnik, *Communist Ministry and Trade Unions in Kerala,* ICFTU, New Delhi, 1959; and West Bengal Youth and Students Committee, *The Kerala Upsurge,* distributors: Writers' House, 211 Park Street, Calcutta-17, no date.

78 See *The Kerala Upsurge,* pp. 31-4, for details of a resolution adopted by a joint convention of the INTUC, HMS and UTUC criticizing the Kerala government's policies.

79 In 1962, both the INTUC and AITUC announced formal plans to start their own national programme of workers' education.

80 The DMK is active in two key centres, Madras and Coimbatore. In the former, DMK leaders have increasingly undermined the position of the HMS leader, Mr. S.C.C. Anthony Pillai, in the textile industry.

81 See D.B. Thengdi, *Why Bharatiya Mazdoor Sangh,* Hindusthan Sahitya, 309 Shaniwar, Motibag, Poona 2, for a statement of this group's position.

82 See *General Secretary's Report,* Third National Convention, February 1 and 2, 1964, Bombay: Swatantra Party, pp. 16-7.

83 The INTUC position, stated in 1952, was as follows: "The concept of free and democratic trade unionism based on nonviolence and truth is totally at variance with the totalitarian outlook of the Communists. No unity in any shape or form with the Communists, or in other words, with the AITUC, is therefore acceptable to the INTUC. It is, however, desirable that closer relationship should be established between the INTUC and the Hind Mazdoor Sabha...." (as reported in *Hindu,*

29 December 1952, from the *INTUC General Secretary's Report*). More recently, such sentiments were reaffirmed in reply to Communist overtures for unity. Mr. Vasavada, the 1956 president of the INTUC, said: "The Communists are appealing for unity of labour. But the Indian workers will think twice before they actually associate and enter into an alliance with the Communist Party. The past record of the Communists is unpatriotic and is of a disruptive nature" (Statement on the occasion of the eighth annual session of the INTUC, as reported in *Hindu Weekly Review*, 14 May 1956). In explanation of the INTUC's attitude towards the HMS, it was stated that the Socialist Party's "purely Marxian approach has undergone radical transformation and the Gandhian philosophy seems to be the new creed of the merged party" (Indian National Trade Union Congress, *Annual Report 1951-52*, p. 3). In 1956, it was similarly asserted that the INTUC would cooperate with those "who believed in democratic methods and work on the lines of truth and nonviolence . . . . " (*Hindu Weekly Review*, 14 May 1956).

84 See exchanges between HMS and UTUC in Mrinal Kanti Bose, *Parties and Paradoxes: Plan of a Labour Party*, United Trade Union Congress (Calcutta, 1953); and also details of unity efforts between AITUC and HMS.

85 See All-India Trade Union Congress, *Twenty-Fourth Session of the All-India Trade Union Congress, Report and Resolutions*, 1954, esp. p. 104. During field interviews in 1962, the same position was reiterated by AITUC leaders.

86 An Indian student of labour problems, writing in 1955, was optimistic on the possibility of some unification among the four federations. He foresaw amalgamation between the INTUC and the HMS, and between the AITUC and the UTUC, leaving "two major rival federations, which could be described as democratic and communist . . . rendering the struggle for prominence rather sharp and keen-edged." Ramesh C. Goyal, "Post-war Trends in Industrial Relations in India," *Eastern Economist Pamphlet* (155), p. 33. However, his hopeful anticipations have not been realized. On the contrary, in July 1955, a fifth labour federation was established by the Akhil Bharatiya Jan Sangh, a political organization to the right of Congress, placing considerable emphasis on the Hindu, as distinct from the non-Hindu, aspects of the Indian heritage. It was claimed that the new labour organization had the support of 76 trade unions, representing 56,000 workers all over India, and that it "is enemy number one of Communism. It is also opposed to capitalism." Furthermore, the new labour body "would oppose rationalization tooth and nail, and endeavour to bring all trade unions on one platform on this issue." "India's Fifth Labour Body: New Organisation Proposed," *Mail* (Madras), 24 July 1955. Another group, the Independent Labour Party, was sponsored in the forties by the late Dr. B. R. Ambedkar, the depressed classes leader, and some adherents were reported during interviews in 1954-55 in Nagpur and Poona.

CHAPTER V

THE CHARACTER OF PRESENT INDIAN UNIONS

Size and Structure

We have seen that approximately 4 million Indian workers are members of trade unions. Table XXVIII presents available figures for an earlier year, 1958, which depict major concentrations of the union strength together with total employment figures. The data are incomplete and are not quite comparable to the 1953 data, reported in the earlier edition, but generally support the impression of weak unionism. The industries covered are in the forefront of union activity, but with the exception of Posts and Telegraphs, a public utility, they report a degree of unionization which is generally about forty per cent or under. The reported figures also generally overstate the extent of affiliation to unions as we shall presently see.

The formal basis for union organization is provided by the Indian Trade Unions Act, 1926. The relevant article reads as follows:

> Any seven or more members of a Trade Union may, by subscribing their names to the rules of the Trade Union and by otherwise complying with the provisions of this Act with respect to registration, apply for registration of the Trade Union under this Act.[1]

This provision in law has led to the formation of a multiplicity of small unions which characterize the Indian labour movement.

A survey of official trade union statistics confirms this observation. The approximately four million trade union members in 1959–60 were shared by 6,594 registered unions submitting returns, or an average of 595 members per union.[2] Incomplete figures relating to the distribution of unions according to size of membership further emphasize the small size of individual unions. In

1959–60 seventy per cent of the unions are in the group with an average membership of from 1 to 299, but these account for only 11 per cent of the total membership. Unions in the 300 to 1,000 category constitute 19.8 per cent of the total number of unions, and 16.8 per cent of the total membership. Unions in the 1,000 and above category represent 9.9 per cent of the total number of unions, but include 72.2 per cent of the total membership of all reporting trade unions.[3]

Trade union membership reports, however, are subject to question. Many unions do not maintain satisfactory records and do not submit returns periodically, as required by law. During 1927–28 (the first year covered by official statistics) and 1944–45, the percentage of unions submitting returns was relatively high, ranging

TABLE XXVIII

TRADE UNION MEMBERSHIP AND EMPLOYMENT IN MAJOR INDUSTRIES, 1958

1	2	3	4
Industry (All India)	Trade union membership 1958	Total for daily employment 1958	Percentage of union membership
Railways	264,128	1,112,754	23.7
Cotton Textiles	260,711	769,000	33.9
Plantations	264,904	1,267,995	20.8
Food, Beverages & Tobacco	283,627	687,000	41.2
Coal Mining	163,905	382,172	42.8
Posts and Telegraphs	40,275	40,332	99.8
Iron and Steel	85,834	49,000	—
Chemical Products	51,718	119,000	43.4
Wholesale and Retail Trade	49,819	1,069,000	4.6
Printing and Publishing	43,217	94,000	45.9

SOURCES:

Col. 2. Government of India, Labour Bureau, *Indian Labour Year Book*, 1958, pp. 128-29.

Col 3. *Ibid.*, pp. 10-12; and *Indian Labour Statistics*, 1962, pp. 14-5, 18, 29, 31.

NOTE: Iron and Steel in column 2 relates to Basic Metal Industry. Figures for Iron and Steel are not available separately. It is not clear whether the figure relates to both ferrous and non-ferrous groups. Since the Union membership figure is higher, the percentage figure is not given.

for the most part between 66 per cent and 96.5 per cent; since 1944–45, however, the percentage has dropped to around 50 per cent (with the exception of 69 per cent of 1952–53),[4] and to around 58 per cent in 1958–59. Furthermore, there is a fairly high mortality rate, which raises doubts whether many unions exist as continuous organizations. This is shown clearly in the following data from two industrial states:

TABLE XXIX

State	Year	New regis- trations	Cancella- tions	Total number of registered unions
West Bengal	1947–48	410	23	985
	1948–49	391	281	1,049
	1949–50	203	135	1,157
	1950–51	161	350	967
	1951–52	205	194	975
	1952–53	321	83	1,213
Bombay	1947–48	166	21	329
	1948–49	149	36	442
	1949–50	221	82	581
	1950–51	155	101	635
	1951–52	158	121	672
	1952–53	145	105	712

a. Figures for West Bengal are calculated from *Annual Reports on the Working of the Indian Trade Unions Act, 1926, in the State of West Bengal,* for the various years, copies of which were made available through the courtesy of the Labour Department of the Government of West Bengal. Figures for Bombay are taken from the *Annual Reports on the Working of the Indian Trade Unions Act, 1926, in the State of Bombay* (for the year 1952-53), (Baroda, 1954) p. 3.

There is little in India comparable to strong craft and industrial unions in the United States and Great Britain. Most Indian unions are plantwide or firmwide unions, embracing all the employees, irrespective of occupational groups. The traditional attitude of paternalism and the master-servant framework in resolving disputes also encouraged the formation of numerous plant-level unions. The employer in particular has been reluctant to negotiate with unions including non-employees. The Textile Labour Association of Ahmedabad is an exception which, since its formation in 1920, had been organized on the basis of several craft unions. Even here a reorganization effected since Independence has transformed the union into an industrial union, within which the former craft unions continue as separate departments.

Of course, there are some craft or occupational unions, mostly in what may be termed single-occupation industries. The Indian social structure undoubtedly plays a significant role in determining which groups enter these occupations. Thus, we have unions of rickshaw-pullers, taxi-drivers, lorry-drivers, journalists, teachers, scavengers, and so on. These tendencies are also observable in commercial firms and government establishments, among low-paid employees (called "peons" according to usage, but more recently termed Class IV employees). A good example is the All-India Postal Workers' Union (representing Class IV employees and postmen from Class III), one of the 9 unions in the National Federation of Posts and Telegraphs Employees formed in 1954-55. In the same federation, the clerks are organized separately. On a lesser scale, craft consciousness is evident—not necessarily in the form of separate unions—in seamen's unions, which are divided between saloon staff and those who work as deck-hands, and in railway unions, where the "ministerial staff," the ticket-checking staff, and the "station-masters"—to take a few examples only—air their grievances by means of special conferences.

Offsetting tendencies towards centralized union structure should also be noted. The pattern of legal regulation and competing political activity in the labour movement account for these developments. In the principal industrial cities, especially in Bombay, Calcutta, Coimbatore, Kanpur, etc., there are citywide unions embracing employees in an entire industry. The employers are well organized in these cases to make representations to the government which plays a key role in resolving general industrial disputes. Union organization along these lines is found in textile (cotton and jute), engineering, chemical, motion picture and hotel establishments, and among transport workers, seamen, and employees in the docks and ports.

There has also been a tendency towards organizing nationwide industrial federations. In some cases, these exist only in name:

and postment from Class III), one of the 9 unions in the National examples include all-India organizations of employees in the tobacco, metal manufacturing, or domestic service industries. Unions have been more active, however, in industries or employment classified by the Industrial Disputes Act, 1947, as falling within the central sphere. These are railways, mines, oil fields and refineries, ports and docks, seamen, banking and insurance, posts and telegraphs, and defence. Whatever strength may accrue to labour is, however, offset by numerous ideological and political cleavages following the pattern set by the four national federations of labour—the AITUC, HMS, INTUC, and the UTUC.

National Federations and Rival Unionism

These four national federations then are at the apex of the organizational forms manifested by Indian unionism. All of these are animated by the universal objective of organizing all labour. The wording employed in the constitution of the AITUC, the oldest of the four federations, is typical:

> To coordinate the activities of all the labour organizations in all the provinces in India, and generally further the interests of Indian labour in matters economic, social and political.[5]

Although reliable membership figures are difficult to obtain, there is no doubt that the four federations together represent a good proportion of the actual trade union membership in the country.

Official figures for 1952–53 indicate that 1,086 registered trade unions with a total strength of 1,218,390 are affiliated to the four national federations.[6] Including the unaffiliated unions, the total membership figures for the same year are 2,064,932 for 2,687 registered unions. It would thus appear that the federations represent approximately 60 per cent of the total union membership, and about 40 per cent of the number of unions. Federation activity appears to be concentrated among the larger unions.

Membership claims of the federations tend, however, to be on the high and unrealistic side. Thus, for the year 1959-60, the four federations claimed a total membership of 1,958,584 for a total of 2,165

unions. For the same year, however, the government's figures of
trade union membership for 2,741 unions was 1,766,175.[7] Since
the latter includes the figures for unaffiliated unions, the claims
made by the federations must be held suspect. This is also the
obvious import of the verification of federation claims undertaken
by the government from time to time. For the year ending March
31, 1953, the affiliation claims of the four federations, contrasted
with the data reported by the government, were as follows :[8]

TABLE XXX

Federation	Number of unions claimed	Membership claimed	Reported by government
INTUC	988	1,347,320	752,909
HMS	574	804,494	208,196
AITUC	784	675,377	172,413
UTUC	485	515,177	84,872
Total	2,831	3,342,368	1,218,390

One major consequence of the presence of these four federations
is the existence in most areas and industries of three or four unions
for the same union territory. The rivalries are acute, and continue
to present problems for trade union unity, despite several attempts
to cut across political lines of division. These divisions counter-
act, as we have already indicated, the advantages to be gained by
the formation of nationwide industrial federations. The earlier
edition noted that only three Indian industrial federations—the
Defence, Railways, and Posts and Telegraphs—are not merely independent of all affiliation to any of the national federations, but also
free—on paper, at any rate—of the existence of rival federations
within the same industry. Even such "paper" unity no longer
obtains, except in Posts and Telegraphs.

The National Federation of Indian Railwaymen was formed in
1953, as the result of a merger of an INTUC railway federation
and the All-India Railwaymen's Federation, an older organization then under the presidency of Jayaprakash Narayan, the
Socialist leader. But unity was achieved in only two of the six
railway zones, and, by January 1955, there was a split in the Western

India zone; followed in June by a split in the NFIR itself. Two competing groups again formed, one led by S. Guruswamy, the general secretary of the NFIR and of the previous AIRMF, and the other led by S. R. Vasavada, president of the NFIR and prominent leader of the INTUC (president of the latter during 1954–55 and 1956–57). The split also affected the one remaining area where zonal accord had been reached, the Central Railway. There were several efforts towards unity, in one of which Lal Bahadur Shastri, then Union Cabinet Minister for Railways, and Jayaprakash Narayan participated.[9] These were unsuccessful and the differences have continued into the sixties.

Rival unionism has caused similar difficulties in the Defence industry, and Posts and Telegraphs. A merger was effected in the former in 1953, but, in 1955, during the course of interviews, the highest officials of the federation stressed that each of the three pre-existing groups (Kanpur, Calcutta-Ichapore, and Poona) was pulling in different directions. One high official commented lamentingly:

> There are three forces—the Congress, the Communists (and pro-Communists), and the Socialists. Today the organization is not a homogeneous body. We cannot act effectively on an all-India basis. All the rank and file workers are O.K., but not the top. I am tired of all this now.[10]

A new defence federation started by the INTUC in the late fifties signalled the end of even this limited phase of unity. The postal federation was formed only in 1954–55. Interviews in India, early in 1955, indicated that rivalries presented a major problem here also. The principal contenders being Congressmen, Socialists and Communists. Interviews in 1958 and in 1962, indicated a central organizational framework which was, however, weakened by ideological factions.

Organizational and Financial Weaknesses of Trade Unions

Rivalries constitute only one aspect of the weaknesses of the Indian labour movement. In spite of politically based rivalries, trade unions could be more effective, if they paid more attention to strengthening their organizations and achieving a higher standard of financial solvency. As we noted in the previous chapter, there are some signs that a change is under way in these respects. By and large, however, Indian unions fail to display minimum standards of viability.

Table XXIX (see earlier) is illustrative in this respect. The data reported there suggest a high rate of mortality. In interpreting the figures, one must keep in mind the reluctance of authorities to cancel the registration of unions even when for all practical purposes they have ceased to exist. Registering officers have explained during interviews the reasons for precipitous drops in membership which may be noted every now and then: they decided to eliminate defunct unions and their moribund membership. Closely linked to the instability depicted by mortality figures are the ups and downs in trade union membership figures and the considerable range in the tenor of union activity. Even the best-known Indian unions have reported a wide range in union membership from one month to another (in the few cases where monthly collection of subscriptions is in vogue) or from one year to another. These fluctuations are attributable to specific crises in labour relations; historically, the ebbs and tides of political activity were a responsible factor through the link with union leadership which will be examined later.

Poor union finances, a general condition prevailing throughout India with occasional exceptions in some of the major cities, reflect another crucial aspect of union weakness. The official figures for 1959–60 indicate that an average union has an annual income of Rs. 2,179.[11] Obviously these figures are inadequate for the maintenance of even one full-time officer per union and for any but the most essential expenses relating to staff and establishment. Many unions do not have regular dues-paying members and no real office or meeting hall. Expenditures on benefits for members constitute only an extremely small part of the total. Even this is only a statistical average. In 1949–50, it had been pointed out that the Textile Labour Association at Ahmedabad alone was responsible for approximately 80 per cent of the total expenditure for welfare (including funeral, old-age, sickness, unemployment, educational, social and religious benefits) incurred by all unions in India.[12] We shall elaborate on the TLA's activities later. Trade unions are poor in part because their practices in regard to financial administration leave much to be desired. Even when employers do not oppose collection of union subscriptions on the premises, few unions enforce collections on a regular basis, and are generally lax in regard to defaulters. Such practices are encouraged due to the climate of competitive unionism, and the attempts to impress the officials, especially on the occasion of a publicly aired labour dispute.

The financial position of the industrial federations is similarly unsatisfactory. Published figures are not readily available, and we can only generalize from one or two examples provided by the leading industrial federations. The financial statement for the first year of the National Federation of Indian Railwaymen (1 August 1953 to 31 March 1954) revealed an income of Rs. 8,244 and an expenditure of Rs. 4,330, of which Rs. 2,860 were spent on salaries and establishment charges. For the following year, the income was Rs. 6,917 and expenditure Rs. 5,074, of which Rs. 2,659 were spent on salaries and establishment charges.[13] Obviously this was inadequate for an industrial federation claiming to be the representative organization of employees in an industry employing more than 900,000. The expenditure on "salaries" could cover at the most the wages of two members of the clerical staff. The financial position of the All-India Defence Employees' Federation was similarly weak.[14] The total income and expenditure for the period May 1953 to October 1954 was Rs. 6,715-14-0. There was, however, no expenditure under the head "salaries." It seems reasonable to inder that both these federations depended on the services of leaders who worked either on an honorary basis or on the basis of other outside support. The report presented by the general secretary of the Defence Federation confirms the validity of this observation. It points out that, although a number of organizers were active, going from centre to centre, offering advice in the name of the Federation, the organization "could not finance them for these tours; therefore the expenses were met by the unions concerned or by themselves."[15]

An examination of the financial position of the national labour federations reveals the same general weakness. We have no published data concerning the UTUC, but its position is probably the weakest. The All-India Trade Union Congress reported for 1952 a total income of Rs. 12,775, of which salaries and establishment charges took up Rs. 4,840, or approximately sufficient to cover the services of two or three paid clerical personnel. This income was obviously inadequate to cover the various needs of the organization, the rents of the various buildings or the salaries of paid organizers. The HMS reported, for the year ending 21 December 1952, a total income including affiliation fees, of Rs. 6,066; the expenditure for the same period was approximately Rs. 4,200. Of the latter, Rs. 1,539 were spent on "allowances," presumably expense allowances to honorary workers. The limitations of the financial base are here again obvious.

The INTUC is in a stronger position than all these federations. Its total income for 1953–54 was Rs. 62,280. To this we must add the strength represented by the Gandhi Memorial Labour Trust, with approximately Rs. 1,100,000 of total funds.[16] The INTUC maintains two all-India organizers and publishes the *Indian Worker,* one of the more regular and better-known labour papers. It has its own headquarters in New Delhi, full-time research staff, and is undoubtedly the best equipped of Indian federations from the point of view of office efficiency, records, and publicity. In addition to quarterly research notes on "rationalization," "wage policy," "managing agency abolition," and so on, it has also published, from the INTUC point of view, detailed comments on the official plans for economic development and resultant statements of labour policy.

What is, then, the national labour federation? It is really nothing more than a coordinating office, maintained for the purposes of representation and publicity. The cohesive force is supplied by the different labour leaders, outsiders with political preferences who group themselves around one or the other national federation.

Union Leadership: Outsiders and Insiders

The weaknesses of Indian unionism noted in the preceding section reflect the lack of a conscious and continuous membership. It is precisely because of this that practically all Indian unions are led by persons who have no background in industry—that is, "outsiders." These outsiders are mostly middle-class intellectuals, with clear-cut political orientation in many cases.

The dominance of outsiders in the leadership of the principal unions in the key industrial cities is reflected in the distribution of offices in the trade union executive. They occupy the key posts of president, general secretary, treasurer, office-secretary, and so on. This is true even of such well-developed and stable unions as the Ahmedabad Textile Labour Association, the Bombay Transport and Dock Workers' Federation, the Bombay Engineering Mazdoor Sabha, the unions affiliated to the UTUC in Trivandrum, and to the City Trades Union Council in Madras, to take just a few representative examples. The general secretary is usually the key, full-time official who runs the union from day to day.

The dominance of outsiders, however, is usually reflected only in the composition of the key posts in the trade union executive. The majority of the office-bearers, in conformity with the law, is composed of insiders—those actually employed in the industry.[17] Nevertheless the dominance of the outsiders is so apparent that signs of real "inside" leadership are difficult to find. The most notable examples of inside leadership are in the Tata Workers' Union in the steel centre of Jamshedpur;[18] the unions in the defence industries in Kanpur, Calcutta, and Poona; the Bombay dockworkers and in some of the railway unions. It is also evident in the middle-class unions representing government employees in posts and telegraphs, in government secretariats, among employees in commercial firms (such as banks and insurance), and in professions such as journalism.

The leadership in all of these cases, however, is drawn from middle classes; in the factories, largely from the supervisory ranks. Furthermore, in the important area of collective bargaining with the government, the key leadership is in the hands of "outsiders," and inside leadership is not evident at the strategic levels. This is clear in leadership at the zonal or federation headquarters of the defence or the railway unions.

There are also a few sporadic cases of "inside" leadership of unions where the leaders are drawn from less skilled workers in the plants. It was apparent during interviews in 1954–55 that these leaders were not very effective, because of low educational standards and poor command of English, which is still the principal language of labour legislation and adjudication. To understand this fully, we must remember that many Indian unions are composite unions, embracing both the supervisory and clerical groups which have higher social and work status than labourers.

To sum up, in none of these cases of so-called inside leadership, at least in the significant areas of union activity, was the outsider dispensed with. Inside leadership, confined mostly to supervisory and middle-class employees, operates only at the local or "uncritical" level of union activity.

There is a secondary category of labour leadership drawn from rank and file workers to serve on the union executive as ordinary office-holders. Occasionally, such workers may even be elected as vice-presidents of their unions. Usually, however, this carries with it little responsibility. Where woeks committees are appointed in consultation with the unions, worker representatives may have some opportunity of exercising responsibility. But it is doubtful whether there is any real delegation of responsibility within the unions so that worker representatives can play an active part. This is due not only to the nature of available worker representatives, but also to the rather limited framework within which such leadership has to be developed.

For example, one leader, whose union had 65 factory committees for the different plants in the city, commented that the worker representative "cannot convey" convincingly decisions of factory committees or of the general council. His comprehension of such technical questions as balance-sheets, audited statements of accounts and the technicalities of labour legislation and tribunal proceedings is limited. For these matters, the outsider's help is clearly necessary. It was also suggested in the interviews that, in view of their low social and educational status, worker representatives may lack the incentive or ability to handle union responsibility. There are few institutional arrangements to train worker representatives; labour training institutes are mostly for the English-educated, although since 1957 the workers' education programme of the Indian Government has made a dent in this situation. Further, few unions have the finances to permit them to engage the most talented or energetic insiders as part of their permanent staff; joining the union staff full-time would invariably involve a financial loss. There is also the age-old fear of victimization and the workers' difficulty in facing the employers on equal terms across the bargaining table.[19] These were the various reasons advanced during interviews in 1954–55, and again in 1962 to explain the absence of inside leadership, and to stress the continued need for outside leadership.

Perhaps the most important stumbling block in the way of developing effective leadership from the ranks is the attitude of persons in leadership positions in industry and government. The authoritarian attitudes prevailing in Indian management will be discussed later, our purpose at present being only to note how this frustrates the development of confident and mature inside leadership. The attitudes in government and the philosophy of "industrial democracy," advocated by official policy, are certainly very different from the approaches taken traditionally. However, the "regulated" nature of the Indian economic and political system often places the trade union movement in conflict with the government and the latter may seek to enforce its position by means of legislation, ordinances, or discretionary administrative action. On such occasions, the outsiders, both those friendly, and the others opposed, to the government, may step in, in effect making the outsider indispensable for purposes of serious negotiation. There is also a lag between the approaches advocated by the top leadership and the attitudes of members of the bureaucracy who handle labour problems. It is a standing complaint of many union leaders that several times the officials are unfriendly or unsympathetic and respond only when trade union pressures are supplemented by the voice of a prominent outsider.

Outside leadership thus plays a definite and useful role today in furthering the activities of the Indian unions. However the outsider's leadership is not an unmixed blessing, and only rarely, as in the case of Mahatma Gandhi, did the outsider attempt to leave a lasting imprint of his association—in the form of a stable and viable trade union organization. In far too many cases, the leadership badge has been a symbol of political activity, rapidly acquired and just as readily discarded, with only a marginal commitment to the interests of the workers concerned.

For one thing, many of the outsiders are associated with more than one union. Sometimes such extremes are reached that one man may be president of more unions than he can remember. A national leader of considerable stature remarked that he was president of about thirty unions, but he added that obviously there was nothing he could contribute to the work of any of these! A labour union weekly drew a remarkable panegyric of a labour leader extolling his presidency of over one hundred unions! These associations would obviously be more useful if the outsider's contribution left a more enduring legacy, or his role was sustained by effective organization. But this has been the exception rather than the rule.

The political orientations and aspirations of outside leaders also represent a source of instability. Further, they often have no unified approach to labour questions, and are considerably divided ideologically. Some of them do develop an independent outlook, and emphasize that they exclude political considerations from the day-to-day running of the union. Even where they are able to make a clear distinction between the two, it will be a rare man, indeed, who will assert the "independence" of the union from financial support and the leadership of political parties.

Party discipline is fairly rigid in the case of the AITUC; and, despite overtures to others, the organization functions as a Communist Party unit in the labour field and discourages outsiders from its inner councils. There have been increasing signs of internal dissension within the Communist Party, especially since the open rupture in Sino-Indian relations in 1959, but the character of communist activity in the trade union field has probably not changed very much. There is again not much of distinction between the union movement and the political parties in the case of the UTUC, as their only substantial activity lies in the labour field. The Socialist theorists emphasize the independence of the labour movement, but difficulties are apparent. One HMS leader pointed out that, when he raises the issue of the independence of the labour movement,

they [the political leaders] think that I am trying to isolate the trade union movement from the political field.... Party leaders also accuse the trade union leaders of setting up their own kingdom, of not contributing to the same extent for party work.

There are similar difficulties in the case of the INTUC also. In 1950, when a group of INTUC leaders broke off from Congress, the latter demanded their expulsion from the INTUC. However, this demand was resisted, but, as a result, a group of loyal Congressmen broke off from the West Bengal INTUC to form a rival unit. At the various regional levels in Jamshedpur, Burnpur, Madras, Punjab, Delhi, and Mysore (now Karnatak), clashes between Congress and INTUC have been open. It was to obviate these difficulties that G. D. Ambekar (INTUC president in 1955–56) secured and announced the following directive of the Congress High Command:

No Congressman will henceforth be permitted to associate himself with any rival organization opposed to the Indian National Trade Union Congress.[20]

We must remember, however, that, though this grants to the INTUC the monopoly of Congress support, it does not necessarily ensure its independence, as the INTUC is primarily a body of Congressmen working within the framework of Congress principles.[21] Prime Minister Nehru made this clear when he said in 1953:

Technically the INTUC and the Indian National Congress are two separate organizations.... Still it goes without saying that the INTUC has been sponsored and nursed mostly by Congressmen and derives its strength from the moral and other support of the Congress. As such it is imperative that in political matters all Congressmen working in the INTUC should treat the Congress as the supreme body and abide by its code of conduct.[22]

In practice also, there has been sufficient disunity within the ranks of the Congress Party, and many individual Congressmen have ignored the directive Ambekar obtained.

The difficulty is that there is no clear distinction between a "political" and a "trade union" matter. Nevertheless the INTUC has made some progress in this respect. During interviews in 1954-55, it was reported that the INTUC is recruiting full-time workers directly without going through political channels, and is using its own funds.[23]   Further, since the Congress is a heterogeneous organization, representing so many diverse economic interests, it is possible for INTUC Congressmen to distinguish between sectional interests affecting their members and the broader interests of the political party. Conflicting ambitions have also led individual INTUC leaders to take direct issue with the stand of the party leadership. A notable development along these lines is represented by the leadership of West Bengal INTUC's, Kali Mukheiju. Generally however such divergence arises from non-trade union matters, and in respect of trade union matters is considerably muted as compared to the positions taken by the rival trade union federations.

Some critics of the present trade union leadership see the problem as too many politicians and a lack of competence in trade union matters. A student of the Indian labour movement writes:

> Becoming leaders of trade unions has become a fashion amongst the politicians of our country. Persons with little knowledge of the background of labour problems, history of labour movement, fundamentals of trade unionism and the technique of industry and with even little general education assume the charge of a labour union and become the self-appointed custodian of the welfare of workers.[24]

Trade union groups freely echo these charges and have frequently talked in terms of strengthening their trade union leadership.[25] However, little concrete progress has been made, and the possibility that this may merely intensify the ideological rivalries should not be excluded. Ultimately further progress will have to await the development of rank and file leadership, which will pay primary attention to the problems of the work environment. Government has indicated an awareness of this problem and undertook in connection with the Second Plan to train workers for trade union work.[26] Also, a legislative amendment in 1956 specified a category of workers as "protected" workers with a view to ensuring freedom of trade union activity.

It would be too much to expect these steps to produce quick results in the form of a more stable and competent group of inside leaders. Field interviews in 1962 indicated the continuing hold of the outsiders in the Indian labour movement. There was no clear evidence to suggest that the designation of a category of "protected" workmen had made any material difference to the conduct of industrial relations or of union affairs. In fact, in many cases, trade unionists were not even aware of this provision or, if aware, appeared entirely indifferent to it. Even under the best of circumstances, a programme of developing rank and file leadership will take a long time before results can be seen. It is certain at present that the trade union movement cannot be deprived of the support and leadership of the outsiders.

Objectives and Policies

The reliance of outside leadership on political channels to further trade union objectives is reflected, as we have seen, in the division of the Indian labour movement into four principal labour federations. All these federations have in common the objective of changing the framework of society as a condition of progress; but there are important differences of approach on the method by which these objectives are to be gained.

The AITUC, at one extreme, emphasizes the class-consciousness of the workers, and the class-basis of the conflict between labour and management. There have been, of course, debates within the Communist Party ranks, on the extent to which the revolutionary potential of the workers' movement may be depended upon.[27] There have also been strategic shifts, or tactical considerations, which have ushered in a policy of direct settlement.[28] However the general approach has been revolutionary, reflective of deep suspicion both of the government and of the employers. The AITUC has therefore been severely critical of any abridgment of the right to strike, and its wrath has been directed particularly at the Industrial Disputes Act, 1947. In a reply submitted in 1952 to a government questionnaire on a suitable industrial relations policy, the AITUC condemned the Act in the following terms:

> The Industrial Disputes Act of 1947 and similar laws in the
> States should be immediately repealed. They are so bad as to
> be incapable of any intelligent and helpful revision. The Acts
> are bad not because the framers would not frame good ones.
> They are bad because they were framed with an evil objective
> ... [to] make the growth of good, strong, democratic trade unions
> impossible ... [to] keep the workers divided and unorganized.[29]

But the AITUC also made it clear that they

> disapprove not only of compulsory arbitration but also the
> suggestion that everything be left to the contending parties
> without *any* State intervention.[30]

What then is the AITUC position? Clearly the AITUC wants
labour to be backed by the state, without accepting, however, any
restriction on its freedom to act. Expressed in another way, the
AITUC would require the state to coerce an employer, but such
coercion cannot be directed against labour.

> In the event of the failure of negotiations and collective bargain-
> ing, the workers should be free either to exercise their right to
> strike or to refer the dispute to arbitration, for which a machinery
> should be at their disposal for use *at their will*.[31]

The UTUC approach is also conditioned by the belief that
"employers generally look down upon the workers as an inferior
species of human beings and ... the workers do not enjoy the
status of equality with employers."[32] The organization favours the
retention of compulsory conciliation and adjudication machinery,
but questions the discretion given to government to refer only some
disputes for adjudication and to include only some points of the
dispute in the referral. During interviews in India during 1954–55,
UTUC spokesmen stressed that they also believed in the "class
struggle." However, it was emphasized that they did not intend to
carry it to the level of the plant. One leader explained as follows:

Don't be carried away by the general impression that simply because we believe in class struggle we don't believe in collective bargaining. We believe in strong unions at first, even to preaching our political ideas. We do the preaching, no doubt. But the worker will be interested, the worker will give his loyalty only if his wages increase.

The fundamental need, the leader added, was to build up trade union strength. In view of the very weak state of Indian unionism, the leader felt that there could not be any genuine difference of opinion on trade union goals.

The original HMS position has undergone several changes. When the organization was established in 1948, the emphasis was on "class struggle," tempered slightly by the position that the methods adopted shall be "democratic" and "peaceful."[33] Since the merger, in 1952, of the KMPP (a group of dissident Congressmen headed by J. B. Kripalani) and the Socialist Party, the talk of class war is officially discounted.[34] The present position is perhaps best indicated in the *Janata* (18 December 1955), the official organ of the Praja Socialist Party, in an editorial captioned "Socialism and Class Struggle." The editorial rejected the notion that "there is a contradiction in the policy which accepts class struggle as an inevitable characteristic of a class society and yet accepts non-violence as a method of achieving a classless society," and continued:

This conflict is visible in the hundreds of negotiations between the representatives of the workers and the managements which go on from day to day all over the country. No industrialist or union leader would be prepared to say that there is no conflict of interest between the workers and those who own the industrial unit.... The means for the liquidation of these relationships are altogether a different matter.... Non-violence is a powerful instrument in bringing out a sudden and definite change in social relationships.[35]

The HMS has also expressed itself as being in favour of collective bargaining, and has criticized the "pathetic reliance on the compulsory adjudication system."[36] During the 1952 election campaign, the Socialist Party promised freedom of "collective bargaining and even strikes."[37] Similarly, in 1952, replying to the government questionnaire on an appropriate industrial relations policy, the HMS declared:

> Collective bargaining is one of the essentials of a democratic form of society. . . . Since collective bargaining cannot be effective without the right to strike, declaration of strikes as illegal would amount to a denial of democracy.[38]

But the parties were not to be left to fight it out. According to the HMS:

> The State should intervene when conciliation fails. In our opinion, conciliation should be made compulsory. . . .Failing conciliation, the dispute should be referred to adjudication if any one of the parties desires that this should be done.

If the emphasis on "nonviolence" distinguished the HMS from the other left groups, it was also clear that the HMS, like the other groups, viewed the strike as a weapon of greater significance than purely for the settlement of plantwide relationships. The editorial quoted above continued:

> Strikes and Satyagraha are the weapons whereby the exploited classes express their determination not to play the role assigned to them. When the class-consciousness grows sufficiently, when class organizations become sufficiently powerful, a decisive action can be fought more effectively under present circumstances through strikes and Satyagrahas rather than through attempts at violent overthrow.

In practice also, the HMS has been more willing to challenge the official position than the INTUC and to sponsor or support strikes which have been declared illegal. The HMS leadership in The Bombay Textile strike in 1950 or in the Central Government Employees strike in 1960, if successful, would have represented a major political gain, although there is no indication that the HMS leaders encouraged violence or insurrectionary activities. The HMS leaders were also active in the efforts to topple the Communist Government in Kerala, notably in 1959. Its ideological position is thus best represented as an unstable compromise between the AITUC and the INTUC, the actual position at any given moment being influenced not only by the approaches of these two federations, but also by shifts in the balance of power among competing groups within the Socialist camp.

By contrast, in its approach and emphasis, the INTUC represents a new element in the pattern of labour-management relations in India. True, like the other federations, the INTUC has pinned its faith on the national ownership of industry; there is also a further antipathy to organized industry in the minds of some INTUC leaders, reflected in their support of the Village Industries Movement, even if it be at the cost of restricting the growth of modern industry.[39] The INTUC leaders have repeatedly stressed their adherence to the Gandhian ideology, and have also indicated in their constitution the importance attached to peaceful and truthful means. Furthermore the INTUC constitution places great emphasis on the "just settlement" of industrial disputes, and the avoidance of work stoppages.[40] The INTUC reply to the government questionnaire in 1952 merely restated this position.[41] Substantially the same points were made during interviews in India in 1954–55, 1957, 1959, and 1962. INTUC leaders explained that they did not place importance on the right to strike; rather it was "the right to secure justice" which was paramount.[42] The harmony of approach between the INTUC and the government is indicated by the following words in a leading article in the *Indian Worker*, the official organ of the INTUC:

> Proper planning should make strikes and lockouts wholly unnecessary in industrial relations.... If, in spite of best planning, a fight becomes necessary, such a fight will not be of the crude, violent, and dislocating type as in the past, but a refined and intelligent fight which will not dislocate the industry, employment or production.[43]

The INTUC emerges therefore among Indian labour federations

as a moderating element, supporting government efforts to curb industrial strife. The support does not mean however uncritical acceptance of government labour policy; for one thing, this would be out of the question where so many different federations compete for the "proprietorship" of labour protest. However, the INTUC approach cannot be categorized as "moderate" by referring to its trade union ideology alone. A major reason for differences in federation militancy is the extent to which the individual federation leadership is associated with the ruling political group. Thus, all over India, INTUC has acted the role of the "moderate" spokesman, advocating cooperation with the law-makers, compliance with tribunal decisions, and discountenancing "illegal" strikes. However, in Kerala, during 1957–59, the roles were reversed when the Communists controlled the state government. The latter, duly supported by the AITUC, advocated "moderation" while, especially in 1959, the INTUC was in the lead of many a trade union struggle aimed at overthrowing the Communist government.

Also, given the prevailing competitive political climate in India, trade unions, even those friendly to the ruling government, must pay attention to the issues of major concern to the workers. These "bread and butter" issues can be ignored or slighted only at some risk as the Kerala government learned to its regret with its abortive labour relations policy in the late fifties. Our concern is rather with the developments over a much wider sphere of industrial India. We shall review briefly some major issues in this context. Special attention will be given to the role of the INTUC which attempts to moderate, channel and contain protest over this vast territory.

At the outset, it should be noted that there are few issues which are settled directly as a result of collective bargaining. This is not surprising, in view of the distance between labour and management. We shall discuss this, with particular reference to management attitudes and policies, in the next chapter. Our discussion here will be confined to an indication of union attitudes and policies on some outstanding issues, and the pattern in which labour protest is directed.

Some Major Issues of Protest

Organized labour in India, like organized labour everywhere, seeks to alter the distribution of income and to protect its members against what it considers evils in the industrial system. In India this protest is focused principally on (1) inadequate wages, (2) labour displacement through "rationalization," and (3) private owner-ship of industry which is held to deny "workers' participation in management."

The demand for a "fair wage" or a "living wage" is in the fore-front of union pressures. The attack is carried on at two levels: (a) through the tribunal system, and (b) through pressures on government for legislation on the subject. During the First Five Year Plan, unions made it clear that they were not satisfied with the official view that further wage increases should go hand in hand with rising productivity and should be confined only to anomalous situations where the wage level is below the prewar real wage level.[44] Union efforts were concentrated in the direction of supplementing the basic wage and dearness (cost-of-living) allowance to advance towards the "living wage" standard. Such steps took the form of annual demands of "bonus" as a means of sharing the prosperity of the industry. These have been settled largely on the basis of the Labour Appellate Tribunal's 1950 "full bench formula," which has become the most authoritative pronouncement on the subject.[45]

The "formula" was based on the principle that where "the industry has capacity to pay ... payment of living wage is desirable; but where ... the industry cannot afford to pay ... bonus must be looked upon as the temporary satisfaction, wholly or in part, of the needs of the employee." The "formula" further indicated that certain "prior charges" must be taken care of before claims for bonus would be allowed. These included depreciation funds and reserves, and fair return for paid-up capital and (at a lower rate) company reserves.

Union dissatisfaction with this procedure came to the forefront following exemptions from payment of bonus that were granted to mills which declared losses.[46] This was partly due to a suspicion of company balance-sheets, and was coupled with the demand that veracity of balance-sheets should be investigated. Criticisms have also been expressed about the "full bench formula," on grounds that allowances made for depreciation and for fair return to capital were too high, and that reserves built "on the toil of labour" should not be treated as management's exclusive property. Further, the position has been taken that profits of an industry in an entire local area should be pooled and distributed among all workers, whether or not the individual firms in which they worked reported profits. There has also been some support for the position that annual bonus payments should give place to higher consolidated wages, free from the vagaries of company profits. Growing dissatisfaction was also reflected in a demand for the abolition of the Labour Appellate Tribunal. The demand itself was not new, but gathered momentum with adverse decisions, principally with respect to bonus.[47]

The Second and Third Five Year Plans do not appear to have altered wage policy appreciably. The Second Plan tried at the same time to appear more liberal in envisaging increases, and more fastidious in tying it to the requirements of planning (by stressing among other things the need for relating wage increases to improvements in productivity) but the Third Plan has not even discussed the issue in formal terms. In the meantime, the trade unions have recognized the need for mounting campaigns with a view to securing general wage revisions. The Second Plan was preceded by a demand for a wage commission, and led in subsequent years to the formation of wage boards for several major industries. Subsequently the unions raised a demand for a full-fledged Bonus Commission which would lay down a more favourable basis for calculating bonus payments. The demand for industrywide wage boards has been supplemented by campaigns for nationwide pay commissions to revise the terms of remuneration of government employees. One of the developments worth recording is the 1957 dispute over the service conditions of postal employees which led to the establishment of a Central Pay Commission which reported in 1959. This recommended revised scales for Central government employees, including workers in railways, defence and postal establishments. In banking, where wages were "frozen" by a Parliamentary Act, union pressure has focused on constituting special national industrial tribunals, and subsequently on the favourable implementation of their awards. As in the agitation over the constitution of the Bonus Commission, the unions have sought to liberalize the principles underlying official wage determination. The most notable of these was the campaign for a Need-Based Minimum Wage, which received "official" and unanimous endorsement from the Indian Labour Conference in 1957. The union strategy has been to gain acceptance for principles which would ultimately be translated into favourable wage decisions when tribunals, commissions, and similar bodies actually recommend wage revisions.[48]

Another important issue on which labour feelings run high centres upon rationalization in industry, which involves new machinery and methods with actual or potential labour displacement.[49] As early as 1949, the general secretary of the INTUC indicated labour opposition in the following terms:

> The Indian National Trade Union Congress is not opposed to any scientific scheme of rationalisation. But it is perfectly clear that we are not willing to accept any rationalisation which leaves industrialists untouched and throws the whole burden on the working class. It is my definite opinion that the future industrial progress . . . is not possible under the old framework. . . . the Managing Agency system is the greatest stumbling block.[50]

However, in 1951, both the INTUC and the HMS agreed to the principles set forth in the "Delhi Agreement" of 1951, which were also incorporated in the Draft Outline of the First Five Year Plan.

A lead was given in Ahmedabad where the Textile Labour Association and the Millowners' Association signed agreements providing for the doubling of loom and ring-frame assignments. It was further provided that the Ahmedabad Textile Industry Research Association, an autonomous research institute supported principally by mill funds, would act as the technical arbiter on the working conditions that were considered a prerequisite to the introduction of rationalization. Implementation proved difficult, however. It was reported during interviews in 1955 that not a single increase in loom assignments had been effected among member mills. Union leaders agreed that implementation was slow, but blamed management for proposing prematurely the installation of automatic looms, with a higher rate of displacement of labour.

This excited the apprehensions of the workers and damaged the climate for introduction of rationalization schemes, according to union officers. Management spokesmen, on the other hand, asserted that rationalization and modernization were necessary for survival, particularly in export markets.

It was clear by 1953 therefore that the issue of rationalization would remain a thorny one and difficult of amicable settlement. Reports of increased unemployment were undoubtedly a prominent factor in the change.[51] The HMS officially attacked the Ahmedabad Agreement and later withdrew its support for the Delhi Agreement. It was explained that the economic conditions of boom, which had facilitated the Delhi Agreement, were no longer present.[52] The HMS, therefore, took the stand that rationalization should centre principally on "organizational" methods, including an elimination of the abuses of the managing agency system, and a consolidation of uneconomic industrial units.

The Communist-led AITUC also took a strong stand against rationalization. Meeting in 1954 for the first open convention after five years, the AITUC adopted the following resolution:

> The AITUC severely condemns the various measures and forms of rationalisation introduced or contemplated by the employers ... in India with the help and support of the Government.... The AITUC further calls upon the entire working class to take note of this new offensive.... The AITUC calls upon its units and affiliated units to take every initiative to forge unity of action with all workers, irrespective of opinion and organisational affiliation.[53]

The AITUC attack against rationalization was carried to the Lok Sabha, but a Communist resolution demanding total ban on rationalization was defeated. Instead the Lok Sabha adopted a resolution to the effect that "rationalization of the textile and jute industries, where it is necessary in the country's interests, must be encouraged, but the implementation ... should be so regulated as to cause the least amount of displacement of labour."[54]

The debate on rationalization was further intensified by the application of an Ahmedabad millowner for permission to introduce automatic looms. S. R. Vasavada, general secretary of the TLA and president of the INTUC, raised the application to the level of a national issue, and demanded during the Planning Commission meeting held to consider the request:

A postponement of introduction of labour saving machinery for ten years, during which period new industries should be started to expand the pool of employment so that labour displaced through future rationalization could be re-employed elsewhere.[55]

Vasavada won a temporary victory, at any rate, as the Ahmedabad millowners' application was denied.

Although the General Council of the INTUC passed a resolution in May 1954, urging government to put a total ban on the introduction of automatic machinery, its approach moderated in 1955 in a memorandum to the Planning Commission which stated:

We do recognize that under certain circumstances certain labour-saving machinery will have to be accepted ... to see that national assets once created by whatever process in the past should not be wasted and new problems of unemployment or closure of industries already existing should not occur.[56]

It is clear that there was sharp resistance and strong opposition at local levels to national INTUC leadership on this issue. In Kanpur, government-sponsored efforts to reach agreement on rationalization failed completely in 1955, and led to the formation of a citywide merger of all the local textile unions, including the INTUC local union, with the avowed objective of fighting rationalization. The INTUC expelled the recalcitrant local INTUC leadership, but employers' efforts to introduce rationalization, in accordance with government instructions, led in May-June-July 1955, to one of the longest strikes in India's labour history.[57] The pattern was repeated in Nagpur, where the textile workers went on a three-month strike early in 1956, protesting against an INTUC agreement with a large mill on rationalization.[58]

Rationalization has continued to be a thorny issue in the last eight years and trade union opposition has not abated. However, employers have proceeded to effect a reduction in their labour force and in only a few cases have the unions given even tacit consent at the stage of the actual implementation of individual schemes. Generally this has taken the form of putting a stop to further recruitment and not replacing "natural wastage" due to retirement, quits, etc. In the Bombay Textile Industry, as reported by Professor Ralph C. James in a competent study based on extensive field work, this was accomplished by "insulating" the textile labour market from the pressure exerted by the city's urban labour surplus. The Tata Iron and Steel Company faced this problem in the context of an expansion to double the steel output undertaken in 1956, with no additions to the labour force. In two other centres where the problem has been dealt with on a continuous basis, namely, the Kanpur Textile Industry, and the jute industry in and around Calcutta, the numbers employed have been progressively reduced. The textile industry in Nagpur also reflects a similar trend.

Although the wage bill reductions were undoubtedly beneficial to employers faced with the need to modernize, the residue of bitterness and disorganization in industrial relations should not be overlooked. Jamshedpur witnessed a disturbing strike in 1958, with a considerable weakening of the INTUC union's command over the steel labour force. The Bombay efforts, it must be noted, proceed under the joint auspices of the Millowners' Association and the Rashtriya Mill Mazdoor Sevak Sangh, which are supported by the Government of Bombay. Nevertheless, negotiations in 1962 over the bonus issue were clouded by disagreement over rationalization; in the background was the threat posed by a rival communist-socialist-led Mumbai Girni Kamgar Union. In the jute industry, even the INTUC has been increasingly militant. In Kanpur, despite several successive attempts initiated by the Government of Uttar Pradesh, the employers have introduced rationalization schemes largely unilaterally, with all the implied benefits and adverse consequences. The suspicion and distrust among the principal industrial relations participants would find few parallels in India.

As one would expect, these are problems mainly with old industries like cotton or jute textile or old firms with surplus labour. It was also to be expected that rationalization would encounter stiff opposition, especially in Calcutta or Kanpur where an agreed framework to govern the actual implementation has been lacking, or when individual employers ignored the conditions implied in the Delhi Agreement providing for "rationalization without tears." Rivalry among unions has also contributed to the difficulties of securing agreement over the introduction of individual schemes. In places like Kanpur, this has meant virtually no one on the union side with whom negotiations could be conducted whether by the employers or by the government. Even where unions have been willing to cooperate with employers, doubts have arisen about their representative character. The model agreement on rationalization provided by the Indian Labour Conference in 1957 skirted the issue entirely, although, as we shall note later in the discussion of government policy, the Code of Discipline has attempted to set guidelines in this respect.

In the preceding review of union objectives, and particularly in the discussion on rationalization, we have mentioned the distance separating organized labour from management. Labour's lack of confidence in private industry is reflected in a variety of demands aimed at curtailing the prerogatives of management. A brief summary of labour attitudes will indicate the direction of these pressures.

First and foremost, there is the historic demand for public, as distinct from private, ownership of all industry. Even as early as in the twenties, the All-India Trade Union Congress, the other rival trade union federations, and the Ahmedabad Textile Labour Association had declared for this goal.[59] This happens to be the objective also of the three new federations established since Independence, the Indian National Trade Union Congress, the Hind Mazdoor Sabha, and the United Trades Union Congress. Labour leaders' dissatisfaction over the labour policies and practices of the nationalized sector in the years since Independence has not led to any appreciable change in this respect.

The demand for increased regulation of the private sector is closely related to the demand for nationalization of industry. The chief object of criticism is the managing agency system which is the principal form of industrial organization. The demand for its abolition was seen in the INTUC 1949 statement already referred to.[60] Leaders belonging to the Communist, Socialist, and Congress labour groups have, especially in the past few years, consistently stepped up pressure for ending the system. The following Socialist statement may be regarded as typical:

> Apart from the obvious malpractices indulged in by some of the managing agents, the system, even if honestly worked, can have no place in a planned economy. It is well known that because of the managing agency system a sort of monopoly capitalism has come into existence in this country. . . . Thus we have neither the advantages of a healthy competitive system nor the fruits of a planned economy. No amount of restrictions contemplated by the Joint Select Committee [Parliamentary authority reporting on changes in Company Law] can deal with this menace. The time has, therefore, come to press for unequivocal abolition of this system.[61]

The INTUC has similarly supported proposals for ending the managing agency system so that "the managing agents of today may function as trustees of the industry, as Mahatma Gandhi wanted them to be."[62]

Closely related to the demand for the abolition of the managing agency system is the demand for worker participation in industry, which seems to go beyond the provisions in the Industrial Disputes Act for "works committees."[63] While this is an objective of both the HMS and the INTUC, the AITUC has not placed any direct emphasis on this demand, presumably because of its limited faith in the reconcilability of the interests of labour and capital. In the 1952 Indian Labour Conference at Naini Tal, the AITUC answered, "If compulsory recognition of Trade Unions by employer and negotiations with them are made statutory, then no such [bipartite] machinery is necessary."[64] Even in its Election Manifesto for the General Elections in 1951–52, the Communist Party of India merely contented itself with the promise that "joint production councils [will be] set up."[65]

Among labour groups, the INTUC has been the most active to campaign for this goal of "worker participation in industry."

Progressive steps for workers' participation in the management of the industry should be taken. It would be in the interest of the industry itself to include workers' representatives in the management, i.e. in the Board of Directors in all concerns. In the beginning such representatives may not be available from rank and file workers but in course of time when workers' knowledge increases it would not be difficult to find such persons even from among them.[66]

Proposals to this effect empowering government to appoint unionists as directors were introduced in the form of amendments to the Companies Bill by K. P. Tripathi, general secretary of INTUC, in the Lok Sabha. It is interesting to note, however, that Tripathi opposed at the same time the suggestion that workers should become shareholders and elect their own directors. It was reported that he felt that this would make the workers

liable to intrigues by the management itself, with the result that the unions might split thereby, and instead of this being a right it might become a liability. He said that Indian trade unions were not in a position to withstand this danger.[67]

It is important to note that INTUC leaders emphasize the Gandhian notion of "trusteeship" with reference to labour's responsibility to the nation. A leading article in the *Indian Worker* argued that the Indian labour movement did not suffer from the "immaturity" governing the "class approach" of the American labour movement.[68] It asserted:

Workers in India do not think themselves as anything but part and parcel of the whole Indian community. They do not imagine their legitimate interests ever to conflict with the true national interests....

Workers' participation in the management is not conceived in India in any narrow class sense, but entirely in a national spirit —to ensure a rationalized management of industry and higher production morale among the workers—both to the good of the entire community.

Whatever the INTUC's feeling for this development, it seems that such enthusiasm is not shared by the other labour groups. HMS leaders, particularly, asserted during interviews in 1954–55 that appointment of labour leaders to directorships and such other co-management schemes may add only to the prestige of some leaders and groups in the labour movement without making them any more effective in protecting labour interests.[69] An important background consideration was of course the apprehension that the INTUC representatives would be favoured in such appointments.

The actual record does suggest that INTUC representatives have almost exclusively represented the labour movement on the boards of directorates of the public sector concerns. However, INTUC leaders have been less vocal in the claims made for this type of representation and this probably indicates a greater awareness of the actual difficulties of influencing managerial policies. In interviews also, the only accomplishments cited were the winning of an occasional concession here and there, reinstatement of a dismissed employee, special payment to commemorate an event or to celebrate a holiday, and so on.

In the meantime, the idea of association of labour with management has led to a more publicized development, namely, the joint councils of management. These were officially launched early in 1958 following a seminar which defined the conditions for their introduction. The schemes were voluntary, and to be introduced only in plants or firms with a good record of industrial relations. Worker representatives' rights were defined in three categories : issues on which they had a right to be informed; those on which they had a right to be consulted; and, mostly welfare issues, in which they had a right to participate in executive action. It was also indicated that issues which infringed on collective bargaining should be kept out of the scope of the council.

So far, the scheme for joint councils has been tried in plants or firms. The Indian labour ministry has from time to time distributed its evaluations of the progress of individual schemes, which have been freely made available to the members of the Indian labour conference. In the government's view, the scheme is an unqualified success. Others are not so sure. One detailed study embracing four individual projects concluded that the joint councils had not worked well. During interviews also, a number of points of friction were raised. One leading official of a state government indicated that they were being bypassed by the Central government and as a consequence some plants were chosen for the scheme even though they did not satisfy an important condition, for instance, peaceful industrial relations. In 1962, during field interviews, it was reported that, in some of the places where councils existed, managements refused to recognize unions, or there were doubts about the representative character of the recognized union, or that the councils did not conform to the structure envisaged by the government scheme. In fact, one of the most successful in the government's roster, the joint committee structure at the Indian Aluminium plant at Belur is different from, and was evolved before the government's scheme. This is actually a healthy sign and indicates that New Delhi is more concerned with substance than form. Nevertheless, a number of critical questions must be raised concerning the functioning of these joint councils.

The Limited Role of Collective Bargaining

Despite the heated debates over bonus and rationalization, and the general air of suspicion with which labour regards private management, some progress has recently been made in settling matters directly with private firms. This has been most notable in Ahmedabad, Jamshedpur, and plants in several other centres, as we shall see in further detail in Chapter VI.

Significant as the Jamshedpur and Ahmedabad agreements are for the future, it is clear, however, that the bulk of unions in India have not succeeded in establishing satisfactory relations with management. On most issues involving wages, discharge and discipline, they either rely on the tribunals provided by the government, or direct their energies to securing satisfactory legislation on the subject.

Even with respect to shop rules, it is unlikely that Indian unions play a very significant role beyond the relatively meagre indications incorporated in the "Standing Orders," certified by government labour commissioners under the Industrial Employment (Standing Orders) Act of 1946 or the different state Acts. These require the employer to submit his "Standing Orders" to the labour commissioner, who may invite labour to submit its views. It is reported that some "bargaining" might take place at this stage, but this is unlikely on any large or effective scale. Also, organized labour has made it clear that it is not satisfied.[70]

The limited role of the union is further indicated in the absence of mutually agreed bipartite procedures for dealing with day-to-day grievances and production problems. This point will be discussed in more detail in Chapter VII where several exceptions to this generalization are also noted. Like many managements, however, some unions have been more active in providing welfare programmes for workers.

The Limited Scope of Union Activities

One reason is that most Indian unions have adopted a very limited view of their responsibilities. Few have done anything to police management actions towards labour on a day-to-day basis, or to service their members in a systematic manner. There is a tendency in unions to become extraordinarily active during strike periods, but only rarely does such enthusiasm get transformed into effective and lasting organizational drives. Union records are generally poorly kept, and, as we have indicated earlier, union funds are inadequate. Few unions collect subscription on a regular monthly basis, or make a conscious effort to keep members apprised of union policy on current or developing issues. Grievance processing suffers by default, and important benefits conferred by law—such as those provided in the Workmen's Compensation Act, the Employees' State Insurance Act, and the Payment of Wages Act—are often not realized simply because of the workers' ignorance of conditions governing these benefits.

There are, of course, a number of exceptions to this practice. The dockworkers' union in Bombay, the INTUC textile union in Bombay, the B and C Mills Union and the Simpson and Company Employees' Union in Madras, the union at the Aluminium plant at Belur near Calcutta, and the Tata Workers' Union at Jamshedpur, must be listed, in varying degrees, as exceptions. Some of the unions in banking, postal services, and railways also constitute exceptions although union representatives—especially with the last two—indicate special problems given the vast and cumbersome nature of government operations. Even the above list of exceptions includes several whose existence is threatened by internal weaknesses and external troubles. Virtually the dominant and exemplary instance of stable unionism is thus provided by the Textile Labour Association in Ahmedabad.

Union Welfare Activities: The Ahmedabad Example

The Ahmedabad Textile Labour Association is outstanding among Indian unions in respect of three key areas of union performance: in its record of organizational adequacy and stability, in the services provided to its members, and in the contribution towards the development of stable labour-management relations. As these points have been developed in greater detail in a number of discussions of the TLA experience, we shall focus attention on the extraordinary range of welfare activities undertaken by the TLA.[71]

The underlying philosophy of unionism at Ahmedabad was indicated by an officer of the TLA in an interview:

One characteristic of the Gandhian trade union movement is that he [Gandhi] has put more emphasis on uplift work than trade union work.... Even though we have brought more rupees [to the worker], we can't say that his standard of living has improved. His [monthly] wages have increased from Rs. 5 in 1914 to Rs. 100 today. But I don't find that his habits have changed that much. Some of them eat carrion meat. We tell them, "We don't mind your eating meat, but eat good meat." We tell them to live decently, have electricity in their homes, and to join housing cooperative societies.

The importance attached to social uplift work is reflected in the following institutions sponsored by the union up to 1954:[72] 25 cultural societies and social centres, 2 study homes, a girls' hostel, 46 reading rooms, and libraries, 8 gymnasiums, and 7 women's welfare centres with a staff of counsellors to visit homes. There is a workers' cooperative bank whose total working funds were reported, as of March 1957, to be as high as Rs. 3,523,180. There are also 28 housing societies, 10 credit societies, and 10 consumers' societies.

The union also provides training classes in tailoring to help workers learn an alternative craft. A municipality section deals with complaints regarding workers' residential areas. Finally, since many workers have a rural background and have a continuing interest in land or have left their families behind in the villages, the union maintains a Rural Relief Section, which deals with such diverse matters as helping workers to secure loans for the digging of wells, implementation of tenancy rights, copies of court records and decisions, certificates of births and deaths, and so on.

These welfare activities, the vigorous grievance processing machinery, and the stable labour-management relations are certainly responsible for the strength and vitality of the Textile Labour Association. It stands virtually alone among Indian unions in its financial strength and organizational continuity. The head-quarters of the union are located in an imposing three storeyed building, erected at a cost of Rs. 300,000 collected entirely from the workers. It is the most important bulwark of the Indian National Trade Union Congress, which depends on the TLA not only for leadership, but for funds amounting to over one million rupees subscribed by the Ahmedabad workers for national labour work.[73] Its membership has shown a steady increase over the years with a total of 95,876 in 1959, making it the largest single union in India.[74] The TLA executive consists of a full-time general secretary and three secretaries who head a union staff of nearly two hundred persons.

Outbursts of Violence

A review of Indian unionism would be incomplete without noting the violence which occasionally mars the Indian industrial relations scene.

In a Calcutta firm, a few years ago, some British managerial personnel were thrust alive into a furnace by a group of enraged workers. This instance is frequently mentioned in interviews. Numerous cases of physical assault of managerial and supervisory personnel, and even of trade unionists, were also reported during interviews in many parts of India. A government conciliator and arbitrator in Uttar Pradesh reported that he had been locked up for a considerable length of time by some disgruntled workers because the employer had not paid their wages in time. Another notable incident occurred during 1956 in Kharagpur, an Indian government railway workshop centre, west of Calcutta. A group of striking workers, dissatisfied with management's attitude on some outstanding demands, entered a moving locomotive, pulled the engineer out, and let the steaming vehicle charge into an assembled crowd, injuring over 60 persons.[75]

These manifestations of violence indicate that industrial conflict is not yet institutionalized along mutually acceptable lines. Weakness of union organization and discipline, with a tendency for feelings to run high and strike situations to get out of hand are also responsible for such a situation. Prime Minister Nehru remarked bitterly on the Kharagpur incident:

> Either it [the Kharagpur union] is directly or indirectly responsible for all that has happened or it is completely incompetent and it has no business to exist. There is no third explanation for this.[76]

Mass demonstrations and violence, including general strikes in Bombay, Ahmedabad and Calcutta, occurred during 1956 in protest against recommendations of the government's States Reorganization Commission on new state boundaries. The Bombay general strike set the Marathi-speaking textile workers against a government proposal to make Bombay City an independent political unit governed from New Delhi, rather than the capital of a Marathi-speaking state, which would have displeased the Gujeratis. When the government later reversed its decision in August 1956, and proposed as new and large bilingual state including Bombay City and both Gujerati and Maharashtrian sections, students of Gujerat University in Ahmedabad led a riotous demonstration which included some textile workers, paralyzed the city, and resulted in many injuries and deaths.[77] Calcutta's third general strike in 1956 occurred on July 7, and was reported to have been organized by "the combined leftist parties, including the Communists . . . in protest against the Indian government's refusal to acknowledge the state of West Bengal's claims to certain areas of the neighbouring state of Bihar."[78]

The industrial relations experience during the Second and Third Plan periods indicate the continuation of the disquieting patterns reported above. General strikes in Bombay in 1963 against the introduction of compulsory saving schemes affecting industrial workers, in Calcutta over price increases in 1959, or in Madras in 1965 over the language issue, indicate the influence of politics and the encouragement for industrial worker protest to make common cause with the grievances of India's low-income urban population. The pattern of assaults, hooliganism, rioting, and police firing have continued to be manifested to a degree that gives little room for comfort. The Indian government has demonstrated some awareness of the dimensions of the problem by bringing these instances of disorderly conduct to the attention of the Indian Labour Conference, and more specifically by evolving a Code of Discipline. Among other matters, the Indian Labour Conference viewed with concern the growing tendency to utilize hunger-strikes in labour disputes.

There is no doubt that the law must be upheld, particularly in the face of criminal transgressions and encouragement to physical and personal violence. At the same time, it is necessary to distinguish the clinical aspects of the problem posed by violent or disorganized protest. Trade unions in this sense may become stabilizing agents of protest and be among the most important intermediaries in channelizing and legitimizing protest in a pluralistic society. It is interesting to note that protest appears in its most destructive form precisely where trade unions are too weak, or are not allowed to function, or waste too much of their energies on rivalries.

As the last sentence implies, a great responsibility attaches to trade union leaders also. Fortunately, there are indications that a few responsible Indian leaders are alive to these weaknesses of the Indian labour movement, and would like to improve the quality of Indian unionism through strengthening the union link with its membership. The Ahmedabad lesson is not entirely lost on the Indian movement, even among those opposed to the TLA. Increasingly union leaders think in terms of building a permanent full-time staff, as we have already seen in our review of Indian labour leadership. During interviews in India, many labour leaders emphasized that unions should lay greater stress on the amicable settlement of disputes, on extending the scope of union services, and on strengthening the basis of union organization. A statement along these lines adopted by the HMS is typical of changing attitudes.

> The HMS is not blind to its own weakness and that of the labour movement of the country in general which has been responsible to a considerable measure for the cavalier treatment it has received in the past. The labour movement has spent too much energy in mutual rivalries; has not given sufficient attention to the strengthening of the Central Organizations, has permitted the growth among workers of the short-sighted obsession with immediate monetary benefits. Above all, a section of the labour movement continues to operate under Governmental patronage and to disrupt independent, militant rival organisations.
>
> The HMS pledges itself to strive for the removal of these weaknesses from the labour movement.[79]

The veiled reference in this statement to the INTUC, however, indicates the continued rivalries within the Indian labour movement and the difficulties in the way of unity among the non-Communist labour federations.

The protective role of government, important as it is to the encouragement of labour organization, has also had adverse effects on the freedom of unions to use whatever economic strength they may possess. We shall examine in Chapter IX the more compelling reasons why government finds it necessary to limit union activities, especially the strike and wage demands. But employer policies and attitudes towards unions and collective bargaining also have a bearing on union strength and the course of action that unions take. In the next two chapters, we shall consider the nature of the employer response to Indian unionism and describe in more detail the nature of plant-level management relations in India.

NOTES

1 Mathrubutham and Srinivasan, *Indian Factories*, pp. 608-09.

2 This represents a consistent decline in the average size of unions. In 1942-47 the average membership was 1,418; and, in 1949-50, it was 946. *Indian Labour Year Book* 1953-54, p. 148. See also *Indian Labour Year Book* 1961, p. 89 for 1958-59 figures.

3 *Indian Labour Year Book* 1960, p. 97.

4 A Bombay government report comments : "It appears that generally speaking unions find it difficult to maintain adequately trained persons on their staff who can properly assist them at the end of the submission of their annual returns. This applies particularly to small unions in the Mofussil." *Ibid.*, p. 2.

5 For text of the constitution (as amended in 1927), see All-India Trade Union Congress, *Report and Congress Constitution* (1928), pp. 144-57.

6 Figures supplied by an official of the Ministry of Labour, Government of India, New Delhi.

7 *Indian Labour Year Book* 1960, pp. 93, 100.

8 Figures supplied by an official of the Ministry of Labour, Government of India, New Delhi. The difference is explained largely by inflated claims of the federations, according to some government officials. A more recent INTUC claim (December 1955) was 1,426,621 members in 1,171 separate unions, *Indian Worker* (Special UNESCO Number), vol. 5, nos. 6-7 (12 November 1956), p. 65.

9 See the following newspaper despatch, "Railwaymen's Federation : Differences Settled," *Hindu Weekly Review*, 19 March 1956.

10 Interview, August 1955.

11 *The Indian Labour Year Book* 1960, p. 98.

12 *The Indian Labour Year Book* 1949-50, p. 159.

13 The National Federation of Indian Railwaymen, *First Annual General Body Meeting*, 20-21 November 1955, pp. 45 ff.

14 All-India Defence Employees' Federation, *First Annual Convention : Speeches, Proceedings, Resolutions*, November 1954, *General Secretary's Report* (Poona, 1955), pp. 25-43.

15 *Ibid.*

16 See later discussion on Labour Leadership.

17 The 1926 Indian Trade Unions Act states that "not less than one-half of the total members of the officers. . . shall be persons actually engaged or employed in an industry." See V. G. Kher, *Indian Trade Union Law* (Bombay, 1954), for the Act as reproduced.

18 The president of the Tata Workers' Union, Michael John, was formerly a supervisor in the Tata Iron and Steel Company.

19 After a field study of trade unionism and collective bargaining in India, Professor Van Dusen Kennedy concluded: "One of the fundamental barriers to an effective in-plant role for Indian unions is the social gulf between worker and management representatives. Looking at Indian industry in general, this gulf is seen to be the result of caste, community and language differences, illiteracy or extremely low

levels of education among workers, and strongly entrenched class or master and servant feeling between those wielding and those subject to authority in industry. Since these barriers are widely reinforced by strong managerial resistance to unionism and a lack of real understanding of collective bargaining, the chances for a free type of daily give-and-take between plant-level representatives of employer and union are rare indeed." "The Role of the Union in the Plant in India," *Proceedings of the Eighth Annual Meeting of the Industrial Relations Research Association* 1955, p. 260.

20 "Loyalty only to INTUC : New Regulation for Congressmen," *Indian Express,* 28 July 1955.

21 The 1947 Delhi conference establishing the INTUC specifically mentioned that the organization shall be run on the basis of the Congress Working Committee resolution of August 13, 1946 (*Proceedings of the Inaugural Conference,* p. 12). For the text of the 1946 resolution, see B. V. Keskar, *Congress Hand-Book,* All-India Congress Committee (Allahabad, 1946), pp. 273-75. Negotiation, conciliation and arbitration, especially vital industries, were emphasized in this resolution.

22 *Hindustan Times,* 31 December 1953. Nehru's views were expressed in the context of open conflicts between the Madhya Pradesh Congress and the Madhya Pradesh INTUC.

23 On the basis of contributions from Ahmedabad textile workers, a sum of approximately Rs. 1,100,000 was collected in 1948 to establish a Gandhi Labour Memorial Trust in 1951. Among the trustees are the top leaders of the Ahmedabad Textile Labour Association, at least three of whom are prominent in the all-India leadership of the INTUC. *Declaration of Gandhi Labour Memorial Trust* (Ahmedabad, 1951).

24 K. N. Srivastava, *Industrial Peace and Labour in India* (Allahabad, 1954), p. 118.

25 See, for instance, Hind Mazdoor Sabha, *Report of the Third Annual Convention* (Bombay, 1952), p. 10, and *Report of the Fourth Annual Convention,* pp. 8, 21-2, where the need for developing a cadre of trained trade unionists is stressed. Similarly, the All-India Trade Union Congress stressed this aspect, but admitted little had been accomplished. *Twenty-Fourth Session of the All-India Trade Union Congress: Report and Resolutions* (Calcutta, 1954), p. 84.

26 Government of India, Planning Commission, *Second Five Year Plan: A Draft Outline* (New Delhi, 1956), pp. 172, 174.

27 Democratic Research Service, *Communist Conspiracy at Madurai* (Bombay, 1954).

28 Strategic considerations, as used here, refer to the allegations of non-Communist labour leaders during interviews that the Communists were settling across the table and working within the government adjudication system because international communism's attitude toward the Nehru government had softened. Similarly, tactics may also change. Leftwing leaders indicated the dilemma confronting them as follows: "Shall we maximize the advantages within the present system, thereby anticipating the fruits of revolution?" or "Shall we minimize our efforts so that revolutionary fervour is maintained at high pitch?"

29 Government of India, Ministry of Labour, *Proceedings of the Indian Labour Conference* (Twelfth Session held in Naini Tal from 8 to 11 October 1952), (Delhi,

1952), p. 237 (referred to hereafter as *Proceedings of the Indian Labour Conference, Naini Tal*).

30 *Ibid.*, p. 242.

31 *Ibid.*, p. 243, italics supplied.

32 For the UTUC reply to the Government of India questionnaire in 1952, see *ibid.*, pp. 255-62.

33 Supra, p. 138.

34 Mr. Kripalani, the Congress president in 1947 and later chairman of the new Praja Socialist Party (1952), in a statement stressed the contribution of Mahatma Gandhi to the evolution of Socialist thought and ideas. He concluded: "To recapitulate, then, the Socialists in India have discarded the Marxian doctrine of dialectical materialism . . . . In addition to material values which no living human being can possibly ignore, the Socialists of India believe in moral values which cannot be sacrificed for the fulfilment of ends . . . . They have repudiated the Machiavellian doctrine that 'ends justify the means.' " *Indian Press Digests*, vol. II, no. 1 (October 1953), Department of Political Science, University of California, Berkeley.

35 *Janata* (Bombay), vol. X, no. 47, 18 December 1955.

36 See HMS comment on the Final Draft of the First Five Year Plan, in Hind Mazdoor Sabha, *Report of the Third Annual Convention* (28 April – 1 May 1952), (Bombay, 1952), pp. 22-3.

37 For the full version, see Socialist Party, *New Deal for Labour* (Bombay, 1951), pp. 15-24.

38 For full text of the answer, see *Proceedings of the Indian Labour Conference, Naini Tal*, pp. 225-36.

39 See, for instance, the speech of Khandubhai K. Desai, INTUC leader (and former Minister for Labour), as reproduced in *Harijan*, vol. XVIII, no. 14 (5 June 1954), p. 116; and also the following extracts from the *INTUC Memorandum* to the Planning Commission: "India cannot afford the luxury of highly mechanised devices involving huge capital outlay except to a limited extent of developing the key industry. . . . The Second Five Year Plan will have to give primary attention to development of village and small-scale industries throughout the country. The industrial expansion . . . will have to be so arranged as to meet the needs of the key industries and the productive industries consistent with the above-mentioned principles, namely, that of creating employment for as large a section of the people as possible by developing village and cottage industries." *Indian Worker*, vol. 3, no. 48 (5 September 1955), p. 10.

40 Article IV of the constitution reads as follows:

   (i) to establish just industrial relations;

   (ii) to secure redress of grievances without stoppages of work by means of negotiation and conciliation and failing these by arbitration or adjudication;

   (iii) where adjudication is not applied and settlement of disputes within a reasonable time by arbitration is not available for the redress of grievances, to have recourse to other legitimate methods, including strikes or any suitable form of satyagraha;

   (iv) to make the necessary arrangements for the efficient conduct and satis-

factory and speedy conclusion of authorized strikes or satyagraha.
SOURCE: *Annual Report,* 1952-53, pp. 225-26.

41 *Proceedings of the Indian Labour Conference, Naini Tal,* pp. 177-224, esp. pp. 182-83, 213.

42 The INTUC emphasis on "justice" stems from the impetus provided by the TLA. This union, as we have seen in the previous chapter, was shaped by the "social justice" standard established by Gandhi in the Ahmedabad strike of 1918.

43 G. Ramanujam, "Strikes and Lockouts in Industrial Relations," *Indian Worker,* 15 August 1955, p. 8.

44 Indian National Trade Union Congress, *Annual Report* (October 1950 to September 1951) (New Delhi, 1951), pp. 123-26. Socialist criticism of the First Plan did not specifically comment on this point; however, the Socialist Election Manifesto (*New Deal for Labour*) specifically promised workers, legislation for "fair wages" in the Socialist state. Criticisms on this point were also voiced by HMS labour leaders during interviews. The AITUC also sharply criticized the Plan. See B. T. Ranadive, *India's Five Year Plan: What It Offers* (Bombay, 1953), pp. 177 and ff. in its Election Manifesto it declared that the Communist government "will grant living wage to the workers." G. D. Binani and T. V. Rama Rao, *India at a Glance* (Bombay, revised edition, 1954), pp. 108-16, for the complete text.

45 For the text of the Labour Appellate Tribunal Award, see *Labour Law Journal,* vol. II, 1950, in the case between the Bombay Millowners' Association and the Rashtriya Mill Mazdoor Sangh (the INTUC "representative" union for the Bombay cotton textile industry). This award is discussed more fully in Chapter IX.

46 It was reported during interviews that such exemptions were granted in Kanpur. In March 1955, the Labour Appellate Tribunal overruled an earlier award by an industrial tribunal, and granted exemption to mills in Madhya Pradesh which declared losses (*Hindustan Times,* 25 March 1955, "Bonus Awards Set Aside: Madhya Pradesh Millowners' Appeal Upheld"). The Bombay "representative" union for cotton textiles, the Rashtriya Mill Mazdoor Sangh, concluded a bonus agreement with the Bombay millowners in March 1956, largely based on the "full bench formula." In this case, worker dissatisfaction in the loss-making mills erupted into wildcat strikes in opposition to the union's agreement. These strikes are described in the *Labour Gazette* (Bombay), vol. 35 (May and June 1956), pp. 9-10.

47 These developments are discussed more fully in Chapter IX in the section on "Wage Disputes under Adjudication."

48 *Hindu Weekly Review,* 14 May 1956, p. 6. The *Review* points out editorially that "the real opposition to it [the INTUC demand]...is likely to come from the Government and the Planning Commission who have prepared their plans on the basis of the State appropriating the bulk of the increase in product ... for purposes of reinvestment." Apparently, however, both the Labour Minister and the Planning Minister have suggested this demand, while employers have opposed it. *Commerce,* 1 December 1956, p. 1021, and 8 December 1956, p. 1075, and *Indian Worker,* 26 November 1956, p. 3.

49 For a further discussion, see Charles A. Myers, "The Labour Problem of Rationalisation: The Experience of India," *International Labour Review,* vol.

LXXIII, no. 5 (May 1956), pp. 431-50, and also Chapter IX.

50 Indian National Trade Union Congress, *Survey and Report, May* 1949 *to September* 1949 (New Delhi, 1949), pp. 2-5.

51 See the various issues of the *Indian Labour Gazette* for 1953 for increases in the figures of registered unemployed. The 1952 average was 383, 991; the 1953 average, 477,575. For October 1953, the total was 514, 975; by December 1953, it had reached a total of 522,360. *The Indian Labour Year Book* 1953-54, pp. 14-6.

52 For the HMS resolution criticizing the Ahmedabad agreement, see *Hind Mazdoor*, January-February 1953, p. 34. In April 1954,the *Hind Mazdoor* demanded that during the current situation of "progressive decline in employment" the government should not permit any rationalization: vol. II, no. 2 (April 1954), p. 1. The Delhi Agreement was termed outmoded by Raja Kulkarni, the HMS representative on the Cotton Textile Working Party. For the detailed Kulkarni statement, see Government of India, Ministry of Commerce and Industry, *Report of the Working Party for the Cotton Textile Industry* (Delhi, 1953), pp. 563-71.

53 *Twenty-Fourth Session of the All-India Trade Union Congress: Report and Resolutions*, 27-29 *May* 1954 (Calcutta), pp. 96-9.

54 "Rationalisation with Least Lay-Off: House Adopts Resolutions," *Indian Express*, 11 September 1954.

55 "Comprehensive Inquiry into Rationalisation Urged: Inconclusive Discussions," *Times of India*, 14 April 1954. The millowner was refused permission, although no decision on principle was taken. But the 1953 amendment to the Industrial Disputes Act (1947) came out of this dispute.

56 *Indian Worker* (New Delhi), 2 October 1955, p. 7. Much of the opposition was concentrated on the introduction of automatic looms, which not only threatened displacement or increased work loads for machine weavers but meant disaster to the handloom weavers in the villages. Other automatic machinery which did not carry the latter threat, such as improved winding, warping and spinning machinery, has been introduced in Bombay and other centres within the last three years without significant labour opposition. For this further information, the authors are indebted to Mr. Ralph James, who spent 1955-56 in India completing a doctoral dissertation on rationalization problems in the Indian cotton textile industry. This dissertation (unpublished) is on file at the New York State School of Industrial and Labour Relations, Cornell University, Ithaca, New York.

57 The strike began on 2 May 1955, and was called off on 20 July 1955. Discussions on the strike were carried up to New Delhi to the attention of Mr. Nehru by Dr. Sampurnanand, the Chief Minister of Uttar Pradesh (see the following issues of the *Hindu*: "Arrests in Kanpur," 30 April 1955; "Kanpur Textile Workers' Strike," 23 May 1955; "Kanpur Textile Strike: Nehru Confers with Dr. Sampurnanand," 6 June 1955; "Kanpur Strike Called Off," 21 July 1955. The Communist Party played up the situation in Kanpur for all it was worth (see the following issues of the *New Age*, the official organ of the Communist Party of India: 12 June 1955, pp. 1, 11, 13, 14, 15; 19 June 1955, pp. 3, 4, 13; and 3 July 1955, pp. 3, 8-10).

58 *Hindu Weekly Review*, 30 April 1956, p. 14.

59 S. D. Punekar, *Trade Unionism*, p. 179; and Nirmal Kumar Bose, *Studies in*

Gandhism (Calcutta, 2nd ed., 1947), p. 211, for the position of the TLA.

60 *Supra*, Note 49.

61 "The Outworn System," editorial in *Janata*, vol. X, no. 29 (7 August 1955), p. 1.

62 "Labour in Second Five Year Plan: INTUC's Memorandum to Planning Commission," *Indian Worker*, 5 September 1955, p. 10.

63 For a discussion of works committees, see Chapter VII, p. 221.

64 *Proceedings of the Naini Tal Conference* (Delhi, 1952), p. 247.

65 G. D. Binani and T. V. Rama Rao, *India at a Glance* (rev. ed. Bombay, 1954), p. 113.

66 *Indian Worker*, 5 September 1955, p. 11. The INTUC emphasis on worker participation was undoubtedly instrumental in inducing the government to send its "Study Group on Worker Participation in Management" to Europe in 1956. The conclusions of the study group are generally in line with INTUC demands in this area. See *Report of the Study Group on Worker Participation in Management*, Government of India (1957), pp. 74-81.

67 *Ibid.*, 12 September 1955.

68 *Ibid.*, 24 October 1955, p. 3.

69 See also "Workers' Participation in Management," in the *Economic Weekly*, 7 January 1956, p. 25, for reported lack of enthusiasm of some labour representatives on the Labour Panel of the Planning Commission.

70 For the INTUC position, see *Indian Worker*, vol. III, no. 49 (12 September 1955), p. 9.

71 For a more detailed treatment of the development of unionism at Ahmedabad, see Subbiah Kannappan, "The Gandhian Model of Unionism in a Developing Economy: The TLA in India," in *Industrial and Labour Relations Review*, October 1962, pp. 86-110. See also "The Ahmedabad Experiment in Labour-Management Relations," *International Labour Review*, April and May 1959.

72 *Annual Report*, 1953-54, esp. pp. 23-7.

73 *Declaration of Gandhi Labour Memorial Trust* (Ahmedabad, 1951).

74 See *The Indian Labour Year Book* 1953-54, Appendix VI, pp. 377-410, for a list of large unions (with 1,000 membership or more). The figures for Ahmedabad are broken up into separate figures for the different craft unions and are also incomplete. Ahmedabad figures are given in the *Annual Report* 1953-54 of the Textile Labour Association, p. 8.

75 "Kharagpur Train Accident: Nehru Condemns Strikers' 'Monstrous Action,'" *Hindu Weekly Review*, 4 June 1956.

76 *Ibid.*

77 *New York Times*, 18 and 19 August 1956. Fortunately the TLA in Ahmedabad opposed the demonstration.

78 *Ibid.*, 8 July 1956.

79 "Hind Mazdoor Sabha: May Day Manifesto," *Janata* (Bombay), vol. XI, No. 14, 29 April 1956, p. 1.

CHAPTER VI

THE MANAGERIAL RESPONSE[1]

MODERN management in India has faced difficult problems in responding to the protest and challenge presented by the growth of the Indian labour movement, by the partially committed industrial workforce, and by evidence of labour indiscipline. We shall examine in this chapter recent attitudes and approaches of management in India with particular emphasis on the utilization of labour and the handling of labour-management relations. We shall analyze the organizational structure of Indian management, stemming from the managing agency together with methods of recruiting managerial personnel. Finally, we shall pay particular attention to the relation between management training and the educational system, and consider the extent to which private and public enterprises in India have concerned themselves with systematic management and supervisory training programmes.

Attitudes and Approaches

There is a continuing view in India, shared by a number of progressive employers as well as by trade union leaders and government officials dealing with labour matters, that many Indian top managements are still relatively authoritarian in their relationships with lower management and with labour.[2] The following quotations are from interview notes in 1954–55, and may be somewhat less applicable today:

There is still considerable short-sightedness and lack of human relations practice on the part of many millowners who think only of the quick profit. This is true even of those who have travelled in Europe and America and have seen different practices. When they get back to India and to their mills, they think of themselves as having sole authority to order people around and do their bidding. [*Official of an employers' association*]
Managing agencies have had a real impact on labour relations,

210

and wartime changes have been unfavourable. Before the war, many managing agencies were interested in building a business on a long-term basis but, during and after the war, with high profits, there was a turnover in managing agencies. Some were bought for quick profits and their purchasers were not interested in building a business for the long term. They did not consider how they treated labour. [*High government official*] [3]

Much of Indian management is not yet convinced of the importance of management's responsibility for developing good industrial relations. They tend to blame government, labour legislation and the unions for their troubles, without realizing their own faults. [*Industrialist*]

Employers in India are still not willing to recognize unions or treat labour fairly. The present difficulties are not labour's fault. Employers must be willing to recognize one union. Indian employers will have to learn this, and it's a matter of time. [*Plant manager*]

The management attitudes required for an expanding economy are slow in coming. The slave-drivers are still favoured, even in appointments to government enterprises. The value of the human approach is not understood; it is dismissed as "too theoretical." Many managing agents got into manufacturing through profits made on the share market [stock exchange]. They still regard quick profits as their major objective: they don't really want to build a business for long-run gains. [*Official in a public enterprise*]

Some Indian businessmen take a professional managerial view of building up the business. But many others are after quick profits; they are not interested in developing their organization within the firm for long-run survival. I am very pessimistic about rapid change here, and I would frankly have to say that a majority of Indian businessmen are in the second category. [*Employers' association official*]

Indian employers haven't yet learned to deal constructively with labour. They are behaving the way American employers did in the early 1900's and they don't know that American employers have changed greatly since then. *Laissez faire* is gone in America and England, but some of our employers don't realize it. [*High government official*]

Changes are occurring in managerial attitudes, principally, under pressure from government, but the above interview statements made during 1954–55 do not differ markedly from the 1947 view of a former president of the Federation of Indian Chambers of Commerce and Industry:

The borderline between authority and autocracy or discipline and docility still seems to elude us. We lack the rudiments of organizational capacity and are far from having mastered the technique of building up and managing institutions. Our industrial organization, for example, is, with certain notable exceptions, still largely in a medieval state and we adopt and follow methods which are individualistic and haphazard.[4]

On the other hand, there has been a feeling of some resentment against criticisms of management implicit in the labour legislation which came largely after 1947. This view was expressed by one industrialist in 1952 in these words:

All the actions of Government during these years (1947–52) were animated by an ideology which conveys pretty clearly to the minds of the people of India the State's concern and anxiety for the so-called downtrodden and ill-treated factory labour, exploited by the unscrupulous industrialists, needing the protecting hand of the guardian angel, the Government.... Thus, with the advent of the National Government, industry entered the labour-management arena in an atmosphere in which an industrial worker was looked upon as the most unfortunate victim of a cut-throat capitalist. It is this spirit which, even today, permeates many of our labour enactments and tribunal awards, and the bias is distinctly in favour of the workers, while the onus of proving innocence is placed on the unfortunate employer.[5]

This reaction, which still finds a sympathetic audience in Indian industry, is no longer so openly expressed. Some management spokesmen, not content to stop here, go further to emphasize in their public utterances the need for good relationships with labour and the importance of working together for the achievement of the nation's planning goals.[6]

In interviews conducted ten years ago for the first edition of this book, many management officials emphasized the changes which they claimed are occurring in Indian and foreign managerial philosophy. These examples will suffice:

In 1947–48, after fabulous wartime profits, the general attitude without exception was, "How much can we cheat the workers?" But, today, times have changed and world trends have made managements here realize that they cannot hope to survive unless they change their attitudes and approaches. Today managements are sincerely interested in their workers and the general welfare. [*Mill managing agent*]

Ten years ago when I was first coming out to India, an "old India hand" got me aside and told me, "Now just forget about these ideas of leadership you have been learning here in Britain. Out there if the workers don't follow instructions, belt them. That will bring them around." But those methods are no longer possible. Leadership is needed, but it can't be a driving leadership. You've got to be firm, but fair. [*Assistant plant manager, English firm*]

I am optimistic about the future here. Changes are coming, and changes in management's thinking and organization to deal more effectively with human relations and labour relations are inevitable in India. Of course, there are still many employers who appear to be reactionary, but in our view of life there is a strong urge underneath to do the right thing—the good thing. I believe this is coming out more and more. [*Managing director of a large firm*]

Workers are more conscious of their rights now and they are stronger, so management can't treat them the way they used to when labour was so cheap and unprotected. But many of my Indian friends don't realize this; they dismiss my talk of human relations as "unpractical" and "won't work." It will take time for them to realize the need for a change, but I can't say how

long. [*Partner of prominent Indian managing agency*]
Indian management is becoming more aware of the need for
good employer-employee relations and for training of lower
management in the better handling of labour. When labour
is plentiful, there is not the same incentive; but workers in
India are expecting better things and are demanding their
rights. [*Chairman of two large Indian manufacturing companies*]

In an increasing number of cases, the newer, expanding firms and
industries with young, dynamic managements are in the forefront of
this change. These are in such industries as heavy metals, chemicals,
pharmaceuticals, engineering, etc. where, as one observer put it, "a
favourable product market inspires production increases and labour
peace, and permits the longer-term investments in training, personnel staffs, organization changes, research, etc." The view of the general manager of a chemical firm was characteristic of this group:

> We work on the theory that incapable management, not poor
> labour, is the trouble in Indian industry. If management is
> competent, the worker can produce more and earn more. But
> we are hemmed in by other managements—especially those
> controlled by big industry associations, which take a different
> approach and blame labour for everything.

These changes, however, are more often expressed in extensive
welfare programmes which reflect a paternalistic concern for
employees than in organizational changes which would help to
make possible a better management structure for dealing with
human problems in the enterprise. The "ma-bap" relationship is
said to be characteristic of Indian rural society,[7] and this is often
cited by management representatives as the reason why the Indian
worker wants to be taken care of and why various welfare and
benefit programmes are necessary. For example, the personnel
officer of one firm asked a worker representative who was demanding
a long list of free amenities, including free shoes, "But why free
shoes?" The worker replied, "Sahib, the Company is our father
and our mother." However, it might be added that in a poor country,
the employer may have to compensate workers "in kind" as well

as in wages, since housing, recreational facilities, medical facilities, etc. are inadequate in the community.

As we have noted in Chapter III, welfare programmes are extensive in the progressive firms, which have far more employee benefits and services than the minimum required by the Factories Act and other laws. While there is an important labour supply consideration in these programmes, to hold workers to the firm when community facilities are inadequate, there is also a strong feeling of management pride in providing amenities for workers. As an example, the founder of one managing agency system, with a number of operating companies which are known for their progressive labour and welfare policies, described his welfare programmes in a language which abounded in "I's." "At first," he explained, "I found that, if workers got a few annas more, they were absent more often; they didn't know how to live properly. So I had to show them how to live better, to keep their houses clean. I started various games and recreation centres. I had to provide these outside interests to soothe the workers' minds."

Some Indian managements have found that paternalism, does not win employee loyalty—or avert unions. A Calcutta industrialist said that, in one of his mills (in another region), "I have bungalows for the workers; I have a school, a children's playground; I have a sports programme and spend Rs. 10,000 a year; I had a provident [pension] fund before it was required by law; I gave them a production bonus so with yearly bonus they get nine months' extra pay. But in spite of all I have done for them, the INTUC union still creates trouble, makes more demands, and says, 'If you don't give us something, the Communists may take over.'" Then he added, "In a nearby plant, I pay just the minimum required, but have four trusty employees who keep out Communists and trouble-makers. We have an INTUC union here, but no trouble. You avoid trouble if you keep all unions out. They're all trying to outbid each other; and, left alone, the Indian worker is as good a worker and as sensible as any."

While these viewpoints still persist, particularly among Indian managers and managing partners who have not been exposed to alternative ways of dealing with employees and unions, the overall pattern of attitudes and behaviour is changing, however slowly.

This is consistent with the view that as industrialization proceeds in a country, pressures develop on employers to change past patterns of behaviour and past policies.[8]

Changing Patterns of Management

The changes which are occurring in Indian management mean that the number of "exceptions" to the still dominant authoritarian and paternalistic management outlook is rising. Over ten years ago, when the interviews with 150 management officials in fifty companies were supplemented with interviews with trade union and government officials, there were clear exceptions to the dominant managerial ideology. There are even more today.

Among the firms listed ten years ago, but not limited to them, were the following: Tata Iron and Steel Company, Jamshedpur; Associated Cement Companies, Bombay; Bombay Dyeing and Manufacturing Company, Bombay; Tata Mills, Bombay; National Rayon Company, Bombay; Calico Mills, Ahmedabad; Sarabhai Chemicals, Bombay; Arvind Mills, Ahmedabad; Delhi Cloth Mills, Delhi; Jay Engineering Works, Calcutta; Ramakrishna Industrials, Ltd., Coimbatore; and the Kirloskar group of companies. At least two public enterprises (Government of India) were then included: Sindri Fertilizers, Sindri; and Indian Telephone Industries, Bangalore. Many, if not all, of these firms would be included in a similar list today.

There was no single distinguishing technical feature about these firms. They were of varying sizes, in producers' and consumers' goods industries, and with management from different castes and business communities. But they did have one thing in common—a top management which believed in the importance of building a lasting organization and developing constructive relationships with employees and trade union representatives. Many of the top officials of these firms had travelled abroad, and some had taken advanced technical or managerial training in Western countries.

It should be noted that these same firms were also generally the progressive firms in other aspects of management—in sales, marketing, production processes and techniques. Their interest in organization building extended to all phases of the organization.

Some of the variations in outlook and policies were attributed to the differences between the Indian business communities. For example, the Parsee businessmen are often believed to be more progressive, and the Tatas (the outstanding Parsee firm) are cited by government officials, labour leaders, and other industrialists as being in the forefront of dynamic management and enlightened labour and personnel policies.[9] The Gujeratis are also well regarded, although there is perhaps more variation in managerial outlook within this group which is concentrated heavily in textiles, and primarily in Ahmedabad. Bombay industrialists, by and large, are frequently cited as more progressive and enlightened than those in other centres, although there are also some in Calcutta, Madras, and Bangalore, among other centres.

The Marwaris, as we have seen in Chapter II, are the fastest-growing of the three big Indian business communities. As they have acquired existing plants and built new ones, it was perhaps inevitable that they would develop a less favourable reputation in handling labour. Any blanket characterization is unfair, but it must be reported that a somewhat critical view of Marwari attitudes and policies is widely held by government, trade union and other business communities. Clearly there are exceptions to these statements. There were individual plants run by Marwari managing agencies which were as progressive and enlightened as non-Marwari companies. A conclusion that some prejudice exists against this rapidly growing and aggressive business community, not unlike similar prejudices in other countries, is inescapable.

Management in certain industries, through employers' associations, has attempted to change the pre-existing pattern of labour-management relationships and deal constructively with unions. The Labour Investigation Committee noted in 1946:

Employers in this country, while they have been showing a much greater internal organization for safeguarding their interests, have not so far, probably with the exception of the Bombay Millowners' Association, shown much enthusiasm for having a properly planned and well-coordinated labour policy. Recently the Jute Mills Association, Bengal, has been thinking in terms of such a policy.[10]

These two associations were in the forefront of efforts to change managerial thinking in the mills and to improve the handling of labour relations. Each had a Labour Relations Officer with high standing in the association, and, in the case of the Indian Jute Mills' Association, a staff of labour officers who worked in assigned districts with the mill managers, mill labour officers, and union representatives in the settlement of grievances. The value placed on these activities was well expressed by the chairman of the IJMA at the 1955 annual meeting:

> The casual reader of the press might get the impression that the normal relationship between employer and employee in this country is one of tension and disagreement frequently punctuated by strikes and other evidence of breakdown in industrial harmony. In the jute industry, at least, this is certainly not the case. Employers are sometimes concerned at the amount of time which it is necessary to give to labour questions, but it is time well spent and the figures which we maintain show what a striking improvement there has been in our ability to settle by peaceful negotiation and conciliation the majority of disputes which arise. This industry was in fact the first in India to set up a Labour Relations Department, and I think that everyone will agree that there have been very few of our activities which have given better or more satisfactory return.[11]

Among employers' organizations, which have done a great deal more recently to improve management competence and labour-management relations, are the Engineering Federation of India (covering engineering firms) and the All-India Organization of Industrial Employers. The various local management associations, as well as the All-India Management Association, have done even more to raise the quality of Indian managers, as we shall note later.

Two associations in Ahmedabad deserve special mention. The Ahmedabad Millowners' Association has a long tradition of direct constructive relationships with a labour organization—the Textile Labour Association, which was organized with the assistance of Mahatma Gandhi in 1920. The history of this relationship began with a strike, and there have been several in intervening years. But it is characterized by a genuine attempt on both sides to settle disputes by direct negotiation or private voluntary arbitration, rather than by resort to government adjudication.[12] One other evidence of management's approach in Ahmedabad is found in the establishment of the Ahmedabad Textile Industry's Research Association (ATIRA), which has pioneered in textile research and in studies of organizational and human relations problems in the local industry.[13] It is financed jointly by the mills in Ahmedabad, many of which participate actively in its research and training programmes. In addition, ATIRA first sponsored an All-India Management Conference in February 1955, and has sponsored many since that time.

Naturally there is considerable variation of outlook between mill managements even in such a centre as Ahmedabad. The managing agents in some firms are authoritarian in their relationships with their subordinates in the management organization, holding information closely, by-passing middle management to give orders directly to supervisors, and blaming labour and labour leaders for their troubles. Others are developing a different philosophy of management, improving their organizational structure by delegating responsibility and authority to junior management for many matters, and seeking agreement with workers and trade union representatives on the difficult problems involved in rationalization.

One observer of the Ahmedabad scene evaluated management's reaction to rising protest in these words written in 1953 which are still relevant :

Two basic questions arise: first, how fast India will be able to improve working conditions; and second, how this improvement will keep pace with the rising westernization of the workers' minds, their sense of the fact that it is a world in which workers are more and more articulate and demanding, and in the long run likely to get most of what they ask. I speak not at all as an expert. I would offer with some caution only the following point : in the first place, there are huge individual differences among the mill-owners in their readiness to modernize, rationalize, reduce noise, dirt, poor illumination, and confusion; their willingness to reduce somewhat the magnitude of their earnings for the workers' welfare; their general sensitivity to the social science approach and their awareness of the terrible pay-off which will come if a modern viewpoint toward labour is not rather early developed. There are in Ahmedabad a few mill-owners who understand that the tide is rising.[14]

Management in the Growing Public Sector Enterprises

In the preceding section, at least two public enterprises were mentioned as having competent, progressive management before 1958. Undoubtedly there were others at that time, although there was a widespread belief (which is still held) that too many top managers of public enterprises were drawn from the Indian Civil Service, with damaging and sometimes disastrous consequences to the management organization and continuity of certain public enterprises.

The Indian Civil Service, of course, has an enviable record of competent *government* administration, which has been of inestimable value to India after Independence. But there is a difference between the kind of administration which supervises a government department or ministry with few shortages of trained personnel and a new or growing *industrial* enterprise which is expected to build new products, hire and train a staff, and show a profit for the public account. Furthermore, in line with transfer policies, it is often assumed that an ICS member can be sent to an industrial enterprise for a couple of years, and then move on to a wholly different assignment in government or in another enterprise. As a retired managing director of one of the most successful government-owned factories said in an interview ten years ago:

Too often the Government Ministries have no conception of the nature of industrial management. They put managing directors in charge, whose experience is not in industry, but rather in various forms of government administration. The ICS [Indian Civil Service] and IAS [Indian Administrative Service] men are nice enough fellows, but they are not equipped in many cases for industrial management.

In the new Industrial Policy statement presented to the Lok Sabha in May 1956, by Prime Minister Nehru, the importance of competent industrial and technical management for the growing public sector was emphasized :

> This programme of industrial development will make large demands on the country's resources of technical and managerial personnel. To meet these rapidly growing needs for the expansion of the public sector and for the development of village and small-scale industries, proper managerial and technical cadres in the public services are being established. Steps are also being taken to meet shortages at supervisory levels, to organize apprenticeship schemes of training on a large scale, both in the public and private enterprises, and to extend training facilities in business management in universities and other institutions.

One of the new arrangements was an Industrial Management Pool, established by the government in 1957, after much prior discussion of an Industrial Management Service comparable with the Indian Administrative Service (successor to the Indian Civil Service). Posts in the Pool were advertised in 1958 and initial appointments made in 1959. But members of the Pool did not have exclusive call on managerial positions in public sector enterprises. The Central Government ministries which watched over these enterprises could still select present or former ICS-IAS officers for deputization. Furthermore the salaries and other emoluments for Industrial Management Pool members did not compare favourably with those of either the civil service officials or of business executives in the private sector, even though much was expected of them in building new public enterprises.

Possibly this explains why only over 200 were selected from 15,000 applicants for the Pool through 1963, and only about 100 were recruited for assignments to public enterprises. The whole experience was aptly summarized in an article in *Economic Weekly* (Bombay) in January 1963:

> The object lesson of this expose is that an entrenched bureaucratic tradition is not likely to be receptive to any fundamental

change which challenges its supreme indispensability and status in all affairs of the Government, direct or indirect, unless the Cabinet and the public are strongly behind the idea.

There is the further difficulty that public enterprises are not simply accountable for final results; they are subject to surveillance from the government ministry to which they report and to committees of the Parliament. Thus, while some of the deficiencies of management in the private sector are perhaps absent (such as nepotism of family or community), public enterprise management finds its initiative hampered and the lines of promotion drawn by membership or non-membership in the government services. While all the management is "professional," it is not always clear that promotion is solely on the basis of competence in industrial management, as it should be.

Indeed there have been some examples of notorious mismanagement of public enterprises, and these perhaps get more publicity than similar examples in the private sector. The published reports of the Estimates Committee of the Lok Sabha (lower house of Parliament) from 1958 onward, concerning specific investigations of public enterprises, are prime examples. Numerous articles in *Indian Journal of Public Administration* have also dealt with the problems of management and control of public enterprises.

One example of a public sector enterprise with management and production difficulties will suffice. In February 1963, the Union Minister for Steel and Heavy Industries announced that an "incentive bonus scheme" was being considered for Heavy Electricals Limited, Bhopal, where production was only 10 per cent of what it should have been, taking into account the original investment. Labour-management relations were poor; there was inter-union rivalry and a strike in 1962. Management appointments were from government civil servants, who on deputation were said to earn higher salaries and allowances than they got in government offices. More recently, however, there have been indications that the situation has improved and, by 1965, it was estimated that the plant would reach full production five years after it was first in operation.

Other examples indicate that the promise of effective management in public enterprises, once the deficiencies of private management were removed, has not been realized. Perhaps there was a doctrinaire expectation that all management difficulties and management-labour friction would be removed when private ownership was not permitted in those industries reserved for the public sector. But good management is not easily developed, whether in public or private industries, and the hoped-for example that public enterprises would set for the whole of India is yet to be achieved.

The Role of Foreign Firms in Management

Management of foreign enterprises in India, principally British and American, cannot be characterized by a single approach or a common set of practices. But, after Independence, there developed somewhat more uniformity than was found within the larger group of Indian enterprises. One reason is that today the "European firms" (as they are usually called) are forced to operate under the spotlight of attention from government, which stresses rapid "Indianization" of the technical and managerial personnel of these firms. Furthermore trade unions often single out the foreign management for special attention.

Ten years ago, among the older British firms especially, there were still "old-timers who came out here twenty or thirty years ago as young men and don't realize what changes have occurred in labour relations back home," as a labour officer of a Calcutta jute mill expressed it. This view was repeated many times in other interviews during 1954–1955. The American training officer of an important American firm, for example, emphasized the same point:

> Our biggest trouble in supervisory training is with the old-type American or British executive who doesn't realize how management has changed in the U.S. or Britain, and still proceeds on the basis of pre-Independence stereotypes in India. Much of our training effort, therefore, has to begin at the top level.

These "stereotypes" varied from the view (quoted earlier) that management had to use the stick on Indian workers to get results, to the widely held view of the importance of the "ma-bap" relationship, mentioned earlier in this chapter. "On the tea plantations,

this was really true," explained the secretary of an employers'
association, "for the workers came to the manager with all the problems, of work and personal. But with trade unions this is passing,
and some of the old-timers have difficulty in adjusting to the new
situation." During the past ten years, there have been fewer of these
"old-timers."

Many trade union leaders and government officials stated in
interviews that some of the "European" firms were in the forefront in their willingness to deal with unions of their employees
and in their whole approach to labour-management relations.
Among these firms today are Esso Standard, Eastern (formerly
Standard-Vacuum) Oil Company, Hindustan Lever, Indian Aluminium Company, Dunlop Rubber Company, Metal Box Company,
Bata Shoe Company, and Union Carbide India Limited. Some
illustrative quotations will indicate the consensus[15]

> European firms are more willing to recognize and deal fairly
> with trade unions than most Indian firms. [*Regional INTUC
> leader*]
> Some of the British employers in the coal industry are better
> to deal with. They are industrialists, whereas many of the Indian
> employers are just businessmen who don't appreciate the value of
> building a lasting relationship with labour or of keeping their
> agreements. [*Coal union official*]
> In the majority of Indian tea estates we are treated worse than in
> the European. The Indian companies have invested recently
> and don't want to spend money. They are also badly organized
> and victimization of workers is common. European employers
> have been more profitable in the past and can be more liberal.
> [*Plantation workers' union official*]
> European employers are often better in dealing with unions and
> workers today than "our own people" [Indian employers]
> because they know the value of good relationships with labour.
> [*Prominent INTUC leader*]
> We have found that employers from the U.K. and the U.S.
> often have better labour relations. They encourage proper trade
> unions and not political jockeys with political ambitions. [*District
> INTUC president*]

In pointing to this change, an Indian industrialist explained it by saying that, "since Independence, foreign firms are trying to develop better labour policies to keep their standing in India." In most of the 14 foreign firms interviewed, the change was implemented through (1) increased top management concern for labour relations problems and personnel policies, (2) a high-level personnel or labour officer (frequently an Indian) with an adequate staff to assist in union negotiations, grievances, and personnel problems, and (3) an extensive personnel programme which included supervisory training, employee induction and training, and full-scale welfare and recreational programmes. Some of the foreign firms were located outside metropolitan areas, where it was necessary to provide housing and other amenities which they would not normally offer to employees in a Western industrialized country. But foreign firms, no less than the enlightened Indian ones, have had to adopt welfare programmes which fit the expectations of Indian workers that they will be taken care of by the employer—or by the State.

Some foreign firms are restless with this welfare philosophy. An American businessman in India said:

Foreign companies in India have not made any major effort to combat the predominant welfare philosophy, and in fact the British pattern has been to encourage it as is evidenced in the jute industry and the tea and sugar plantations. American companies, coming later on the scene and concentrating primarily in built-up industrial areas, have not had the facilities to follow many welfare practices, and made a conscientious but none too successful attempt to promote a policy of paying wages to obviate the necessity of major welfare commitments.

The dilemma facing both foreign and Indian private enterprise in Indian economic development was posed by two Indian economists:

In recent years increasing responsibilities for labour welfare have been imposed upon private industries, which have resisted this trend on the ground that it has a depressant effect upon the rate of reinvestment of profits. In considering this problem, one

must realize that a backward economy undergoing rapid industrialization faces different conditions than do advanced countries. . . . The present climate of social opinion differs from that of
150 years ago. Unless private business realizes that welfare
measures are essential to the maintenance of a democratic
system in the country, a "mixed" economy will be able to function only with difficulty. The case for private enterprise in un-
developed countries rests upon willingness to accept a large
share of social responsibilities. Labour welfare measures are a
condition of public support for private enterprise. The transition
would be smoother if enlightened sections of the Indian business
community understood more fully the implications of acceptance
of a mixed economy in a backward country.[16]

Some foreign firms and some Indian firms understand these
implications, and have developed advanced employee welfare
programmes.[17] But, as we shall see, fewer have been concerned
with the relation of organizational structure to the development of
human resources.

Organizational Structure of Management

Within the past ten years, there have been changes in the organizational structure of the more progressive and efficient firms,
particularly in the private sector. We have already noted some of
the organizational problems of public enterprises, under ministerial control, but here, too, organization structures and procedures
are improving. The need for more attention to organization structure has been emphasized by Professor H. C. Ganguli in his recent
book, *Structure and Processes of Organization.*

The importance of adequate organizations is central to rapid
industrialization, and consequently organization-building ability
becomes the critical skill. This organization-building function
largely belongs to the managerial staff, and the most important
single fact about foreign companies, especially American, seems
to be their emphasis in attaining depth in management by invest-
ing heavily in large management staff and for impressive manage-

ment-development programmes. . . . This is also one of the most pressing problems of India today—development of managerial skill for the proper integration of persons and functions in the entire organization for achievement of its overall objective. Fortunately, steps are being taken now toward building up adequate and skilled managerial resources for Indian industries.[18]

The growing interest in management training and development, which will be discussed later in this chapter, should be distinguished from the development of managers through their *experience* in organizations. Whether the organization is definitely hierarchical in nature, with strong central control from the top, or whether it is flatter, with considerable delegation of authority to subordinate managers, will affect the opportunity for managers to develop greater competence. In this sense, there is less evidence that most Indian firms (and indeed, perhaps as many firms in other industrializing and industrialized countries[19]) have undergone fundamental organizational changes. Centralization of top management is still the rule, despite claims of delegation and despite the proliferation of staff departments like industrial engineering or work study, personnel or industrial relations, etc.

At this point, it may be well to recall our earlier analysis of the character of the managing agency system, which is the basic decision-making unit in Indian industry. The Indian trading and money-lending castes and communities adopted the managing agency form of organization as a way of maintaining and extending family control of investment in business and industry. Thus they retained in their own hands the major financial decisions affecting the operating companies which the agency controlled.

Even though the private limited company form of organization has increasingly replaced the proprietorship and partnership, the officers of the managing agency are often members of the same family, or of the same caste. Not infrequently, sons follow fathers in positions of responsibility, and this is expected even if the sons may not possess the requisite ability. Staff appointments to other important positions in firms controlled by the managing agency are also frequently made from among the joint family, or within the community or sub-caste, to which the principal officers belong.

The managing agency, in turn, controls at least one operating company, and frequently, more than one. Some general observations about the organizational structure of these operating companies will help to fill out a picture of the management hierarchy.[20]

In some cases an officer of the managing agency firm may also be the top executive officer of the operating company. This officer may have had special technical training himself, or have acquired a working knowledge of operations sufficient to enable him to be the operating manager, in fact. In these cases, another man designated as "manager" in the operating company may be no more than a glorified head clerk.

More often, however, the mill manager (in the textile industry) or the plant manager (in an engineering firm, for example) has direct control of the internal operations of the mill or the plant. This type of hired mill manager in the textile industry has been described as follows :

> He arranged the details of the production schedule, given production requirements; the technical heads were responsible to him in the first instance, although he did not appoint or dismiss them; the powers of appointment and discharge in relation to other members of the technical and supervisory cadre were larger, although not final; he acted as the liaison between the managing agents and the technical and other members of the non-worker group of employees. In respect of workers, his powers of dismissal were the widest and usually final. In many routine and purely technical matters he represented the mill company.[21]

This managerial role is found more often in the large firms and in situations where the managing agents are physically distant from the operating companies and must therefore delegate more responsibility to the manager on the spot. Regional factors are important here, and companies in larger cities like Bombay are more likely to have professional managers than those in smaller cities like Ahmedabad. Size alone is not the sole explanation, however; Bombay has always been regarded as more cosmopolitan and progressive than most other Indian cities.

Below the operating manager is frequently a group of "technicians." Some of these are line management officials at the second or third level, heading operating departments or divisions such as the weaving or spinning department in a cotton textile mill, or serving as assistant department heads or supervisors. Others are staff specialists, such as accountants, statisticians, chemists, and labour welfare officers. Because of lack of delegation, the middle management level as a whole is relatively "thin" in many companies. The view expressed in 1947 by Mr. G. L. Mehta, leading Indian industrialist and former Ambassador to the United States, may still be relevant in many firms:

The place of the technician and managerial executive is, in fact, yet to be recognized in the world of Indian industry. Those who have studied Indian industrial organization have noted that there is a gap between the "top men" and the lower rungs of management in many factories and plants. In a large-scale organization, not only are people wanted to formulate policies and give orders but also an intermediate category of persons who would seek to translate such policies in terms of concrete measures and who would try and see that those policies are implemented in practice.[22]

The failure of Indian management to delegate authority was stressed by one of India's leading industrialists, G. D. Birla, in his inaugural address to the Sixth Management Conference in Ahmedabad in 1960:

Unfortunately in this country we do not delegate powers . . . if business is to grow in this country, then businessmen must learn how to delegate powers. It is a wrong thing . . . to go into smaller details for which your technicians are free. They are paid for that purpose.

The adequacy of first-line supervision is another problem in Indian industry. The first level of supervision in the cotton textile industry, the jute industry, and a number of others is the "jobber"

or "mukadam" group. Originally these were recruiters of labour
for the mills, with considerable power to hire and fire and many
opportunities for petty graft and favouritism, as we indicated in
the discussion of commitment of an industrial labour force. They
usually came from the same social level and sometimes even the
same community or sub-caste as the workers, and they had no
formal education. Today their powers are curtailed, largely because of the growth of labour officers with recruitment and disciplinary responsibilities and the development of new intermediate
levels of supervision. Their position is now anomalous; they cannot
advance to the next higher levels of management, and their role is
increasingly rejected by the workers.

In the words of one authority:

> The workers treat him [the jobber] as belonging to the camp of
> the employer and liable to be suspected as such, whereas his
> acceptance in the opposite camp is strictly limited, and of a low
> order. This lack of a sense of belonging weakens the faith of the
> management, and adds to the feelings of defiance in the worker,
> in relation to the jobber. . . .The jobber, we may then conclude,
> is the weakest link in the organizational set-up of India's cotton
> mills.[23]

This characterization may be less applicable outside the cotton
textile and jute industries, but effective first-line supervision is a
major need in Indian industry. As we shall see, an increasing number
of companies are concerned with supervisory training, and even
within the cotton textile industry the more progressive mills have
replaced jobbers with technically trained supervisors.

The qualities of an effective supervisor in Indian industry do not
appear to differ markedly from those found in an advanced industrial country. For example, a special study of the nature of supervision in a government engineering factory in 1955–56 concluded
that good supervisors, in the opinion of their seniors as well
as their workers, generally, tend to identify themselves more
with the workers than with the company and also look upon
their men as human beings rather than as instruments of production
only. Yet the good supervisor has unfulfilled aspirations; his job

satisfaction is less than that of the poorer supervisors. More specifically, the study points out, he is somewhat dissatisfied with the work he does, and substantially dissatisfied with his income and scope for further training.[24]

Some Consequences of Inadequate Organization

The way in which organizational structure is related to the delegation of authority and responsibility, to communication patterns and to the practice of consultation is illustrated by a special study done in two mills in Ahmedabad by the Ahmedabad Textile Industry's Research Association.[25] In Mill *A*, authority was highly centralized in the managing agent, and the senior staff felt that they did not have enough authority to work effectively. Many were not clear about their responsibilities, and orders were frequently given by the managing agent directly to the second or third level of supervision, by-passing the mill manager and department heads. Sometimes a jobber received instructions from two different supervisors. The atmosphere for free communication upwards was limited. Jobbers did not freely go to department heads, nor department heads freely to the managing agent—only to the production manager. There was little formal consultation between superiors and their subordinates. Supervisors and assistants were transferred from one shift to another without a corresponding change of the rest of the work-group.

In contrast, Mill *B*'s managing agents delegated considerable authority to the mill manager, who in turn gave a fairly free hand to his department heads. Most members of the management hierarchy were clear about the scope of their responsibility and authority, and were satisfied with the degree delegated to them. The formal channel of communication was generally used by top management in giving instructions or receiving information; there was little or no "by-passing." Yet lower management people felt free in bringing their problems to higher levels. Consultation was practised not only at the higher levels of management, but also at the intermediate level, where department heads held monthly meetings with their assistants and supervisors to discuss departmental problems. Jobbers, supervisors, and assistants were all

transferred together from one shift to another systematically, so
that there was continuity of the same work-group.

What was the result of these differences? In Mill *A*, subordinate
levels of management showed considerable hostility and resentment
towards top management, and there was a widespread sense of
instability and insecurity. Lower management had little understanding of or identification with top management goals. Despite
higher-than-average salary levels for department heads, turnover
was high and people were leaving for jobs that were less attractive
financially. In Mill *B*, the situation was almost the reverse. Subordinate management staff understood top management policies and
goals and on the whole were satisfied with them. There was a sense
of stability at all levels, and turnover was very low, despite salaries
which were at the average for the industry.

Mill *A* is probably more typical of the majority of management
structures in Indian industry than is Mill *B*. Certainly there has
been a high turnover within the middle management group in
the cotton textile industry,[26] as dissatisfied technicians and even
mill managers seek other positions through the columns of the
trade journals. The bitterness of this group towards the managing
agents was revealed in the comments made by a group of technicians
in a major Indian textile centre late in 1954:[27]

> The managing agency system is a hereditary system, and sons
> take on responsibilities for which they are not adequately pre-
> pared. In some cases this is changing, so that technicians can
> discuss matters more than formerly, but it is a sort of halfbaked
> knowledge which also makes for difficulties. The agent may
> interfere, and then if things go wrong, he blames the technician.
> There is inadequate delegation of responsibility to department
> heads.
>
> Within the managing agency, two brothers may vie for control;
> give contradictory or conflicting orders. And this is reflected and
> sensed all along down the line. There is also conflict between
> sales and production; and managing agents listen more to sales,
> which bring in the money. Managing agents are still interested in
> quick profits—still speculators. They are not interested in
> building a business through quality, to make a long-run profit.

Similar views were expressed in interviews with middle management in jute, engineering, steel, and other industries. As long as there is substance in these views in the eyes of middle management in Indian industry, the sense of teamwork which is so important for effective functioning of the management organization will be lacking. The gulf between the middle and the top is still wide in many instances, and this is also true between the first-line supervisors (jobbers) and the technicians or middle level of management. The gulf is the result of differences in educational background, family connection, and social caste and class, all of which are reflected in the organizational structure. It will not easily be narrowed.[28]

Organizational Changes in Several Firms

A small minority of the fifty firms interviewed ten years ago was concerned with these problems of organizational structure, and were attempting to move in the direction suggested by the example of Mill *B* above. One large textile firm, for example, was devoting considerable top management time to a review of the responsibilities of different levels in the management organization. A proposed reorganization would make a managing agent, one of two general managers, with manufacturing and development reporting to him, and sales and finance to the other general manager. But the real problem, one management official explained, was to get the managing agent (general manager) "to delegate responsibility; not to keep his hand in everything. He was a master of detail and nobody could take action without consulting him. But now he is delegating more, and lower management can't yet believe he means it."

The new mill manager of another large firm, in the jute industry, has started a programme of weekly meetings with operating superintendents and staff specialists. Broad and detailed problems were discussed and responsibility for making decisions was increasingly pushed down the line. The superintendents, in turn, held weekly meetings with the supervisors reporting to them. A staff adviser commented: "The superintendents' group is too inclined to make policy without consulting subordinate levels; it regards itself as a little too omniscient. But we are working towards 'joint consultation' within the whole management group." The older supervisors resisted this method, for under the former manager there were no intermediate levels of management—just the manager and a number of supervisors who carried out orders. With the retirement of older supervisors, however, younger, better-educated ones were appointed and the new organizational structure could be introduced.

A third example is the case of a large multi-plant company, an amalgamation of four previously separate managing agencies, which found through the work of an outside consultant that its plant managers and technicians were completely in the dark on the company's vast plans for expansion. In the absence of one top managing director, apparently no one took the responsibility for communication of company-wide plans to the branches. When a new managing director was finally appointed, one of his first moves was to hold information and discussion meetings at central locations throughout India for branch-plant management officials.

The Tata Iron and Steel Company has also pioneered in certain organizational changes designed to bring middle and lower management into better communication with top management. Among these are (1) a week-long "Company Information Course" for foremen, in which questions are encouraged and the Resident Director periodically meets with the foremen to answer their questions; and (2) a Management Consultative Committee of 25 elected representatives of foremen, general foremen, and assistant superintendents meeting bi-monthly with the general manager, general superintendent, personnel director, and head of the Management Research Unit. The latter unit was established to make a continuous study and review of company organization structure and management practices.

These examples indicate the importance of the relationship between organizational structure, communication channels, and the development of management personnel. It should be noted again that organizational structure is equally important in public enterprises, not only within the enterprise but also between the enterprise and the government ministry in charge. The need for greater delegation of responsibility to the public enterprises, and less minute control from the Centre, has been stressed by students of public administration.[29]

Development of Management Personnel

Methods of selecting and training management are important enough to deserve separate treatment in the light of Indian experience. Key managerial positions in Indian private industry are still filled, too often, from members of the particular business community to which the managing agents belong; and, as we have seen, preference may even be given to members related to each other through the joint family. The importance of the business community in management selection, and its limitations, were well put by a leading Indian business publication:

> The sectional outlook of the Indian business communities— like the Parsees, Gujerathis and Marwaris—in the choice of managers and partners in an enterprise was more relevant to the earlier conditions of ordinary risk-bearing in trading and the initial manufacturing stages. It is no surprise that they have not been able to create a class of the more versatile type of business managers required by modern industry. Thus India has, even with the middle class component in the social structure which has produced enough able lawyers, politicians, administrators, doctors, engineers and teachers, proved unable to face up to this problem successfully.[30]

Charges of nepotism are frequent, particularly on the part of those outside the family or the community who feel frustrated and blocked by lack of opportunity within the management structure. But nepotism does not always result in bad management; for there are some family enterprises in which sons have been sent abroad for special training in engineering and business administration and have returned to become competent managers and innovators, expanding the family businesses into new fields. Two examples stand out among the firms interviewed: one textile firm in South India in which the U.S.-educated son branched out into the manufacture of textile and printing machinery and the publication of a daily newspaper; and an electrical products firm, in which a similarly educated son developed a small motors and transformer plant. The important distinction within the family-dominated enterprise is this: have the most competent family members been chosen for managerial advancement, and have they been given professional training for these responsibilities? Or is the managerial hierarchy staffed with family or community members of varying degrees of competence, whose only claim to these positions is their family or community membership as such?

Probably more typical of much of Indian private industry is the case of a textile firm in which two brothers were partners in the managing agency. Each had a son, recently graduated from the local university college of commerce with undistinguished record. The sons joined the fathers in the managing agency during 1954. They were given authority over much more competent, technically trained managers, who resented having to take orders and instructions from these inexperienced and cocky young men.[31] Another example of inadequate selection and training of management is the story told by a Bombay millowner who explained the presence of a young man sitting at a nearby desk in his office. "This is my nephew," he said, "and he is learning the business just the way I did from his grandfather years ago. I sat at the desk he is at now, and I listened to everything the old man did, the people he met, and the problems he discussed with them. This is the way I learned the business, and that's the way he is learning it now from me."

Another aspect of management development in the private sector is in the "Indianization" of the staffs of foreign firms operating in India. One of the criteria for establishment of new foreign enterprises is the extent to which they will train and give employment to Indians. While there is no rigid policy or set of rules, the Government of India does encourage the utilization of Indian personnel in the technical and managerial ranks, and requires periodic reports from foreign firms on their progress in this respect. The American oil companies have a good record in developing Indian personnel increasingly to take over responsible positions. For example, Esso Standard Eastern, Inc. (formerly Standard-Vacuum Oil Company) reported in November 1964 that the number of Indians in key posts in its marketing organization had increased from 3 to 4,538 since 1942. Of the 110 key technical and managerial positions, 107 were filled by overseas personnel.[32] Indianization of technical and managerial positions in the company was over 62 per cent in 1956, as compared to 3 per cent in 1942, and in November 1964, it was almost 99 per cent.

Foreign firms in other industries may or may not have an equally satisfactory record,[33] but all are faced with the challenge and the opportunity to train Indian nationals for responsible managerial positions. This is also in the financial interests of these companies, for salary levels and allowances for overseas personnel are generally much higher than for Indians in the same positions. The difference is a source of dissatisfaction which tends to be destructive of morale among Indian personnel.

Management Training and the Educational System

In the past, one of the difficulties in developing a professional managerial class in India lay in the nature of the educational system. The leading Indian universities, distinguished as they were for their contributions to other areas of knowledge, paid little attention to the type of training which, in the experience of more advanced industrial nations, develops competent industrial managers. Until recent years, there were relatively few first-rate engineering schools and technological institutes. Furthermore the imprint of the British emphasis on university training in the humanities and law was strong in the great Indian universities, many of which were founded by the British.[34] This training was useful for those entering the professions, or the government civil service under the British and later in independent India. But it did not prepare a man adequately for the complexities of modern industrial management, or for the administrative skills required for building organizations.[35]

The nature of the Indian system of higher education in 1950–51 and changes in the intervening years are shown in Table XXXI. Enrolment in universities and colleges increased threefold in the 12-year period, 1950–51 to 1962–63. In the earlier year, enrolments in faculties of arts and low accounted for half of all enrolments, as compared to about 37 per cent in faculties of science, engineering and technology, agriculture, and veterinary science (combined). By the end of the period, enrolments in arts and law had declined to 45 per cent of the total, but this still exceeded the 39 per cent enrolled in the other faculties listed above. In

TABLE XXXI

ENROLMENT IN UNIVERSITIES AND COLLEGES ACCORDING TO FACULTIES, 1950-51 TO 1962-63

Year	Total	Enrolment according to faculties									
		Arts	Science	Commerce	Education	Engineering and Technology	Medicine	Agriculture	Veterinary Science	Law	Others
1950-51	396,745	180,806	127,168	34,067	4,135	12,094	15,260	4,744	1,101	13,649	3,721
1951-52	459,024	212,923	142,666	41,458	4,982	13,900	16,942	4,856	1,219	16,746	3,332
1952-53	512,853	253,494	148,676	46,279	6,104	14,162	17,929	4,798	1,332	17,118	2,961
1953-54	580,218	293,677	163,234	53,124	7,046	15,613	18,756	5,053	1,642	18,706	3,367
1954-55	651,479	333,412	182,161	58,718	8,699	16,935	19,767	6,378	2,035	19,491	3,883
1955-56	712,697	361,899	197,475	64,167	11,371	19,899	21,405	8,230	3,052	20,162	5,037
1956-57	769,468	395,672	210,039	66,674	13,000	21,237	23,431	10,389	3,572	20,707	4,741
1957-58	827,341	415,313	229,899	69,570	14,357	27,534	25,591	12,475	4,139	22,424	6,039
1958-59	928,622	461,081	256,145	78,762	15,297	32,809	27,537	16,828	4,524	24,376	11,263
1959-60	987,319	477,636	285,130	87,098	15,989	39,072	33,253	17,515	4,988	25,770	868
1960-61	1,030,384	487,016	294,329	92,802	18,990	45,139	34,139	23,389	4,788	27,240	2,552
1961-62	1,155,440	511,940	336,722	125,142	21,718	58,168	39,569	24,794	5,214	29,401	2,712
1962-63(P)	1,272,666	543,841	386,374	129,951	25,638	68,589	49,546	31,427	5,524	28,944	2,832

P—Provisional.

SOURCES: (1) *Education in Universities in India*, Ministry of Education.
(2) *University Development in India*, University Grants Commission.

other words, a system of higher education perhaps appropriate for an earlier period of Indian development was changing only slowly in response to the pressures for industrial and agricultural development.[36]

These data, of course, are quantitative, and give no indication of qualitative improvements. For example, the Indian Institute of Technology at Kharagpur and the Indian Institute of Science at Bangalore, two of the earlier institutions of higher education in these important fields before 1950, were supplemented by three new higher institutes of technology in Bombay, Madras and Kanpur subsequently. Whether these institutes provide technically trained people with a competence in industrial management, however, is less certain.

Table XXXI also shows enrolments in "commerce" faculties, which were twice as high in 1950-51 as the combined faculties of engineering and technology, agriculture, and veterinary science. By 1962–63, commerce enrolments had nearly quadrupled, and still exceeded the combined enrolment of the other specified faculties.

Does this high enrolment in "commerce" indicate a source for future business and industrial managers? Unfortunately the answer is generally "No." Commerce colleges, with a few exceptions, typically do not provide programmes centered in industrial management, and typically do not give students a background which adequately prepares them for modern industry.[37] The "B. Com." degree in India is not held in particularly high repute.

Recognition of these weaknesses in the present system of higher education led the Government of India to appoint a committee in May 1950 to study "management education." This was headed by Sir Jehangir Ghandy, then Resident Director of the Tata Iron and Steel Company. Surveys under the auspices of the committee in the Calcutta region during 1950–51 were discouraging about the prospects of getting the cooperation of most managing agents in releasing junior management personnel for special postgraduate short courses. Nevertheless, one was started in February 1953 at the Indian Institute of Technology at Kharagpur, West Bengal. A Department of Management Studies (later called Industrial and Business Administration) had earlier been established there with the assistance of a British management engineer and educator under the auspices of the Colombo Plan. The first short course for "General Management" attracted 40 senior men; and this was later followed by a one-week Production Management course in 1953, a year-long postgraduate course in Industrial Engineering and Management with eight students, beginning in January 1954, and a two-week residential study course in Works Management in January 1955.

In the meantime, more ambitious plans for postgraduate training programmes in management were being developed under the auspices of the Central Ministry of Education, with the advice of an All-India Council of Technical Education, composed of representatives of state governments, universities, industry and commerce, various government ministries, and professional associations. A Board of Management Studies, headed by Sir Jehangir Ghandy, was given the specific responsibility of approving postgraduate full-time or part-time courses in Business Management at University Schools of Economics, and similar courses in Industrial Administration at Schools of Technology.[38] Another committee was appointed to investigate the possibility of establishing an Administrative Staff College, patterned after the British one and, by 1956, plans were completed for a college in Hyderabad which started its first programme the following year. The significant fact here is that the central government was coordinating and even dominating these efforts, in large part because the financial resources were to come from public funds.

Recent Developments in Management Education [39]

In the eight years since the first edition of this book appeared, there have been further developments in management education in India. The three-year part-time postgraduate diploma courses in business management and industrial administration have continued in the schools of economics and institutes of technology. As an example, the extensive programme at the Delhi School of Economics involves not only formal lectures, which are common to Indian higher education, but also seminars, plant visits, case discussions, use of films, etc. Admission requirements include at least two years' experience at the junior executive level in a com-

mercial or industrial establishment, and sponsorship by the employer.

The Administrative Staff College at Hyderabad was the first
residential management training centre in India, with approximately 50 participants nominated from private and public enterprises, as well as from government ministries, for the 12-week
sessions, repeated three times each year. By 1965, the College had
completed eight years of operation, and over 1,000 managers had
participated in its programmes. Originally the "syndicate" method
of instruction was used, but subsequently case studies and other
teaching methods have been introduced. The first cases dealing
with Indian management problems were developed there with
assistance from a Ford Foundation consultant.

In an effort to reach an even broader group of managers and
potential managers, the Government of India (with financial
assistance from the Ford Foundation) took steps to establish two
new Indian Institutes of Management in 1962, with faculty guidance
from two graduate centres in the United States. These are now
operating with full programmes, including research and consulting
by faculty members. One is the Indian Institute of Management,
Calcutta (with faculty assistance from the School of Industrial
Management at the Massachusetts Institute of Technology) and
the other is the Indian Institute of Management, Ahmedabad
(with faculty assistance from the Harvard Business School).
The Ahmedabad institute drew some staff and guidance from the
earlier activities in the management training area of the Human
Relations Division of the Ahmedabad Textile Industry's Research
Institute, which had conducted earlier annual management conferences. The Calcutta institute supplements earlier management
training efforts, particularly by the Calcutta Management Association.

Both new institutes have two-year residential postgraduate
management programmes at the master's level. They also conduct
special shorter residential programmes for junior executives and,
separately, for senior executives in special areas. The faculties are
predominantly Indian, with Indian directors, even though there
are a few visiting professors from the cooperating American
institutions.

The Indian Institute of Management, Calcutta, now conducts the four-week residential Advanced Management Programme held each summer in Srinagar, Kashmir, under the auspices of the All-India Management Association. This programme started in 1960 with the faculty largely from the Massachusetts Institute of Technology. About 30–40 top managers are selected each year by the AIMA from nominations by private and public enterprises through local management associations. This is an outstandingly successful executive programme, judging by the responses of the participants and the enthusiasm of former members for continuing their exposure to modern management concepts and techniques.

All of these efforts, plus those to be reviewed in the next section, will hardly meet the projected needs for managerial manpower, although *quality* (which the newer programmes stress) is more important than quantity. Preliminary estimates reported by the Institute for Applied Manpower Research indicate that the quantitative requirements for technical, commercial and general management during the Fourth and Fifth Five Year Plans are at least 110,000. The report adds that this estimate "is a very broad one erring towards underestimation rather than overestimation."[40] An earlier projection by the National Council of Applied Economic Research was 500,000, and even this estimate was challenged by some who thought 700,000 might be nearer the right one for the period 1960 to 1980.[41] It is clear that competent management at all levels is likely to be in short supply in India for some years in the future.

Other Management and Supervisory Training Efforts

Supplementing the university, graduate institutes and the residential management training programmes are such activities as those of the National Productivity Council, the Training Within Industry (TWI) Centre, the local management associations, and some intra-company management training programmes.

The Government of India established the National Productivity Council in 1958, as an "autonomous" body under the Ministry of Commerce and Industry. It was patterned after the Japanese Productivity Council, and has financial assistance from the Indian government and the U.S. Technical Cooperation Mission in India. In addition to meetings and conferences, it sends "productivity teams" of managers abroad for study tours, and management specialists from abroad for specific assignments. It has also encouraged the establishment of local productivity councils on a tripartite basis.

The TWI effort preceded this, beginning in 1953 when an ILO specialist on the training-within-industry methods was sent to Ahmedabad to work with cotton textile mills there. He trained training officers in twenty-two mills, and they in turn conducted TWI courses for supervisors in their own mills.[42] The programme was later extended by two ILO specialists to firms in Baroda, Bombay, New Delhi, Bangalore, and Nagpur during 1954–56. A national TWI Centre was established under the Ministry of Labour, in Bombay, and the 1963-64 activity included supervisory training sessions in a tobacco firm, two Tata firms, and two other Bombay enterprises. These efforts, it must be said, still only scratch the surface of supervisory needs in India. Perhaps many Indian managers still do not appreciate the need for competent first-line supervisors, as a part of management.

Local management associations have been attempting to meet some of the need for better middle management through various evening meetings and, in some cases, longer conferences. The management associations in Bombay and in Calcutta have been particularly active, especially in organizing more extended training conferences for managers from member firms.

An effort to reach a different management need in small firms has been made by the Small Industries Extension Institute in Hyderabad, with assistance from two former staff members of the Harvard Business School. Some of the professional associations, such as in accounting and in personnel management, have also conducted conferences and training programmes for staff specialists in their fields. The Indian Institute of Personnel Management, with headquarters in Calcutta, is particularly active.

Finally, but not least, there are a few organized management training programmes within Indian and foreign enterprises. These are the larger and more progressive firms, which have recognized the importance of management development as an important activity *within* the company organization. Obviously the climate of management and the organization structure will have the primary impact, as noted earlier. But organized management conferences are also helpful as a communication device, as well as to improve the managerial competence of junior managers. Some efforts have aimed even higher.

One of the first was the Management Conference started by the Tata group of firms in 1955 for key management officers from various Tata companies. At the initial three-day conference, held at a hill hotel away from Bombay, papers were given by participants, company directors met with the group, and the conferees concluded with specific proposals for improving the managerial organization within their companies. During 1956, a Tata Staff College was established to provide four-week residential training for small groups of selected managerial personnel drawn from Tata enterprises. The first group discussed in detail two topics: "the difficulties of organizational interrelationships and means of overcoming them," and "the management of the individual." Speaking to the Second Tata Management Conference, Mr. J.R.D. Tata, the Chairman of Tata Industries, expressed the guiding philosophy behind these efforts:

> Today, in judging management, I certainly attach the greatest importance to the capacity that has been shown by a particular individual or group of individuals to train men under them. However efficient a manager may be in doing the work himself, I always feel that the man who is not only capable of doing the work, but who has shown propensity and enthusiasm in training men under him even to do the work that he himself does, is a more valuable member of management. In expanding industries and companies, the careful and successful training of under-studies and of men to take your place does not mean that your usefulness will be diminished but, on the contrary, that you will free yourself for opportunities to undertake higher tasks in management.[43]

Another Indian firm interested in management training is the United Commercial Bank, which has been training about twenty junior officers a year for six-month periods,[44] and the Indian Overseas Bank which maintains a staff college. Other examples are some of the foreign firms in India which have brought over supervisory and management training programmes already developed in their home countries. As early as 1954, Standard-Vacuum Oil Company, for example, had a full-time training director who used training programmes in "Conference Leadership" and "Basics of Supervision" with management and supervisory personnel. The latter programme was also translated into Hindi and given to first-level terminal supervisors. Some changes were made in the content of these programmes to fit Indian conditions, particularly the examples used, but the essential framework was unchanged. In the judgment of the training supervisor, "supervisory problems are almost identical with those in the United States and the same skills are needed. People respond to the same kind of treatment everywhere, and Indian workers are no exception."

Authoritarianism and paternalism still too often characterize the approach of many managements in India in utilizing human resources and in dealing with labour problems. Changes are occurring, however, under the impact of an increasingly articulate labour movement and a government which supports the aspirations of industrial labour.

Exceptions to the prevailing pattern of management ideology and approach in handling labour problems can be found in almost every industrial region in India. These firms vary in size and in other environmental characteristics; they have in common a top management which believes in the importance of building an effective managerial organization and in developing workable relationships with employees and trade union representatives.

Many, but not all, of these progressive firms are foreign-owned or foreign-managed companies. Specific foreign firms are often cited favourably by Indian trade union, government and management officials. Perhaps there is more pressure on foreign firms to develop enlightened managerial policies in utilizing labour, as a means of maintaining their right to continue to operate in independent India.

The organizational structure of Indian management is highly centralized and often family-oriented, with the result that many in middle management appear to regard their opportunities for participation in management decisions and for promotion to top ranks as rather limited. Caste, class and family differences are factors accounting for the gulf which exists between different levels of management, but organizational changes in several of the firms interviewed indicate that these barriers are not insurmountable.

Charges of nepotism in the selection and promotion of higher management personnel are frequent, but the recognition of the value of professionally trained management (regardless of family connection) is growing. Foreign firms are also increasing the proportion of competent Indians in their middle and higher managerial ranks, partly under pressure from government. Public enterprises are drawing on trained administrators for their top managerial posts.

The relationship between management training and the educational system is changing. There is growing recognition of the value of postgraduate training programmes for selected groups of middle-management personnel; but the facilities available do not yet match the present and potential need. Too many law and arts graduates relative to the requirements of a developing industrial society are still being turned out by Indian universities.

The new Indian Institutes of Management in Ahmedabad and in Calcutta have met a real need for management education at the postgraduate level, as well as providing opportunities for experienced managers to get up to date on new management concepts and techniques. The Administrative Staff College in Hyderabad pioneered in this executive seminar activity, and the later Advanced Management Programme in Kashmir has also appealed to higher levels of management in India.

Management in India has also turned in some companies and in some centres to in-plant supervisory training programmes. This development has been stimulated greatly by the successful Training Within Industry (TWI) programme started in 1953 by the International Labour Organization at the request of the Government of India.

The development of management associations, in addition to professional societies for certain phases of management, indicates the growing interest and concern for professional as opposed to patrimonial management.

NOTES

1. The revision of this chapter has benefited from comments and suggestions from Professor Ramesh C. Goyal of the Indian Institute of Management, Ahmedabad; and from Dr. Theodore M. Alfred, visiting professor during 1963–65 at the Indian Institute of Management in Calcutta.

2 This characteristic may grow, in part, out of the authoritarian nature of the Indian social structure, in which there is a hierarchy of castes and a joint family system with a patriarchal head.

3 Compare these statements with the one by United States Ambassador to India, Chester Bowles: "There are many competent and forward-looking Indian businessmen who understand the dynamic role of modern American capitalism. Unfortunately, there are a good many others who cling to the old traditions of monopoly, with its pattern of high prices and low wages, who grasp for the quick profits of trading and speculation rather than for long-term productive investment. The Indian government is certainly justified in being tough with destructive elements of this kind." *Ambassador's Report* (New York, 1954), pp. 167-68.

4 G. L. Mehta (former Indian Ambassador to the United States), "Industrial Management," in C. N. Vakil, ed., *Papers in Economics*, Silver Jubilee Memorial Volume, University of Bombay, School of Economics and Sociology (Bombay, 1947), p. 131.

5 Naval H. Tata, "Our Present Labour Laws—Are They Based on Economic Realism?" *Commerce Annual Review Number,* December 1952, p. A-40.

6 See presidential address of Shri B. M. Birla at *The Twenty-Eighth Annual Session of the Federation of Indian Chambers of Commerce and Industry,* New Delhi, 5 March 1955.

7 McKim Marriott, "Technological Change in Overdeveloped Rural Areas," *Economic Development and Cultural Change,* no. 4 (December 1952), pp. 261-72.

8 For a discussion of this point, see Frederick Harbison and Charles A. Myers, *Management in the Industrial World: An International Analysis* (New York and London, 1959); and Clark Kerr, John T. Dunlop, Frederick Harbison, and Charles A. Myers, *Industrialism and Industrial Man: Labor and Management in Economic Growth* (New York and London, 1964).

9 This view is widely held outside India also. "Some firms, foremost among them, the house of Tata, have been notable exceptions to the speculative outlook. The Tata group has undertaken all manner of long-term industrial investment, including India's pioneer iron and steel industry. There are some signs that their example is being increasingly followed by other firms. Such a development is essential if a solid, progressive, socially acceptable business leadership is to emerge in India." "India: Progress and Plan," *Economist* (London), Supplement to vol. CLXXIV, no. 5813 (22 January 1955), p. 7.

10 *Main Report,* Labour Investigation Committee, pp. 384-85.

11 M. J. Gardner, quoted in *Capital* (Calcutta), 24 March 1955, p. 439.

12 After a breakdown in the arbitration machinery during 1953-55, the Mill-owners and the Textile Labour Association reached agreement in July 1955, on the

resumption of the machinery. Earlier the arbitration machinery had been by-passed between 1939 and 1952, when the parties used the dispute machinery provided under Bombay state legislation. The TLA was reportedly in favour of the Bombay Industrial Relations Act as a threat to maintain private arbitration in Ahmedabad.

13 Examples of these studies are: *The Group Norm Chart Method as an Incentive to Increase Production in the Loom Shed* (November 1952); *Motivation to Work: An Improvement in Motivation of Winders and Warpers and Its Effect on Loomshed Efficiency* (August 1953); and *An Analysis of the Attitudes of the Textile Workers and the Effect of These Attitudes on Working Efficiency* (September 1953). Subsequently the Psychology Division of ATIRA has undertaken a study, in collaboration with the Industrial Relations Section at MIT of the organizational structure and communication patterns in two textile mills, summarized later in this chapter. An article on this study was subsequently published in *Human Organization* (see foot-note 25, *infra*).

14 Gardner Murphy, *In the Minds of Men* (New York, 1953), p. 214. Dr. Murphy supervised a UNESCO study of human behaviour and social tensions in India and one of the studies was done in Ahmedabad by ATIRA.

15 A minority view, expressed several times in interviews with government officials, was that some foreign employers (British were mentioned specifically) prefer to deal with Communist unions because (a) government would take the employer's side in any dispute, to avoid strengthening the Communists, and (b) the employer can get a better agreement with Communists for this reason, because the Communists want to hold on. It is sometimes said that these employers fail to see the advantage of dealing fairly with INTUC unions and building up their strength. The impression gained from interviews with some of the employers so charged is that they would prefer to deal with an INTUC union but cannot refuse to discuss problems with Communist union officials who show evidence that they represent a substantial number of employees, particularly clerical workers.

16 C. N. Vakil and P. R. Brahmananda, "Reflections on India's Five Year Plan," *Pacific Affairs*, vol. XXV, no. 3 (September 1952), pp. 254-55.

17 For further examples of this type of employer response to labour problems, see George B. Baldwin, *Industrialization in South India: Case Studies in Economic Development*, Center for International Studies, Massachusetts Institute of Technology (Cambridge, Massachusetts, 1957).

18 H. C. Ganguli, *Structure and Processes of Organization*, Asia Publishing House (Bombay, 1964), p. 61.

19 For widely discussed contrast of two types of management, see Douglas McGregor, *The Human Side of Enterprise*, McGraw-Hill Book Company, Inc. (New York, 1960).

20 This information comes partly from interviews during 1954-55 and partly from the excellent study of the cotton textile industry by S. D. Mehta, *The Indian Cotton Textile Industry: An Economic Analysis*, The Textile Association (Bombay, 1953), pp. 52-85.

21 *Ibid.*, pp. 62-3.

22 G. L. Mehta, "Industrial Management," *loc. cit.*

23 S. D. Mehta, *The Indian Cotton Textile Industry: An Economic Analysis*, pp. 70-1.

24 H. C. Ganguli, *A Study on Supervision in a Government Engineering Factory*, Indian Institute of Technology (Kharagpur, 1957). Also reported in Ganguli, *Structure and Processes of Organization*, 1964, Part II. The study was conducted in the machine shop of a government-owned and -operated railway workshop employing 11,500 workers. Interviews were held with a sample of 140 workers, 13 first-line supervisors (of a total of 31 in the machine shop), all of the "chargemen" (next higher level of supervision), three of the four assistant foremen, and the foreman of the shop.

25 Fixed-question, free-answer interviews were held with the managing agents, the mill managers, and twenty-four department heads, assistants and supervisors (but not jobbers) in the weaving and spinning departments of these two mills during the first half of 1955. The study was done in collaboration with the Industrial Relations Section at Massachusetts Institute of Technology. For a brief report, see Kamla Chowdhry and A. K. Pal, "Production Planning and Organizational Morale: A Case from India," *Human Organization*, vol. 15, no. 4 (Winter 1957), pp. 11-6.

26 S. D. Mehta presents a tabulation showing 313 changes in departmental head level and higher in 357 cotton textile mills between 1946 and 1947, *op. cit.,* p. 75.

27 Group interview, 23 November 1954. *The Report of the Working Party for the Cotton Textile Industry*, Government of India (New Delhi, 1953), deplores management's "anarchical relationship" with the technicians. Chapter IX, p. 58. There are exceptions, of course, but the general pattern persists.

28 An Indian psychologist has offered a further explanation for the gulf between supervisors and subordinates in Indian industry: "A recent study of inter-group relations revealed the tremendous damage that a policy of drift is doing to human relations in government and business administration. Most administrative heads, especially in small places, like to be guided by the written regulations. Many of the day-to-day problems of discipline can be solved easily through the conference method and through the officers maintaining a personal contact with men committed to their charge. This is avoided because it requires more intelligence, effort and time. The conventional method of demanding written explanation for minor lapses, quoting regulations in reply to the grouses and complaints of the staff, continues to be in vogue. In fact, many officers promote, in the name of efficiency, a spirit of impersonality in the establishments under their charge. This practice makes for charging the social atmosphere with suspicion. Many juniors who look for personal friendship with their colleagues feel frustrated and build phantasies of being rejected and persecuted." Dr. Pars Ram, "Human Relations on the Indian Scene," Presidential Address, Section of Psychology and Educational Science, 39th Indian Science Congress, 1952, *Indian Journal of Psychology,* vol. XXVII, parts I-IV (Calcutta, 1952), p. 7.

29 Professor J. K. Galbraith of Harvard University, U. S. Ambassador to India in the early 1960's, has forcefully expressed a similar view. He concludes that "the public corporation should have autonomy in decision-making .... Autonomy ...

is a requisite of success." J. K. Galbraith, "Public Organization," *Studies Relating to Planning for National Development Economic Planning in India: Five Comments,* Indian Statistical Institute (Calcutta, March 1956), pp. 9-10.

30 *Eastern Economist,* Annual Number, 31 December 1954, p. 1057.

31 When one of these was asked by the mill manager to sign letters of appreciation to department heads who had recently completed a special supervisory training course in Job Relations (JRT), he replied, "Why should we thank them? It was their duty to take the course." Yet his father, in introducing the invited speaker to assembled mill superintendents and department heads, stressed the very great importance of "good human relations"!

32 Statement by Clifford B. Marshall, vice-president, Standard-Vacuum Oil Company, reported in *Times of India,* 20 November 1954. In the new Bombay refinery, Indians were able to take over 90 per cent of the production and technical jobs, under the guidance of United States technicians brought over on short-term assignments, within eighteen months. Data supplied by the company since 1950 for all employees show that the number of American employees has been declining at the end of each year.

	1950		1951		1952		1953		1954	
	A	*I*	*A*	*I*	*A*	*I*	*A*	*I*	*A*	*I*
Marketing	55	4,950	58	5,199	68	5,268	75	5,399	65	5,354
Refining		none		none	9	22	18	74	80*	598

	1955		1956		1957		1958		1959	
	A	*I*	*A*	*I*	*A*	*I*	*A*	*I*	*A*	*I*
Marketing	60	5,408	48	5,332	27	5,291	20	5,229	20	5,167
Refining	38	715	24	754	24	751	14	731	10	679

	1960		1961		1962		1963		1964 (*Oct.* 1)	
	A	*I*	*A*	*I*	*A*	*I*	*A*	*I*	*A*	*I*
Marketing	22	4,829	20	4,838	18	4,827	15	4,723	14	4,538
Refining	9	631	7	589	6	562	6	534	6	508

(*A*–American personnel; *I*–Indian personnel)

* Number of American overseer employees at start of refining operations, June 1954.

33 By 1963, nearly 94 per cent of the salary group of Rs. 1,000-2,000 in foreign-owned or foreign-controlled firms had been "Indianized." In all salaried groups earning Rs. 1,000 and above in foreign firms, 92 per cent were Indianized in public utility firms, 91.3 in oil companies, nearly 82 per cent in cotton mills, but only 57 per cent in banking companies, and 65 per cent in transit and transport companies owned or controlled by foreigners. *Economic Times,* Bombay, 27 February 1964.

34 S. Mathai, "The Structure of University Education," Chapter I, in *The Teaching of the Social Sciences in India,* UNESCO, Paris (1956), pp. 25-35. See also essays by Humayun Kabir and C. N. Vakil in this volume.

A study of 69 postgraduate male students at Delhi University in 1956 emphasized the preference that students have for continuing their studies instead of finding employment. Unemployment among the educated groups was partly responsible, but the implication was clear that many students liked the easy life of coffee houses and other recreation. The first preference of the students was for a government job, then a university post, and only 19 per cent wanted a job in business or industry. *New York Times,* 27 January 1957, p. 5.

35 Maurice Zinkin has pointed out the value of Indian universities in training clerks for the complex paper-work tasks of modern business and industry, but he calls attention to the "overproduction of lawyers" and the failure of parents to look ahead for careers of future importance. *Development for Free Asia* (Fair Lawn, New Jersey, 1956), Chapter 14.

36 For a fuller discussion of the relation of education and economic growth, with references to India, see Frederick Harbison and Charles A. Myers, *Education, Manpower and Economic Growth. Strategies of Human Resource Development* (McGraw-Hill Book Co., Inc., New York, 1964).

37 See C. N. Vakil, "The Teaching of Economics" in UNESCO, *The Teaching of the Social Sciences,* pp. 48-9 (on commerce courses).

38 This distinction between "business management" and "industrial administration" grew out of a belief that a similar distinction existed in United States and British management education. The grounds for this were questionable, and the distinction was later dropped.

Postgraduate evening programmes were started at the School of Economics and Sociology, University of Bombay; Delhi School of Economics, Delhi University; All-India Institute of Social Welfare and Business Management, University of Calcutta; Department of Economics, University of Madras; Victoria Jubilee Technical Institute, Bombay; and the Indian Institute of Science, Bangalore. Most of these programmes drew junior management people as students in the part-time evening courses, with some of the staff also recruited from business and industry. Only Bombay started a full programme in 1955; the others followed later in 1955, 1956 and 1957.

39 This information is drawn from a number of sources, some of them unpublished. Perhaps the most recent published survey is by Nanabhoy S. Davar, *Management Training in India.* Progressive Corporation Private Ltd., Publishers, Bombay, 1962. "Recent Developments in Management Training in India," *Indian Journal of Public Administration,* vol. IV, no. 2, April-June 1958, pp. 154-64. Some perceptive

recent comments have been made by A. P. Paul in two unpublished papers presented at seminars at the Shri Ram Centre for Industrial Relations, in Spring 1965: "Management Development Work in India—A Critique," and "New Perspectives for Management Development Work in India."

40 *Preliminary Estimates of Requirements for Managerial Personnel in India during Fourth and Fifth Five Year Plan Period*, Institute of Applied Manpower Research, New Delhi, Occasional Paper no. 2, 1964, p. 16.

41 P. S. Lokanathan (Director-General, National Council of Applied Economic Research), "Importance of Management Education: Training Programmes Need to be Broad-Based," Supplement to *Capital*, 19 December 1963, p. 61.

42 For a review of the early history of the TWI movement in India, see *Development of Supervisory Training in India*, T.W.I. Centre, Ministry of Labour, Government of India, Bombay, 1957.

43 Quoted in *Tata Monthly Bulletin*, vol. XI, no. 5 (May 1956), p. 3.

44 G. D. Birla, "Education for Business Management," *Hindustan Times*, 30 May 1953, pp. 1, 10.

CHAPTER VII

LABOUR-MANAGEMENT RELATIONS AT THE PLANT LEVEL

MANAGERIAL attitudes, organization and development, which reflect in part the response of management to the labour problems of industrialization, help to explain the character of labour-management relations at the plant level. The organizational role of the Personnel or Labour Welfare Officer is our first concern in this chapter, for it highlights both the problems and the possibilities of more effective utilization of human resources in Indian industry. Following this discussion, we shall turn to more specific aspects of handling labour-management relations at the plant level. These include negotiations with unions, leading in some cases to written agreements; discussions with works committees; and settling grievances.

The Role of the Personnel or Labour Welfare Officer

The Factories Act of 1948 required the appointment of a labour welfare officer in every firm of 500 or more employees.[1] This was an attempt to extend to all manufacturing industry a managerial function which had earlier been developed by some of the more progressive firms and employer associations.[2] The Bombay Millowners' Association, for example, had a labour officer as early as 1934, and many member mills appointed labour officers before statutory requirement. The Indian Jute Mills' Association started a labour office in 1937, and several managing agencies in the jute industry appointed labour officers as early as 1941. But the term "labour welfare" suggests the difference between the concept embodied in the law, and the personnel (or labour) officer appointed on management initiative as part of the managerial staff.

Responsibilities for labour welfare officers were spelled out in special "rules" issued by the state governments under the Factories Act of 1948.[3] For example, they were expected to see that the provisions of the Act relating to labour welfare and working

conditions were observed by management, that harmonious relations between labour and management were established, and that
grievances of workers were settled promptly. New appointees to
these positions, furthermore, were to be selected by management
from those who had earlier received special training at approved
training centres, such as the Tata Institute of Social Sciences at
Bombay, the Xavier Labour Relations Institute at Jamshedpur,
the All-India Institute of Social Welfare and Business Management
in Calcutta, or centres run by state governments, as in Bombay.[4]
The role of the labour welfare officer, therefore, was structured by
government rules; and his training was prescribed in a manner
not found in advanced industrial countries. Despite this apparently
enhanced status, however, many labour welfare officers during
interviews in India expressed frustrations which highlighted their
dilemma.[5]

On the one hand, they are supposed to keep on good terms with
workers and to interpret workers' problems to management; and,
on the other, they are often expected by management to be the
"axe men" in disciplining and discharging offending workers.[6] Or
they are expected to organize and supervise the welfare activities
which the firm provides for workers, and also to appear before
labour tribunals as management's spokesmen in opposing demands
by union representatives on behalf of the firm's workers. Yet few
said that they were consulted by top management in formulating
company labour policies or before taking actions which create new
labour problems.

Some labour walfare officers are driven by this dilemma to the
conclusion that they ought to be appointed by government and
partly or wholly paid by government in order to give them independent status. In some places, they have formed trade unions and
from time to time have voiced demands for legislative protection.
However, most labour welfare officers recognize that they would
have less influence with top management in private enterprises
if they were paid by government, because they would not have the
trust of management and would be even more completely excluded
from management policy discussions.

Another consequence of the dilemma is a view of the personnel
function in management which may be peculiar to the Indian

scene. In the words of the personnel officer of an American firm in India:

There is a fundamental difference between thinking in India and in the United States concerning the function of the Labour Officer. In my opinion, the Indian theory of the function of the Labour Officer is that he is a kind of "third force" or independent liaison officer between the conflicting groups of Management and Labour. In the US the Industrial Relations Officer is advisory or staff to line management—he is definitely identified with Management and has no neutral status. It is his duty to advise Management as well as employees on any phase of industrial relations policy or procedure of the Company for which he works. He exercises his function at all Management and staff levels.[7]

The difference between the American concept of a personnel officer as a staff expert advising and assisting the line management in handling personnel and labour relations and the Indian "third force" concept is further sharpened in this analysis of the Indian labour or labour welfare officer by an American:

Although employed by and answerable to management, the labour officer is supposed to occupy a middle ground between workers and management and to interpret each to the other. He is thought of as performing something of a social work function and much of the academic training designed for him has this orientation.[8]

The "third force" concept is appealing to those who feel either that top management does not give them enough support or that identification with management weakens their position with workers and the trade unions. This is a reflection, of course, of the low opinion which even many company labour welfare officers have of top management. "Not more than 1 per cent of the employers in India understand the relationships between good labour relations and higher production," was the collective view of one group of labour welfare officers in an open meeting. Another group said: "Some managements use labour officers to carry out decisions which have already been made and give them no leeway to negotiate or mediate." One embittered labour welfare officer in the coal industry said, "We are expected to legalize illegal actions or get out." The idea that the labour officer should have some leeway to work out his own solution to a labour management conflict is the essence of the "third force" concept, which is implicit in the rules specified under the Factories Act for labour welfare officers. This concept was also prominent in a 1956 symposium conducted by a branch of the Indian Institute of Personnel Management. The participants concluded that collective bargaining should be used to settle disputes, and that "the role of the personnel officers in this connection should be that of a conciliator."[9]

Nevertheless, there is a growing recognition in some Indian firms and in European firms operating in India that the staff role for the personnel administrator or even labour welfare officer is the most effective one.[10] In a number of cotton textile mills in Bombay, for example, the labour officer is in direct contact with the managing agents, who listen to his advice before taking disciplinary action, or before taking a position on a major grievance or demand raised by the union. The status and influence of the labour officer, more frequently called the Chief Personnel Officer, was even higher in most of the British and American firms interviewed. There was a carry-over of the organizational structure for personnel administration found in the home countries of these firms. Similarly, in three public corporations, the role of the personnel officer was clearly that of a high-status advisory and service officer. The personnel manager of the government-owned Sindri Fertilizer Factory, for example, wrote in the company newspaper:

It should be obvious . . . that members of any Personnel Department, if they are to fulfil their role effectively—can only be guided by a spirit of service and mission. The concept of authority must be foreign to those who believe in personnel principles and practices. They should accept that their authority can at best be only a reflection of the confidence that they can create in the minds of all as regards the soundness of the advice they render.[11]

In this firm, the managing director meets daily with the personnel manager to discuss union grievances and any problems involved in securing uniformity in handling labour relations problems in the line organization. Line-staff relations have been improved through a series of meetings with department heads on their personnel problems.

Further developments also indicate that a more realistic view of the labour officer's functions is gaining greater acceptance. In January 1957, the Ministry of Labour convened a Special Committee to consider whether any changes were necessary in the rules pertaining to the recruitment, conditions of service, and the duties of welfare officers.[12] The rules in question were those published in 1951 [Labour Officers (Central Pool) Recruitment and Conditions of Service Rules] covering government undertakings. Under these rules, the labour officer was to "act as a negotiating officer with trade unions," while at the same time he was required "to maintain a neutral attitude during legal strikes or lockouts and to help in bringing about a peaceful settlement." The Committee felt that these provisions were contradictory and recommended the abolition of the principle of neutrality and substituted the words "act as a liaison officer between management and labour" for the words "as a negotiating officer with trade unions." An underlying pressure for this change is the desire to strengthen the personnel role as an integral part of top managerial decisions.

Handling Labour-Management Relations

The dilemma confronting the labour welfare or personnel officer in Indian industry is also reflected in the handling of labour-management relations.

Concurrently with legislation designed to settle labour disputes, the Indian government has also been encouraging bipartite relations through indirect means. Since the commencement of planning, the government's efforts have been directed towards encouraging direct negotiations, joint consultation and orderly settlement of grievances at the work place. Industry-wide settlements have been encouraged through tripartite wage-boards in which concerned management and workers' representatives play a dominant role; negotiated collective agreements on *ad hoc* or general issues as well as agreements to arbitrate differences have received public support. Since 1958, the government has also attempted to further joint consultation in selected plants by means of joint management councils. Model grievance procedures have also been recommended with a view to encouraging orderly resolution of plant-level complaints. These are supplementary to the compulsory procedures provided by legislation and have been promoted mainly under the auspices of the tripartite Indian Labour Conference. These steps will be discussed briefly later in this chapter and elaborated in greater detail in Chapters VIII and IX dealing with government policy.

It must be noted here that the resultant pattern of labour relations reveals great variety. There is no dominant pattern because of variations in managerial attitudes, the approaches of unions and, finally, the positions taken by the affected governments in the centre or the states. Four types of industrial relations situation may be distinguished.

The first centres in essentially chaotic situations, characterized by poor or weak management, employing primarily unskilled labour or engaged principally in manual occupations. Only rudimentary efforts have been made by the employers to develop the personnel function, and neither the employers' nor the producers' associations have been active in promoting defined policies for stabilizing labour relations. This characterization is applicable to isolated employers of labour, particularly in such areas as the coal or manganese mining centres, where externally sponsored organizing drives can be easily checked and it is unlikely that the ill-educated workers will themselves develop sufficient cohesiveness and discipline to protest effectively against employer policies. The result for the employer has not, however, been an unmixed blessing as the manifestations of protest have tended to be irrational, violent and destructive.[13]

A second and more hopeful type is presented in particular local or regional situations where employers are relatively well organized for the purposes of handling questions of industrial relations. Even here three sub-categories should be distinguished. There are associations which are organized only for the purpose of providing legal or similar advice or representation to their constituents; secondly, there are associations which employ a pool of personnel (or labour) officers who serve as trouble-shooters and attempt to provide expert personnel advice for their members; and finally, there are associations which actually negotiate with unions on selected general issues.[14]

A third type of employers are those in the "All-India" industries like Ports and Docks, Banking, Railways, Posts and Telegraphs, Defence, etc., where the Central rather than the state authorities play the key role.[15] The Central government's involvement arises from one of the three circumstances : as an exclusive employer (railways, defence); as the principal employer (the banking industry, where the employer's role is shared with private enterprise); and as *de facto* employer, as in Ports and Docks, where the Central government nominees have assumed effective authority through Port Commission or Dock Labour Boards.[16]

The last type consists of individual employers, rather than employers' associations or the government as a collective constitutional body. We are concerned with two categories within this group, the group of companies representing the private sector and a growing number of manufacturing enterprises in the public sector. Generally the private units belong to one or more employers' or producers' associations, and all are affected by industry or area-wide decisions by tribunals or wage boards. The private units in this group deserve to be distinguished from the rest of the private employers, however, because of their keen interest in labour harmony and commitment to progressive personnel management as a high-level management responsibility. A well-organized personnel department, including more or less orderly procedures of consultation and grievance handling, constitutes one of the observable characteristics of this group. There is a keen desire to adopt relatively more sophisticated tools of management, including works study, job evaluation, formal selection, induction and training programmes, and incentive schemes. These firms are also in the forefront of employers who have laid considerable stress on training at various ranks, including in such training responsibility for handling personnel. Relations with the unions are not always smooth, but a surprisingly large number have made progress here too.

It is important to stress, however, that the limited and more or less formal relationships with labour organizations in India are conducted within the framework of an extensive set of rules and procedures embodied in various Central government and state labour relations laws. The pioneer piece of legislation, bringing the government into the labour-management relationship directly, was the Bombay Industrial Disputes Act of 1938, which provided for compulsory conciliation of disputes, recognition of "representative" trade unions by employers, and the approval by the Bombay Commissioner of Labour of plant rules (called "Standing Orders") formulated by the employer.[17]

The principle of government intervention in labour-management relations was extended during World War II by an amendment to the Bombay Act enabling the government to refer almost any dispute to a court of arbitration, and the Central government achieved the same powers to declare strikes illegal through promulgation of Rule 81A of the Defence of India Act. This wartime legislation set the pattern for the two postwar industrial dispute settlement Acts: the Bombay Industrial Relations Act of 1946 and the Central government's Industrial Disputes Act of 1947. The Bombay law modified and extended the 1938 Act by strengthening the requirement of compulsory recognition of a "representative union" and other categories of unions,[18] providing for union representation at hearings before the Labour Commissioner on approval or modification of the employer's "Standing Orders," requiring the establishment of joint works committees in each plant, and providing for reference of unsettled disputes over these or other matters to labour courts for binding awards.[19] Thus collective bargaining in the sense of direct dealings between management and unions without the intervention of a third party (the government) was made difficult—unless both management and a dominant union really preferred direct relationships.

The Industrial Disputes Act of 1947, like the Bombay law, provided for limitation of the right to strike and reference of disputes to conciliation or industrial tribunals.[20] Even if the government does not refer a dispute to a tribunal, either party may request reference and the government is bound to refer "if it is satisfied that the persons applying represent the majority of each party." Provision for appeal of tribunal decisions to newly established Appellate Tribunals came in a 1950 amendment,[22] and the Bombay provisions on "Standing Orders" were included for all India in the Industrial Employment (Standing Orders) Act of 1946. Finally, the 1947 Act also provided for the establishment of works committees in plants under Central government jurisdiction and empowered state government to require such committees in firms employing 100 or more workers.

The typologies noted above may help us identify the progress made in Indian industries towards plant-level relationships. The fourth category is a distinct minority among the firms involved but nevertheless influential and in the forefront. The limited progress towards plant-level relationships generally, as well as the achievements of the noteworthy exceptions, may be discussed within the following framework :

   (i) negotiations or disputes settlements between employers and unions representing their workers ;

  (ii) consultation or coordinated action at the plant or shop level ; and

 (iii) grievance settlement procedures.

The significance of each of these with examples from Indian experience will be discussed in the following pages.

Negotiations with Unions

Collective bargaining, or, more accurately, collective relations with unions, tends to be industry-wide in a particular locality in such industries as cotton textiles, jute, and engineering. The law of industrial relations favours this type of bargaining. For example, the Bombay Millowners' Association deals with the Rashtriya Mill Mazdoor Sangh, which is the INTUC union with "representative" status under the Bombay Industrial Relations Act of 1947.[23] Until 1956, however, there was no signed collective agreement between these two parties; major issues were referred to the industrial tribunal for decision, and after 1950 these decisions were frequently taken to the Appellate Tribunal with consequent delays.[24] The labour office of the Millowners' Association represents member mills at every stage of a dispute with the union after the mill management has been unable to settle it. In 1956, the Bombay Millowners'

Association and the INTUC union signed a five-year agreement for determination of "bonus," similar to the earlier one in Ahmedabad, as discussed below.

In the jute industry in Calcutta there is no single dominant union, and the Indian Jute Mills' Association does not officially recognize any of the several competing unions: INTUC, Socialist or Communist. But its labour officers have informal relations with representatives of these unions in the different mill areas as worker grievances are brought up for discussion and settlement. The value which the IJMA places on these informal relations with union representatives has been cited earlier. Another major function of the IJMA labour office is that of representing member mills in cases before industrial tribunals. Basic wages and dearness allowance were increased by a Special Bench of the Labour Appellate Tribunal in June 1956.

The most striking example of collective relations between an industry association in a local area and a strong union, however, is the long experience of the Ahmedabad Millowners' Association and the Textile Labour Association, referred to earlier in this and the three preceding chapters. Except for a breakdown during 1938–52 and a period of difficulty in 1953–55, these parties have had a voluntary arbitration system for settlement of all disputes since 1920, when Gandhi first encouraged the arbitration of the strike which followed the formation of the union and its initial wage demands. The arbitration agreement, to be sure, is procedural; there is no agreement on substantive issues as such. But it is a voluntary signed agreement between two responsible parties,[25] and it has been supplemented by specific agreements providing for the introduction of increased workloads under certain conditions. These latter supplementary agreements are substantive, since they cover the specific circumstances under which any mill may introduce higher weaving or spinning work assignments. For instance, in 1955, the TLA and the Mill owners reached an agreement on the matter of year-end bonuses.[26] Direct collective bargaining in Ahmedabad has also taken place on other major issues.[27]

Direct negotiations involving comprehensive agreements or sustained collective bargaining relationships between individual employers and unions are still rare in India, but they are found under two conditions: (1) when the employer is genuinely interested in developing constructive relations with a union representing his employees, and (2) when such a union exists without serious threats from rival unions. These two conditions, it may be noted, are not unrelated for, in several of the instances reported below, the employer encouraged and nurtured a new union to a point where it represented a majority of the firm's employees.

Some examples from the interviews in 1954–55 will illustrate the nature of individual company-union collective bargaining relationships in India today.

A British company recognized a newly formed union in 1946, and signed an agreement with it covering Standing Orders, grievance procedure, year-end bonus and other matters. As the manager explained, "We had a tradition of negotiating with unions in the UK and we wanted to do the same here." The union was subsequently affiliated with the INTUC, and the president of the union became a member of the INTUC national executive. The union represented 90 per cent of the workers, collected dues on company premises immediately after workers were paid, and had 20 elected representatives who served as shop stewards (in addition to the six elected officers). There was a joint piecework committee, to which unsettled disputes over rates were referred, and several union representatives received training in time-study methods. The union president used to spend about two days a week at the plant, since he was an "outsider" active in other unions also, but he had complete and easy access to the plant manager and other officials. There had been no cases referred to industrial tribunals, and the original agreement had been modified in annual negotiations. There were unresolved problems such as restriction of output in one section of the plant, but the management was moving slowly because the union president "might lose control of the union if the Communists are given a good talking point."

Another British company insisted at the outset when two unions were formed that it would deal with the one which had the largest membership certified by the Bombay Registrar of Unions. This resulted, however, in two rivals—an intra-company union and an HMS (Socialist) union—uniting to form a joint negotiating committee. After tribunal decisions on the 1950 and 1951 bonuses, the company and the union negotiated a "package" on the 1952 and 1953 bonus amounts, and this pattern continued. The chief personnel officer of the company frequently held informal meetings with the union negotiating committee, apart from contract discussions, to discuss ideas for proposed changes in policy or programmes. He explained his approach:

> I tell them that I've been thinking over a problem and may take some action, but that I'd like to get their reactions and sugges-tions. This is participation, but there is too little of it in Indian industry. Don't let any labour officer or employer say that these things can't be done in India because of the illiteracy of the Indian worker or the irresponsible union leaders. These are just alibis for the failure of labour officers to be effective in selling their ideas to top management, or of management's failure to make a genuine effort to build good relations. The Indian worker, who is often blamed, is the least to blame for the present conditions.

An Indian-owned and -managed engineering firm, with an out-standing reputation for progressive management, has had an agreement with a Communist union representing 80 per cent of its employees. This followed a strike in 1953, and the basis for the present relationship is the insistence of the management that the union follow the Soviet Labour Code in which the responsibility of workers' unions for good discipline, observance of production standards, and low absenteeism is stressed! Management believes that it is better "to sit around the table and discuss plant problems with this union than to refuse to recognize it." There is also a works committee comprising ten elected worker representatives, which meets once a week for discussion of grievances, but this was first established in 1945 and is separate from the union. Appeal to the union is the final step in the grievance procedure; but, according to management, no cases have gone beyond the works committee level. This case illustrates the separation which is found in some firms between the union and the works committee, and their rela-tions to the grievance procedure.

In a European firm in the same region, the Communists were in a majority in the union executive, but non-Communists held the top positions. Following three strikes in 1946, the union was recognized and an agreement concluded. An adviser to the company was subsequently made a full-time officer to handle labour relations, and he served both as chairman of the company negotiating committee and as chairman of the works committee which has union representatives on it. The managing director of the company also spent about half of his time in negotiations and in works committee meetings to discuss grievances; but the responsibility for company decisions was in the hands of the full-time labour relations officer. As the Managing Director explained, "Because he takes personal interest in labour matters and spends his full time on them, we have had little trouble in reaching agreements or in implementing them." There had been no tribunal cases since 1947. Labour peace in this firm had its costs, however, for some line management people were restive under the unusual delegation of responsibility to a staff officer. He also was not entirely convinced of line management's good faith, and was concerned about the future of the union. "I have to nourish it," he explained, "and even after all these years it hesitates to take responsibility for saying 'no' to weak cases. I could break the union any time I wanted to."

An American company with branches in several Indian cities had begun to negotiate long-term agreements in 1954 and 1955 with non-Communist unions, representing either its clerical or labour employees, and in at least one case with a Communist union. Terms of these agreements included an annual bonus related to the levels prescribed by earlier tribunal awards, working hours, lunch breaks, a slight increase in base rates, and other similar terms of employment. The real objective of management here was to avoid costly and time-consuming appearances before tribunals, and evidently the unions also preferred voluntary agreements. By early 1956, three-year agreements were concluded in all of the company's Indian plants and offices.

The Indian Aluminium Company, affiliate of the Aluminium Company of Canada, negotiated two collective bargaining agreements with an INTUC union when a new managing director came in 1949.[28] There had been strikes under the previous management, and he was determined to change the relationship, bringing a competent industrial relations director to the company a year later.

One of the two written agreements provided for a monthly production bonus scheme and an annual productivity bonus, and
terms were being re-negotiated in 1955. The other agreement,
covering the major works of the company, ran for five years and
contained a number of clauses similar in some respects to an
American collective bargaining agreement. Among these were:
(1) a list of management's rights; (2) a grievance procedure;
(3) a joint pledge to avoid unfair labour practices; (4) specification of
production standards; (5) conditions under which employees may
be transferred by management; (6) payment of one month's basic
wage or salary as an advance on the annual productivity bonus,
or in addition to it "if peaceful conditions, spirit of wholehearted
cooperation and good relations are maintained throughout the
year and the stipulated output for the year is obtained"; (7) recruitment of eight new workers from among refugees and among present
employees' "near relatives"; (8) establishment of a Joint Personnel
Relations Committee and a Joint Production Committee; (9) acceptance of a wage structure developed by a management engineering
firm; (10) a no-strike, no-lockout clause; and (11) withdrawal
of certain disputes pending before the Labour Appellate Tribunal.
This agreement expired in March 1956, and a second five-year
agreement was signed on 1 September 1956. Like the first agreement, this is a remarkable document of thirty-seven printed pages,
similar in scope and content to many union-management agreements in the United States.[29]

Both the Managing Director and the Personnel Manager believed
that these agreements had improved relationships and avoided
strikes and slowdowns.[30] The union was regarded as strong and
responsible. It claimed 90 per cent of the 1,200 workers as members,
and the company provided facilities for collection of dues and bulletin board notices. Only one "outsider" was a member of the union
executive; the others were company employees. Subsequently,
the management of the Indian Aluminium Company has attempted
to negotiate similar agreements with unions in its other plants in
various parts of India.[31] On 3 December 1956, a five-year agreement
was reached with the Muri Aluminium Factory Workers' Union at
the Muri Works in the Ranchi district of Bihar state. The report
of the personnel manager is illuminating:

Here we had to deal with a union different in many respects from the one in Belur (near Calcutta). Nevertheless, we are convinced from our own experience that, given the proper climate, it is possible to negotiate such agreements with unions in India though they differ from one another in ideology, outlook and other matters. The Muri Agreement, as the one in Belur, has the same pattern with a "No strike–No lockout" clause and provision for fair incentive bonus. Here also the union declares that profit-sharing bonus is not conducive to the advancement of the interest of labour, management or industry.[32]

An important public enterprise, the Sindri Fertilizer Factory, reached an agreement in June 1954 with the Fertilizer Factory Workers' Union, affiliated to the INTUC and representing many of the firm's 7,000 employees. This provided for : (1) collection of dues near the place of payment of wages ; (2) a grievance procedure with specific steps up to the Managing Director; and (3) the right of the union to send a representative to "every enquiry affecting a worker." The Personnel Manager held weekly meetings with the union officers to discuss outstanding problems and grievances, and a few cases went to the Managing Director. All except one disagreement had been settled up to mid-1955, and this was referred to a state labour department official for arbitration.

The Tata Iron and Steel Company in Jamshedpur has had one of the best union-management relationships in Indian industry, beginning with recognition of the Tata Workers' Union in the twenties. There was a stormy initial period, but stability in the union came after the war with the presidency of Michael John, former employee of the company and president of the INTUC in 1953. The Tata management has been concerned about the need for higher productivity in the mills and also about the continued stability of the union in the face of rival threats. A series of agreements covering wages and incentive schemes was reached after the war, and a new path-breaking three-year agreement was signed in January 1956.[33] Among the provisions new to labour agreements in India were: (1) joint determination to explore ways of progressively associating employees with management at various levels; (2) agreement in principle to maintain union membership and check-off of dues ; (3) union recognition of the right of the company to introduce new methods and equipment and to fix the number of men required, subject to binding arbitration if there is union disagreement after a trial period; (4) a company pledge of no retrenchment as a result of rationalization; (5) revision of the wage structure, particularly between mill and town employees ; and (6) construction of additional housing and hospital space for company employees.[34]

A supplemental agreement, providing for "workers' participation in management," was signed by the Tata Iron and Steel Company and the union in August 1956, with effect from 1 October 1956. The Preamble expresses the hope that the agreement will help to satisfy the workers' urge for self-expression and, at the same time, promote increased productivity. A three-tiered system of joint councils is established. At the base are joint departmental councils, one for each department, and above these are a joint works council for the entire works and a joint town council dealing with matters relating to the company's town, medical, health and education departments which administer these services in Jamshedpur. At the top of these is a joint consultative council of management. While all of the councils are advisory, the agreement was hailed by Michael John, president of the Tata Workers' Union, as a "major advance towards the national objective of a socialistic pattern of society. . . . The workers of Jamshedpur are the first in India to give concrete shape to the concept of workers' participation in management."[35] But Sir Jehangir Ghandy, Director-in-Charge of the company, said that the agreement avoided the extreme of "co-determination" in Germany and "is fully in keeping with our middle-of-the-way philosophy of life." [36]

Our summary indicates that collective bargaining agreements in individual firms are more frequent among foreign than among Indian companies. This squares with the statements of Indian trade union leaders quoted earlier in the chapter. The Tata management and a few others, however, are clear exceptions to this generalization, and the same could be said of a few public enterprises, such as Sindri. There is also some collective bargaining by the Central government employing ministries, such as Posts and Telegraphs, Defence and Railways.[37] An agreement was signed between the

Bombay State Transport Corporation and the State Transport Workers' Union, covering nearly 20,000 workers and recognizing the union as the sole collective bargaining agent.[38] This was characterized as a "landmark in collective bargaining in the public sector ... which has hitherto been neglected."[39] Wage and salary classifications were established for different grades of labour, free uniforms were provided, earned leave and paid holidays were specified, and wage or salary advances were to be given prior to certain religious holidays.

In the absence of formal collective relations with bona fide unions, however, many employers deal with works committees on matters which would normally be handled by a local union.

Experience with Works Committees

We have already noted the legal requirement for the establishment of works committees, as in the Bombay Industrial Relations Act of 1946 and the Industrial Disputes Act of 1947. According to the latter Act, the committees are consultative; they are to promote measures for securing and preserving unity and good relations between the employer and the workmen and to that end to comment upon matters of their common interest or concern and endeavour to compose any material difference of opinion in respect of such matters.[40]

Workers' representatives are to be appointed in consultation with a trade union, if any exists. But this practice is not always observed and friction results, as in one important plant where the state government insisted upon open elections for works committee members instead of union-appointed members. A rival faction within the union was able to capture the works committee in 1954, and repudiate the working arrangements which had been reached earlier by the management and the former works committee. In Bombay state, this is avoided by giving representative unions the right to nominate employee members on the works committee.

Disputes have also arisen over whom the recognised unions may nominate to represent the workers on the works committee. For instance, in 1952, the Engineering Mazdoor Sabha in the Premier Automobile plant in Bombay got the members of the works committee to agitate for its secretary's presence in all its meetings. The management yielded, resulting in the participation of a key "outsider" trade unionist in the deliberations of the committee.[41] Some of the advantages of a joint consultative forum, as distinct from bargaining sessions, were obviously impaired.

The spread of works committees under this legislation has not been rapid, despite earlier reports.[42] A special tabulation of works committees in plants in undertakings coming under the jurisdiction of the Central government legislation showed that there were only 657 such committees in December 1954,[43] and 367 of these were in coal mines. During 1962, there were 871 works committees functioning in the central sphere.[44] The total number of committees in undertakings under central and state government jurisdiction was 2,095 for the year 1953–54.[45] The grand total of works committees, production committees and joint committees in the various states taken together was 2,434 for the year 1962.[46]

These data seem to corroborate the widespread opinion, at least in management circles, that the committees have been ineffective. As one spokesman at the management conference put it, "Many firms have either given up trying or continue to have them on sufferance." Part of the difficulty is the confusion over the proper role of works committees; and this is evident from the different purposes for which works committees have been used in Indian industry.

In a few cases, works committees deal with actual production problems. In a machine tool plant, for example, one meeting of the committee in 1954 dealt with quality problems and bottlenecks in the assembly department, the need for a quality control system, and the difficulties in getting government approval for import of parts necessary to keep production schedules moving. Grievances were not discussed in this meeting, for management had good relations with an HMS engineering union. The union representatives on the committee were young, alert, and better educated than the average Indian worker. A similar experience was reported by a large jute mill, where the management discussed re-allocation of production and its impact on the workforce with the works committee, and had a separate joint Training Advisory Committee to develop criteria for the selection of trainees and methods of training for skilled jobs. A final example is the Advisory Development and

Production Committee established in several departments of Tata Iron and Steel Company, to discuss departmental costs and how they might be reduced through avoidance of waste, damage to equipment, and so on.

A second and more frequent use for works committees is in negotiating outstanding differences between management and labour, in the absence of established union-management relations and sometimes in place of them. A Bombay company, for example, refused to recognize a Communist union following go-slow and violence, and began negotiating with a works committee. Since 1953, the year-end bonus has been negotiated without going to an industrial tribunal, and other subjects on which agreement has been reached through the works committee included grade wage scales, new leave rules, and changes in the Standing Orders. However, at one committee meeting of this company, several requests from the worker's side were to be "referred to the manager for action." Much of the meeting was taken up with reading the manager's written comments on questions raised by worker representatives at the last meeting, action on applications by individual workers for grants from the plant welfare fund to meet emergency expenses due to sickness, discussion of individual complaints from members about the water cooler, poor ventilation, and other problems.

A second example of negotiations with a works committee was the case of a large textile firm which refused to continue negotiating year-end bonus with a union whose president led it out of the INTUC and into a Communist union. The 1953–54 bonus amount was then discussed with the works committee, and an agreement was reached late in 1954. Periodic meetings of the works committee also discussed worker's grievances, but on some questions the committee was only advisory, or was so regarded by top management. A lower management representative on the committee explained :

Since recommendations are not binding on management, the company representatives on the committee feel, why oppose worker suggestions among the people we have to deal with every day? So we agree to many worker proposals, knowing that management will turn them down—but we don't get the blame.

In another plant the works committee was authorized by its constitution to deal with problems of discipline, method of payment of wages, distribution of working hours and holidays, questions of physical welfare, ways and means of increasing efficiency, settlement of grievances, and elimination of defective work and waste. The minutes of a February 1955 meeting showed that the chairman (the company Works Manager) started with a review of production and sales for the month, then took up problems of safety, mobile canteen in the shop, fortnightly payment of wages instead of monthly, cleanliness of factory premises, and misuse of water-closets.

Discussion and settlement of grievances is the third, and most frequent, activity of works committees. This is evident from the examples cited earlier. It is not unusual for the works committee to hear grievances for the first time, brought up by worker representatives in the absence of some specific step-by-step grievance procedure. In one large Bombay cotton textile mill, for example, the management attitude was to "allow workers to express themselves in these meetings; bring out their full grievances." Sample complaints at one monthly meeting included: (1) earnings had dropped because warp beams were poor; (2) experienced weavers were being bypassed by supervisors in job assignments; (3) a drilling machine in the mechanical department was out of order. Presumably these complaints could have gone to the supervisors, department heads, labour officer, or mill manager; but they were first brought up in the works committee, where the worker representatives were appointed by the representative INTUC union. Nonetheless, management in this mill regarded the works committee as "good, because it airs all grievances before they get too serious."

Further information has been revealed in recent surveys and may be briefly summarized. A survey conducted in six companies in Bombay in 1961,[47] showed that in three of them there were no works committees. Its findings also show that in the remaining companies the committees were not functioning well. In one of them, where there was no union, the committee was nominated by the management. Moreover, the committee did not meet at regular intervals. In another company there was a strong union, but this was not recognized, although their leaders were elected to the works committee. It is said that owing to this the top officials, including the chairman of the company, attended its meetings. However, most of the problems could not be settled by the committee, in part because the management was attempting to evolve the works committee as an alternative to the union. After four years of participation in the works committee, the union successfully opposed its further continuance. The works committee (called the Departmental Representative Committee) was active in only one company.

Another study based on the records available at the Bombay Labour Commissioner's Office of undertakings of different sizes ranging from 60 to 3,800 workers, in various types of concerns in industry, trade and administration was made in 1959.[48] After a study of the records, the investigating staff attended some meetings of the works committees and conducted interviews. The study reported that in 63 per cent of the undertakings interviewed covering 55 per cent of the workers no difficulties were experienced in the functioning of the works committees. Of the managements interviewed, 26 per cent (covering 38 per cent of the workers) expressed difficulties which included outside union influence, rival unions, lack of fruitful discussions, and lack of interest among workers. Nevertheless, they reported satisfaction with the works committee. However, a close reading of the report reveals that there is considerable scope for improvement in the functioning of the works committee. One conclusion that emerged from the study was that the managements did not regard the committees as harmful—a conclusion that is at odds with the more detailed plant-level survey mentioned above. At the same time the study points out that both management and labour agreed that "it would be desirable and *possible* to make their committees more active and effective by bringing up regularly on the agenda reviews of their production, efficiency, wastage, consumer complaints, facilities required for work and discussions of the ways and means for improving their productivity."

Two public sector concerns are the subject of recent studies. In the meetings of the Hindustan Housing Factory Limited, a number of issues were discussed,[49] including modes of payment to

casual workers, sale of wood scrap, payment of dearness allowance
to canteen staff, unsettled past payments involving a grant of Rs. 5
as interim relief, promotion of workers to higher posts, etc. Here
it appears that the works committee was in effect a negotiating
machinery and functioned in a climate of considerable industrial
unrest and tension. It appears to have ceased to function after an
initial trial period. The report of the experience of another concern,
The Hindustan Insecticides Limited, is not more encouraging.[50]

At this point, it may be helpful to summarize the preceding
discussion by suggesting several categories of labour-management
relationships at the plant level, involving either unions or works
committees or both:

1. Some managements deal with or negotiate agreements with
   unions representing their employees, and there is no separate
   works committee despite the statutory requirement. We have
   seen that the spread of works committees throughout Indian
   industry is by no means complete.
2. Other managements may deal with unions, frequently in
   connection with cases before industrial tribunals involving
   part or all of the industry in a locality. But in their plants,
   these same managements may also deal with works committees
   on plant welfare problems and individual grievances. In
   these cases, the works council may be (a) controlled by the
   dominant union, (b) fought over by rival unions, or (c)
   nurtured by the employer in preference to an outside union
   acting as a rival to the union.
3. In the absence of recognized or strong unions, many managements deal only with works committees at the plant level,
   and in some cases they negotiate oral and written agreements covering wages and working conditions with these
   committees.

Some attempts have been initiated in recent years to secure a
coordinated development of works committees and to define their
functions more clearly. The 17th session of the Indian Labour
Conference held in 1959 decided to constitute a Committee consist-
ing of the government, employers, workers and an observer from the

Indian Institute of Personnel Management, to examine the material on the subject of the works committees. The Committee, which met in November 1959, drew up "guiding principles" relating to the composition and functioning of works committees. It decided that it was not practicable to draw an exhaustive list of the functions of works committees, and advocated some flexibility of approach for the system to work properly. An illustrative list of items which a committee will normally deal with, and those which it will not deal with, are briefly as follows: It will deal with (*a*) conditions of work such as ventilation, lighting, temperature, etc.; (*b*) amenities such as canteens, drinking water; (*c*) safety and accident-prevention; (*d*) adjustment of festival and national holidays; (*e*) administration of welfare and fine funds; (*f*) promotion of thrift and savings; (*g*) educational and recreational activities; and (*h*) implementation and review of decisions arrived at in its meetings. On the other hand it will not deal with (*a*) wages and allowances; (*b*) bonus and profit-sharing; (*c*) rationalization and fixation of work loads; (*d*) fixation of standard labour force; (*e*) planning and development programmes; (*f*) retrenchment and lay-off; (*g*) victimization for trade union activities; (*h*) provident fund, gratuity schemes and other retiring benefits; (*i*) incentive schemes; and (*j*) housing and transport services.

It appears from the above list that the "guiding principles" aim at focusing attention of the works committees on day-to-day problems and away from bargaining issues or intractable items like victimization. However, it was also agreed that the two lists were not rigidly demarcated but were flexible in scope.[51] This may continue to be quite important in the absence of institutionalized and functioning alternatives. Thus in many plants the works committee may have considerable potential as an ultimate "clearing house" which embraces discussion of all affected issues. The works committee may thus be an ultimate internal forum to handle unresolved issues. In fact, the First Five Year Plan especially states that works committees should be "the culminating step in the grievance machinery."[52] The objectives of a well-functioning grievance system will continue, however, to be the resolution of grievances on a step-by-step basis at the lowest levels—a condition, as we shall see presently, rarely attained in Indian practice.

Grievance Procedures and Settlement of Grievances

Formal grievance procedures, with well-defined steps to be followed, are fairly rare in Indian industry, even among the Indian plants of foreign firms. The most frequent procedure is a highly compressed one: the worker goes with his complaint to his jobber or supervisor, and failing to get a satisfactory answer, goes directly to the labour or labour welfare officer. Discussion and settlement of grievances is, as we saw earlier in the chapter, one of the major duties of the labour or labour welfare officer in most firms. Sometimes this is the first and final step in the procedure; for, as one explained, "When workers come directly to me with a complaint, and I find that they haven't even seen their supervisor about it, they tell me that he won't listen; and if I don't hear it, nobody will." Occasionally, in a firm characterized by a benevolent paternalism in the top management, the managing agent will allow individual workers to come directly to him to air their grievances and seek redress. As in the case of the labour officer, this encourages short-circuiting of lower levels of management, but may permit hearing of grievances that would otherwise not be expressed to anyone.

The most successful area-wide grievance procedure is found in Ahmedabad, where the Textile Labour Association states in its *Annual Report:* "It is the primary function of a trade union to endeavour to redress the grievances of its members."[53] Here the union clearly took the initiative in establishing grievance machinery. Through a system of elected shop representatives and full-time union "inspectors," grievances are handled within the individual mills and, if not settled there, are taken up by the officers of TLA with mill managements or with the Millowners' Association. The conciliation and arbitration machinery mentioned earlier in Chapters IV and V is the final stage in this procedure. In contrast, grievances in the jute industry around Calcutta are settled more or less informally through the initiative of the Labour Department of the Indian Jute Mills' Association. Labour officers in various districts meet with union representatives (though there is no recognized union) and with workers about their complaints and grievances, and then attempt to reach a settlement in subsequent consultation with mill management officials.

A few of the firms interviewed had formal procedures, sometimes announced unilaterally in the absence of any recognized union, or developed jointly with a union. In one government-owned plant, for example, where the management refused to recognize a union dominated by "outsiders," the grievance procedure included the following steps: (1) worker to foreman; (2) worker to superintendent; (3) worker to department head or Works Manager; and finally (4) worker to Personnel Manager, acting for the Managing Director. There was also a works committee in this plant, and grievances involving more than one worker were brought up in these meetings. According to one management representative, "the works committee is not popular with the union because either it is regarded as a stooge of management or it arrogates to itself subjects which the union feels it should discuss with management."

Two large privately owned firms, one Indian and the other European, had grievance procedures involving joint committees which included union representatives. Both companies considered their labour-management relations excellent, although there was some evidence in the first that the power given to the joint committees to reverse grievance settlements made by the lower line management was a source of much discontent in managerial ranks The grievance procedure in this firm included the following steps:

1. The worker brings his complaint to the plant personnel officer, who discusses it with the foreman and the superintendent. The decision is made by the superintendent, although the personnel officer may transmit it to the worker and his union steward.

2. If dissatisfied, the worker and the union representative go to the General Superintendent of the Deputy Director of personnel. They take up the problem with the full-time general secretary of the union.

3. Unsettled grievances then go to plant works committees, which have four management representatives and four union representatives elected by the union executive committee. These plant committees have the power to investigate the facts of the case and try to reach a decision. If the decision is unanimous, it is usually accepted by both the union and the

management. The committees meet weekly.

4. A central works committee, composed of four representatives of top management and four top officers of the union, meets weekly to handle grievances on which the plant works committees have split. Unanimous decisions are binding.

5. Final authority to decide a grievance rests with the managing agent, who, however, gets few cases, since the great majority are decided at the joint committee level.

Most of the grievances which came before the joint committees in this company during 1954 were over disciplinary action and promotions. For example, at a meeting of one of the committees in November 1954, there was unanimous agreement to reduce or commute four of six appealed disciplinary decisions of lower management. At another, a committee voted unanimously to retain the written warning given to a millwright who had "refused to obey orders and behaved insolently," but it failed to reach an agreement on several other disciplinary actions, which were then referred to the general committee for decision. This committee frequently reached decisions upholding earlier management action; but, as one member explained, "A modicum of cases has to be conceded by management representatives in order to prevent the union representatives from walking out."

In the other firm, a similar procedure had been set up in 1952, terminating in two Mill Labour Advisory Committees and one top Central Advisory Committee. The full-time paid officer of the union (an "outsider") served on the top committee with three elected union representatives from different departments, and four representatives were appointed by management. The mill committees comprised entirely inside union representatives and management appointees. During the first year, 143 grievances were taken up at the departmental level, between supervisors and elected union representatives, and 88 decisions were termed "favourable to workers."[54] These involved, in order of frequency, working conditions, leave, seniority, wages, work-load, punishment, transfer, promotion, unfair treatment by supervisory staff, working clothes, and others. Only 15 of the departmental decisions unfavourable to workers were appealed to the mill committees. But 36 additional cases were brought directly to the committees, as they involved dismissals in which the mill manager rather than department heads had made the decision.

The decisions in the mill committees were "advisory" to top management, which took action favourable to workers in 16 of the 51 cases. But only 11 were appealed by the union to the Central Labour Advisory Committee, which decided five against workers. This decision, however, was really the decision of management members of the committee, following discussion in the top committee, and subsequently communicated to the union. For example, the minutes of one meeting of the Central Committee in 1954 showed that the outside union representative had brought up five grievances, four of which involved individual promotions and a fifth wage rates on a particular job. Management representatives on the committee raised numerous objections to the union's demands, and subsequently the secretary of the committee (a management representative) notified the union representatives in writing of the "decisions of management" on the grievances—all of which were unfavourable to the union's position.[55]

The higher proportion of settlements favourable to workers at the departmental level may have been the result of conscious management policy to encourage use of the procedure as an "alternative to lightning strikes in sections of departments on account of petty grievances, real or imaginary," in the words of one management spokesman. He explained further:

At times, workers' representatives do bring in cases which have no merit, but in order to keep the scheme going satisfactorily, I feel that occasionally we should be prepared to depart from rigid adherence to rules and regulations without in any way compromising principles and make a few concessions at least to make the workers feel that the departmental representatives are doing some good to them. Otherwise, these departmental representatives will lose their hold on the workers on which the success of the scheme largely depends. So long as the workers have faith only in their elected representatives, we must see that the elected representatives are able to keep the confidence of the workers. This is in the interests of the management as well as the workers.

Both these examples of joint committees at the final stage of the grievance procedure, therefore, indicate an approach in which management appears consciously to desire the building up of a workable union-management relationship, even at the cost of concessions which depart from a strict application of rules or involve reversal of lower managerial decisions. The strength of the unions in these two cases, however, was enough to force management to make this choice instead of running the risk of short strikes or a major shut-down.

In the absence of union strength, the direct approach to the labour officer or the plant manager is the usual grievance "procedure" and the types of grievances brought are often personal and in the nature of "petitions" to management. An analysis of 200 complaints brought to the labour officer of a firm of 3,000 employees between May and July 1953 illustrates the kinds of problems which individual workers had in this company :

TABLE XXXII

	(per cent)
Medical advice and treatment	13
Housing accommodation in company colony	12
Admission to state insurance hospitals	9
Retirement	8
Granting or non-granting of leaves	8
Financial aid	7
Shortage of water in company housing	6
Lack of work (for part-time workers)	6
Employment of relatives	4
Repairs of quarters in company houses	3
Cattle nuisance in company housing	2
Transfers from one department to another	1
Miscellaneous	21

The works committee in this firm was also a forum for the airing of grievances, and some of those brought initially to the labour officer also reached the committee. There was no recognized union, however, and management's approach to labour relations was best characterized as benevolent paternalism. Under these circumstances, which are more prevalent in Indian industry than the two cases discussed above, the grievance procedure is informal and often highly personal.

Further, even formal attempts to establish grievance procedures may fail without a much greater willingness of the management to decentralize their practices and of the union to respect the progression of steps indicated in the procedure. Thus a grievance committee established in the Hindustan Insecticides Limited in 1960 failed leading ultimately to the boycott of the committee in 1962 by the union.[56] The management blamed the union, especially its bypassing of the committee in favour of direct representation to the Managing Director. It is not unlikely that management policy contributed indirectly to this result to the extent that management structure was highly centralized—a condition common to many public sector enterprises.

However, another illustration of what can be accomplished by managements intent on reducing frictions arising from grievances is provided by a report of a study team which in 1962 examined the handling of grievances in several manufacturing firms with an average employment of 3,000.[57] All the firms concerned had separate personnel departments which functioned in an advisory capacity. Excepting for a couple of cases referred to conciliation, it was found that all of the grievances were settled within the organizations concerned which did not have a record of strikes. For three organizations for which more detailed data were available concerning the settlement of grievances at different stages of established procedures, the breakdowns were as follows: two of them settled 90 per cent of the grievances at the first stage, and the third, 10 per cent at the first stage, another 30 per cent at the second stage, and the rest at the third stage.

Another and more striking exception to the Indian pattern is the orderly procedures in the Ahmedabad textile industry. This arrangement owes much to the positive role played by the union in Ahmedabad in the handling and processing of grievances. In the Textile Labour Association there are five "group heads" who handle complaints involving the sixty-five mills. It is a policy to put two persons to work together, whether an industrial worker as group head, with a graduate assistant, or vice versa. Next to the group head are various inspectors, one for every two or three mills, whose principal function is to handle complaints. In addition to these persons attached to the union office, there are also for each plant elected shop stewards (*pratinidhis*) who also handle grievances. Of course, where these efforts fail, the "outside" general secretaries step in, and the voluntary machinery of the 1952 agreement may be set in motion. Precise statistics of the degree of plant-level settlement, unaided by union intervention, are not available. However, it is interesting to note that for 1952–53, of 17,975 complaints, only 155 were referred to the conciliation board;[58] for 1953–54, only 404 cases (including those pending from the previous year) were referred of a total of 16,521.[59] For 1954–55, 456 cases out of a total number of 18,020 were referred to conciliation.[60] Whatever these figures may mean, it is clear that direct settlement plays a major part in the industrial relations pattern in Ahmedabad. Despite its varied welfare activities described in Chapter V, the TLA states: "It is the primary function of a trade union to endeavour to redress the grievances of its members."[61]

Before concluding this section, mention must be made of the efforts of the Ministry of Labour and Employment to secure improvements in handling grievances.[62] A model procedure for speedy disposal of workers' grievances was formulated in 1958 in accordance with one of the clauses of the Code of Discipline in industry. This was done in consultation with the representatives of the workers' and employers' organizations. The procedure provides for the setting up of a grievance committee at the level of the undertaking and detailed procedures for handling grievances. The implementation is in the hands of the Central Implementation and Evaluation Division, which received twenty complaints during 1961–62 regarding non-establishment of grievance procedures. Two of these were not substantiated on enquiry; in four, the management set up a mutually agreed grievance procedure on intervention by the Division and, in the rest, the matter was under correspondence with the managements or their central organization.

Joint Management Councils

We have already referred to the study group on worker participation in management which toured Europe. It consisted of representatives of government, employers and workers and it favoured a scheme of joint management councils for introduction in the country.

The suggestion of the study group referred to above was accepted at the Indian Labour Conference in 1957 and after a discussion in a seminar the scheme of Joint Management Councils was formulated. A feature of the scheme had been that there is no legal sanction, and tripartite agreement formed the sole basis for the introduction of this voluntary scheme.[63] It was further stipulated that these councils may be instituted only in plants or firms where there has been a tradition of healthy industrial relations.

The following framework can be adopted for an examination of the principle of joint management councils : (1) the question of representation; (2) the question of the scope of the functions of these councils; (3) their place and role in the sphere of plant-level relationship.

The Question of Representation

The Seminar on Labour Management Cooperation[64] held in 1958 discussed the problem of representation. They suggested that the council should be composed of not more than twelve members with equal representation from both management and labour. An essential criterion for the formation of the council was the presence of a well-established and strong union in the undertaking. It was recommended that, where there was a registered union which was representative, it would nominate the employees' representatives in the council. However, where there was more than one established union, representation to the council would be decided by agreement among the unions involved. The seminar also recommended that there should be no bar on the members of the supervisory and technical staff being nominated as employees' representatives on the council. Also, it was suggested that the trade union could appoint non-employee members to the extent of 25 per cent of its quota.

In this connection, an observation by the study group which toured Europe is particularly relevant for highlighting one of the problems of representation. The group points out :

In Belgium, as elsewhere, the question of drawing a precise line between workers and managerial staff is a difficult one. We in India have developed no particular theory on the subject but the recent amendment to the Industrial Disputes Act includes supervisors, drawing less than a prescribed rate of pay and excluded those performing managerial functions. No clear principle can be evolved from this as to which side of the table certain categories of the lower managerial staff should occupy.[65]

The problem of representation is closely bound with the question of union recognition. It is not easy for an employee to put aside his trade union ties especially if his union has not been recognized. In some cases the council deliberations can take ugly turns resulting in a battle between labour and management instead of a mutual participation.[66]

The Ministry of Labour and Employment brought out 23 evaluation reports and an assessment report on the working of the joint management councils.[67] It points out: "The management representatives on the Joint Council are invariably nominated by the management. In most cases the workers' representatives are nominated by the union . . . . In a few cases a complaint was voiced by worker representatives that management was nominating to the Joint Council comparatively junior officers who had often to plead ignorance or want of instructions in some of the problems discussed." The assessment report says that, in those cases where the council was functioning successfully, the management representatives were from the top cadre.

We may conclude our discussion of this point by noting that the problem of representation has a direct bearing on the interest that will be evinced by both management and labour in the constitution of the council and in attending its meetings.

Scope of the Councils

The 1957 Labour Conference accepted the following recommendations of the study group relating to the functions of the councils. The main objectives of the councils will include provision of means of communication, improvement of working conditions as well as of productivity, encouragement of suggestions, and assistance in the administration of laws and agreements. It was recommended that the list of functions should be flexibly determined by the councils, but the exclusion of wage and bonus items and individual grievances was favoured. Three specific roles were envisaged for the joint councils:

1. The councils may be consulted regarding matters like alteration in standing orders, retrenchment, rationalization, closure, reduction in or cessation of operations, introduction of new methods and procedures for engagement and punishment.
2. They may have the right to receive information about the general economic situation of the concern, the state of the market, production and sales programmes, annual balance-sheet and profit and loss statement, etc.
3. The councils may also be entrusted with some administrative responsibility for some areas such as welfare measures, safety measures, vocational training, etc.

Clearly these arrangements depend greatly on the mutual confidence and goodwill between the parties.

The Place of Joint Councils in Plant-Level Relationship

The scheme for forming joint management councils has been clearly prompted by the desire on the part of the government to promote industrial peace with a view to increasing efficiency and productivity. The realization of these objectives depends on a number of factors, such as the nature of the union-management relationship, the degree of responsibility on both sides, the desire to eschew long drawn-out conflicts, and the parties' appreciation of the issues that can be reasonably tackled at the council level. An encouraging sign, however, has been the realization of the need for some kind of machinery to guide plant-level relationships. The question whether this should be the joint management council itself or some other machinery has been raised. A committee set up in December 1959, on the suggestion of the Indian Labour Conference Sub-Committee on Worker Participation in Management and Discipline in Industry, reports that, out of 396 units, 360 units favoured the setting up of a suitable machinery in some form or other with a view to raising efficiency and welfare of the workers. An interesting feature of the realization is the reported view that the general preference was for setting up a special machinery other than the works committee and the joint management council.[68]

Since the scheme was established in 1958, a number of councils have been constituted. As of late 1963, it has been reported that 66 councils were functioning, as many as 25 in the preceding year, in both public and private sector firms.[69] Twenty of these reports having subcommittees dealing with production, safety, welfare and suggestions.

Information as to their performance is, however, less encouraging. One detailed study of the experience in four units ranging in employment from 245 to 3,600 workers concluded that

> one is led to doubt the very sincerity of the experiment, the very keenness of the management to understand the new idea and to make a success of it in actual practice.[70]

The study further observed:

> It was convincingly proved by this study that contrary to the official belief, it is the top management that needs education, for the success of this scheme.[71]

A somewhat more general indictment is given by a distinguished former civil servant, now an important industrial spokesman. He says :

> When, in July 1963, Government put out a list of 56 councils, it was at best not more than 36 or so. Out of these, more than half were in small and unimportant undertakings. In the field of works committees also, the movement had almost come to a standstill. Although the number of committees was quite large on paper, many of them were not functioning at all.[72]

Government spokesmen are, however, understandably more inclined to stress the progress made.

Among the complicating factors were the adverse emotional reactions given rise to by the term "participation" and the rigid attitudes of the parties involved. Management reacted adversely to the term "participation." A former President of the Indian Institute of Personnel Management seems to have said that sharing of the executive responsibility and decision-making by the workers were outside the scope of the existing councils. The workers in turn appear to have been disappointed with the "limited participation" in management actually provided by these councils. Part of the problem is that both workers and managements have reacted primarily to the question of "who has the final power to decide" and have, therefore, concentrated on drawing sharp lines demarcating the rights of these councils, and in turn attempting to distinguish these from the earlier ventures to encourage works committees.[73] Dealing with this problem, the ILO points out :

> This confusion, however, seems to arise from the lack of intelligent appreciation of the functions of joint councils, which should more appropriately deal with policy matters leaving subjects arising from the day-to-day working of the undertaking for discussion in the works committees. In small industrial concerns, however, it may be advisable to combine the functions of the joint council and works committee in a single body.[74]

Problems in Labour-Management Relations

Some of the difficulties facing Indian management in developing systematic and constructive labour-management relationships have been indicated in this and the preceding chapter, and can now be summarized and supplemented with additional material from the interviews.

Managerial attitudes in many cases still have strong overtones of authoritarianism and paternalism; unions represent an invasion of managerial rights, and the presence of "outsiders" in the union executive is especially resented.

A survey, conducted in 1961 of six companies in Bombay,[75] showed that the first dispute seemed to determine the future relations with the union. One company took the decision to negotiate with the union and arrive at a mutual settlement though the dispute was under conciliation. This relationship continued for twelve years and the area of mutual relations seemed to widen. Another company in their first dispute decided against recognition of the union and negotiations. For the next ten years, their relations with the union continued to be one of conflict. A third company dealt with their first dispute by staging a lock-out and dismissed the workers and recruited new labour. After this incident in 1938, there had not been any union in the company. A fourth company decided to submit the dispute to conciliation, and when it failed, showed itself unwilling to negotiate with the union or even to recognize it. The study also revealed a case of multiple unions. The company sponsored a union (which the study says was not representative) and entered into an agreement with it in a wage dispute, while the workers had submitted it for conciliation. The conciliation proceedings were then terminated on the grounds of mutual settlement. But the company failed to implement the mutual settlement and the workers went in search of a new union. When the new union took a dispute for conciliation, the company resorted to retrenchment on a large scale resulting in clashes, criminal cases, complaints to the conciliation officer, etc. The study shows that the legal structure prevailing at the time of the study gave a greater scope to the companies than to the unions for initiating action for regulating industrial relations and initiating negotiations. By the same token, the companies seemed to have a greater share of responsibility for determining the nature of the industrial relations desired by them.

Important exceptions to this picture may be found but there are still few managements which realize the long-run adverse implications of an early history of conflict and bitterness. Although legal regulation is extensive, there is surprisingly little pressure on managements to negotiate with unions. Also, however much managements are exhorted to change their practices, it is likely that due to the relative weakness of unions, change will be slow. Also, given the present stage of industrial and economic development characterized by unemployment, small firms, and inadequate professionalization of management, the firms which face the pressure of rationalizing their labour relations policies are likely to be few.

Traditional managerial attitudes are reinforced by the existence of rival unions claiming to represent various groups of employees in a particular firm or industry. As we have seen in the discussion of the Indian labour movement, rival unions are often affiliated to political parties, and the managerial reaction is understandably critical of the shifting affiliation of union leaders. A frequent experience reported by a number of firms was movement of a key outside union leader from one party to another, taking with him the union members he claimed to represent and making possible the development of a rival faction attached to the original party. Some managements have taken a firm stand for negotiating only with a unified union group, but the employing government ministries seem to have been more successful in this than private employers.

Faced with these difficulties, a number of managements have favoured direct negotiations with a works committee, or with a union confined to the particular plant and headed by the firm's employees. Their approach and policies are designed to nurture and strengthen this labour-management relationship. Union officers are given time off for handling grievances or union business; management stands ready to talk with these union representatives at any time in order to build up their prestige and discourage bringing in "outsiders." Even in some firms with bona fide unions, management makes concessions to the union leadership in the handling of grievances, as we have seen, in order to maintain a systematic procedure and avoid direct action. Perhaps this approach is no different from management's effort to develop constructive labour-management relations in any other country; but it is reinforced in India by the desire to avoid more radical forms of union activity.

The availability of compulsory adjudication through the state Acts and the Industrial Disputes Act of 1947 means that unions can take unsatisfied demands to a tribunal and force the employer to participate in protracted hearings. While employers widely report that this discourages collective bargaining, it is not always certain that they would benefit from an abandonment of compulsory adjudication or that more collective bargaining would result. The labour officer of an important employers' association asserted that compulsory adjudication was "absolutely necessary in the present state of rival unions and weak unions. There would be

complete chaos without it." When employers and unions have
negotiated agreements directly, as in the cases reported above,
they have often done so to avoid the delays and the hazards that
are involved in lengthy tribunal hearings and awards. This aspect
of Indian labour-management relations will be discussed more
fully in the following chapter, but its relevance to employer policies
needs emphasis here.

In the present state of labour-management suspicion, a well-
intentioned management which attempts to develop constructive
relations with a union runs a risk of weakening the union and
encouraging a rival union to come to the fore. One of the most
progressive and enlightened managements in India negotiated an
agreement with a Socialist union, and proceeded immediately to
settle all outstanding differences with it. Concessions were made
by management on a number of points, and the outside union
president was invited to participate in discussions on management
problems in meeting competition from other companies in the
industry. Two months later, the union membership voted this
president out of office and elected a Communist leadership. The
disillusioned manager's explanation was that "the workers thought
that, because things were so peaceful, the union leadership must
have 'sold out' to management or have been bribed. I was naive;
I should not have given in so easily."

In view of these difficulties, it is perhaps all the more remarkable
that there are cases of lasting union-management relationships
comparable with the experience in more advanced industrial
countries. The forces at work encouraging the growth of these
relationships have already been discussed. However, these are still
the exceptions in Indian industry; they give promise of becoming
more general as industrialization proceeds, and as unions and
government develop means to put more pressures on management.
But the character of union-management relations in the next
five, ten, or twenty years will be importantly shaped by the role of
government, to which we turn in the next chapter.

NOTES

1 Article 49 of the Act. For text of the Act, see Mathrubutham and Srinivasan, *Indian Factories and Labour Manual, Madras Law Journal* (Madras, 1952).

2 For an account of the development of personnel management in India, see Indian Institute of Personnel Management, *Personnel Management in India* (Asia Publishing House, New York, 1961), especially pp. 45-7. It is pointed out that personnel management as understood today had its beginnings in the cotton textile mills in the years just before the Second World War. The interaction of government policy and the initiative of the leading employers' associations in the mills was responsible for its rapid development.

3 See, for example, *The West Bengal Factories (Welfare Officer) Rules* 1950, Labour Department, Government of West Bengal, 1954. Ten broad duties are listed.

4 The Inter-University Board at its 1947 annual meeting urged expansion of training programmes for labour welfare officers in existing universities. *Indian Labour Gazette,* vol. VI, no. 1 (July 1948), p. 31.

5 For a good discussion, see "Whither Personnel Officers?" *Industrial Relations,* Journal of the Indian Institute of Personnel Management, vol. IV, no. 6 (November-December 1954), pp. 232-40.

6 Instances are reported where labour officers were assaulted by infuriated workers. In one jute mill, for example, a labour officer checked the timekeeper's wage records and found that he was paying absent workers their wages and taking a 50 per cent cut. The guilty timekeeper then told the workers that the labour office was docking their pay, and they swarmed into the office, overturned furniture and physically assaulted the senior labour officer.

7 P. J. Collins (Employee Relations Manager, Standard-Vacuum Oil Company, Bombay), "Training of Labour Welfare Personnel," address given at The First All-India Conference of Labour and Welfare Officers, Bombay, April 1953.

8 Van Dusen Kennedy, "The Role of the Union in the Plant in India," *Proceedings of the Eighth Annual Meeting,* Industrial Relations Research Association, 1955. p. 13. (Professor Kennedy spent thirteen months in India during 1953-55 in a study of Indian industrial relations.)

9 "The Role of Personnel Officers in the Second Five-Year Plan," *Industrial Relations,* vol. III, no. 4 (July-August 1956), p. 186.

10 In a resolution on "Organization of a Personnel Department in Large Industrial Undertakings," the All-India Conference of Labour and Welfare Officers recommended at its December 1955 meeting that ". . . the duties of the Personnel Department are primarily advisory in character except in the administration of welfare activities which are executive in nature." *Industrial Relations,* vol. VII, no. 6 (November-December 1955), p. 222.

11 P. C. Chakravarti, "Personnel Management," *Sindri News,* May 1954, p. 7. Reprinted in *Industrial Relations,* Journal of the Indian Institute of Personnel Management, vol. VI, no. 6 (November-December 1954), pp. 229-31.

12 Details from Indian Institute of Personnel Management, *Personnel Management in India,* Asia Publishing House, New York, 1961, Appendix I.

13 A number of reports for 1957, including plantations and mines, have been cited in Subbiah Kannappan, "Some Thoughts on Our Quest for Industrial Peace," *Current Problems of Labour in India,* Government of India, 1959, note 6, p. 82; in 1962, the situation was no better and a special tripartite conference on the problems of lawlessness in the mines was convened by the Labour Ministry. See also Government of India, Ministry of Labour and Employment, *A Study of the Strike in the Premier Automobiles Ltd., From the Point of View of the Code of Discipline,* 1960. The report condemns the union for unruly and abusive behaviour.

14 The most prominent of the third type is the Millowners' Association, Bombay and the Ahmedabad Millowners' Association. The *Annual Reports,* Textile Labour Association, Ahmedabad, and the *Annual Reviews of the Labour Situation in the Bombay Cotton Mill Industry* (R. G. Gokhale of Millowners' Association, Bombay) give relevant details. The Indian Jute Mills' Association is a good example of the middle type (see, for instance, IJMA, *Report of the Committee,* 31 December 1960, 1961, esp. pp. 81-6). The Employees' Association of Northern India at Kanpur is principally of the first type although it has taken an active role in general negotiations on rationalization.

15 A number of tribunals or special commissions have been appointed: a partial listing is given in *Indian Labour Year Book,* Appendix IV, 1, C, under the heading "Reports by Special Officers, Adjudicators, Courts of Enquiry, etc." Thus the publications in recent years include numerous reports for banking, docks, defence, Central government employees (pay commissions), etc. Prominent recent recommendations include one for all Central government employees (1959) and for 69 leading banking companies, including the Reserve Bank of India, in 1962. Several volumes of a mimeographed Bibliographical Series entitled *Labour Literature: A Bibliography,* issued by the Librarian of the Ministry of Labour and Employment provide a helpful guide to the controversies surrounding each major reference.

16 In the banking industry, the government-owned State Bank of India and affiliated banking units commanded in 1961 slightly over 31 per cent of the deposits of all banks in India. See Reserve Bank of India, *Statistical Tables Relating to Banks in India for the Year* 1961, Bombay, pp. 8-9. A brief indication of the scope of the dock labour boards is given in *Indian Labour Year Book* 1958, pp. 256-58.

17 For full discussion of the significance of this Act, see N.S. Pardasani, "The Bombay Industrial Disputes Act, 1938," *Indian Journal of Economics* (Allahabad), vol. 21, no. 80, July 1940, pp. 49-66. This Act was preceded by the Bombay Trade Disputes and Conciliation Act of 1934 and the Central Government Trade Disputes Act of 1929. In neither piece of legislation was the labour-management relationship structured as much as in the 1938 Bombay Act.

18 A "representative union" was designated as any union with at least 15 per cent of the employees in a particular plant or industry in a local area, and if two unions so claimed, the one with the greater membership was selected. Failing to meet this membership test, a union with at least 5 per cent could be registered as a "primary union," and failing this, a "qualified union" with at least 5 per cent membership among the workers in a given occupation could be registered. The single dominant union among these had the right to represent workers in discussions with employers

and in proceedings before conciliation and adjudication. An "approved union" category was also established, with special privileges accruing to it in return for voluntary submission of disputes to arbitration. INTUC unions usually qualified as "approved" unions, if they met the other tests.

19 For a fuller discussion of this and other dispute settlement Acts, see Chapters VIII and IX.

20 Reference was required in "public utility" industries such as railways, posts and telegraphs, power, light, water, public sanitation, and certain others declared a public service (coal, cotton textiles, foodstuff manufacturing, iron and steel, and other transport). Strikes and lockouts were prohibited in these industries.

21 Section 10(2) Charges of favouritism to INTUC unions under this Section have been made by other unions.

22 The Appellate Tribunals were later abolished in September 1956, when the Industrial Disputes (Appellate Tribunal) Act, 1950, was repealed.

23 The INTUC union claims between 20 and 30 per cent of the 230,000 Bombay textile workers as members; the HMS and Communist union groups were much weaker. According to one association official, "We are definitely much better off with the INTUC. The workers are less rowdy, there is a better attitude and fewer strikes. In the past, Bombay workers were used to spectacular leadership, but the INTUC has calmed them down." A 1950 strike called by the HMS (Socialist) textile union was broken, and the HMS never regained its strength.

24 During 1954, for example, a case involving action taken in 1950 was being argued before the Bombay Bench of the Appellate Tribunal. The Tribunal's decision was handed down early in 1955.

25 For the text of this agreement, see Appendix A of the earlier edition.

26 For further discussion, see Chapter IX and also Appendix A (full text).

27 *Indian Worker*, vol. 5, no. 8, 19 November 1956, p. 161.

28 See especially Subbiah Kannappan and associates, *The Belur Report*, 1958, pp. 22-32, for a detailed account of the evolution of collective bargaining during 1941-57 at the company's works at Belur.

29 The agreement was summarized in these words: "Firstly, it is distinctive because it is all-comprehensive. Secondly, it clearly defines the respective functions, duties, responsibilities and privileges of both sides, the lack of understanding of which by management and unions leads to many a strike in this country. Thirdly, without paying lip homage to many common sentiments that have crept recently into the field of industrial relations, it effectively associates the workpeople with the management in scientifically setting standards of production in all the machine centres, in job evaluation and fixing of rates and also in the day-to-day running of the industry by an elaborate grievance procedure. Fourthly, not only the wage rates and bonus rates are scientifically linked to production, but here for the first time a union proclaims in unambiguous terms that bonus payment made by industry on the basis of profits is unsound, unscientific and not to the interest of the workers." P.N. Krishna Pillai, "Highlights of the Second Five Year Agreement," *Indalumin Bulletin*, Special Issue, 3 September 1956 (Indian Aluminium Company, Calcutta), p. 2.

30 According to the company's personnel manager, the 1951 agreement "was the

first freely negotiated labour-management contract ever to be signed by a management and a trade union in this country which covered the comprehensive terms and conditions of employment. The experience gained by both sides in these five years has reassured us of the great potentiality in collective bargaining and settling of differences by direct negotiations. In these five years, though there had been occasions where there were strong differences of opinion between the management and the union, we had never approached the conciliation machinery or adjudication machinery of the state to settle the differences. We always settled them by mutual negotiations. The experience thus gained convinces us that effective collective bargaining does not breed mutual hatred, but, by the interplay of forces and mutual respect of the respective rights and responsibilities of parties, creates a mutuality of interest which will guarantee higher standards of living for workpeople and greater productivity for industry." *Ibid.,* p. 2.

31 See also Subbiah Kannappan and Eugene W. Burgess, *The Case Study of Aluminium Limited in India,* Washington, D.C., National Planning Association, 1962, pp. 52-5.

32 Letter from P. N. Krishna Pillai, personnel manager, Indian Aluminium Company, Calcutta, 25 January 1957.

33 The full text of the agreement is reproduced in Appendix D of the earlier edition.

34 *Janata,* official organ of the Praja Socialist Party, has described the agreement as follows: "... [The] Jamshedpur Agreement ... is the hope for higher standard of life, good working conditions ... job and social security that become the basis for cooperation. That is the reason why ... [it] is more significant to the labour's interest than the Ahmedabad experiment. ... The Jamshedpur Agreement, in short, is a fine piece of collective bargaining. It will open a new chapter in the labour-management relations in our country. It will also have wide repercussions on the methods and practices of trade unions in promoting labour interest. Apart from ensuring industrial peace ... the agreement has shown how a trade union should combine its protective functions with the representative functions in a harmonious blending of labour interest."

"The Jamshedpur Agreement," *Janata,* vol. X, no. 51 (15 January 1956), p. 1.

35 *Indian Worker,* weekly political journal of the INTUC, to which the Tata Workers' Union is affiliated, commented editorially: "The recently concluded agreement between the Tata Workers' Union and the Tata Iron and Steel Company is a landmark not only in the history of the Union, but also in the history of trade unionism in India. ... In our view the agreement is a pointer to the social change which is taking place in India. It gives concrete shape to the concept of workers' participation in management of industries, thereby implementing the resolution on the subject adopted at the Eighth Annual Conference of the INTUC at Surat." In the words of Michael John, president of the Tata Workers' Union, "The agreement would provide opportunities to the workers to acquire knowledge and skill so essential for managing industries and when India achieved her goal of socialist pattern of society, they would be well prepared to play a full and effective part in running the country's industries"—vol. 4, no. 45 (20 August 1956), p. 3. (Compare this interpretation with that of Mr. J. R. D. Tata, chairman of the company, in the next note.)

36 "Tata Steel Company: Workers' Share in Management", *Hindu Weekly Review*, 13 August 1956, p. 15. For text of this agreement, see Appendix E. J.R.D. Tata, chairman of the company, subsequently stated: "The question whether the Company should not have waited until all-India policy had been evolved on the subject was discussed by the Company's Board who ultimately decided to ratify the draft agreement. This decision, which I am convinced was right, is in consonance with the accepted view that freely negotiated agreements are much to be preferred to imposed settlements. The Agreement was negotiated in a fine spirit of mutual frankness and cooperation and represents an honest attempt to devise means of understanding each other better and working closer together. I have every hope that it will prove workable in practice, provided both parties respect the intentions recorded in the Agreement and try to read into its provisions neither more nor less than they contain. This will apply particularly to the Joint Consultative Council of Management. . . . So far as we are concerned, we shall not seek to fetter the discretion of this Council in discussing such matters as will enable its members, and particularly those representing labour, to acquire a better understanding of the industry and its problems. At the same time, the Company has no intention of surrendering its managerial functions and responsibilities." Speech of the chairman at Forty-Ninth Annual General Meeting, 30 August 1956, reported in *Economic Weekly* (Bombay), vol. VII, no. 35 (1 September 1956), p. 1050.

37 No specific studies were made of these experiences, but efforts have been made by each of these ministries to establish collective relationships with one union by pressing for unity among competing unions. On their part, the unions have also favoured unity, as in the All-India Defence Workers' Union, and, until the recent split, the Railwaymen's Federation. When unity involves the Communist unions, however, there are dangers. One critic has commented: "It is a fact that while in private industries there is a terrific conflict between democratic trade unions and the Communist unions, in nationalized industries, the conveniences and requirements of the nationalized management often pressure the rival unions into forced unity. This has happened uniformly in the Posts and Telegraphs, in the Defence industries, and this process will continue in all nationalized industries in the glorious name of 'One Union, One Industry.' In many instances the nationalized industry's owner, the State, hands over hundreds of thousands of good workers on a gold plate to the disruptors of the country and labour to suit the conveniences of the nationalized management." *Free Labour Herald* (Journal of the Association of Free Trade Unionists, Bombay, no. 26, November-December 1955), p. 5.

38 *Memorandum of Settlement Filed by the Parties between the Bombay State Road Transport Corporation, Bombay and its Employees (except Class I and II Officers) Employed under it Represented by the State Transport Workers' Union (Federation)*, dated 25 April 1956.

39 Editorial in *Indian Worker* (weekly journal of the INTUC), 18 June 1956. The editorial contains a scathing denunciation of management in public enterprises: "There is little doubt that a chosen set of Government representatives who head the administration in various capacities in public undertakings are not very well equipped to view the industrial relations in the fashion it is possible and it should

be done. As it is, the administrative powers and the control rest with high Government officials of the IAS and ICS cadre who have scant experience in running industries and handling the industrial relations. A man who works in an administrative capacity for as long as twenty years could not be expected to handle the delicate question of industrial relations effectively and efficiently. There is no surprise, therefore, that an employer in the private sector would any time prefer to have conditions which today obtain in the public sector with a view to avoiding trade unions. It would not be far wrong to say that unions, wherever they exist, are either bypassed or attempt is made to form a rival union. Another grouse which the workers nurse is with regard to the fact that their grievances are attended to in a bureaucratic manner."

Corroboration of this view comes from Walter Reuther, who visited India in May 1956, at the invitation of the INTUC. An account of his visit reports that Reuther "told a New Delhi Press Conference how shocked he had been to hear from the manager of the government's Chittaranjan locomotive plant that union organizing is not permitted, warning that 'the bosses there may be bureaucrats, but they're still bosses.' " Selig S. Harrison, "Reuther in India," *New Republic*, vol. 134, no. 21 (21 May, 1956), p. 11.

40 *Industrial Disputes Act,* 1947, Section 3(2).

41 Government of India, Ministry of Labour and Employment, *A Study of the Strike in the Premier Automobiles Ltd., from the Point of View of The Code of Discipline,* New Delhi, 1959, p. 7.

42 *Indian Labour Gazette* reported that 1,196 works committees had been established by September 1950.

43 Provided by the Ministry of Labour, New Delhi, June 1955.

44 *Indian Labour Year Book,* 1962, p. 108.

45 *Ibid.,* 1953-54, p. 172.

46 *Ibid.,* 1962, p. 109.

47 Gujarat Research Society, *Case Studies in Industrial Relations,* Samsodan Sadan, Bombay-52, 1962, pp. 188-89.

48 Government of India, Ministry of Labour and Employment, *A Survey of the Functioning of the Works Committees in Bombay City* (conducted by the Statistics Division of the N. C. Corporation Pvt. Ltd.), 1959, New Delhi, pp. vii, ix.

49 Government of India, Ministry of Labour and Employment, *Industrial Relations in the Hindustan Housing Factory Limited: A Case Study* (1956-62), New Delhi, no date, p. 31.

50 Government of India, Ministry of Labour and Employment, *Industrial Relations in Hindustan Insecticides Limited,* 1955-62 *: A Case Study,* New Delhi, no date, esp. pp. 19-20.

51 Government of India, Ministry of Labour and Employment, *Second Seminar on Labour-Management Cooperation,* New Delhi, 8-9 March 1960, pp. 44-8.

52 Government of India, The Planning Commission, *First Five Year Plan,* 1952, p. 577.

53 *Annual Report,* 1953-54, Textile Labour Association, Ahmedabad, 1954, p. 9. For further details on this experience, see Van Dusen Kennedy, "Union in the

Plant in India," *Proceedings of the Eighth Annual Meeting of the Industrial Relations Research Association* (Madison, Wisconsin, 1955), pp. 249-64.

54 According to statistical summaries supplied by the company, "favourable" meant that some or all of the worker's claims were upheld.

55 A summary of the Central Labour Advisory Committee's work during a twelve-month period in 1953-54 showed that, of 37 cases, 9 decisions were favourable to workers, 11 were unfavourable, 1 was not pressed, and 16 were still under consideration. Punishment (dismissals and discharge) and claims for re-employment with unbroken service after suspension of illness or physical unfitness were involved in 27 of the 37 cases. Fewer of the department-level decisions were favourable to workers than during the preceding year. Sixty-three of 81 cases were decided against workers in the departments, but only 24 were taken up by the union to the Mill Labour Advisory Committees.

56 Government of India, Ministry of Labour and Employment, *Industrial Relations in Hindustan Insecticides Ltd., 1955-62: A Case Study*, p. 33.

57 *Report of the In-Country Study Team on Discipline and Grievance Handling in Selected Industrial Undertakings In and Around Calcutta, February-March* 1962, Jamshedpur: Jamshedpur Productivity Council, 1963, pp. 11-2, 20-1.

58 Textile Labour Association, *Annual Report,* 1952-53, pp. 43-4.

59 Textile Labour Association, *Annual Report*, 1953-54, pp. 56-7.

60 Subbiah Kannappan, "The Gandhian Model of Unionism in a Developing Economy: The TLA in India," *Industrial and Labor Relations Review*, vol. 16, no. 1, October 1962, p. 96.

61 Textile Labour Association, *op. cit.,* p. 9.

62 Government of India, Labour Bureau, *Indian Labour Year Book* 1962, p. 107.

63 *Ibid.,* pp. 115-16.

It is said that, since the formation of the scheme, management councils have been set up in 53 undertakings, 16 in the public and 37 in the private sector. Of these, only 46 were functioning by the end of 1962.

It is interesting to note that public sector undertakings have not shown any conspicuous initiative in setting up such councils. Major employers like ordnance factories, railways, the state steel works are not among these. "Workers' Participation a Misnomer," Letter from Calcutta, *Economic Weekly,* April, 7, 1962, p. 577.

64 Government of India, Ministry of Labour and Employment, *Seminar on Labour-Management Cooperation,* 31 January and 1st February 1958, New Delhi, 1958, pp. 14-5.

65 *Report of the Study Group on Worker Participation in Management,* 1957, Manager of Publications, Delhi, p. 43.

66 The joint management council introduced in the Hindustan Machine Tools in 1958 soon became extinct, after the union complained that unilateral actions were taken by management without the consultation of workers' representatives. Union rivalry has also been cited in this case, *Statesman,* 22 October, 1959.

67 The information on these was obtained from the Evaluation Reports on 23 management councils supplied by the Ministry of Labour and Employment.

68 Government of India, Ministry of Labour and Employment, *Report on the*

Proposed Code of Efficiency and Welfare, 1961, p. 27.

69 *Economic Times,* November 25, 1963, p. 2.

70 *Worker Participation in Management: The Indian Experiment*, Institute of Economic Growth, Delhi, 1962, p. 69.

71 *Ibid.,* p. 71.

72 Nabagopal Das, *Experiments in Industrial Democracy,* Asia Publishing House, New York, 1964, p. 152.

73 *Report of the Study Group on Worker Participation in Management*, 1957, Manager of Publication, Delhi, p. 74.

74 International Labour Officer, New Delhi, *Supplement to Labour News Digest,* 1961, no. 1, January-March 1961, *Workers' Participation in Management* (mimeographed), p. 17.

75 Caution is needed before generalizing from the experience of these companies which were selected from a particular region within Bombay city for operational convenience. Two units with less than 250 employees, two with about 500 employees and two with more than 1,000 employees were selected. A criterion for selection was the "general level of industrial relations," Gujarat Research Society, *Case Studies in Industrial Relations,* Samsodan Sadan, Bombay, 52, pp. 186-88.

SOME COLLECTIVE AGREEMENTS

Name of the concern	Date and duration	Contents	Source
1. Assam Oil Company	1957	Bonus	Industrial Relations,[1] vol. X, no. 4, July-August 58, p. 213.
2. Bata Shoe Company	July 1957—1-1/2 yrs. November 1948	Dearness Allowance Comprehensive. Work standing orders and rules incorporating terms and conditions of service. Recognition of union. Rules regarding residential quarters	Do Industrial Relations, vol. VII, no. 6, November-December 1956, p. 269.
3. Burma Shell Refineries,[2] Limited, Bombay and their clerical workmen	1960—4 years	Bonus, *ad hoc* increments, annual privilege leave rules changes, changes in service conditions could be met by new demands by workmen who otherwise agreed to exercise restraint	
4. Burma Shell, Madras[2]	1958—3 years	Wages, bonus, D.A., leave rules, grievance procedure, conditions binding on either party	
5. Burma Shell, Bombay[2]	1958—3 years	Wages, bonus, dearness allowance, leave rules, grievance procedure, conditions binding on either party	
6. Caltex. Bombay[2]	1959—3 years.	Wages, bonus, dearness allowance, leave rules, grievance pro-	

(*Appendix contd.*)

Name of the concern	Date and duration	Contents	Source
		cedure, conditions of service binding on either party	
7. Hindustan Lever Ltd.	1956 Bombay factories—4 years	Wages, bonus, provident fund, etc.	*Industrial Relations*, vol. IX, November-December 1957, p. 238.
	1957 All offices, field force, etc.—3 years		
8. Hindustan Heavy Chemicals, Limited.	1955—2 years	Wages, increment, dearness allowance, bonus, acting pays, higher grade vacancies	*Industrial Relations*, vol. VIII, no. 6, November-December 1956, pp. 270-71.
9. (a) Indian Aluminium Company, Limited, Alupuram	1957	Comprehensive. Orderly collective bargaining, grievances disposal, prevention of strikes, lock-outs, wages, hours of work, joint committees, holidays	*Industrial Relations*, vol. IX, no. 3, May-June 1957, pp. 109-10.
(b) Indian Aluminium Company, Limited, Calcutta, Belur Works	March 1951—5 years	Comprehensive terms and conditions of employment	*Industrial Relations*, vol. VIII, no. 5, September-October 1956, p. 232.
10. Indian Aluminium Company, Limited, Muri	January 1957—5 years	Similar to Belur agreement above	
11. Indo-Burma, Bombay[2]	1958—3 years	Wages, bonus, dearness allowance, leave rules, grievance procedure, conditions binding on either party	
12. Joint Steamer Companies	1954 April 1955	- Bonus for shore staff Introduction of direct recruit-	

Name of the concern	Date and duration	Contents	Source
		ment and employment of inland seamen in place of old contract system	
13. Joint Steamer Companies of North-East India	June 1957—$2\frac{1}{2}$ years	Wage scales and amenities Pay, allowances, pensions for certified ranks, crew service records and allowances for workshop employees	*Industrial Relations*, vol X, no. 4, July-August 1958, pp. 213-14.
14. Lever Brothers (India), Limited	July 1955	Terms and conditions of employment. Increments for hourly rate staff, leave, dearness allowance, transfer	*Industrial Relations*, vol. VIII, no. 5, September-October 1956, p. 233.
15. National Newsprint and Paper Mills, Nepanagar, M.P.	March 1956—5 years	Joint consultations on welfare and amenities and regulating market prices in Nepanagar. Pay and allowance, medical aid, conveyance, accommodation and house rent	
16. Srrith Stanistreet and Company. Limited. Calcutta	April 1960—3 years	Wages, bonus, working hours, holidays	Text of agreement
17. Standard Vacuum, Madras[2]	1958—3 years	Wages, bonus, leave rules, dearness allowance, grievance procedure, conditions binding on either party	
18. S. V. O. C. Madras[2]	1959—$2\frac{1}{2}$ years	Wages, bonus, dearness allowance, leave rules, grievance procedure, conditions binding on	

(*Appendix contd.*)

Name of the concern	Date and duration	Contents	Source
		either party	
19. Tata Iron and Steel Company. Limited, Jamshedpur	January 1956	Recognition of union as sole bargaining agent, union membership, security. Rationalization without retrenchment, fixation of standard force by agreement or arbitration. Job evaluation through joint committee and promise to revise wage structure. Discipline, grievance procedure, promotion to supervisory posts, *ad hoc* increase in pay	
20. Tata Iron and Steel Company. Limited, Jamshedpur	August 1956	Workers' participation in management through 3-tiered consultative councils	
21. Transport Operators, Bombay	1955—1 year	Wages for drivers and cleaners, overtime wages. holidays, gratuity, reinstatement of victimized workers	Text of agreement (mimeographed)

SOURCES:

1 *Industrial Relations*, Indian Institute of Personnel Management, Calcutta.

2 "Analysis of Long Terms Agreements signed by the Oil Companies during 1958-59," *Petroleum Worker*, vol. 2, no. 6-12, May-November 1960, Bombay, pp. I-XXXII.

3 Mrs. M. Sur, "A Study of Trends in Recent Collective Agreements," Eighth All-India Conference of the Indian Institute of Personnel Management. *Souvenir*, New Delhi, 7-9 February, 1958, p. 56.

CHAPTER VIII

THE ROLE OF GOVERNMENT

THE pattern of labour-management relations in India has increasingly been structured by government. The difficulties in developing a committed industrial labour force, the rivalries and weaknesses of the Indian trade union movement, the failure of many Indian and foreign employers to deal fairly with workers or constructively with trade unions, and the resultant labour discontent and strife have encouraged government intervention in order to contain, channel and redirect incipient and actual labour protest. Increasingly, planning objectives for rapid economic development have been given priority and the pattern of labour-management relations has been expected to conform to these objectives. While there are opposition parties, the Congress Party (often called the "Party of Independence") has been in power since Independence in 1947; and the 1957 and 1962 elections gave it renewed five-year mandates.

Government was not always so active in guiding labour-management relations in India. Before Independence, or at least before the war, the role of government was passive, as we shall see in a brief examination of labour legislation prior to 1947. But, faced with the problems of a new nation and post-war labour unrest, government became an active intervener with the passage of a number of new laws, beginning with the Industrial Disputes Act of 1947. We shall review the major steps in the intervention process, and then turn to a fuller discussion of such problems as compulsory adjudication versus collective bargaining, wage disputes under adjudication, handling rival unions and protecting union growth, rationalization and unemployment, and effective utilization of foreign technical assistance programmes. These are problems which have required increased attention from government in its role as active intervener in structuring labour-management relations.

Government as Passive Regulator: Before 1947

We shall not attempt to make an exhaustive compilation of the progress of Indian labour legislation.[1] Rather, our major objective is to focus attention on the limited role of government in dealing with labour-management relations before World War II. The earliest legislation was not really labour legislation. The foreign government's main concern was to assist employers interested in enforcing the work contract and with the maintenance of order and security. In this category belonged the Workmen's Breach of Contract Act of 1859 and the Employers' and Workmen's Disputes Act of 1860.[2]

Soon, with the beginnings of Indian industrialization, several voices were raised in behalf of protective labour legislation. Among the strongest influences were the Lancashire and other British interests which faced the competition of manufacturing centred in India.[3] Factory commissions were appointed (mostly in Bombay) during the eighties and nineties; and, as a result of their deliberations and recommendations, several laws were passed protecting woman and child labour. The first comprehensive regulation of adult male labour was the Factory Act of 1911, limiting the working day of textile factories to twelve hours.

Further progress was suspended until after the First World War, when labour legislation received fresh impetus from various economic and political pressures.[4] An important factor in the development of Indian labour legislation was India's membership in the International Labour Organization.[5] Important laws passed during the twenties were: the Indian Factories Act, 1922; the Indian Mines Act, 1923; the Indian Workmen's Compensation Act; the Indian Trade Unions Act, 1926; and the Trade Disputes Act, 1929. The last-named Act prohibited lightning strikes, and provided for the establishment of *ad hoc* conciliation boards.

The appointment of the Royal Commission on Labour in India, which reported in 1931, represented a more positive approach. But its significance for labour reform was blunted because of the business depression and unsettled political conditions. The principal labour enactments of the British Indian Government during this period were: the Indian Railways Act, 1930; the Tea Districts Emigrant Labour Act, 1932; the amendment to the Workmen's

Compensation Act in 1933; the amendment to the Indian Factories Act in 1934; the amendment to the Indian Mines Act in 1935; and the Payment of Wages Act of 1936. The 1934 Factories Act reduced working hours in "perennial factories" to fifty-four a week, and prohibited completely the night work of women as contrary to the social custom in India. The Payment of Wages Act of 1936 represented the first move to protect Indian industrial labour from numerous chisellings in their earnings by their employers. Special mention may be made of a regional enactment, the Bombay Disputes Conciliation Act in 1934. This provided for the appointment of a Government Labour Officer to look after the interests of workers and to promote better relations between employers and employees. A Conciliation Board, with the Commissioner of Labour as the ex-officio chief conciliator, was established; and it was made illegal to obstruct, or picket against, conciliation proceedings.

Government's labour policy during the major part of the period from 1919 to 1940 was that of a passive regulator of labour in industry. All legislative and governmental intervention was designed essentially to achieve two ends: (1) to ensure labour the minimum of protective legislation against the more flagrant abuses of the industrial environment; and (2) to ensure that labour-management friction did not overtly disturb the peace and security of the state. To the first category belonged most of the protective legislation already referred to, and to the second category the Trade Disputes Act of 1929 and perhaps even the Bombay Trade Disputes Conciliation Act. The current detailed attempts to regulate working conditions, define shop rules, and determine the pattern of labour-management relations by comprehensive state machinery for conciliation and arbitration had no parallel in those days. Indeed, as an important government-appointed committee, the Labour Investigation Committee, remarked in 1946 :

Unfortunately, it is to be feared that the State in India, all these years, has done very little besides merely passing laws and seeking to enforce them through various agencies. Except in recent years, it has stood aloof from any active work in the field of labour, mainly on the ground of lack of funds and also on the doubtful theory that the State cannot afford to spend on any particular class or section of the population.[6]

This "doubtful theory" was also challenged earlier by the Indian National Congress, the largest party in the country. In 1929, Jawaharlal Nehru, as president of the Indian National Congress, argued :

> The Congress, it is said, must hold the balance fairly between capital and labour.... But the balance has been and is terribly weighted on one side. The only way to right it is to do away with the domination of any one class over another.[7]

The All-India Congress Committee adopted in 1929 a resolution to the effect that

> the great poverty and misery of the Indian people are due not only to foreign exploitation in India but also to the economic structure of society. . . . In order, therefore, to remove this poverty . . . it is essential to make revolutionary changes in the present economic and social structure of society and to remove the gross inequalities.[8]

The Karachi "fundamental rights" resolution, as amplified at Bombay in 1931, stated in part:

> The State shall safeguard the interests of industrial workers and shall secure for them, by suitable legislation and in other ways, a living wage, healthy conditions of work, limited hours of labour, suitable machinery for the settlement of disputes between em ployers and workmen, and protection against the economic conse- quences of old age, sickness, and unemployment. Peasants and workers shall have the right to form unions to protect their interests.[9]

Congress policy was further clarified in the succeeding years. It opposed "loose talk" along the lines of confiscation and class war, which were declared to be "contrary to the Congress creed of non- violence."[10] It was also declared that the Congress "contemplates a healthier relationship between capital and labour."[11] *The Congress Election Manifesto* of 1936 guaranteed "the right of workers to form unions and to strike for the protection of their interests," but only "as far as economic conditions in the country permit."[12]

There followed a brief interlude when Congress exercised power in 1937–39. We have already seen in Chapter IV the main outlines of official policy and indications for the future. The Bombay Industrial Disputes Act of 1938 (in part an extension of the Bombay Trade Disputes Conciliation Act of 1934) and the various enquiry committees appointed by the Congress signalled that, in an independent India, under the rule of the Congress party, the government would play a much more active role in industrial relations.[13] The restrictions on the right to strike in the Bombay Act and the emphasis on compulsory and comprehensive arbitration of industrial disputes similarly heralded an era when industrial grievances would be settled through comprehensive state machinery.

The Impact of the Second World War

But Congress stayed in power for only a short while ; for the Second World War intervened and the different Congress provincial administrations resigned in protest against the British Indian government's wartime policy. Wartime exigencies and consideration of post-war development, however, actually carried the country further along the road to compulsory arbitration and greater intervention by the government in the "structuring" of industrial relations.

Developments during the war under the auspices of the British Indian administration may be briefly reviewed. In 1941, the Bombay Act of 1938 was amended, empowering the provincial government to refer any dispute to compulsory adjudication by an industrial court if, in the government's view, the continuation of a dispute was likely to lead to a breach of the peace, or to result in serious hardships to the community, or likely to affect seriously the position of the industry and thereby curtail the prospects of employment.[14] The Government of India, by a series of regulations promulgated under the Defence of India Act, empowered itself to forbid strikes or lock-outs and further to alter working and employment conditions and wages paid to the industrial workers.[15] Earlier labour standards were relaxed, to permit underground work by women (in the mines) and increases in working hours.

Several positive steps were also initiated by the British Indian government, which began technical training programmes, and toward the end of the war established the nucleus of a national employment exchange service, at first with only the limited objective of resettling demobilized personnel.[16] To facilitate the development of a broad-based and acceptable labour policy, a national tripartite machinery (the Indian Labour Conference and the Standing Labour Committee) was established as a forum for discussions on labour policy in which representatives of government, industry, and labour participated.[17] Subsequent developments in the field of labour legislation concerning health insurance, trade union protection and industrial disputes regulations may be traced to the deliberations in this forum. An important offshoot of the tripartite machinery was the appointment of the Labour Investigation Committee (referred to as the Rege Committee, after the name of the chairman), which recommended in its 1946 Report:

> If "maximum good of the maximum number" is to be achieved, the maximum number in India, as anywhere else, consists of the labouring classes; and, therefore, if the common man is to get his due, a frontal attack on the problems at issue will have to be made with the State in the vanguard of such a movement.[18]

As we can see, official attitude had changed in the direction of a more active role for the government even before Independence. Independence hastened the process, and so radically altered the tone and content of governmental policy as to usher in a new phase in the development of industrial relations in India.

Government as Active Intervener: After 1947

When independence came to India in 1946–47, conditions on the labour front were unsatisfactory. As we have already noted in Chapter I, real earnings of industrial workers had declined from an index of 109 in 1940 to 73 in 1946. Labour organizations were very militant; the Communist-led AITUC, which had opposed work stoppages during the war, now led the call for strikes. The total of workers involved in industrial disputes reached a new high, as Table XXXIII indicates.

TABLE XXXIII

INDUSTRIAL DISPUTES IN INDIA, 1921-47[a]

Year	Disputes	Workers involved	Working days lost
1921	396	600,351	6,984,426
1922	278	435,434	3,972,727
1923	213	301,044	5,051,704
1924	133	312,462	8,730,918
1925	134	270,423	12,578,129
1926	128	186,811	1,097,478
1927	129	131,655	2,019,970
1928	203	506,851	31,647,404
1929	141	532,016	12,165,691
1930	148	196,301	2,261,731
1931	166	203,008	2,408,123
1932	118	128,099	1,922,437
1933	146	164,938	2,168,961
1934	159	220,808	4,775,559
1935	145	114,217	973,457
1936	157	169,029	2,358,062
1937	379	647,801	8,982,795
1938	399	401,075	9,198,708
1939	406	409,189	4,992,795
1940	322	452,539	7,577,281
1941	359	291,054	3,330,503
1942	694	772,653	5,779,965
1943	716	525,088	2,342,287
1944	658	550,015	3,447,306
1945	820	747,530	4,054,499
1946	1,629	1,961,948	12,717,762
1947	1,811	1,840,784	16,562,666

a Comparable data since 1947 are presented in Table XXXVI.

SOURCE: For 1921-37, International Labour Office, *Industrial Labour in India* [Studies and Reports, Series A (Industrial Relations), no. 41] (Geneva, 1938), p. 138; for 1938 and 1939, *Indian Labour Problems,* by A.N. Agarwala, ed. (London, 1947), p. 215; for 1939-47, *Indian Labour Gazette,* vol. VIII, no. 3, (September 1950), p. 215.

Industrial production dropped substantially from the wartime peak of 1944. Additional problems were presented by inflationary pressures and by bottlenecks in transportation, in foreign exchange, and in the critical area of food supplies. The partition of the country imposed another serious strain on its economy. It was under such trying circumstances that the labour policy and outlook of the newly established Congress administration evolved.

In 1946, the Working Committee of the Indian National Congress had recommended that Congressmen work in close cooperation with and accept the guidance of the Hindusthan Mazdoor Sevak Sangh, started originally in 1938 "with a view to giving wider application to the Gandhian principles in the field of labour."[19] In another resolution the Working Committee urged government and employers

> to take early steps to satisfy the legitimate needs and aspirations of the working class and to remove every cause of genuine discontent by arranging for an impartial examination of the conditions and complaints of the employees and by prompt settlement of points of disagreement by process of conciliation and arbitration.[20]

The committee further noted that "the undesirable features of the labour situation are due in part to the efforts of certain individuals... to exploit the ignorance of the workers," and pointed out:

> Avoidable strikes cannot have the backing of public opinion, and in view of the dire need of the country for more goods and services, hasty or ill-conceived stoppages and the refusal to take advantage of the available means of settlement by negotiation, conciliation and arbitration, constitute a distinct disservice to the community and the working class itself.

This in brief constituted the Congress testament for labour. As we have already seen, Congress and government dissatisfaction with the Communist-led AITUC led to the formation of the INTUC as a "central organization of labour" more in accord with the objectives of the Congress for labour.

The outstanding features of Congress official policy during the initial years of administration have already been reviewed in Chapter IV. The Industrial Disputes Act of 1947 continued the restrictive aspects of wartime labour policy. But the government was committed to a greater role as arbiter of social justice. The Five Year Labour Programme announced in 1947, and the Industrial Truce Resolution of 1947, representing the mutual decisions of representatives of labour, management and government, defined the goals of social policy. Other important enactments were the Industrial Policy Statement of 1948, accepting the principle of associating representatives of labour in the consideration of problems of industrial production; and the Limitation of Dividends Act of 1948, as the counterpart of a policy of wage control. All of these, together with the appointment of two important committees on profit-sharing and on fair wages, were indicative of government's intention to hold the balance between labour and capital in its efforts to rehabilitate the country's economy. The rationale behind government policy was explained as follows:

> The new labour policy of the Government of India is thus designed to steer clear of all ideological and class conflicts and keep the two arms of production—labour and capital—contented. Its main object is to foster mutual respect among employers and workers as well as the realization that they are equal partners in a joint enterprise and that by serving the country they serve their interests best.[21]

Major Labour Legislation After 1947

The more important legislative enactments may now be briefly described. The Industrial Disputes Act of 1947,[22] was enacted over the bitter opposition of labour representatives in the Central Legislative Assembly. It empowered the government to refer any "dispute" or "difference" to adjudication by industrial tribunals. Strikes were forbidden during the pendency of conciliation or arbitration proceedings, and during the period when an award was in force. The Act further provided for the establishment of works committees in all industrial establishments employing one hundred workers or more.

An important regional Act, the Bombay Industrial Relations Act, deserves special mention. Although it provided for compulsory conciliation and adjudication of industrial disputes, the procedures were more elaborate. It forbade any alterations in the conditions of employment without a "notice of change" to be given the union concerned and the government. The Bombay Act provided further, for different categories of unions: (1) a "registered" union, which would be a union registered under the all-India Act, registered separately under the Bombay Act; (2) the "primary"union, that is, a registered union with 15 per cent membership in any undertaking; (3) a "qualified" union, a registered union claiming 5 per cent membership of employees in an industry; and (4) a "representative" union, a registered union claiming 15 per cent membership of employees in an industry.

There is also a further classification, the "approved" union, which undertakes the following obligations: (a) to submit every dispute to arbitration, if settlement is not reached;[23] (b) not to resort to strike unless all the procedures provided for in the Bombay Act are exhausted and unless a majority vote of the members by ballot is taken in favour of the strike; (c) not to resort to or sanction any stoppage which is illegal under the Bombay Act. In return, the Bombay Act grants the approved union the following privileges: (a) to collect union dues on the premises where wages are paid; (b) to put up notices on the premises of the undertaking where members are employed; and (c) to hold discussions, for the purpose of preventing or settling an industrial dispute, with members of the union and employers' representatives, and also to inspect an undertaking for the same purpose. Further, the approved union is entitled to legal aid at government expense in any determination of the legality of a stoppage, or of an important question of law or fact.

The Bombay Act also stated clearly that "no employee shall be allowed to appear or act in any proceedings under this Act except through the representative of the employees." Similarly, works committees under the Act can be established only in concerns where there is a representative union or a registered union with at least 15 per cent membership. Also, the worker-members of the works committee shall be nominated by the union.

A special institution provided in the Bombay Act is the Government Labour Welfare Officer, really a continuation of the authority first established in the 1934 Bombay Act. The Labour Welfare Officer is statutorily authorized and required to: (*a*) "watch the interests of employees and promote harmonious relations between employers and employees"; (*b*) "investigate the grievances of employees and represent to employers such grievances and make recommendations to them." He is also empowered to appear in any proceedings under this Act. He may neither so appear nor investigate grievances where there is an approved union, except at the latter's request.

The procedures and regulations embodied in the Bombay and all-India Acts constitute in essence the industrial relations law which has guided the government's approach to industrial disputes settlement in the years since Independence.[24] In 1950 the Industrial Disputes (Appellate Tribunal) Act was passed establishing a Labour Appellate Tribunal to ensure uniformity and to provide for an appellate authority over numerous, often uncoordinated, decisions of different industrial tribunals throughout the country.

The Industrial Disputes Act itself was amended in 1953, following reports of rising unemployment and retrenchment in industry. The amendment provided for gratuities to those laid off on the basis of one half-month's basic wages plus dearness allowance for a maximum period of forty-five days in a year. In cases of retrenchment, the compensation was to be fifteen days' average pay for every year of completed service. The Industrial Disputes Act was again amended in 1956 with a view to expediting decisions and introducing a more rational structure as we shall later note; a special category of "protected workmen" was also introduced to protect active trade union workers.

The other salient features of the labour code established since Independence deserve brief comment. The Factories Act of 1948 introduced for the first time the fortyeight-hour week, abolished the distinction between "perennial" and "seasonal" factories, and required all industrial establishments employing 500 or more workers to appoint "Labour Welfare Officers"; employers were also required to provide canteens, lunch rooms, and "creches" (day nurseries for the children of working mothers). The Act further established a weekly day of rest, double pay for overtime work, and paid annual holidays.

Similar requirements were also included in the Mine-workers (Hours of Work, Leave, Hygiene, Safety) Consolidation Act of 1952. The Plantations Labour Act of 1951 regulated for the first time working and employment conditions in the tea, rubber, and cinchona plantations. The Act established a fiftyfour-hour week for adults, and a forty-hour week for children and young persons. Welfare facilities required included the provision of schools and recreation facilities. The Dock Workers (Regulation of Employment) Act of 1948 was again the first of its kind, empowering the Central government, in the case of major ports, to frame schemes to ensure regularity of employment to the dock workers.

A comprehensive measure to regulate job relations within the plant was the Industrial Employment (Standing Orders) Act of 1946, borrowing the concept of "Standing Orders" originally incorporated in the Bombay 1938 Act. The Act required the firms employing one hundred or more workers to frame standing orders which defined terms of employment, including discipline. Standing orders were to be submitted to the government for certification, and, once certified, could not be changed unilaterally.

New legislation in the field of social security should also be mentioned. The Employees' State Insurance Act, passed in 1948, covered all "perennial" (non-seasonal) factories employing twenty or more persons. It was a contributory scheme, drawing funds from employers and employees as well as from the state and Central government. Medical assistance, sickness and maternity benefits, in addition to workmen's compensation (as in the 1923 Act) were provided.[25] The Coal Mines Provident Fund and Bonus Schemes Act, 1948, also a contributory scheme, entitled every coal-miner to a bonus at one-third of his earnings, provided he had fulfilled a minimum attendance qualification. The Employees' Provident Fund Act, 1952, also a contributory scheme, provided for lump sum retirement benefits to the industrial worker or to his dependants.[26]

This all-inclusive code of labour and social legislation, largely expanded and developed in the years since Independence, was clearly designed to provide some of the benefits which workers in more advanced industrial countries enjoyed and, at the same time, to control and contain the possibility of further labour strife. But doubts began to emerge whether a country like India, in the early stages of planned economic and industrial development, could afford to move too rapidly in this direction. The emphasis in the subsequent years after Independence thus shifted away from fresh legislation to consolidating and extending the benefits envisaged in the earlier labour legislation. Also, the interposition of an external authority with direct and pervasive responsibility for preventing or settling industrial disputes was essentially an immediate response to the disturbed conditions just before and after Independence. As the country began to think in terms of development plans and orderly political evolution, the long-term objectives of industrial relations policy commanded increased attention. These concerns found expression in the several Five Year Plans.

Labour Policies of the First, Second and Third Five Year Plans

Considerations of planned economic development were assigned an important place in the shaping of government labour policy in the Plans. The general approach may be summed up best in the following words of the First Plan, a final draft of which was made public in December 1952:

> On the side of labour, there should be a keen realisation of the fact that in an undeveloped economy it cannot build for itself and the community a better life except on the firm foundations of a higher level of productivity to which it has itself to make a substantial contribution. The role of labour in promoting better standards of living for the community involves acceptance of greater regularity in attendance, disciplined behaviour and meticulous care in discharge of duties. To ensure this, much greater attention has to be paid to the spread of literacy and the healthy development of trade unions so that workers are not exposed to exploitation and can act with a greater sense of responsibility.[27]

This concern with the requirements of a developing economy was further evident in the discussion on most of the substantive issues such as wages, social security, rationalization and productivity, protective labour legislation and the regulation of industrial disputes. A very clear statement of official philosophy along these lines is to be found in the section dealing with industrial relations policy:

> Economic progress is . . . bound up with industrial peace. Industrial relations are, therefore ... a vital concern of the community. ... In normal times and in ordinary cases, whether right to strike or lock-out should be circumscribed is an open question. An economy organized for planned production and distribution, aiming at the realisation of social justice and the welfare of the masses, can function only in an atmosphere of industrial peace. India is moving in this direction. It is also at present passing through a period of economic and political emergency. Taking the period of the next few years, the regulation of industrial relations in the country has to be based on these two considerations and it is incumbent on the State to arm itself with legal powers to refer disputes for settlement by arbitration or adjudication, on failure of efforts to reach an agreement by other means. ... The restrictive aspects of any existing or future labour legislation must be judged in the light of these considerations.[28]

The labour section of the First Plan also stressed the importance attached by the state to direct settlement. Labour and management were exhorted to conceive of their relationship "as a partnership in a constructive endeavour." It was emphasized that "the representatives of employers and trade unions should be associated at every step in the implementation of the Plan."[29] In a special section devoted to public enterprises, the First Plan proposed:

1. The public sector "should set the pace and serve as models" in respect of wages, working conditions and welfare amenities;
2. The board of directors of public undertakings should be persons possessed of a sympathetic appreciation of labour problems;

3. The benefits of all labour laws applicable to private undertakings should be made available to workers of public undertakings, and as a rule exemptions from such labour legislation
should not be granted;

4. There should be progressive participation of labour in the
running of the "many matters of the undertaking" so that the
workers "feel that, in practice, as well as in theory, they are
partners in the undertaking;"

5. There should be encouragement of healthy unionism, and there
should be no restrictions on industrial and commercial
employees exercising their trade union rights like any other
employees;

6. Agreements should be entered into "for increasing output
and reducing cost, combating absenteeism and checking
offences against discipline."

On wage increases, the Plan stated:

On the side of wages, any upward movement at this juncture will
further jeopardize the economic stability of the country if it is
reflected in costs of production and consequently raises the price
of the product. For workers too, such gains will prove illusory
because in all likelihood they will soon be cancelled by a rise in
the general price level, and in the long run the volume of employment may be adversely affected. Such an increase in wages
should, therefore, be avoided. Workers can be expected to agree
to such a course only if restrictions are also placed on the
distribution of profits.... Any steps to restrict wage increases
should, therefore, be preceded by similar restrictions on the
distribution of profits. Subject to this, wage increases should
be granted under the following circumstances:

(i) to remove anomalies or where the existing rates are abnormally low;

(ii) to restore the pre-war real wage, as a first step towards
the living wage, through increased productivity resulting
from rationalisation and the renewal or modernisation of
plant.[30]

With respect to social security, the First Plan merely enumerated measures already undertaken by the state without suggesting any major alteration. On protective labour legislation, the Plan referred to existing legislation as "sufficient for the purpose" of improving working conditions "in order to get the best out of a worker in the matter of production."[31] The Plan concluded: "The emphasis in the next five years should, therefore, be on the administrative measures needed for the implementation of such legislation."

Special attention was also devoted to improving the quality and distribution of manpower in industry, and to raising the levels of productivity. The policy statement in the First Plan called for improvements in the methods of recruitment and technical and vocational training of labour. It was felt that the services rendered by the government-operated employment exchange organizations should be considerably expanded. Increasing utilization of national and international experts (including the experts provided by the ILO) and greater attention to "training-within-industry" programmes were recommended. On the controversial question of rationalization, the Plan recommended the adoption of certain safeguards, as we shall discuss more in detail later in this chapter.

Encouragement of Tripartite and Bipartite Consultation

In concluding this review of labour policy in the First Plan, special mention must be made of the Plan's conception of the role of trade unions and employers' associations in a planned economy:

> The trade unions and the employers' associations can play a positive and important role in the execution of plans. . . . For the successful implementation of the Plans in India, cooperation from trade unions and employers is absolutely essential . . . the representatives of employers and trade unions should be associated at every step in the implementation of the Plan.[32]

Various steps have been taken by the government to encourage the participation of representatives of labour and management in the formulation and implementation of labour policy. The tripartite machinery at the Centre, comprising the Indian Labour

Conference and the Standing Labour Committee, has already been mentioned in the review of government policy during World War II. In 1954, direct national bipartite consultation was encouraged, with the revival of the Joint Consultative Board. Those represented on the board included, besides employer representatives, officials of the Hind Mazdoor Sabha, and the Indian National Trade Union Congress. G.L. Nanda, the then Cabinet Minister for Planning and a veteran Ahmedabad TLA leader, acted as chairman of the board in his personal capacity. More recently, in connection with the Second Plan, a Labour Panel has been established as an advisory body to the Planning Commission. The body is fully representative, and is composed of delegates from all the four labour federations, the different employers' federations, and the ministries principally concerned.

Labour representation has also been provided for in the implementation and administration of legislative policy. The Industries (Development and Regulation) Act of 1951 (including an amendment in 1953) affords the most notable instance of the kind. Labour representation is provided for both in the Central Advisory Council of Industries and in the Development Councils appointed for the different industries. Labour representatives have also been associated on the directorates of the various public enterprises and on the statutory authorities created for the implementation of various enactments. All of these represent a persistent and widespread use of the technique of tripartite consultation in industry and in the formulation of official policy.[33]

The statement of labour policy as outlined in the First Plan is continued in most basic essentials in the Second and Third Plans. However, there have been modifications, reflecting pressures that the government had had to contend with. One of these centred around the merits of the compulsory adjudication system.

Compulsory Adjudication and Collective Bargaining

The compulsory adjudication system is, as we have seen in the preceding review, the corner-stone of labour dispute settlement procedures in India. The tripartite Labour Panel of the Planning Commission re-examined in 1956 possible modifications of the system in the light of criticisms; other efforts have been made mainly under the auspices of the Indian Labour Conference. But compulsory adjudication survived one effort to reverse the trend toward government intervention; and it seems likely to survive others. A review of the earlier effort and the reasons for its failure is instructive.

When V. V. Giri, a union leader with long experience in the railway industry, succeeded Jagjivan Ram as Minister of Labour in New Delhi in 1952, he became an articulate spokesman for the view that voluntary negotiation between the parties was generally preferable to taking a dispute before a tribunal for decision. He held, further, that the availability of compulsory adjudication discouraged genuine collective bargaining.[34] This view became known as the "Giri approach" and received wide publicity and discussion in India during 1952–53.

There was a favourable response from some employer groups, though not all, but the four labour federations were opposed. Even the Communist-dominated All-India Trade Union Congress, which had consistently attacked the compulsory adjudication system, urged freedom for workers to strike or to take a case to a tribunal.[35] More effective opposition to the "Giri approach" developed in the dominant trade union federation (INTUC) and in the state labour ministries, particularly. Between the twelfth session of the Indian Labour Conference in October 1952, and the Labour Ministers' Conference in February 1953, Giri was forced to recognize this opposition; and subsequently he withdrew his earlier proposals for substantial change of the compulsory adjudication machinery in accord with the majority view, even though his personal views had not changed.[36] His resignation later in August 1954 came over government modification of an Appellate Tribunal award in a dispute involving salaries for bank employees.[37] He was succeeded by Khandubhai Desai, former general secretary of the Textile Labour Association in Ahmedabad and former president of the INTUC. Mr. Desai clearly indicated his preference for retaining the essentials of the compulsory adjudication system.[38]

The reasons for opposition to the "Giri approach" and support of the compulsory adjudication system were elaborated in many interviews with government officials, employers, and trade union leaders in India during 1954–55. They can be summarized as follows:

1. India faces many difficult problems in rapid industrialization under her Five Year Plans, and she cannot tolerate work stoppages which would interfere with the achievement of her production goals.

2. If strikes were permitted to occur in important industries or sectors, this would play into the hands of the Communist trade unions, which are adept at manipulating grievances and capitalizing on discontent.

3. Trade unions are generally too weak and workers lack sufficient resources to survive long strikes. So, if compulsory adjudication were not available, workers and their unions would be at the mercy of employers, most of whom would refuse to deal with unions or make any concessions voluntarily.

4. The labour ministries in the various states want to keep a firm hand on the labour situation and avoid trouble. Their present power to refer disputes to adjudication gives them a substantial measure of control which they would lose under a system which permitted work stoppages on a large scale.

5. The government has an obligation to all people, and if the parties cannot reach an agreement voluntarily, it is better to let an impartial third party decide what is right than to permit management and labour to decide the issue by a test of strength. A decision imposed by one party on another through brute strength is immoral.

Some quotations from the interviews will illustrate these views and bring out the strong feelings involved.[39]

I am against a trial of strength. Today it is capital which may be unjust, but are you sure that tomorrow, if labour wins and is strong, it will do the just thing? And we have no guarantee that labour and capital will not combine at the expense of the nation. Between labour and capital, of course, I am on the side of labour; but the nation's interests must be superior to those of labour. For these reasons, I still prefer adjudication to strikes. [*Labour minister of an important industrial state*]

If your object is to build a powerful trade union movement and encourage collective bargaining, you might favour less resort to compulsory adjudication. But if your objective is economic development and political stability, then you must have a measure of discipline. Perhaps in twenty years, when we can afford strikes, we can afford to try free collective bargaining. [*Member of the civil service*]

Collective bargaining is almost a repugnant idea to me. The "right to strike" and the "right to hire and fire" all meant more before the adult franchise and the democratic welfare state developed. But today in twentieth century India, we must think in terms of the "right to work" and the duties and responsibilities of management and labour to the public welfare, represented by the consumer. Therefore, the state must retain the power to prevent mere strength of either management or labour determining the conditions of employment, including wages. Work stoppages, which are part of the Western concept of collective bargaining, are costly, and India can't afford them now when it needs more production desperately. So the state must intervene in almost every dispute except the minor ones.[40] [*Central government official*][41]

Since direct settlement has not been fruitful, we find the need for a friendly third party, who has a thankless task, however. There was voluntary arbitration under the Mysore Labour Act, 1941, but it did not work because neither employers nor labour would ever agree. Now there is too much suspicion, and neither has sufficient respect for the other. [*High state government official*]

The Giri approach was not only premature, but it misread the whole trend in India of planned economic development. The liberal democratic outlook which characterized the handling of labour relations in advanced industrial countries in the West cannot be applied without qualification to an industrially underdeveloped country. [*Prominent Indian economist associated with Five-Year Plans*]

Compulsory adjudication is the only workable solution so long as the leadership of the trade unions of India is allowed to remain a free-for-all scramble of persons using trade union activities to further their own political and personal ambitions. We would prefer voluntary negotiations but, in the present unbridled competition for leadership of the workers, practically every voluntary or negotiated improvement has been promptly followed by much more extravagant demands. So compulsory adjudication now offers the only machinery which, by the independent establishment of fair working conditions and wages, gives employers some hope of at least a little period of some certainty about production costs, and by establishment of these standards, some hope of resuming the voluntary negotiation method of settling future disputes when both workers and employers have such standards to guide them as to what is desirable and what is practical. [*Leading employers' association official*]

While many employers and employer spokesmen favoured the Giri approach, I was more cautious. Looking at the broad picture, I felt that collective bargaining was premature in India because of the strong possibility that industrial strife would encourage Communist unions, and that strikes would disrupt our production goal under the Five Year Plan. [*Secretary of an employers' federation*]

Compulsory adjudication is necessary because trade unions are not strong-enough to bargain with employers. Except in Ahmedabad, no union really has sufficient staff to prepare data and present cases to tribunals. Unions are even now at a disadvantage with employers before tribunals, although lawyers are entering the unions. Without compulsory arbitration, unions would be even worse off than they are now. [*Government official*]

Tribunals are absolutely necessary for protecting weaker unions. We don't need them where unions are strong, but most unions in India aren't strong. Giri had been out of touch with the real trade union movement so long that he didn't know what was happening outside of railroads. [*Regional INTUC union leader*]

I have urged abolition of the Appellate Tribunal because of added expense and delays, but I feel that Industrial Tribunals are necessary to get justice for workers who are still too weak. [*HMS union official*]

Unions are strong enough to forego compulsory adjudication
only in a few industries like textiles, cement, and railways. But in
others, workers can't afford to strike because employers are much
stronger. Are these workers to remain at the mercy of employers?
There must be machinery to give justice if the employer denies it
and there must be compulsion. When a strike can easily be broken
by hiring new employees now unemployed, adjudication is our
only hope. [*Local INTUC union officer*]

A succinct summary of the government's attitude toward com-
pulsory adjudication was presented by Shantilal Shah, Labour
Minister of Bombay State and Indian government delegate to the
June 1955 Conference of the International Labour Organization.

In an economy where development is planned to achieve a
definite target under regulation of the State, it would obviously be
impracticable to leave the vital field of labour-management
relations entirely to chance. Labour-management relations has
been a subject of debate in India for the last few years. We have
come to the conclusion that, though every encouragement should
be given to collective bargaining and voluntary settlement of
disputes, the State should be prepared to intervene whenever
the voluntary machinery fails to work. We believe that the best
way of resolving labour-management differences which are not
solved by mutual negotiations is not a trial of strength by strikes
and lock-outs but by an award by an impartial body.... The
success of voluntary negotiation and collective bargaining presup-
poses the existence of a united trade-union movement and an
enlightened outlook on the part of the employer elements, which
it has taken the advanced countries of the West long years to
develop. An underdeveloped economy moving forward to
achieve a planned target cannot afford the hazards involved in
leaving labour-management relations beyond the pale of state
action. We propose to profit by the experience of the Western
world in the earlier stages of industrialization and avoid as far
as possible the malaise that it created. We have planned our
development, and regulation of labour-management relations
is also a part of our Plan. I need hardly emphasize that in our

planning we have scrupulously avoided regimentation and tried to combine the principle of freedom with that of social direction.[41]

Proposals for Change

To be sure, the emphasis which Giri put on voluntary negotiation and agreement, and his criticism of compulsory adjudication as discouraging collective bargaining, still find sympathetic agreement in India. Some managements point out that, so long as unions can take a case to compulsory adjudication, there is no incentive to negotiated agreements.[42] And some union leaders particularly among the Socialist unions, are critical of the effect of compulsory adjudication in weakening or hampering the growth of strong, independent trade unions.[43] These leaders also charge that in making referrals to adjudications, some of the state labour ministry officials or conciliators tend to favour INTUC unions as opposed to unions affiliated to other political parties. This charge is just as vehemently denied by INTUC officials, by some State Labour Ministers, and by the Union Labour Minister.[44]

But all union groups have united in criticizing the delays which accompany the adjudication process and especially the availability of the Appellate Tribunal, which (it is charged) has frequently reversed or modified lower tribunal decisions which were more favourable to labour.[45] Employers have also been critical of the delays but have looked upon the Appellate Tribunal as bringing some semblance of consistency and uniformity to the body of decisions flowing from the lower tribunals.

Nevertheless, the Central government was sympathetic to the protest of the unions, and presented a bill to amend the Industrial Disputes Act (1947) in September 1955. This was subsequently passed by the Lok Sabha on 24 July 1956. In the "Statement of Objects and Reasons" accompanying the bill, Khandubhai Desai, the Labour Minister, summarized one of the changes as follows:

There is a large volume of criticism that appeals filed before the Appellate Tribunal take a long time for disposal and involve a great deal of expenditure which the workers cannot afford. It is proposed to repeal the Industrial Disputes (Appellate Tribunal) Act, 1950, and at the same time, to substitute the present system of original tribunals, manned by personnel of appropriate qualifications. References to the National Tribunals will be made by the Central Government and they will cover disputes which are of such a nature that establishments situated in more than one State are likely to be interested in, or affected by, the disputes.[46]

The three-tier system included, in addition to the National Tribunals, a system of labour courts to pass on standing orders and disputes over them, discharge or dismissal of employees, and other disciplinary action; and industrial tribunals to hear disputes over wages, allowances, hours, leave, bonus, wage classification, rationalization, and so on—except when these were of national importance and would be referred directly to the National Tribunals.[47]

Another change incorporated in the new Industrial Disputes (Amendment and Miscellaneous Provisions) Act was designed to meet strong employer opposition to Section 33 of the Industrial Disputes Act, 1947. This prohibited any disciplinary action being taken against workers during the pendency of conciliation or a dispute before a tribunal, even though the misconduct might be wholly unconnected with the particular dispute, unless express written permission were given by the conciliator or tribunal judge. Employers contended with good reason that the delays in taking disciplinary action under this provision were disastrous for maintenance of good discipline within the plant or establishment. The change provided that the employer could take the necessary disciplinary action against workers in offences not connected with a pending dispute, but, "where the action taken involves discharge or dismissal, he will have to pay the workman one month's wages and simultaneously file an application before the authority before which the proceedings are pending, for its approval of the action taken."[48] It is perhaps indicative of the difficulty under which employers operate that a proposal such as this, generally approved by labour and management representatives on the Joint Consultative Board as early as 1954 and widely agreed as necessary, was not enacted into law until July 1956, and even then was not immediately put into effect.

Other criticisms of the system of settling labour disputes have centred upon the inadequacy of existing conciliation services and the tendency of some state labour ministries to refer disputes too readily to adjudication. A group of company labour officers expressed this view:

> Many cases now go to young, inexperienced conciliation commissioners who don't know how to mediate. They get both parties together in the same room and ask each to state its position which just makes the situation worse. If we suggest separate meetings, they say, "We don't have time." They are just rubber stamps and often refer cases directly to adjudication.

Other instances were cited by employers of inexperienced or biased conciliators holding joint meetings, listening to the union's demands and then turning to the employers present and commenting, "These sound reasonable to me. What are your objections?" In some of the state labour dispute settling agencies, there have been cases where the "conciliator" and the "adjudicator" was the same person— sometimes a recent university graduate—with rather arbitrary powers.

On the other hand, one of the most successful former chief conciliators for the Central government explained his technique as fact-finding and trying to understand each party's position in separate meetings, then making recommendations if a mutual settlement did not emerge. He summarized his final comment to the parties in these words: "I will be happy if you accept my recommendations, but I will be even happier if you reject them, for then you will not feel a settlement has been imposed and if I am right you will learn through a strike or other difficulties that you should have followed the suggestion, and after that you will be better able to settle your own problems."[49] This man added that "adjudication has made a mockery of conciliation; conciliation must recommend or reject reference to adjudication, so all effort is pointed in that direction and not in bringing agreement."

Another former state Labour Commissioner, now the Personnel Officer of a large private firm, stated that, despite the discouraging effect of compulsory adjudication, "the improvement of conciliation services is the single most important thing which could be done to assist the development of direct collective bargaining. Many conciliators intervene too early, and they lack the training and experience which is necessary for effective assistance." This same view was expressed in a resolution passed by the Third All-India Conference of Labour and Welfare Officers late in 1955, part of which stated:

> Conciliation proceedings should be preceded as far as possible by a preliminary investigation by the Conciliation Officer for equipping himself with the full facts of the case and generally preparing the ground for a proper approach to conciliation. Conciliation should be undertaken only if every possible avenue of the internal machinery for the settlement of a dispute has been tried before.
>
> The Conciliation Officer's report should be factual as far as possible and not contain any recommendation on the question of reference of the dispute to a Tribunal. Should the case be referred to a Tribunal, the report of the Conciliation Officer should not be passed on to it. Before assuming full responsibilities as a Conciliation Officer, he should undergo suitable training which should include practical work as an under-study to a full-fledged Conciliation Officer for a reasonable period.[50]

Even though much remained to be done to improve conciliation services, there were encouraging reports in 1955 that the labour ministers in several important industrial states were scrutinizing more carefully than before the cases proposed for adjudication and refusing to refer them when the employer's offer appeared to be genuine and reasonable. In one state the Chief Labour Commissioner even stated: "There will be no collective bargaining if disputes are readily referred to tribunals. A strike or lockout threat helps bring agreement, and I say this knowing that it is not the New Delhi view."[51]

The official Central government view, however, is that conciliation proceedings are highly effective. The Union Labour Minister reported in July 1956 that in the Central sphere 75 per cent of the cases referred to conciliation machinery during 1955 were settled, although in the state sphere the comparable figure was only 44 per cent.[52]

The Record of Dispute Settlement

Statistical evidence to validate these claims is difficult to get, and what is available is still more difficult to evaluate. For example, if labour and management do reach agreement, the written document is frequently initialled and approved by the state Labour Commissioner, and this case then may be reported as "settled through conciliation." Furthermore, the reports from some industrial states, where the reputation for good conciliation services is relatively low, claim a higher percentage of disputes settled through adjudication than in other states, where employers say that references to adjudication are scrutinized more carefully.

Data supplied by the labour ministries of the states of West Bengal and Bombay are illustrative of the claims and the difficulties of evaluation. In Table XXXIV, we see that the percentage of disputes settled through conciliation in West Bengal was as high as 72 per cent in 1951; yet the number of cases referred to adjudication in that year was considerably less than 28 per cent of the total. Table XXXV shows that the percentage of cases settled by conciliation in the same year in Bombay state was much lower than in West Bengal; but

TABLE XXXIV

DISPUTES SETTLED THROUGH CONCILIATION AND
ADJUDICATION IN WEST BENGAL STATE, 1948-53

Year	Number of disputes	per cent settled	Referred to adjudication	Awards made
1948	3,177	56.2	192	161
1949	3,366	54.2	123	115
1950	2,904	63.5	160	172
1951	3,062	72.5	141	124
1952	3,158	56.9	235	200
1953	3,813	63.7	293	243

SOURCE: Labour Ministry, West Bengal, 1955.

TABLE XXXV
DISPUTES SETTLED THROUGH CONCILIATION IN BOMBAY STATE, 1947-48 TO JULY 1954

Year (fiscal)	Under Bombay I.R. Act, 1946		Under Central I.D. Act, 1947		
	Number of disputes	Per cent settled	Number of disputes	Per cent settled	Referred to Adjudication
1947–48	417	11.5	449	41.6	(not available)
1948–49	534	21.1	750	39.4	134
1949–50	1,142	30.3	1,077	28.7	195
1950–51	1,132	28.9	1,168	24.1	226
1951–52	784	26.7	1,006	23.9	241
1952–53	859	24.1	1,077	22.8	174
1953–54	613	19.4	1,299	27.2	153
Jan-June 1954	441	23.6	615	13.3	105

SOURCE: Labour Ministry, Bombay State, 1954. Since Bombay has a separate Industrial Relations Act applying to certain industries, data are reported separately above. No data for cases referred to adjudication under the state Act were supplied. Obviously, not all the disputes which were not settled by conciliation were referred to adjudication. There were part settlements in some, but most were dropped or closed, according to the fuller report supplied. Some disputes were minor, involving individual workers; others were industry-wide in one area. No distinction is made between these in the official data.

this does not accurately measure the difference in the quality of the conciliation services in these two states—in fact, the circumstantial evidence and reported impressions are the reverse. Furthermore, while the number of disputes and the number referred to adjudication have been on the increase in West Bengal, the reverse has been occurring in Bombay; and this is confirmed by other reports.

Comparable figures are not available for more recent periods at least in the issues of *West Bengal Labour Gazette* (January 1962 to January 1963) and *Bombay Labour Gazette* (September 1962 to August 1963) which were available. Supplementary figures are available for West Bengal which further illustrate the points made in the previous paragraph.[53] A large number of disputes are handled without work stoppages, but the Labour Commissioner's role may be substantial. Thus, during the year 1957, there were 6,118 disputes (including 1,600 carried over from the previous year), of which 4,616 were disposed of during the year. Of these 4,616, in 2,122 cases (or 47 per cent) settlement followed intervention by the Labour Commissioner and 540 cases (or 11.6 per cent) were referred to the tribunal. The total number of disputes "on the books" has increased steadily almost every year from 3,945 in 1948 to 6,118 in 1957. The statistics regarding disputes involving work stoppages are perhaps more instructive as to the role played by formal conciliation efforts.

TABLE XXXVI

DISPOSITION OF CASES IN DISPUTES INVOLVING
WORK STOPPAGES

Year	Number of disputes	Disputes settled by							
		Conciliation		Negotiation		Unconditional resumption	Otherwise	Total settlement	
		Number	Per cent	Number	Per cent			Number	Per cent
1948	197	85	43.14						
1949	158	84	53.16	34	21.51	24	9	151	95.56
1950	116	66	56.89	11	9.40	25	5	107	92.24
1951	174	116	66.66	24	13.79	22	5	167	95.97
1952	139	86	61.87	16	11.51	26	8	138	99.28
1953	266	119	44.73	35	13.15	96	2	252	94.73
1954	164	103	62.80	29	17.68	6	8	146	89.02
1955	352	276	78.40	23	6.53	43	7	349	99.14
1956	177	101	57.06	29	16.38	38	1	169	95.48
1957	227	138	60.79	30	10.83	47	3	218	96.03

EXPLANATION: All percentage figures are in terms of the total number of disputes reported in column 2.

Of the 218 cases settled in 1957, only one case was settled by reference to adjudication.[54] Generally, the reference to adjudication is limited and comprises the category "otherwise" in column 8. The total references to adjudication in 1957, thus, were 541 as opposed to a total of 4,843 outstanding disputes. The absolute number of adjudicated settlements have, however, registered a consistent increase as seen from the figures in Table XXXVII.[55]

On the all-India basis the record of man-days lost through indus-

TABLE XXXVII

Year	Number of awards	Year	Number of awards
1947	42	1953	328
1948	145	1954	454
1949	170	1955	388
1950	192	1956	481
1951	188	1957	555
1952	223		

trial disputes shows as improvement since the post-war years of 1946 and 1947. Table XXXVIII illustrates this trend, with the 1950 total an exception because of the long Bombay textile strike in that year. Compulsory adjudication and the pressure used by the government authorities have undoubtedly been a positive influence in reducing time lost due to industrial disputes.[56] In 1957, for instance, nearly

TABLE XXXVIII
INDUSTRIAL DISPUTES IN INDIA, 1947-56

Year	Number of disputes	Workers involved	Working days lost
1947	1,811	1,840,784	16,562,666
1948	1,259	1,059,120	7,837,173
1949	920	685,457	6,600,595
1950	814	719,883	12,806,704
1951	1,071	691,321	3,818,928
1952	963	809,242	3,336,961
1953	772	466,607	3,382,608
1954	840	477,138	3,372,630
1955	1,166	527,767	5,697,848
1956	1,258	722,334	7,095,960
1957	1,630	889,371	6,429,319
1958	1,524	928,566	7,797,585
1959	1,531	693,616	5,633,148
1960	1,556	982,868	6,514,955

SOURCE: *Indian Labour Gazette,* vol. XIV, nos. 3 and 9 (September 1956 and March 1957), pp. 266 and 753. For years 1957-60, *Indian Labour Year Book,* 1961, Labour Bureau, Government of India, p. 96.

50 per cent of the disputes involving work stoppages were settled in less than 5 days and nearly 60 per cent in 10 days.[57]

While conciliation and adjudication may reduce the number of overt disputes, the basic causes of conflict between labour and management are not thereby removed. As one student of Indian labour problems has put it:

Thus the main defect in industrial relations in this country is the

INDUSTRIAL DISPUTES ACCORDING TO DEMANDS[a]

(per cent)

Year	Number of Stoppages	Type of demand involved (per cent of total)					
		Wages and Allowances	Bonus	Personnel	Leave and hours	Other	Not known
1939	406	57.3	0.5	18.2	2.9	21.1	
1940	322	62.7	2.8	16.8	3.1	14.6	
1941	359	60.7	2.5	15.3	4.2	17.3	
1942	694	51.9	11.3	9.1	1.0	26.7	
1943	716	47.8	7.7	7.4	1.9	35.2	
1944	658	56.5	7.6	12.5	5.3	17.9	
1945	820	43.4	13.4	17.7	6.8	18.0	0.7
1946	1,629	37.1	4.9	17.2	8.0	32.8	
1947	1,811	31.7	10.8	19.3	5.2	32.1	0.9
1948	1,259	30.5	9.0	28.8	8.7	22.1	0.9
1949	920	30.1	5.7	23.6	9.1	25.5	6.0
1950	814	27.4	9.0	22.8	8.2	28.5	4.1
1951	1,071	28.1	6.5	28.1	7.9	25.2	4.2
1952	963	29.4	9.8	33.8	7.5	16.4	3.1
1953	772	26.0	9.9	35.8	4.5	18.4	5.4
1954	840	30.0	6.7	37.0	10.3	16.3	
1955	1,166	24.6	17.3	32.6	5.2	20.3	
1956	1,258	25.9	8.1	27.7	5.2	16.1	8.3
1957	1,360	29.6	13.6	27.8	3.1	5.0	20.9
1958	1,524	30.5	11.5	29.2	3.8	3.2	21.8
1959	1,531	27.1	10.3	29.1	3.7	29.8	
1960	1,556	37.1	10.5	24.7	2.4	25.3	

a Disputes involving less than ten workers are not included here. Figures for 1939-49 are from S. D. Punekar, *Industrial Peace in India*, pp. 41-2; for 1950-51, from *Indian Labour Year Book* 1951-52, Government of India (Delhi, 1954), p. 168; for 1952 and 1953 from *Indian Labour Year Book*, 1953-54, p. 160; for 1954 to 1960 from the issues of *Indian Labour Year Books*, 1954-55 to 1961.

lack of co-operation at the lowest level, i.e., between an individual employer and his employees. In the absence of this co-operation industrial peace cannot be achieved, in spite of full co-operation at the higher levels and adoption of various methods such as conciliation and arbitration.[58]

There is no statistical classification of the type of issues involved in disputes under adjudication, but some indication can be seen in the tabulation of industrial disputes according to the demands presented by unions. Table XXXIX shows quite clearly that disputes involving wages, allowances and bonus comprise the largest percentage in most recent years, with "personnel" issues taking a second place. These include disciplinary cases and retrenchment due to mill

TABLE XL

INDUSTRIAL AWARDS IN WEST BENGAL 1947-1957, CLASSIFICATION OF DISPUTED ISSUES

Year	Wages	Bonus	Cols. 2 and 3 as per cent of col. 10	Personnel	Service conditions	Cols. 5 and 6 as per cent of col. 10	Welfare	Rest	Total
1	2	3	4	5	6	7	8	9	10
1947	48	7	47.8	20	20	34.7	3	17	115
1948	140	24	39.8	59	97	37.8	36	56	412
1949	229	80	32.7	93	263	37.7	179	99	943
1950	133	51	42.7	76	108	42.7	28	34	430
1951	94	38	44.5	61	61	41.2	14	28	296
1952	108	44	43.6	70	87	45.1	14	25	348
1953	129	60	38.4	145	113	52.5	20	24	491
1954	134	71	30.9	265	154	63.2	7	31	662
1955	125	60	29.3	275	107	60.5	21	43	631
1956	170	57	29.7	305	175	63.0	13	44	764
1957	167	68	28.6	360	173	64.9	9	44	821

SOURCE: *West Bengal Labour Year Book* 1957, pp. 99-102. Issues covered under "personnel" include "Discharge and Dismissal including Termination" which constitute the most numerous of five categories; issues covered under "Service Conditions" include disputes over retiring benefits and recruitment, tenure, promotion, etc.

closures. Disputes over leaves and hours are somewhat less frequent, and "other" causes include disputes over lack of amenities, quantity or quality of food, and so on.[59]

More detailed figures for West Bengal confirm the importance of Wages, Bonus, and Personnel issues. The 227 disputes for 1957 were thus classified as follows according to the principal demands underlying the disputes: Wages—22; Bonus—31; and Personnel—85. This picture, including the intractable nature of disputes involving personnel and service questions, is confirmed by an analysis of adjudication awards between 1947 and 1957 in terms of the issues covered. (See Table XL.)

Further Developments in Public Policy: Government as Active but Indirect Regulator

Much of the preceding section was written on the basis of impressions of the Indian situation obtained from the literature or from field interviews in India prior to the commencement of the Second Five Year Plan. Subsequent developments have done little to alter the salient elements in the Indian scene. As before, the government is committed to a policy of stabilizing industrial relations but is confronted with industrial relations of sufficient severity which will yield only slowly to changes initiated from above. This is clear both from a reading of the relevant literature, greatly augmented by the growth of Indian scholarship in the intervening period, and from field interviews undertaken in India by both of the authors during the Second and Third Plan periods. It is also clear that difficulties continue to arise from the compulsory adjudication system as it is presently administered.

Employers continue to voice criticisms of the discouragement to collective bargaining and the quality of conciliation services. Increasingly, in protest against tribunal awards, many individual employers have also taken their cases in appeal to the civil courts, including the Supreme Court of India. Trade union criticisms have focused on delays in securing adjudicated settlement and the lack of an adequate machinery to ensure the implementation of these settlements. Charges of pro-INTUC favouritism also continue to be made. However, as we have noted in the earlier chapters, there has been a small, but perceptible, improvement in the practices of unions and managements and a growth in the number of mutually negotiated agreements. Some of these simply incorporate principles which have found widespread acceptance as part of the "industrial jurisprudence" of the compulsory adjudication system.

Government officials continue to stress the need for public regulation of labour-management relations and cite the record of decline in man-days lost due to industrial disputes as supporting the wisdom of public policy. However, there is no reason to suppose that the government's position is rigid. Where there is no alternative to public intervention—and there is reason to believe that in many situations labour-management relations are far too chaotic to justify an opposite presumption—the government has been ready to intervene through the machinery of tribunals and conciliation. As in the case of the amendment of the Industrial Disputes Act in 1956, the government has also been willing to modify the basis for its intervention on a pragmatic basis; it has further taken the initiative to develop "model" principles of adjudication under the auspices of the Indian Labour Conference so as to spell out more clearly the circumstances in which public intervention would be appropriate. Finally, even while maintaining the role of enforcement officer in the sphere of labour-management relations, the government has turned increasingly towards creating a consensus on industrial relations issues (which the parties concerned will respect), and towards auxiliary efforts at training and research.

The Second and Third Plan periods thus record an increasing emphasis on indirect measures designed to raise the "moral" commitment of industrial relations participants to national requirements.[60] These in turn reflect a growing feeling that extensive government intervention to police the behaviour of labour and management could not take place of more purposive relationships between the parties. Conceptually and teleologically at any rate, public intervention took the second place, being justified mainly as a consequence of the failure of management and labour to agree. The search for consensus which organized labour, management, and government could support has taken several forms as follows: tripartism, voluntarism, and moral suasion and public pressure.

Special mention must be made of the tripartite principle extensively employed in India as a mechanism of consultation with employers' and workers' representatives and as a device to ensure that the public interest is represented in industrial relations settlements.[61] This principle, mentioned favourably in the First Plan, has since been systematically encouraged ; the various tripartite bodies, including particularly the Indian Labour Conference, now constitute a major means of encouraging public discussion on government policy. Since 1952, when the Labour Minister, V. V. Giri, turned the conference into a general debate on the government's labour policy, a succession of well-publicized conferences have debated virtually every aspect of the government's labour policy. A number of special conferences have been called to discuss the problems of specific industries or other particular topics. ILC resolutions or recommendations, as in the case of rationalization or the abolition of contract labour, have been accepted as guiding principles by tribunals, commissions, or wage boards.

The development of many new public sector enterprises, under the authority of the Central or state government, posed a problem initially, but it was decided to make them integral parts of the ILC, in part due to the pressures generated by participants at the Conference that labour laws and principles of public policy should apply to all units, public or private. It has also been proposed to include representatives from the public—especially research scholars, economists, consumers, etc. It should be noted further that the tripartite machinery has been widely duplicated at the state and industrial levels, although in these cases the groups do not meet as regularly and are not as predictably representative.

Another major innovation is the adoption of several codes, dealing with discipline, inter-union rivalry, and industrial efficiency and welfare.[62] The Code of Discipline, which is the only operative Code, should be discussed. Briefly, the Code is an attempt to prohibit or curb specific practices, either by labour or management, which are likely to worsen industrial relations. The text of the Code contains provisions for recognition of unions and verification of membership, although these are vague and are weakened by the absence of a clear requirement that managements recognize "representative" unions and negotiate with them in good faith. The experience since the adoption of the Code has raised the issue of management's obligation to deal with unions inasmuch as the latter do assume some responsibility, and may suffer withdrawal of recognition, in the event of code violation. These developments have also implied a constraint on the role of the government in view of allegations by rival unions that government officials, particularly in some of the states, have supported or bolstered INTUC unions on a discriminatory and exclusive basis. In appealing for support to the Code, Nanda (Labour Minister until Prime Minister Nehru's death in 1964) assured the Indian Labour Conference that there would be no discrimination on a political basis in the administration of the Code.

Both management and labour have come under pressure for certain activities which were considered inimical to industrial relations even though they were merely availing themselves of procedures permitted by, or loopholes in, the law. For example, "screening" bodies have been established to discourage appeals to the higher courts against decisions of lower-level tribunals, especially if the matters at issue are not "substantive" or "material." In regard to discharge cases, it has been contended that the spirit of the Code required more than a mechanical adherence to the legally required procedures of inquiry and that managerial decisions should also be judged in the light of their substantive validity. Although the ILC did not explicitly ban the hunger-strike, the considerable antagonism towards its use compelled the union representatives to disown responsibility for its use.

The third and final aspect of the changed direction in public policy is its emphasis on voluntarism. Partly, this consists of an effort to encourage negotiations within the framework of the compulsory adjudication system. Thus, during interviews, government officials have stressed their reluctance to refer disputes for adjudication if they felt that serious negotiations had not taken place. Also, the amendment to the Industrial Disputes Act in 1956 provided for legal recognition of negotiated settlements. Progress in terms of collective agreements has further received many words of praise from distinguished government leaders. The second plan ushered in a policy of extensively publicizing these developments. Some government officials have been notably flexible in the administration of labour laws with a view to encouraging genuinely constructive relationships. Labour-management disputes have also been mediated by the intervention of prominent public officials acting in their individual capacities. Thus, in the Kanpur rationalization dispute, Dr. Sampurnanand, formerly Chief Minister of the state of Uttar Pradesh, stepped in to provide a compromise award. This echoes similar interventions in the Bombay textile industry bonus disputes in 1955 and 1962, first by the Central Labour Minister and later by the state Chief Minister. The major lacuna in Indian industrial relations has, however, been at the plant level where it has been difficult to secure rapport between unions and managements.

To meet this need, the Indian Labour Conference devised "model" grievance procedures which it was hoped would be widely adopted. The Government of India has also adopted a policy of favouring workers' participation in management; however, in contrast to the provision for works committees in the 1947 Industrial Disputes Act, the scheme was designed to be voluntary. An all-India tripartite conference in 1958 endorsed a limited programme of joint management councils which would have certain rights to information, to be consulted, and to take executive action in defined (mainly welfare) spheres. The workers' education scheme launched in 1957 had from the beginning, as one of its objectives, the task of training union representatives to handle the responsibilities of worker participation in management. The progress in these respects has been slow, as one would expect. The scheme for worker participation in management was further clouded by divergent expectations. Managements reacted adversely to the implied sharing of managerial prerogatives, and workers felt let down as the councils provided only for an advisory role. The scheme for workers' participation in management nevertheless reflects a widespread concern for the spread of consultative practice at the workplace. There is also no doubt about the need for improvement of plant level personnel procedures. Some of the most important advances in these respects have been displayed by a handful of managements. These have been supported by government officials in line with their policy of supporting progressive managements.

Any listing of steps initiated by the government to improve the quality of industrial relations in the community should also include measures of training, research and publicity, which are likely to yield results only after some time. We mentioned earlier the government-sponsored workers' education schemes providing mainly training in principles of trade unionism. One should further note the institution of national and regional productivity councils, and a wide range of training activities to improve the quality of management and supervision.[63] Attention has also been given to the training of government officials responsible for the administration of public policy. In 1962, the Indian government announced plans for the establishment of National Labour Research Institute in collaboration with Indian universities and employers' and workers' organizations. These programmes have benefited greatly by sending members of Indian organizations abroad as well as by inviting qualified personnel from foreign educational and research institutions and from workers' and management organizations to visit India. These training activities have been assisted by a number of organizations, both Indian and foreign.

Several international organizations, notably the International Labour Organization, have given aid; in addition to the Labour Ministry, several other ministries have been active; Indian universities have also developed programmes in industrial relations and management; and recently two All-India Institutes of Management have been established with the active association of the Massachusetts Institute of Technology and Harvard University. Leading private enterprises have also established research institutes of their own. Special mention must be made of the Ahmedabad Textile Industry Research Association and similar research institutes established by the Bombay and Coimbatore textile industries. An All-India Administrative Staff College, sponsored by the government and private industry provides training in management and personnel relations to senior executives from private and public sector enterprises. Recently, an ambitious industrial relations research centre has been established in New Delhi to honour the memory of a leading industrialist, the late Sir Shri Ram. Finally, the principal workers' organizations, the AITUC and the INTUC, have announced plans to adopt formal training programmes in trade unionism for their own cadres. All of these point to the increasing importance attached to research, training, and publicity with a view to promoting more orderly industrial relations practices.

Concluding Remarks

Although compulsory adjudication and extensive public regulation of labour management relations constitute the corner-stone of the Indian industrial relations system, it is clear that government authorities place a great deal of importance on the development of stable bipartite relationships between labour and management. Inevitably progress is slow, and this justifies the additional steps to train and to improve the quality of unions and managements. Thus a number of key disputes, especially those involving wages, allowances, and bonuses, continue to be settled mainly through the adjudication system. It is also in respect of these disputes that the labour policy of the Indian government impinges closely on the over-all issues of developmental plan priorities. Disputes involving these items thus merit further discussion in the next chapter.

NOTES

1 For a survey of the progress of Indian labour legislation, the following standard works may be consulted: R.K. Das, *History of Indian Labour Legislation,* University of Calcutta (Calcutta, 1941); Sir Atul C. Chatterjee, "Federalism and Labour Legislation in India," *International Labour Review,* vol. 49, nos. 4-5 (January-June 1944), pp. 415-45; P. S. Narasimhan, "Labour Reforms in Contemporary India," *Pacific Affairs,* vol. XXVI, no. 1 (March 1953), pp. 57-68; International Labour Office, *Recent Developments in Certain Aspects of Indian Economy* (New Delhi, 1955), esp. pp. 1-11, dealing with "Labour Legislation in India, 1953-54." *Indian Labour Gazette* and *Indian Labour Year Book* may also be consulted for dependable summaries of Indian legislation. For well-edited, annotated introduction to Indian legislation, consult S.N. Bose, *Indian Labour Code* (Central), (Calcutta, 2nd ed., 1950). *Labour Law Journal* (Madras), published regularly since 1947, is another excellent non-official publication.

2 An authority on Indian legislation points out: "What little legislation there existed ... was confined to making breaches of certain acts of service criminal offences." Alan Gledhill, *The Republic of India: The Development of Its Laws and Constitution* (London, 1951), p. 254.

3 For a good treatment of this early phase of Indian labour legislation up to World War I, see R. K. Das, *The Labour Movement in India* (Berlin, 1923), Chapters I and II, pp. 1-20.

4 On the economic situation in the country, particularly as it affected workers, see Vera Anstey, *The Economic Development of India* (London, 1942), esp. the section

dealing with "Prices, Wages, and the Cost of Living," pp. 445-69.

5 On the impact of the ILO, see V.K.R. Menon, "The Influence of International Labour Conventions on Indian Labour Legislation," *International Labour Review*, vol. LXXIII, no. 6 (June 1956), pp. 551-71; and Subbiah Kannappan, "The Impact of the ILO on Labour Legislation and Policy in India," in *Labour Management and Economic Growth*, Robert L. Aronson and John P. Windmuller, eds., Institute of International Industrial and Labour Relations, Cornell University (Ithaca, New York, 1954).

6 Government of India, Labour Investigation Committee, *Main Report* (New Delhi, 1946), p. 10.

7 *Congress Presidential Addresses* (Madras, 1934), pp. 895-96.

8 Indian National Congress, *Resolutions on Economic Policy and Programme, 1924-54*, All-India Congress Committee (New Delhi, 1954), p. 3.

9 *Ibid.*, pp. 3-6, 8.

10 *Ibid.*, pp. 10-1.

11 *Ibid.*, p. 10.

12 *Ibid.*, p. 14.

13 For an indication of the Congress approach, see R.K. Das, *Principles and Problems of Indian Labour Legislation*, University of Calcutta (Calcutta, 1938), Appendix "Congress Labour Programme," pp. 270-76. Das concludes that " ... it must be said that the Indian National Congress has adopted a very progressive policy and drawn out a bold programme for action." For a somewhat opposed view, see S. D. Punekar, *Trade Unionism in India*, pp. 103-06.

14 For details, see N. S. Pardasani, "Labour Conciliation and Arbitration in India," in A. N. Agarwala, ed., *Indian Labour Problems* (Allahabad, 1947), p. 92.

15 *Ibid.*, pp. 92-3; see also "A Decade of Labour Legislation in India, 1937-48, Part II," *International Labour Review*, vol. 59, January-June 1949, pp. 513-14.

16 International Labour Office, *Wartime Labour Conditions and Reconstruction Planning in India* (Montreal, 1946), p. 37.

17 "The Institution of a Tripartite Labour Organization in India: The Influence of the I.L.O.," *International Labour Review*, vol. XLIII, no. 1 (January 1943), pp. 1-21.

18 *Main Report*, p. 10.

19 From a speech by former Union Labour Minister Jagjivan Ram, "Congress and the Workers," in *Jagjivan Ram on Labour Problems*, Shachi Rani Gurtu, ed. (Delhi, 1951), p. 14.

20 B.V. Keskar, *Congress Hand-Book*, 1946, All-India Congress Committee, Allahabad, pp. 273-75.

21 Government of India, Publications Division, *Square Deal for Labour* (1951), p. 7.

22 For complete text of the Act, see Mathrubutham and Srinivasan, *Indian Factories and Labour Manual* (Madras, 1952), pp. 647-82.

23 An "approved" union also has the right to submit disputes to arbitration; while unions under the Central government's Industrial Disputes Act have only the obligation to submit disputes to arbitration.

24 For the subsequent developments relating to the Industrial Disputes Act,

see *Indian Labour Year Book* 1953-54, pp. 119-25; on the Bombay Act, *ibid.*, pp. 127-30. Although not strictly a labour relations statute, the Preventive Detention Act of 1950 has been invoked by the government in major labour disputes when union (usually Communist) leaders were jailed to prevent local or national disorders affecting the peace. This extreme measure was renewed, after debate, in 1955.

25 Implementation of Employees' State Insurance was delayed until February 1952 and then introduced initially in only a few states. By September 1956, it was in force in 31 centres and covered slightly over one million workers. *Indian Worker*, vol. V, no. 47 (3 September 1956), p. 1.

26 For a fuller discussion, see V. Jagannadham, *Social Insurance in India* (Amsterdam, 1954).

27 Government of India, *The First Five Year Plan* (New Delhi, 1952), p. 571. For full texts of the labour sections of the First and Second Five Year Plans, see Chapter XXIV of *The First Plan* and Chapter XXVII of *The Second Plan*.

28 *Ibid.*, pp. 572-73.

29 *Ibid.*, pp. 573, 81.

30 *Ibid.*, p. 583.

31 *Ibid.*, p. 586.

32 *Ibid.*, p. 581.

33 For a brief indication of the progressive use of the tripartite machinery, see *Indian Labour Year Book*, 1953-54, pp. 167-79, and also previous issues. Very little is known, however, about the actual functioning of the Development Councils under the Industries (Development and Regulation) Act of 1951.

34 In his opening speech at the twelfth session of the Indian Labour Conference held at Naini Tal in October 1952, V. V. Giri said: "Compulsory adjudication has cut at the very root of trade union organisation. . . . If workers find that their interests are best promoted only by combining, no greater urge is needed to forge a bond of strength and unity among them. But compulsory arbitration sees to it that such a bond is not forged. It stands there as a policeman looking out for signs of discontent and at the slightest provocation takes the parties to the court for a dose of costly and not wholly satisfactory justice. The moment the back of the policeman is turned, the parties grow red in the face with redoubled determination, and the whole cycle of litigation starts all over again. . . . Let the trade unions become strong and self-reliant and learn to get on without the assistance of the policeman. They will then know how to organize themselves and get what they want through their own strength and resources. That will also be the means of their achieving greater self-respect. It may be that until the parties have learnt the technique of collective bargaining, there are some unnecessary trials of strength, but whoever has heard of a man learning to swim without having to drink some gulps of water?" *Proceedings of the Indian Labour Conference* (Twelfth Session held in Naini Tal on 8 to 11 October 1952), (Delhi, 1952), pp. 6-7. The Ministry of Labour had distributed a questionnaire to labour and management organizations prior to the conference, seeking their views on compulsory adjudication.

35 *Ibid.*, pp. 237, 243. See Chapter V *supra* for a fuller discussion.

36 Subsequently, Giri, as a member of the Labour Panel of the Planning Commission and as a member of the Lok Sabha, resumed his plea for abolishing compulsory adjudication and encouraging direct collective bargaining. *Hindustan Times* (New Delhi), 22 July 1956. Replying to this view during the debate on the Industrial Disputes (Amendment and Miscellaneous Provisions) Bill in July 1956, Khandubhai Desai, Union Labour Minister, stated that he had always felt that voluntary agreement to refer questions to arbitration was the best solution, and the Bill provided that such agreements should be given legal sanction. But, he added, "Complete *laissez-faire* is out of date. Society cannot allow workers or managements to follow the law of the jungle. Therefore, as a last resort, the Government has taken powers to refer disputes to adjudication." *Hindustan Times,* 25 July 1956.

37 In his public letter of resignation, 30 August 1954, Giri asserted that modification of the Bank Award meant that workers and their organizations would lack confidence in the integrity of tribunal awards in the future. He also charged that government had failed as "model employer." "It has been my fervent wish that Government should be the model employer, inspiring other employers to follow its example. But I have to confess that the possibility of this hope being fulfilled has become remote.... There is a growing feeling among the employing Ministries [such as Railways, Communications, Irrigation, and Public Works] that each can have its own way and its own labour policy, thus rendering the Labour Ministry almost superfluous in shaping Government policy in their behalf." *Times of India,* 9 September 1954.

38 See notes 36 and 40.

39 No less a person than Prime Minister Nehru has taken a strong position in favour of limiting the right to strike or lock-out. He has developed this theme in a number of speeches, emphasizing that, in a planned economy such as India's, there is little justification for strikes. In his talk to the tenth annual meeting of the Association of Scientific Workers of India, he said: "While it is necessary to have trade unions for protecting workers' rights, at the same time it is also necessary to look to the bigger interests of the country....I do not see any wisdom in trying to solve problems in the industry by indulging in fights and clashes or by the show of force or strength. All problems must be solved by mutual consultation in an atmosphere of goodwill and friendship." *Hindu Weekly Review,* 9 January 1956, p. 14.

40 The influence of Gandhi's emphasis on duties and obligations, pointed out earlier in connection with his role in the development of the Textile Labour Association in Ahmedabad, is important here. For views similar to the one quoted, see the 1950 and 1952 addresses of Khandubhai Desai as president of the Indian National Trade Union Congress (Union Labour Minister 1954-57). In 1950 he contrasted the two approaches to labour-management relations: "The one based on principles of conciliation and arbitration initiated and worked out by Gandhiji ... has proved successful, while the other [direct action] has not suited our country." In 1952 he said: "We have, however, to admit that the objective conditions in our country differ to a great extent as compared to Western countries. Workers are illiterate, their unions with a very few exceptions are not very strong, and very few unions have

trained personnel to combat resources and intelligence that the employers can utilize. While, therefore, aiming at self-reliance and evolving trade union sanctions, we in our own interest cannot agree to elimination of compulsory adjudication in cases where employers are recalcitrant. When the country is trying to increase its wealth by planned economy on the one hand, it has to be given due protection by state intervention in industrial disputes which would otherwise strengthen disruptive elements among labour or die-hard capitalists." (1952 *Address,* p. 7.)

While it is critical of some aspects of government labour policy, as we have seen, INTUC officials still emphasize the right to secure justice as opposed to the right to strike. G. Ramanujam, a member of the Working Committee of INTUC, has written: "There can be no lawful strikes or lockouts in industrial relations. At best, it can only be a strike or lockout which is 'not illegal.' For the right to strike . . . is gradually becoming an outmoded conception. . . . With the attainment of our freedom, the conception of strike and lockout . . . had to undergo a further change; i.e., instead of . . . being weapons of *last* resort, they had to be the weapons of *least* resort. This necessity became particularly pronounced as we entered an era of planned economy. Proper planning should make strikes and lockouts wholly unnecessary in industrial relations." "Strikes and Lockouts in Industrial Relations," *Indian Worker* (INTUC, New Delhi), 15 August 1955, p. 8.

41 International Labour Conference, *Provisional Record, no.* 11, 10 June 1955. In the summer of 1957, Prime Minister Nehru was forced to address himself to the question of what to do when the goal of strong, independent trade unions comes in conflict with economic planning. Strikes for wage adjustments were threatened among such heterogeneous, yet strategic, work groups as the Bombay Dock workers, the Civil Aviation employees, and the Posts and Telegraphs workers, Nehru lashed at "the language of threats and defiance," expressed the view that "these demands for higher wages . . . however justified they might be, are at the present moment more in the nature of a political rather than an economic approach." *Hindu Weekly Review,* 22 July 1957. p. 3. The Bombay dock workers called off their strike threat one hour before their deadline. *Ibid.* However, a Presidential ordinance outlawing walk-outs in essential services, making participants subject to penalties of imprisonment, or a fine, or both, was necessary to forestall the strikes in Civil Aviation and Posts and Telegraphs. See *New York Times,* 9 August 1957, p. 5; and *Hindu Weekly Review,* 12 August 1957, p. 3.

42 Private employers in India do not often give the "management prerogative" reason for opposing compulsory adjudication, but this view was forcefully put forth by a former high official of the Railway Ministry, who said: "Government has the final responsibility for running railroads, and it can't delegate any part of this to a tribunal. I favour direct negotiation, and I am willing to permit the right to strike. One good strike might mean there would be no more later, and anyhow the possibility of a strike may help bring agreement." (Interview, February 1955.)

Apparently a majority of employers, however, favour continuance of the present system of compulsory adjudication. In its "Analysis of Indian Business Opinion" based on a poll of business leaders, the Indian Institute of Public Opinion concluded: "The present system of compulsory adjudication is generally believed to be working reasonably well and the alternative might easily be a combination of exploitation by the more unscrupulous employers and violence by the more extreme workers." Certain modifications, similar to those to be discussed later, were suggested by the respondents. *Quarterly Report* of the Indian Institute of Public Opinion (New Delhi), vol. 1, no. 4 (January 1955).

43 For example, one union leader stated in an interview: "The tribunal system is bad; it encourages legalism and results in unions depending on the tribunal rather than developing their own strength. The best way is to settle things around the table." Yet even the Socialist union leaders are not willing to leave weak unions at the mercy of strong employers, and they favour ultimate access to the tribunal system.

44 Data provided by the Ministry of Labour, Bombay State, show that, in 1950, 1951, and 1952, the percentage of cases in which adjudication was granted was about the same for INTUC and HMS unions, but higher than that for Communist and "Independent" unions. In 1953 the percentage of cases referred to adjudication for INTUC unions was 68 per cent, as compared to 54 per cent for HMS unions, but in the first six months of 1954 (the latest then available) the percentage was again almost identical–72 as compared to 70 per cent. The Labour Minister of another large state, however, said in an interview that "the INTUC is wedded to and allied with the Congress."

Replying to charges in the Lok Sabha of favouritism to INTUC, Khandubhai Desai, Union Labour Minister, said these were "absolutely baseless." He stated that during 1954-55 INTUC unions requested adjudication in 2,243 cases, but only 1,063 or 47.4 per cent were referred to adjudication. Comparable figures for the other union groups were: AITUC—1,769 cases, of which 874 or 49.4 per cent were referred; and HMS—1,077 cases, of which 592 or 55 per cent were referred to adjudication. Desai concluded : "I think this is the last charge, and it will not be repeated." *Hindustan Times,* 25 July 1956.

45 A series of cases in 1955 brought the union demand for abolition of the Appellate Tribunal to a head. One of the most important of these involved the closure of the Madras Electric Tramways. In 1953, an industrial tribunal awarded the workers a 50 per cent share in the reserve funds of the company, with half a month's basic wage for every completed year of service up to a maximum of six months' salary as retrenchment compensation. In August 1955, the Appellate Tribunal reversed the lower tribunal's decision, and denied the workers any share of the reserve funds of the company. *Mail* (Madras), 10 August 1955. For a full history of the events leading to the abolition of the Labour Appellate Tribunal, see B. S. Narula, *The Abolition of the Labour Appellate Tribunal,* The Indian Institute of Public Administration, New Delhi, 1963, pp. 57-196.

46 *The Gazette of India Extraordinary,* part II, section 2, no. 39 (New Delhi, 21 September 1955), pp. 431-32.

47 The Bill also contained a provision (Sec. 8) for private voluntary arbitration if the parties chose this at any time before a dispute had been referred to a labour court or tribunal or national tribunal. Draft Outline of the Second Five Year Plan commented on this and the other provisions of the Bill as follows : "Considerable emphasis should be placed on mutual negotiations for the settlement of disputes and on voluntary arbitration. Government intervention should be resorted to only in

intractable cases. The proposed amendment of the Industrial Disputes Act is therefore a move in the right direction." *Second Five Year Plan: A Draft Outline,* Planning Commission, Government of India (February 1956), p. 272.

48 "Statement of Objects and Reasons," *The Gazette of India Extraordinary,* p. 431. A "limited number" (1 per cent of the total employed, but not less than 5 or more than 100) of representatives of workers were to be given protection against discharge regardless of whether their action was connected with the dispute or not. This was intended to prevent "victimization" of union leaders. Despite this, during the debate in the Lok Sabha, Communist members were opposed to any change in Sec. 33. *Hindustan Times,* 22 July 1956.

49 Interview, March 1955.

50 Quoted in report on conference in *Industrial Relations* (journal of the Indian Institute of Personnel Management, Calcutta), vol. VII, no. 6 (November-December 1955), p. 22.

51 Interview, February 1955.

52 Reply to debate in the Lok Sabha on the Industrial Disputes (Amendment and Miscellaneous Provisions) Bill, *Hindustan Times,* 25 July 1956.

53 Government of West Bengal, Labour Directorate, *West Bengal Labour Year Book,* 1957, pp. 89-102.

54 *Ibid.,* p. 95.

55 *Ibid.,* p. 98.

56 This has been frequently implied by the Union Labour Ministry. For instance, Khandubhai Desai stated in the Lok Sabha in July 1956 that the number of adjudications ordered in 1955 was 2,804 by both the Central and state governments. The success of the industrial relations machinery, he added, could be judged by the number of strikes, which accounted for 16.5 million man-days lost in 1947 and "the number has now come down to about 33 lakhs." *Hindustan Times,* 25 July 1956.

57 *West Bengal Labour Year Book,* 1957, p. 93.

58 S.D. Punekar, *Industrial Peace in India,* Library of Indian Economics (Bombay 1952), p. 110.

59 "Hartals," the short work stoppages (usually a day) to register protest or express sympathy for a particular event, usually unconnected with industry, are not considered industrial disputes as such. They are likely to be political in character, in protest against arrests of political leaders (as in pre-Independence days) or in sympathy for the death of a prominent leader. such as a depressed classes leader. Sometimes "hartals" have also been resorted to in protest against delays in referring a labour dispute to adjudication or in making an award. See Punekar, *Industrial Peace,* p. 40.

60 Government of India, *Third Five Year Plan,* 1961, p. 250.

61 For details, see Government of India, *Consultative Machinery in the Labour Field,* (Labour Bureau Pamphlet–Series 1), 1959. See also Government of India, Ministry of Labour and Employment, *Tripartite Conclusions,* 1942-62, Delhi, 1962.

62 The texts of the Codes have been reproduced in S. A. Palekar, *Problems of Wage Policy for Economic Development,* Asia Publishing House, Bombay 1962, pp. 313-17.

63 See, for instance, Government of India, Central Board for Workers' Education, *Lectures and Synopses of Lectures* (ed. by S. D. Punekar and B. C. Desai), Nagpur, Government Press, 1960, pp. 418. The gathering of an unusually well-qualified group of speakers for the purpose of training teacher administrators is surely a worthwhile achievement. Some of the lectures are only in outline form, but it is clear that the lecturers between them represented a wealth of experience not available in the form of class texts. Similar opportunities have been extended to trade union nominees, and rank and file workers.

CHAPTER IX

PROBLEMS OF GOVERNMENT LABOUR POLICY

As we have seen in Chapter I, levels of industrial wages in India are low. It is not surprising, therefore, that disputes over wages have been frequent. In the early years after Independence, official policy favoured wage increases which would push industrial real wages up to the pre-war 1939 "minimum" levels. Since then, a more liberal policy has been subscribed to, with the usual caveat that wage increases must be tied to increases in productivity. However, there have also been steady price increases throughout most of the post-war and post-Independence periods, which justified compensatory payments. A principal means of reconciling conflicting claims has been through the compulsory adjudication[1] system which has been flooded with disputes pertaining to (a) the basic wage, (b) the amount of bonus, and (c) dearness allowance (for changes in the cost of living). We shall discuss the issues raised by each of these briefly. Attention will also be given to the related efforts undertaken by the government to improve the climate of industrial relations for its bearing on productivity as well as the smooth resolution of wage disputes. The issues brought to the forefront by employer efforts to "rationalize," unions' demand for recognition, and government-sponsored efforts to improve the functioning of unions and managements will be included.

Wage Disputes under Adjudication

The basic wage, usually paid monthly to industrial workers in India, has been established by industrial tribunals according to the principles summarized in the 1949 Report of the Fair Wages Committee, appointed by the Government of India. The lower limit (of basic wage plus dearness allowance) is the "minimum wage" which provides "not merely for the bare sustenance of life but for the preservation of the efficiency of the worker by providing some measure of education, medical requirements and amenities."[2] This is presumably ordered, regardless of the alleged capacity of the

firm or industry to pay; but, as we shall see later, subsequent increases in cost of living have not been fully matched. The upper limit is
the "living wage," representing "a standard of living which provides
not merely for a bare physical subsistence but for the maintenance
of health and decency, a measure of frugal comfort and some
insurance against the more important misfortunes." Between these
limits, a "fair wage" is ordered according to ability to pay and the
prevailing rates of wages in the same or similar industry or locality
with the latter given more importance. "Capacity to pay" is determined with reference to the industry as a whole, and in an early case
(Buckingham and Carnatic Mills, 1951) the Labour Appellate
Tribunal denied labour's contention that this more profitable firm
should pay higher wages than other units in the same industry.
Frequent demands for revision of basic wages are discouraged,
and claims growing out of profits made in a particular year are
usually denied. In other words, changes in wage incomes have come
in bonus and dearness allowance, rather than in basic wages.

The amount of annual year-end bonus is generally related to
profits. The nature of bonus as a part of the wage structure is
indicated by the key 1950 decision of the Labour Appellate Tribunal
in the 1949 bonus dispute between the Bombay Millowners'
Association and the Rashtriya Mill Mazdoor Sangh (INTUC),
Bombay:

> Bonus is cash payment made to employees in addition to wages.
> It cannot any longer be regarded as an *ex-gratia* payment, for it
> has been recognized that a claim for bonus, if refused, gives rise
> to an industrial dispute, which has to be settled by a duly consti-
> tuted Industrial Court or Tribunal.... Where the goal of living
> wages has been attained, bonus, like profit-sharing, would
> represent the cash incentive to greater efficiency and production.
> We cannot, therefore, accept the broad contention that a claim to
> bonus is not admissible where wages have (as in the case before us)
> been standardized at a figure lower than what is said to be the
> living wage. Where the industry has the capacity to pay, and has
> been so stabilized that its capacity to pay may be counted upon
> continuously, payment of "living wage" is desirable; but where
> the industry has not that capacity or its capacity varies or is

expected to vary from year to year, so that the industry cannot afford to pay "living wages," bonus must be looked upon as the temporary satisfaction, wholly or in part, of the needs of the employee.[3]

This same decision went on to spell out the principles governing the amount of bonus to be awarded in a particular case. These may be summarized as follows:

1. A normal depreciation allowance "for rehabilitation, replacement, and modernization of machinery" is the first charge on gross profits. The usual allowance is based on what the tax authorities have permitted for corporate income tax purposes.
2. A fair return on paid-up capital (6 per cent) and on reserves employed as working capital (2 per cent) should be the next charge.
3. Only if there is a residue after these deductions should bonus be paid to employees. If a particular firm has losses, although the industry as a whole in the region shows profits, no bonus is to be awarded to employees in the losing firms.
4. The amount of bonus depends on "the relative prosperity of the concern during the year under review," as revealed in the "residuary surplus" after the above deductions; and on "the need of labour at existing wages," as revealed by the gap between the wages paid and the "living wage."

Two years later, in another bonus dispute in the textile industry, the Labour Appellate Tribunal emphasized the "social justice" considerations which motivated its earlier decision:

That decision is broad, based on principles of social justice. By that decision we lifted bonus out of the category of gratuity ... and we held that labour was entitled as of right to a share of the available surplus, by way of bonus for the year so long as a living wage had not been attained. The scheme of our formula was to do social justice; our full bench was moved by a desire to give a fair deal to labour, and the resultant formula was the best that we could devise in the circumstances to do justice to the parties.[4]

While in later cases, where ability to pay was not disputed, the tribunals have awarded higher bonuses than usual, most awards have been related to the bonus amounts already paid elsewhere in the industry or in the locality. "Care has also been taken," one Labour Appellate Tribunal award declared, "to see that the bonus which is given is not so excessive that it creates fresh problems in the vicinities, that it upsets emoluments all around or that it creates industrial discontent and the possible emergence of a privileged class."[5]

When the recession in cotton textiles in 1953-54 brought losses to some mills, these were exempt from paying bonus under the formula outlined above. Labour's reaction was critical, as we have seen in Chapter V; and there were demands that profits of firms in an industry in a particular area be pooled, and bonus be distributed to all workers regardless of individual mill profits or losses.[6] The bonus issue remains a continuing source of dispute, and the INTUC has raised doubts about the validity of the losses claimed by certain employers.[7] It has also urged that basic wages be raised to avoid recurrent disputes over bonus, and that dearness allowance be merged with basic wages.[8] These points have also been made by the other labour federations.

Employers, on the other hand, have opposed these proposals, although deploring the continuing disputes over bonus.[9] Some have made a successful effort to offer bonus amounts sufficient to induce unions to accept them rather than take their chances through the delayed procedures of compulsory adjudication. One of the most hopeful signs, although still a small one, is the increasing number of agreements between individual firms and unions on the bonus question. These include both Indian and European firms, and they reported during 1954-55 that the consistency of Labour Appellate and Industrial Tribunal decisions on bonus in earlier disputes had helped to establish the limits within which voluntary agreement could be reached more speedily in current disputes. This view, it must be admitted, was not shared by national trade union leaders, who had urged abolition of the Labour Appellate Tribunal.[10]

After difficulties in the application of the voluntary arbitration machinery in Ahmedabad in 1954, the Textile Labour Association and the Millowners' Association reached agreement in June 1955 on "principles, procedure and method" for granting of bonus for the five years, 1953–57, in the case of each individual member mill. The claim for bonus could be made when a mill had an available surplus of profits after providing for all prior charges according to the 1950 Labour Appellate Tribunal formula, and in this case the bonus would be no less than 4.8 per cent of basic wages and no more than 25 per cent. But if more were possible, this could be set aside in a bonus reserve for future lean years. Similarly, if the amount available under the formula were less than the required minimum of 4.8 per cent in one year, the difference could be offset against any larger amount payable in a subsequent year. Finally, a mill which has no available surplus or has made a loss "will, as a special case, for creating goodwill among its workers and for continuing peace in the industry but without creating a precedent, pay to its employees a minimum bonus" of 4.8 per cent of basic wages earned during the year, to be offset against future years' bonuses.[11] Determination of the amount of bonus was to be made by the TLA and the Mill-owners' Association jointly, from published balance-sheets and other data supplied by the mills; and, failing agreement, reference could be made to the president of the Labour Appellate Tribunal or to an umpire from a panel established by a separate arbitration agreement signed also in June 1955.

Similar agreements have been signed in several firms and industries throughout India. One of the more notable is the long-term "bonus" agreement in the Bombay cotton textile industry in 1956 which was renewed, after some difficulties, in 1962. The Tata Iron and Steel Company has also had a profit-sharing bonus agreement for some time. A number of firms in the expanding manufacturing sector have also concluded bonus agreements, although some of these are not specifically related to profits: examples are the several agreements concluded by the Indian Aluminium Company, Limited, in its plants in various parts of India. Some of these, notably the Bombay agreement, were aided by a clear knowledge of the limits set by adjudication and close participation by concerned government leaders acting in a mediatory capacity. Nevertheless, there have been continuing problems. There was uncertainty about the renewal of the Bombay agreement, and this was aggravated by disagreement over rationalization and threats posed by the rival socialist-communist union; indeed a final settlement was made possible only by what amounted to a third-party "unofficial" award. Elsewhere in India the situation has been much less satisfactory. Unwillingness among employers to negotiate, rivalry and instability among unions, conflicts over closely related issues such as rationalization, and distrust of company financial statements, have been among the factors which have made it difficult to secure agreements. The Kanpur textile industry represents one of the worst situations in India and incorporates all of these complicating circumstances.

Agreements on bonus in individual cases have been aided by skilful conciliation efforts of some state labour ministries, or their refusal to refer exorbitant union demands to adjudication. For example, in one important industrial state, a high official of the labour ministry explained: "Several times when genuine offers are made by employers, we tell them, 'If you will implement the offer made during conciliation, we will not send this case to adjudication.'" But the active role which government officials can play in forcing agreement is illustrated by this further comment: "There is another way we handle this problem. Suppose three months' bonus is offered at first and the union demands seven months'. We look into the data and conclude that four months' bonus is fair, and we say, 'If you will offer four months,' there will be no adjudication.'"

The annual bonus has nevertheless continued to cause considerable friction in labour-management relations. An indication of the complexity of the problems raised by the bonus issue, as well as the efforts currently under way to minimize friction, is given by the omnibus terms of reference to the Bonus Commission which was established by recommendation of the eighteenth session of the Indian Labour Conference. It was decided that the Bonus Commission should determine the general principles governing the payment of bonus and work out suitable norms for the settlement of bonus claims in the different industries.

Accordingly, in December 1961, the Government of India appointed a Bonus Commission to be headed by M. R. Maher. In addition, there were two independent members, and two representatives each of the employers and the workers. The Commission was asked:

1. To define the concept of bonus and to consider, in relation to industrial employments, the question of payment of bonus based on profits and recommend principles for computation of such bonus and methods of payment;
2. To determine the extent to which the quantum of bonus should be influenced by the prevailing level of remuneration;
3. (*a*) To determine what prior charges should be in different circumstances and how they should be calculated; (*b*) to determine conditions under which bonus payments should be made unit-wise, industry-wise and industry-cum-region-wise;
4. To consider whether the bonus, due to workers beyond a specified amount, should be paid in the form of National Savings Certificates or in any other form;
5. To consider whether there should be lower limits, irrespective of losses in particular establishments, and upper limits for distribution in one year and, if so, the manner of carrying forward profits and losses over prescribed periods;
6. To suggest an appropriate machinery and method for the settlement of bonus disputes;
7. To make such other recommendations regarding matters concerning bonus that might be placed before the Commission on an agreed basis by the employers' (including the public sector) and the workers' representatives.[12]

The Commission signed its 350-page report on 21 January 1964, recommending a minimum bonus of four per cent of a worker's total annual wages, including dearness allowance, in all industrial employments. The Commission's formula was that 60 per cent of the "available surplus" was to be allocated as bonus subject to the above minimum. In arriving at the minimum, other allowances, production bonuses, and attendance bonuses were excluded. This minimum limit was not to fall below Rs. 40 in the case of adults and Rs. 25 in the case of children. The available surplus referred to gross profit for the year less depreciation, income-tax and super-tax and the return on the actual rate payable on preference share capital and at 7 per cent on ordinary shares, plus 4 per cent on reserves.[13] The maximum limit of bonus was set at twenty per cent of the total annual earnings of the worker.[14] Although, up to this time, bonus awards had been expressed as multiples of basic wages, it is too early to say whether, in practice, this will make a material difference.

The Commission has also fixed the maximum bonus payable to workmen. Its recommendation is that the portion of the "available surplus" allocated for bonus should include bonus to employees drawing a total basic pay and dearness allowance (taken together) up to Rs. 1,600 per month. Further, the bonus payable to employees drawing total basic pay and dearness allowance over Rs. 750 per month was to be limited to what it would be, had their pay and allowances been only Rs. 750 per month. The government accepted the recommendations of the Commission subject to certain modifications. One of the main modifications related to the calculation of the "available surplus." All direct taxes were to be deducted as prior charges. Similarly, tax concessions made to industry to provide resources for development were also treated as prior deductable charges. The government also decided that beyond a certain maximum, bonus was to be paid in securities or investment.[15]

Though the government has accepted the recommendations of the Bonus Commission, it cannot be said that the matter has been settled. A former president of the INTUC commented that the government's decision amounted to saying that there would be no bonus except for the minimum recommended. He predicted that there would be demand for bonus other than on profit, and that he himself would not compromise on the demand for cost of living bonus and rationalization bonus.[16] On the side of the employers, too, it cannot be said that the Commission's recommendations had been favourably received. As of October 1964, Bombay mill-owners had not granted the interim bonus of four per cent of total annual earnings according to the Commission's recommendation. A strike by the textile workers was postponed only after the intervention of the State Chief Minister.[17]

In order to safeguard the existing rates of bonus which in some cases may be higher than those payable under the Commission's recommendations, and to specify principles for the guidance of tribunals, the government announced that it would draft a bill to be enacted into law.[18]

During interviews, some employers and, occasionally, even trade unionists have expressed themselves in favour of entirely eliminating the annual profit-sharing bonus. Arguments advanced against it stem from a feeling that its incentive effect is questionable, that it needlessly exacerbates industrial relations, and finally on purely business grounds, that it is an inefficient mechanism for sharing the firm's prosperity with its employees.[19] Alternatives suggested include straight wage increases and production bonuses. However, it is unlikely that the bonus practice will be generally displaced in the foreseeable future. For one thing, the practice of a lump sum bonus payment is too ingrained a part of current industrial relations to be abandoned easily.[20] The annual bonus negotiations also provide occasion for workers to let off some steam and for employers to press forward with solutions for related industrial relations problems, such as rationalization. Variations in the level of bonus payments also provide the government some means of controlling the wage level and structure in a planned economy; it is interesting in this connection to note the repeated attempts to pay part of the bonus in the form of national savings certificates. Finally, any effort to rationalize Indian wage payments must contend with the much larger role played by dearness allowances, and the diversity in regard to its payment.

Dearness allowance was introduced into the Indian wage structure during the war to neutralize in part the rise in the cost of living as prices rose rapidly. Full neutralization was not permitted, however, on the theory that wage-earners like other groups must share in the burden of inflation. Tribunals have upheld the principle that full neutralization is not possible, but there has not been any agreement on the percentage of neutralization to be recommended. "This varies with adjudicators, and is worked out after making allowance for factors like basic wage, the financial capacity of the industry, the practice prevalent in the industry or in the locality, the extent of rise in the cost of living, etc. Within this broad framework, each case is decided on its merits, with the result that at times the rates of dearness allowance vary between centre and centre, and between different industries in the same centre, and occasionally, even between different units of the same industry in a centre."[21] Table XLI shows the wide range of variation to be found.

There have also been substantial differences from region to region in regard to general practice. In some centres, as in Bombay,

TABLE XLI
DEARNESS ALLOWANCE IN SELECTED INDUSTRIES AND AREAS

Industry and area	Date		Rupees	Dearness allowance Per cent of basic wage
COTTON				
Bombay City	Sept.	1954	66/2	220
Ahmedabad	Sept.	1954	64/9	231
West Bengal	Sept.	1954	30/0	149
Hyderabad	Sept.	1954	26/0	100
JUTE				
West Bengal	Dec.	1953	37/6	144
Kanpur	Dec.	1953	49/4	410
DOCKYARDS				
Bombay (Unit 2)			61/12	237
Bombay (Unit 4)			40/0	133
West Bengal (Unit 5)		1952	31/0	74
CEMENT				
Banjari	Dec.	1953	22/0	116
Chaibasa			26/0	100
CHEMICAL				
Bihar	April	1953	35/0	166
Bombay (II)	April	1953	66/10	213

SOURCE: *Indian Labour Year Book* 1953-54, pp. 176-86; for December 1957, the D.A. and per cent of basic wage figures for cotton in Ahmedabad was Rs. 71.92 or 257 per cent; and in West Bengal Rs. 30 or 149 per cent. *Indian Labour Year Book* 1957, pp. 61-2.

dearness allowance payments were linked to fluctuations in the cost of living index, while in other centres, for instance Calcutta, the payment schedules were revised only periodically. It is also generally agreed that for many centres the cost of living index is unsatisfactory. Consumption weights in most cases were also based on outdated family budget studies and it is only recently that new studies have been completed for the major employment centres. Fresh working class family budget surveys were conducted on an all-India basis in 1958–59, in 50 selected centres. On the basis of these surveys, a new series of working class consumer price index numbers, with base 1960, are being currently compiled. As of now, beginning with the December 1962 issue of *Indian Labour Journal,* index numbers for 24 of these centres have been published.

The relative importance of dearness allowance in the wage structure has led many unions to demand that all or part of the dearness allowance be merged with basic wages. Merger would leave the workers' earnings in a more secure position in the event of a fall in the price level. Furthermore, where pension and other gratuities have been tied to basic wages, the workers would receive higher benefits. In July 1952, the Central government appointed a Dearness Allowance Committee (Gadgil Committee) to consider the question of treating some part of the dearness allowance of government employees as basic wages. The Committee recommended that 50 per cent of the dearness allowance should be merged with basic wages or salaries. This recommendation was accepted by the Government of India.[22]

For the private sector, the Central Wage Board for the cotton textile industry set the pace by recommending that the dearness allowance should be consolidated with the basic wage. This was to be done at an index which would yield an amount equal to three-fourths of the average dearness allowance of the first six months of 1959 and the remaining 25 per cent should as before continue to be linked with the cost of living. The difference between the point at which the current index was merged and the total dearness allowances due were to be paid according to the existing method and at the existing scale.[23] However, an analysis of industrial awards in recent years reveals the reluctance of tribunals to accept the idea of merger.[24] The position thus appears to have changed little since the last edition.

The absence of accurate wage data led the Government of India to undertake a wage census in forty-four industrially important centres on a sample basis. The main field survey was launched in July 1958 and was completed by the end of August 1959. Late in 1956, the government also announced its intention of establishing

wage boards to set new minimum basic wages in several industries.[25]
Khandubhai Desai, Union Minister of Labour and former INTUC
president as well as general secretary of TLA, explained the purpose
of these boards at the Fortieth Foundation Day of the TLA in
Ahmedabad, when the union's demand for a substantial wage
increase was reiterated:

> The Wage Boards will examine how to allocate increased pro-
> duction to workers and national investment. Even if the workers
> had not demanded a wage raise, the Government would have
> taken up the problem for the simple reason that the increased
> production had to be used for promoting the general welfare
> of the people at large.[26]

Since the establishment of wage boards has become an integral part
of government labour policy, we shall consider them in some detail.

Wage Boards

The Second Plan recommended the establishment of tripartite
wage boards for individual industries as a means of setting wages
on an industry-wise basis. The industries for which wage boards
have been established include working journalism (May 1956),
cotton textiles (March 1957), sugar (December 1957), cement
(April 1958), jute (August 1960) and plantations (tea in December
1960, and rubber and coffee in July 1961). A wage board for iron
and steel started functioning from January 1962. It has also been
decided to set up a wage board for the coal industry.[27]

Mention must be made of the report, published in March 1960,
of the Central Wage Board for the cotton textile industry. The
government accepted its recommendations, and urged that employers, workers, and state governments implement the Board's
unanimous recommendations. In their resolution dated 3 March
1960, the government drew attention to the Board's emphasis on
the importance of speedy rationalization and modernization of
the cotton textile industry.[28]

The textile industry wage board divided the mills into two
categories. Category I included mills in Bombay, Ahmedabad,

Baroda, Delhi, Calcutta and Madras, and a few other centres, whereas Category II included mills in other centres. It recommended an increase in wages for all clerical and manual workers in the composite and spinning mill sector of the industry. For Category I, starting in January 1960, the increase was to be at an average rate of Rs. 8 per month per worker, and a further flat increase of Rs. 2 per month, starting January 1962. For Category II, the increases were to be Rs. 6 and Rs. 2 respectively. Dearness allowance was to be linked to the cost of living by suitable machinery.[29]

As regards the Wage Board's recommendations, 393 (357 fully and 36 partly) out of 416 cotton textile mills have implemented the recommendations. An enquiry was reported to be in progress into the reasons for non-implementation in the remaining mills.[30]

In January 1961, the wage board for jute industry unanimously recommended the grant of interim relief at the rate of Rs. 2.85 per month beginning October 1960, to all workers, permanent, temporary or *badli*.

Similarly, the wage boards for tea plantations, rubber plantations, sugar and cement, have all given their recommendations for the revision of wages. Twentythree out of 33 cement factories, and 66 out of 170 sugar factories have implemented the recommendations. Seven cement factories and 39 sugar factories have complied partly with the recommendations.[31]

Recently the composition and terms of reference of the wage board for port and dock workers at major ports have been finalized.[32]

The Representative Union Problem

Disputes over wages, bonus and other matters might be easier to settle directly between employers and unions if there were one majority or representative union with which an employer or employer-association could negotiate. But, as we have seen in Chapter IV, a multiplicity of small and rival unions plagues labour-management relations in India. A method of determining the representative union exists in Bombay under state legislation, as we have noted in Chapter VIII. But the Industrial Disputes Act of 1947, which still applies to certain industries in states with their own disputes legislation and to all industries in those states (like West Bengal) without any separate law, has no provision for determining the most representative union among competing unions. There have been proposals to amend the 1947 Act in 1950 and again in 1954,[33] but the 1956 Industrial Disputes (Amendment and Miscellaneous Provisions) Act contains no provision on this question. In fact, the Union Labour Minister expressed opposition to the principle of compulsory recognition of trade unions when he replied to debate on the bill in July 1956.[34] This opposition also explains why a post-war amendment to the trade union legislation, providing for compulsory recognition, was never brought into force.

The reluctance of the Central government to proceed with legislation along the lines of the Bombay Act is explained by officials in New Delhi on the grounds that unions in India generally (possibly outside of Bombay state) are weak and unstable, and almost any test devised by law to determine a representative union is difficult to meet. Furthermore, one observer explained, "Determining the representative union would require elaborate governmental machinery and run the risk of victory by Communist unions. Of course, it is more difficult for the employer to bargain collectively when he doesn't know which union to deal with, but when government is not sure what will happen if it tries something new, it is cautious and tends to leave things alone."[35] Another reason for governmental caution is that there is no general agreement on how to determine a "representative union."

The Draft Outline of the Second Five Year Plan states that the "present trade union legislation needs to be revised with the object of . . . giving unions statutory recognition under certain conditions," but the manner in which this might be done is not further spelled out.[36] The Labour Panel of the Planning Commission was reported to have reached agreement in February 1956 that "a condition for recognition of a representative union should be at least one-third of the membership of the total number of workers,"[37] presumably as determined by a check of membership rolls. But Central government legislation on this question is still lacking.

The Bombay procedure involves inspection of union membership lists (presumably current dues-paying members) by the Registrar of Trade Unions, and certification of the "representative union" on the basis of this inspection. Charges have been made that the Registrar tends to favour INTUC unions as opposed to others,[38] and certainly, one of the most frequent objections to a secret ballot procedure for determining the representative union is that the Communists would win elections by extravagant promises and irresponsible attacks on rival unions.[39] Some quotations from the interviews illustrate the conviction with which this view is held:

> The Indian worker is easily subject to whim, and is usually swayed by the labour leader who can make the most extravagant demands and promises. In a secret ballot the Communists would be more likely to win, therefore. [*Deputy state Labour Commissioner*]
>
> We might be willing to try a secret ballot experimentally, but the danger is that the Communists will win by extremism. A secret ballot assumes a certain level of education. The comparison with general political elections is not valid because there are no corrective forces available to offset extravagant claims. [*State Labour Minister*]
>
> If you had a secret ballot, the vote would not be on trade union issues but on Communist issues, political issues, etc. And the power of demagogic appeal is greater in trade union issues than in political parties where national leaders are the vote-getters. [*INTUC union officer*]

Those who favour the secret ballot for determining the representative union include some leaders of HMS unions. One charged that the membership list check is "a legal fiction and leads to a large number of abuses. The so-called 15 per cent union forces its will on the other 85 per cent." But he favoured protection of minority union bargaining rights. Another argued that "the union with whom the employer signs the contract should be a union which is accepted by workers with a 75 per cent majority through a secret ballot vote." Such views are rare exceptions, however; most government officials, many employers, and certainly nearly all INTUC union leaders (who benefit from the present system) oppose the secret ballot and favour the Bombay system, if they favour any.[40]

An alternative procedure which is reported to have had some success in determining the representative union is the extra-legal one developed in 1951 in the state of Bihar through the bipartite Labour Advisory Board. The details of the procedure are worth nothing, for they indicate the difficulties involved in a conscientious effort to deal with the problems of union recognition and rival unions.[41]

1. Any number of unions can be registered in a plant, but before registering a new one, the Registrar of Trade Unions examines carefully the claims of the one claiming registration. (Under the Trade Union Act, 1926, any union representing seven members can be registered.)
2. The employer must recognize at least one of the registered unions, and in granting this recognition he must take care that he recognizes the one most representative of the workmen. The employer should deal only with the recognized union on questions affecting all workers, such as bonus, hours, leave, etc. but he should be willing to hear individual grievances presented on behalf of its members by minority or rival unions.
3. When there is a dispute about the representative character of unions for purposes of recognition, the Labour Commissioner will try to determine the representative character after taking into consideration the membership and such other evidence as may be produced before him.
4. Voting by secret ballot will be taken only in extreme cases, and as a last resort. Voting, if necessary, will be restricted only to members of the registered unions and the rival union should secure at least 75 per cent of the vote of all member workmen before it can dislodge the existing recognized union. Casual and temporary employees of less than twelve months' continuous service are excluded from voting.
5. Recognition granted to the most representative union, as a result of a vote, is not to be disturbed for one year.

While there is general agreement that some method should be developed to select a representative union when two or more are competing, some present and former government officials seem to favour trade union "unity" as the answer. Employing ministries, for example, have insisted that rival unions combine and join in one bargaining group for collective relations with the ministry, as in the case of Posts and Telegraphs. This view was also expressed by a former high official dealing with labour matters in the Government of India:

I don't favour the secret ballot or the determination of the representative union. When there are rival unions facing a management, my prescription is: Bring them together and urge them to unite for collective bargaining fairly and openly with management. I am opposed to any form of compulsion, including the denial of rights to minority unions.

Trade union unity between the INTUC and the Socialist unions may be possible in particular industries or areas, as we have seen in Chapter IV, but unity with Communist-dominated AITUC unions is not generally welcomed either by the INTUC or the Socialist unions. As a real solution to the problem of the representative union, this does not seem very promising at this stage in Indian industrial relations.

The latest effort to deal with the problem is provided by a Code of Discipline adopted in 1958. According to the Code, which was accepted by the principal employers' organizations, and subsequently by individual employers, managements agreed "to recognize the union in accordance with the Criteria (Annexed) evolved at the 16th Session of the Indian Labour Conference held in May 1958." The full text of these criteria is reproduced below:

1. Where there is more than one union, a union claiming recognition should have been functioning for at least one year after registration. Where there is only one union, this condition would not apply.
2. The membership of the union should cover at least 15 per cent of the workers in the establishment concerned. Membership would be counted only of those who had paid their subscriptions for at least three months during the period of

     six months immediately preceding the reckoning.

3. A union may claim to be recognized as a representative union for an industry in a local area, if it has a membership of at least 25 per cent of workers of that industry in that area.

4. When a union has been recognized, there should be no change in its position for a period of two years.

5. Where there are several unions in an industry or establishment, the one with the largest membership should be recognized.

6. A representative union for an industry in an area should have the right to represent the workers in all the establishments in the industry, but if a union of workers in a particular establishment has a membership of 50 per cent or more of the workers of that establishment, it should have the right to deal with matters of purely local interest such as, the handling of grievances pertaining to its own members. All other workers who are not members of that union might either operate through the representative union for the industry or seek redress directly.

The underlying expectation was that this procedure, which was adopted on a voluntary basis along with the Code of Inter-Union Harmony (also adopted in 1958), would minimize the impact of the "representation" problem by encouraging a measure of trade union unity as well as by providing criteria to guide union recognition on a national scale. As we have seen before, union rivalry continues to be a major unresolved problem; and there is little evidence that the Code of Inter-Union Harmony has made any dent on this situation. The recognition procedures indicated by the Code of Discipline, although they have gained general acceptance, have in practice been weakened due to the prevalence of the same factors which have frustrated earlier attempts.

Firstly, there is disagreement as to what constitutes a satisfactory procedure for verifying membership claims by unions. The established procedures do not call for a secret ballot; further, there is considerable diversity from state to state. Opposition charges that, in particular states or in particular instances, the procedures employed are not a satisfactory method of assessing worker sentiment cannot be dismissed. Field interviews also reveal some confusion arising from uncertainty as to what constitutes, in American parlance, the bargaining area. The rights of minority unions have also been an issue of critical importance inasmuch as few Indian unions can muster a commanding majority. This is particularly important where industrial relations questions are determined on an industry-wise basis. The representatives of the Indian Jute Mills Association, for instance, base their refusal to recognize any union on an industry-wise basis on the ground that representative status accorded to any single union would aggravate rather than mitigate labour relations problems. Unions for their part have argued that they cannot be held responsible for violation of Code provisions if employers refuse recognition. The absence of a statutory requirement for recognition and direct federal machinery to implement the provisions of the Code have thus enabled many of the parties concerned to stand firm by their traditional positions.

However, it may be premature to expect clear-cut and unambiguous legislation on this point considering the divergent objectives and views among the participants. The Code has nevertheless been helpful in bringing to the forefront the issues posed by union recognition and satisfactory determination of the representation problem. During interviews in several centres in India in 1962, labour spokesmen of varying ideological persuasions also agreed that the Union Minister for Labour (then G.L. Nanda) had been personally fair in seeking an unprejudiced implementation of the Code. The Central Evaluation and Implementation Machinery, under the leadership of R. L. Mehta, Additional Secretary, has also been conscious of the need for rationalizing procedures. Despite this progress, it is most likely that the representation problem will continue to be a major unresolved issue of the foreseeable future. As of 1962, the impact of the Code in stimulating recognition of unions, and in adjudicating upon competing claims of rival unions, was minimal.[42]

Protecting and Encouraging Union Growth

Government is also confronted with the problem of protecting and encouraging the growth of the trade union movement in India, in line with professed aims, but not letting it get out of hand. We have seen in Chapter IV that important government officials and Congressmen were present at the formation of the INTUC and we have noted charges from non-INTUC unions that state labour ministry officials have favoured INTUC unions in references to adjudication and in the determination of the representative union. These latter charges are difficult to evaluate factually, but there is certainly a widespread belief in India that the INTUC unions receive more encouragement from government than do other unions.[43]

In the 1947 Amendment to the Trade Union Act of 1926, the Central government further provided for protection and encouragement of union growth through a list of five-employer "unfair labour practices" almost identical in wording to those in the National Labour Relations (Wagner) Act of 1935 in the United States. However, as we have seen, this provision was never implemented, and no official explanation has ever been given. Unofficially, it is reported that the reasons were that civil servants were not expressly exempted so that the protections would have applied to unions of government employees (which the government did not want), and further that enforcement would have required an elaborate governmental machinery which did not exist. Subsequently, no effort has been made to implement this provision or to enact an amended version, and it may be presumed that this method of protecting and encouraging union growth is not favoured by the Government of India.[44] A revealing interview comment from a government official indicates the clash of objectives which are regarded as paramount:

> If your object is to build up a powerful trade union movement, then you would protect unions through "unfair labour practice" procedures, select majority unions by secret ballot, and all the other methods tried in the United States. But if your main objective is rapid economic development in a planned economy, you wouldn't do these things. You must have a measure of discipline. Perhaps in twenty years, when we can afford strikes, we can afford to try free collective bargaining.

In two respects, however, the government has concerned itself with protection and development of strong trade union leadership.

First, union officials presumably have been protected against "victimization" by employers under Section 33 of the Industrial Disputes Act, which places severe limits on the ability of employers to discipline or discharge any workers so long as a labour dispute is pending before an industrial tribunal.[45] The 1956 Amendment Act, modifying this section in cases not directly connected with a pending dispute, specifically exempts "protected workmen" who are defined as officers of registered trade unions.[46]

Second, the government has also been concerned about reducing the domination of "outsiders" in the leadership of trade unions—a characteristic of Indian unions which we have noted earlier. The Trade Union Act of 1926 specifies that not less than one-half of the members of the trade union executive shall be employed in the industry, but this does not prevent the outsiders from holding the leading offices.[47] As we saw in Chapter V, comparatively few "insiders" who have come up through the ranks of the particular firm or industry are able to handle trade union matters effectively. Dependence on outsiders, therefore, seems likely to survive for a considerable time, despite various suggestions to legislate on this matter.[48] The existing programmes, which scarcely meet the need if inside leadership is to develop, are confined to the limited programmes of the Textile Labour Association in Ahmedabad, an INTUC school in Indore, the Tata Workers' Union, and the Asian Trade Union College, sponsored by the International Confederation of Free Trade Unions, in Calcutta.[49] Some of India's well-known schools of social work and institutes which offer degree programmes in labour and social welfare have also taken a lead in this matter but, generally speaking, these are confined to English-speaking trainees and are not in many cases specifically oriented towards trade union requirements. About the best known is the training provided by the Tata School of Social Sciences. A promising programme was initiated in 1962 under the leadership of Professor S. D. Punekar and S. R. Mohan Das, two well-known specialists on Indian labour problems. The inadequacy of these private ventures prompted the Government of India to launch its own scheme in 1957. A national programme of workers' education in trade unionism is currently being run in several centres throughout India, following the general outlines of a programme recommended by a joint team of Indian and international specialists. The latter included persons with considerable experience in running union-associated education programmes in the United Kingdom, Sweden, and the United States. The programmes are being run for three levels of trainees: teacher administrators; trade union activists; and rank and file workers. The latter two are conducted in the local languages, and appear generally to have been well received. There are problems arising from lack of equipment, instructional material, and transport (especially for teacher administrators who have a wide territorial span to cover) as well as insufficient decentralization in the administration of the programme. Although these problems must be looked into to assure greater effectiveness, the programme has clearly filled an important need. Much credit must go to the determination and sincerity with which the officials concerned with implementing the programme   all the way from the Central Board of Workers' Education down to the lowest level of teacher administrators— have proceeded to extend the scheme to various centres and plants in India. The principal spokesmen of the national federations have, however, been critical and, during interviews in 1962, expressed major reservations concerning the programme. In part it stems from a lukewarmness towards the "official" dominance over the programme and the shortcomings noted above. Also, since a government programme must avoid overt partisanship or active support to organizing campaigns, it is inevitable that the federations should feel the need for their own programmes. In 1962, both the INTUC and the AITUC announced plans for national trade union education programmes under their own auspices.

Adequate financial support for carrying on legitimate trade union activities is lacking in most Indian unions, as we have seen, because of the failure of Indian workers to pay membership dues regularly or even to maintain membership interest except at times of crisis. This is, of course, not confined to Indian trade unions, but in some other countries compulsory union membership has been given governmental blessing, and the checkoff of union dues has been legal. Since the passage of the Payment of Wages Act in 1936, however, the legality of checkoff of union dues has been in doubt and is probably unlawful. Despite some agitation by a few union leaders to permit the checkoff,[50] nothing has been done.

From this review of government's role in the protection and encouragement of trade unions, as well as in the determination of the representative union, it is difficult to conclude that a strong, independent union movement, similar to those in the United States, Great Britain or Scandinavia, is among the top priorities in government's present labour policy. This is understandable, for there is little general agreement within government or outside about the best ways to build such a labour movement. Some observers have suggested abandoning compulsory adjudication so that unions will rely on their own resources for their gains, and be forced to develop internal strength. However, this is a minority view even among trade unions.

Rationalization and Unemployment

Another problem for government as intervener in labour-management relations is the effort of Indian management, particularly in the cotton textile and jute industries, to increase work-loads and introduce more modern, automatic machinery as part of a cost-reduction programme. Rationalization of machinery and equipment, with its threat of labour displacement, is a major issue of labour protest, as we have seen in Chapter V. The Socialist and Communist labour federations have opposed any further rationalization, and even the INTUC has been forced to urge a total ban until employment increases in other areas and sectors sufficiently to absorb displaced workers.

Here, then, is the dilemma facing the government. On the one hand, organized labour and individual workers are opposed to rationalization which would immediately add to the large volume of existing urban unemployment.[51] On the other hand, at least some cabinet ministers recognize the validity in management's contention that modernization is necessary if export markets (particularly important in jute, and to a lesser extent in cotton textiles) are to be retained. The post-war competition of modernized Japanese, Hong Kong and Pakistan cotton textile industries and the newer Pakistan jute industry is cutting into these export markets.

The First Five Year Plan proposed a number of "safeguards" to "facilitate the progress of rationalisation," such as standardization of work-loads and working conditions, stopping new hiring so that displaced workers can be absorbed, maintaining workers during a re-training period for other jobs, and sharing the gains from rationalization with workers affected.[52] These safeguards were followed by a number of progressive employers in their rationalization programmes before April 1954, when growing unemployment and the union objections led the government to deny further requests for installation of automatic looms. Protection of the handloom industry, which is labour-intensive and provides employment in the villages, against competition of mill-produced cloth, is also involved in the government's decision. This is evident in the Second Five Year Plan, which permits some expansion of mill production, particularly for export markets, but envisages a much greater expansion of the handloom industry as part of the household and hand industries which are expected to provide additional employment in the next ten years.[53]

The dilemma is not easily resolved.[54] In established industries employing large numbers of workers, such as cotton textiles and jute, it is difficult to introduce automatic machinery which is labour-saving unless there is planned expansion within the firm (preferably) or within the industry in the locality. The "safeguards" suggested in the First Five Year Plan are reasonable. The alternative is the strong possibility of labour protest erupting into strikes which would be politically unstabilizing and economically costly. The dimensions of this problem have been explored in detail in Chapter V.

Even with the best intentions, however, private employers have considerably less freedom to work out the labour problems of rationalization than did their predecessors in the older industrial nations at an earlier stage of economic development. The role of the state is necessarily larger in industrialization than it was then, and the existence of the adult franchise means that political pressures from unemployment and urban discontent must be reckoned with. The price of political stability in India today may well be some slowing down of the pace of modernization in the older established industries. New industries, of course, can more easily adopt modern techniques since there is no presently employed labour to be displaced and to protest.[55]

Problems of Choice in Public Policy

A major implication of the foregoing survey of the patterns of government involvement in labour-management relations, although the point is never specifically made by responsible government officials, is that in the government view strikes and lock-outs are unnecessary in a planned economy, where the government is looking after the just interests of the workers as well as other groups in society. In other words, a government concerned with rapid economic development considers it essential to have some control over the "protest" represented by strong, independent trade unions. On the other hand, it has become increasingly clear that such "control" is not easy in a democratic society where industrial grievances will be mobilized under auspices opposed to the government. It has also become clear that efforts must be made to legitimize protest patterns lest these display an increasing degree of alienation. Social and cultural attitudes are also involved which tend to regard industrial disputes as wholly destructive or avoidable with, in the eyes of some observers, a tendency to place hopes on utopian solutions.

These points merit serious attention and present an uneasy dilemma for India's policy-makers. The emphasis on the moral requirements of an industrial relations policy, the reliance on tripartite procedures to promote a consensus, and the encouragement to collective bargaining even while retaining the compulsory adjudication system represent pragmatic, if not entirely satisfactory, endeavours. The actual techniques of government intervention also suggest considerable flexibility; this has been brought out also in the discussion of several industrial relations typologies in Chapter VII. The prevailing public policy is a complex mix of various techniques: compulsory regulation, encouragement to voluntary settlements, emphasis on promoting a tripartite consensus, direct wage control through centralized authority, more decentralized control through tribunals and tripartite norms, etc.

The complexity of the public policy mix is thus influenced by the variety of prevailing industrial relations situations. It arises also from the diversity of objectives—political, economic, and social—that an industrial relations system may serve. A necessary objective of public policy must also be to economize on the time of the government, for trained officials are few and must increasingly perform in more challenging roles. In the consideration of appropriate policies, short- and long-term considerations necessarily intermingle.

India's commitment to planned economic development within a democratic framework is genuine and stands as one of the outstanding features of the development of new nations in the second half of the twentieth century. India's planners must contend not only with alternative prescriptions suggested by each major objective but also with the possibility that the realization of one objective may well be at the expense of another, at least in the short run. If the economic objective is interpreted as one of suppressing or strictly controlling protest, this is likely to be at the expense of the political objective of legitimizing protest under responsible leadership. Conversely, the latter objective may be interpreted as standing in the way of the former. Even if it were possible to ignore the problem raised by protest in a political sense, this may be at the cost of sacrificing workplace morale and productivity. This may add greatly to the cost of enforcement, not only for the government and the police, but also for the plant-level management interested in ensuring a smooth operation of the enterprise. In a country as vast as India, further problems are likely to arise because the different key actors in the industrial relations system—the Labour Ministry, the employing ministries, the individual managements in the public sector, the Planning Commission, the Finance Ministry, and the several state governments, to name only the heterogeneous elements in the government sector—may not always agree on the appropriate prescriptions or the extent to which primacy should be accorded to any one objective at any given time. There is, in addition, Parliament, the trade union federations, and the various groups comprising private management. The scene is likely to become increasingly complex as the years roll by after Prime Minister Nehru's death in 1964.

A fundamental difficulty in the Indian situation arises from the conflicting fact that the forces which urge India's modernization—those which provide the external environment to the developing industrial relations system— themselves stand as major constraints within which industrial relations policy must evolve.

The evolution of India as a parliamentary democracy inevitably implies freedom of political activity. Accompanying the disintegration of the Congress party which provided the "umbrella" for various political movements, there is now a great proliferation of political activity competing for the meagre rewards which the Indian economy can now offer. This has appropriately been called by a distinguished student of Indian affairs as the "politics of scarcity." Industrial workers who, as we have noted in Chapter I, have always been politically important, constitute a pivotal group in this development. Industrial relations policies which are, explicitly or implicitly, based on a docile role for the labour movement must contend with this factor. One necessity then is for policies which would lessen the chances of the labour movement becoming implacably associated with groups hostile to the ruling party and losing faith in constitutional methods of advance.

The economic constraint also constitutes a parameter which cannot be ignored. Industrial development is predicated on manpower shifts towards new areas, new skills, and new forms of discipline. Despite the existence of what is generally identified as manpower surpluses, workers needed for a massive programme of industrialization command significant economic premiums and possess bargaining power. Industrial development also implies a substantial draft on available non-human resources. Desired levels of productivity and commitment in industry cannot be secured without some improvements in the standard of living. Indian development priorities may, however, mean slow rates of advance in agriculture, in the provision of social services, and in the availability of food and consumer goods. There may thus develop pressures to hold down the real wage, even as the workers begin to press for improvements in their standard of living.

A final constraint is imposed by enhanced expectations. Many writers in the field of economic development have indeed argued that it is desirable to have this change as a method of stimulating the demand for income. It is, however, a mistake to consider this as a change only with respect to current material or income returns. People are interested in the growth possibilities in their own lifetime as well as in the possibilities of advance for their offspring. The desire for improved material prospects is also part and parcel of a desire for advance in respect of non-material matters. Ideals of social equality or natural justice which, in present-day industrialized countries, were recognized after a long struggle, command popular support. Complacent and mechanical denial of these aspirations is unwise, even though the prospects of fulfilment may be discouraging. Further, the transference of workers to employments in which income from human wealth plays an increasing role is likely to be facilitated where opportunity exists to preserve the human asset at levels of functioning efficiency, to protect rights of access to complementary inputs in the form of tools and equipment provided by the employer, and to build up the earning power of one's progeny.

The external environment, which represents the ingredients of progress, may thus at the same time be an inhibitory influence on the development of orderly industrial relations.

A central conclusion which emerges is that accelerated advances in particular directions may yield progressively only diminishing returns due to the restrictive conditions imposed by lags in other directions. For this reason, it may be unwise to ignore the need for parallel efforts until after some far-off and indefinable stage when development has been reached. Rational consideration of policy thus must recognize that the several objectives of development may constitute short-run conflicts, but long-run support for one another.

Fortunately, the Indian government displays in this sense a high order of realism and pragmatic experimentation. India's planners certainly do not view economic growth as being achieved in a social vacuum of stagnation and apathy. It is recognized that economic growth requires increases in productive inputs as well as improved attitudes towards work and discipline which in turn depend on equitable treatment in the workplace.

One of the most hopeful signs on the current scene is the extraordinary increase in the attention given to technical training, research, and adaptation from the experience of the developed democracies. Some of this has already been noted in the previous chapter. The earlier edition also noted the active role of the Indian government in channelling external technical assistance. The range and breadth of these programmes has increased so greatly that it will be uneconomical in terms of space to attempt a complete catalogue of the programmes currently under way. What follows will be a thumb-nail sketch of the principal directions of development.

Building Technical Skills for Better Industrial Relations

The major outlines of the present efforts may be noted. The Indian government, through its various official and quasi-official agencies, has stimulated advances in the following directions: industrial relations and management research; technical training for managements, unions, and officials connected with labour directorates; and application of scientific techniques to improve productivity in the workplace. Major institutional innovations of the government include the National Institute for Labour Research and a similar institute for Manpower Research; the All-India Administrative Staff College; the Central Board for Workers' Education; the National and Regional Productivity Councils; and several semi-official agencies at the national and state level. One state programme that deserves special mention is the Labour Institute run by the Government of Bombay. In many of these cases, external assistance provided by the International Labour Organization,[56] Ford Foundation, and the governments of the United Kingdom and the United States have been important. The Indian government's role in industrial relations has also been a major influence in stimulating private groups to take an active responsibility in this matter. Some of this has been simply a consequence of the growth of government activity in industrial relations; in many cases active government support has been a material factor.

Apart from the schools of social work already mentioned, one of the pleasing developments is the increased attention given to industrial relations by India's universities. The major development here has been in the direction of management education: Madras, Bombay, and Delhi have been in the forefront. Bombay University has also initiated a trade union training programme. Some of the newer institutions like the Indian Institute of Technology at Kharagpur, and the Indian Institute of Sciences at Bangalore have also been active in research pertaining to management. Osmania University, under the leadership of Professor V. V. Ramanadham, has made some notable contributions to the study of the developing public sector. Other institutions active in this sense include the Indian Law Institute, which has published detailed studies of the functioning of the compulsory adjudication system, and the Indian Institute of Public Administration which has pioneered in studies of the public sector enterprises. In recognition of its pioneering work, the Tata School of Social Sciences was recently elevated to the status of a national university by government action. Two noteworthy developments which deserve mention are the All India Institutes of Management established with the active association of the Massachusetts Institute of Technology at Calcutta and of Harvard University at Ahmedabad.

Private industrialists have acted in concert with these developments. Textile Industry Research Associations have been established in Ahmedabad, Bombay, and Coimbatore, three major textile centres. The Ahmedabad Textile Industry Research Association in particular deserves credit for its pioneering application of scientific techniques to assist in the solution of specific industrial relations problems as well as in research oriented towards the Indian scene. Creditable work has also been done by the South India Textile Research Association located in Coimbatore. The Administrative Staff College, already referred to, is headed by a private industrialist and enjoys considerable financial and technical support from private industry. The Indian Institute of Personnel Management has been a noted leader in encouraging personnel management and defining standards for the profession. It runs its own training programme and publishes a competent journal, *Industrial Relations;* further, by means of publicity and representations, it has sought to gain acceptance for the need for trained management to handle difficult labour problems. In recognition of its contributions, the Indian Labour Conference has admitted the Institute as an observer. In 1963, an ambitious industrial relations research centre was established in India to honour the memory of a leading industrialist, the late Sir Shri Ram, who, during the greater part of his career, had urged employers to develop a humane point of view in handling employees. It is proposed to develop the institute as an autonomous research institute which, one may hope, will increasingly devote itself to thorough investigations of Indian industrial relations problems.

These are in addition to specific programmes undertaken by individual enterprises for their own employees which are too numerous to be mentioned here. Thus, as opposed to ten years ago, a number of firms have established their own staff training programmes; several of the larger banks have their own staff training colleges; the government-owned State Bank of India and the Life Insurance Corporation also have similar arrangements. In a number of cases, these include training abroad. One of the better examples is provided by the managerial development programme in Geneva, Switzerland, to which the Indian Aluminium Company Limited, sends select persons with management potential.

As already noted, a number of these programmes are dependent in a critical measure on assistance from abroad. This involves consulting and technical advice as well as provision for training required high-talent manpower. It is noteworthy that a preponderant fraction of such assistance has come from Western sources, notably the United States and United Kingdom. These reflect not only traditional allegiance of the Indian elite but also the growing ties since Independence. Commercial channels which provide for various levels of industrial training have been largely with the West, despite the growing involvement of the Soviet Union and East Europe with India's industrial involvement. Far more striking is the role played by contacts with U.S. universities. These have influenced virtually most of the major developments in industrial relations and management education and research. A number of the men in key positions in the new institutions and developments noted above have been trained in U.S. universities.

These developments reflect in a very basic sense India's commitment to constitutional lines of advance. Yet it would be a mistake to assume that India's development can be a carbon copy of earlier developments in the West. Also, despite this assistance, and India's own concrete progress in several desirable directions, it would be a mistake to assume that the industrial relations problems confronting present-day India are capable of easy solution. In underdeveloped countries, even with the best will and the best effort, and the most imaginative and successful programmes, one must keep in mind that conflicting objectives can be reconciled only at a low level of fulfilment. The considerations which argue for a balance among competing objectives or for priority for any one of them at a given point in time are complex, and often unique to the specific circumstances of each country.

We noted at the commencement of this book the "fateful" character of the Indian experiment. It is no less fateful after the intervening years of progress since Independence. The issue at stake is India's ability to sustain steady progress under democratic auspices.

NOTES

1 See A. S. Mathur, "The Labour Judiciary in India," *The Journal of Industrial Relations*, Industrial Relations Society of Australia, vol. 6, no. 3, November 1964, pp. 239-55.

2 *Report of Fair Wages Committee*, p. 32.

3 This is generally known as "The Full Bench Formula," *Labour Law Journal* (Madras), vol. II, 1950, p. 1247. The Industrial Disputes (Appellate Tribunal) Act of 1950 specifically for the first time established bonus as a legitimate issue before the tribunal system.

4 "Textile Mills of Madhya Pradesh *versus* Their Workmen," 1952, reported in V. B. Kher, *Companion Volume to Digest of Labour Law Cases* (Bombay, 1954), pp. 509-10.

5 "Burmah Shell, Bombay *vs.* Their Workmen," *Labour Law Journal*, vol. II, 1953, p. 246. Following this decision, an industrial tribunal in Bombay refused to increase the 1952 bonus above the amounts awarded in 1950 and 1951 ($3\frac{1}{2}$ months' basic wage) to clerical employees in three foreign oil companies. The Petroleum Workers' Union in Bombay had demanded seven months' bonus, based on basic wages plus dearness allowance. The tribunal's decision stated: "In the matter of bonus, we have to be guided by certain set formulae and certain set principles enunciated by the Labour Appellate Tribunal. The employees of a monopolistic concern cannot have a higher quantum of bonus merely on the ground that they happen to be the employees of such a concern. . . . Nothing worth the name has happened during the year 1952 necessitating a deviation from those principles. . . . To grant a token advance (over what was awarded last year) would be a step in the wrong direction and would have no principle on which it can rest. In the *Tata Oil Mills* case the Labour Appellate Tribunal condemned the practice of granting token advances without justification as having an unhealthy effect on industrial relations." *Bombay Government Gazette*, Part 1-L, 25 March 1954, pp. 644-46.

6 The 1952 voluntary arbitration argeement in Ahmedabad broke down over the settlement of the 1953 bonus when twenty of the city's sixtysix mills showed losses. In February 1954, the Bombay State Government introduced a bill to pool profits for bonus determination, but it was subsequently withdrawn following strong criticism from industry. *Commerce*, 3 April 1954, p. 610.

7 A resolution adopted at the Seventh Annual Session of the INTUC in January 1955, stated: "The conduct of some concerns in each industry creates difficulties for the workers by their showing losses instead of profits, especially when the price atmosphere indicates profits and even when a majority of the concerns show handsome profits. The question of these loss-making units has created an atmosphere of distrust, suspicion and discontent." *Seventh Annual Session: A Brief Review,* Indian National Trade Union Congress (New Delhi, 1944), Appendix A, pp. 5-6.

8 *Annual Report* (New Delhi, 1955), pp. 6, 100-01. The INTUC textile union in Bombay made these part of its major demands in the 1952 bonus case, heard by the Appellate Tribunal in 1954. The Tribunals' January 1955 award made a concession in the direction of raising basic wages and merging dearness allowance, but other union demands were rejected.

9 Sample opinions are found in *Quarterly Report* of the Indian Institute of Public Opinion (New Delhi), vol. 1, no. 4 (January 1955). For example, one group of replies opposed a major change, except that the Labour Appellate Tribunal formula should be made statutory, pending a full enquiry by an expert commission and recommendation of a better formula, if necessary. But another section held that the rate of bonus should be entirely controlled by the prosperity or profit earned by the company. Some respondents favoured a profit-sharing scheme, and others believed that bonus should be abolished. One view was that the "annual wrangle on the question of bonus . . . is the greatest single cause of industrial unrest in this country. Any alternative would be preferable."

10 At the Seventh Session of the Indian National Textile Workers' Federation in April 1955, G. D. Ambekar, president of the INTUC, asserted that the bonus formula of the Labour Appellate Tribunal had caused great discontent among workers and, in calling for abolition of the Tribunal, he said that, "instead of introducing uniformity of principles, the Appellate Tribunal had ... made confusion worse confounded and helped the capitalists to exploit consumers and workers more and more." Quoted in *Mail* (Madras), 24 April 1955.

11 Text of "Agreement," signed on 27 June 1955, by H. G. Acharya, secretary, Ahmedabad Millowners' Association, and S. R. Vasavada, general secretary, Textile Labour Association. (Vasavada was also president of the Indian National Trade Union Congress.) The agreement covers twelve folio-sized printed pages, and contains detailed examples of the computation of bonus under hypothetical situations. The Arbitration Agreement, signed by the same principals, is a renewal of the earlier agreement.

12 Government of India, Labour Bureau, *Indian Labour Year Book,* 1961, pp. 114-15.

13 "Bonus Commission Explains Basis of Formula," *Economic Times,* 4 March 1964. The formula was to be applied retrospectively with effect from the accounting year 1962 and was not to apply to new units for a maximum period of six years.

14 Indian Press Service, New Delhi, 21 January 1964.

15 "Delhi Modifies 'Available Surplus' Definition, Bonus Panel Report Accepted," *Economic Times*. 28 August 1964.

16 "'There will be serious unrest,' says Ambekar," *Economic Times,* 28 August 1964.

17 "Textile Workers Postpone Strike to Oct. 31," *Economic Times*, 26 October 1964.

18 *Ibid.*, 22 September 1964.

19 Many employers, of course, also object to the year-end profit-sharing bonus for business reasons. They report that some profits for the year are set aside in a reserve for bonus awards applying to that year handed down by tribunals several years later. If the award is larger than estimated, prices cannot be raised retroactively and, in any case, funds which might otherwise be reinvested or paid out in dividends are immobilized pending the bonus award. These points have considerable validity, but are not likely to hold much weight in bonus discussions centred on the labour relations aspects exclusively.

20 As an illustration, it is widely reported by trade union officials and company labour officers that workers count on the payment of an annual lump sum bonus to get them out of debt (or reduce their indebtedness) and to provide funds for such important family obligations as the marriage of a daughter or a son, religious festivals, and other events.

21 Datar and Mongia, *Industrial Awards in India*, p. 71.

22 Government of India, *Report of the Dearness Allowance Committee*, New Delhi, 1952.

Recently there has been a discussion supporting a scheme for payment of part of the wages in kind. But the scheme has not taken any concrete shape. It is understood that a bill is to be introduced as an alternative, compelling all industrial establishments employing more than 300 persons in both the private and public sectors to supply to their employees some of the prescribed consumer goods at wholesale and controlled prices through their own fair price shops or cooperatives. The distribution cost, it is suggested, will be borne by the employers. The worker will be entitled to buy from his cooperative store or fair price shop these commodities to the total value amounting to 40 per cent of his monthly earnings or Rs. 150 whichever is less. The bill includes a penal provision applicable to an employer for continued offence in not setting up a fair price shop. "Wages-in-Kind Scheme Goes: Fair Price Shops To Be Made Compulsory," *Economic Times*, 14 November 1964.

23 Ministry of Labour, *Report of the Central Wage Board for the Cotton Textile Industry*, Manager of Publications, Delhi, 1960, p. 23.

24 See *Supplement to Industrial Awards in India*, 1961. This relates to awards given during 1953-58. See esp. p. 58.

25 *Indian Worker*, vol. 4, no. 47 (3 September 1956), p. 1.

26 *Indian Worker*, vol. 5, no. 11 (10 December 1956), p. 2. On 28 January 1957, a tripartite Central Wage Board was established for the cotton textile industry.

27 Government of India, Labour Bureau, *Indian Labour Year Book* 1961, p. 113.

28 Labour problems of rationalization are likely to be less serious in newer industries like bicycle and sewing machines than in older industries like cotton textiles. For a further elaboration of this view, see Charles A. Myers, "Labour Problems of Rationalization: The Experience of India," *International Labour Review*, vol. LXXIII, January-June 1956, pp. 431ff.

29 Ministry of Labour, *Report on the Central Wage Board for the Cotton Textile*

Industry, Manager of Publications, Delhi, 1960, pp. 22-3.

30 Government of India, Labour Bureau, *Indian Labour Year Book* 1961, p. 114.

31 *Ibid.,* pp. 113-14.

32 Reserve Bank of India, *Indian News Digest,* vol. XVII, no. 403, 1 November 1964, p. 241. The date of finalization is probably October 1964.

33 The 1954 Bill, which was prepared by the Labour Ministry but never reported out of the Central Cabinet because of the opposition of other ministries to some of its Sections, contained a provision for an "industry bargaining agent" when a union represented not less than 25 per cent of the workers in all establishments in a specific industry in a local area and not less than 10 per cent of the workers in each of not less than 75 per cent of the establishments in the industry in the area. Such a union would have sole rights to bargain on wages, dearness allowance, bonus and leave. Failing to attain this status, a "recognized union" was a registered union (under the Trade Union Act of 1926) with not less than 15 per cent of the workers in a particular establishment. It could bargain for all workers in the establishment on all matters. The 1950 Bill, which contained somewhat similar provisions, was introduced in Parliament, but lapsed when adjournment occurred without passage.

34 *Hindustan Times,* 25 July 1956. He stated that there were about 4,000 registered unions and 90 per cent were recognized. He offered his "good offices to bring about voluntary recognition" and said a law would not be necessary.

35 Interview, October 1954.

36 *Second Five Year Plan: A Draft Outline,* Planning Commission, Government of India, February 1956, p. 172. The other suggestions for "strengthening the trade union movement" include "restricting the number of outsiders in the trade unions ... protecting office-bearers against victimisation, and improving the financial base for the trade union movement from within its own resources," but no further detailed suggestions are given.

37 *Industrial Relations,* vol. VIII, no. 1 (January-February 1956), p. 42.

38 This charge has come particularly from unions affiliated to the HMS and AITUC, but claims are difficult to evaluate. One student of the Indian labour movement reports that the INTUC cotton textile union in Bombay was designated the "representative union" by the Registrar, only a few months after a one-day protest strike called by the Communist and Socialists in December 1947, brought out 209,000 workers and closed all but one of the city's mills. See Morris David Morris, "Labour Discipline, Trade-Unions and the State in India," *Journal of Political Economy,* vol. LXIII, no. 4 (August 1955), p. 303. Morris goes on to point out that in 1950, the Socialist-Communist groups called a protest strike against the 1950 bonus award, which lasted 63 days. This was subsequently broken and the INTUC "Congress-supported union, although itself reduced in membership, emerged with no effective opposition against it. Since 1951 the union has increased its ability to force workers to operate through the formal channels of protest, over which it has a government-supported monopoly." (p. 302.)

39 Curiously, the Communists do not appear to favour the secret ballot or even recognition of the most representative union to the exclusion of others. A Communist member of the Lok Sabha introduced a bill in March 1955, providing for compulsory

recognition of all registered trade unions, provided they had 5 per cent membership of the employees in the industry or in a company under the same management. The Union Labour Minister, Khandubhai Desai, opposed this on the grounds that it would perpetuate eternally the rivalry among unions in the same industry." The bill was rejected by a voice vote. *Statesman* (New Delhi), 19 March 1955.

40 Some of these differences of opinion came out in a one-day seminar held in Bombay in December 1954, under the auspices of the Association of Free Trade Unionists, which had published a paper on "Problems of Indian Trade Unionism and Labour Relations," by Van D. Kennedy, Associate Professor of Industrial Relations at the University of California (Berkeley) and a Fulbright scholar who spent some thirteen months studying industrial relations in India during 1953-55. Kennedy had proposed an integrated programme to strengthen Indian unions and promote collective bargaining. One of his proposals was to "make worker support as shown by secret ballot vote, not membership, the test of a union's majority status and the deciding factor between rival unions."

41 Resolution of the Bihar Central (Standing) Labour Advisory Board, Labour Department, Government of Bihar, Patna, 23 January 1952. According to one official, "absolute impartiality between competing unions, whether Congress, Socialist, or Communist, is necessary to make this procedure work." A similar procedure has been developed in Mysore state, where it applies to the individual plant and not to the industry in the region as in Bombay.

42 At a meeting held on 20 September 1958, the Central Implementation and Evaluation Committee suggested that a tripartite Inquiry Committee should study the Calcutta Tramway Workers' strike from the point of view of the Code of Discipline in Industry, (The dispute under inquiry can be traced back to 12 March 1958, when a 14-point charter of demands was submitted jointly by three trade unions.) For further details, see Government of India, Ministry of Labour and Employment, *A Study of the Strike in the Calcutta Tramways Company Limited, Calcutta, From the Point of View of the Code of Discipline,* New Delhi, 1961, pp. 1-54.

43 The following statement in an article in *Indian Socialist Journal* is an extreme example of this point of view:

"One of the principal causes of the stagnation and frustration in labour today is the obstinate refusal of Government to permit workers to freely choose their own bargaining agents, to build up their own organisation without official interference and its refusal to exercise elementary administrative fairness and impartiality as between various trade unions. The Government continues to show the most flagrant favouritism to INTUC unions, gives the INTUC disproportionate representation on tripartite bodies and virtual monopoly in I.L.O. conferences and committees. The administrative and even the law and order apparatus of the Government are freely and ruthlessly used to disrupt and crush non-INTUC unions. Decisions of the INTUC unions are foisted on unwilling workers even in the face of High Court rulings and even when it leads to work stoppages as in Nagpur recently. Such favouritism and interference in trade union matters undermine the very foundations of industrial peace and negate progressive labour policies.

"It is idle for Government spokesmen to deny the favouritism shown to the

INTUC. Instances can be cited from every industry and State. If an impartial inquiry is undertaken into this question, the case against the Government can amply be proved." "Labour Policy in Second Five-Year Plan," by "Mehnatkash," *Janata,* vol. IX, no. 28 (15 August 1956), p. 5.

44 During the debate on the Industrial Disputes (Amendment and Miscellaneous Provisions) Bill in July 1956, V. V. Giri, the former Union Labour Minister, pointed to the absence of any provision for compulsory recognition of unions. He recalled the 1947 Amendment and said: "I do not see why the Government should not consider and see that the law is not in a state of suspended animation, but is put into effect. If necessary, a tripartite conference could be called to remove deficiencies of that measure and bring it into force." *Hindustan Times,* 22 July 1956.

45 There are conflicting reports on how effective this protection has been. Possibly officials of the stronger unions, which can more easily bring cases before tribunals, are protected more than officials of minority unions.

46 *The Gazette of India Extraordinary,* part II, section 2 (21 September 1955), p. 424. The number of "protected workmen" in any establishment would be limited to one per cent of the total number of workers employed, with a minimum of 5 and maximum of 100 protected workmen. This provision was opposed in a memorandum to government from the Indian Institute of Personnel Management, which stated: "The Institute also views with apprehension the introduction of a privileged class of 'protected workmen' in industry, since it will be neither to the advantage of industry nor a sound trade union movement to have persons with a vested interest in trade union leadership. It is the experience of Institute members that the plea of unfair·labour practice is nowadays raised in practically every case of dismissal that goes to adjudication. Therefore, management is not in a position to dismiss lightly any employee known to be an active member of a union. This is sufficient deterrent to unfair discrimination against an active trade unionist." *Industrial Relations,* vol. VIII, no. 1 (January-February 1956), p. 36.

47 The Mysore Labour Act, 1942, provided that "associations of employees in private industrial undertakings may take on two members who are not employed in the industrial undertaking, with a view to their appointment as officers. Associations of employees of Government concerns may for a similar purpose admit two Government servants, employed elsewhere as honorary members." Quoted in *International Labour Review,* vol. XLVI, no. 4 (November 1942), pp. 458-59.

48 A proposal discussed in New Delhi in 1955 involved restricting certain offices in the union to those who were either employed in the industry at present, or who had been so employed for a specified number of years. Exceptions might be made for office-holders of ten years' service or more. The Draft Outline of the Second Five Year-Plan suggested "restricting the number of outsiders in trade unions," but no specific proposals were made. Subsequently, the Industrial Relations subcommittee of the bipartite Labour Panel of the Planning Commission was reported to have reached agreement that the number of outsiders on the executives of primary unions should be reduced from 50 per cent to 25 per cent or to 4, whichever was higher. Persons who had worked for at least five years in the same industry were not to be considered as outsiders.

For an alternative proposal, requiring a "recognized" trade union to have paid officers holding government diplomas in trade unionism from government-approved one-year courses at universities, see K. N. Srivastava, *Industrial Peace and Labour in India* (Allahabad, 1954), p. 165.

49 Union officers from all countries in South Asia and the Far East can attend this school for the 13-week residential training programmes. By February 1955, some sixty Indian union leaders had completed the programme, and a number of rank and file unionists from the Tata Workers' Union in Jamshedpur had benefited especially from this programme.

50 Michael John, president of the Tata Workers' Union and former president of the INTUC, has urged the check-off and the union shop as a way of providing stability of trade union membership and finances. *Presidential Address*, Bihar Branch of Indian National Trade Union Congress, February 1955. Subsequently, his union signed a notable three-year agreement with the Tata Iron and Steel Company in January 1956, one provision of which noted the company's agreement "in principle" to measures of union security such as maintenance-of-membership and the check-off. The company expressed its willingness to join the union, if necessary, in approaching government for any alterations that may be required in the law to permit the bringing into effect of such provisions. For the full text of the agreement, see Appendix D.

Other union leaders, however, have objected to the check-off on the grounds, as one put it, that it "would prevent even the very limited contact the union leaders have today with workers through collection of subscriptions [dues].

51 Opposition to rationalization which involves the introduction of new machinery also springs from the pronouncements of Mahatma Gandhi. He favoured the development of self-sufficient villages, with the use of machinery only in its proper place. Specially concerning textiles, he wrote, "I think that machinery is not necessary for us at all. We should use khadi [home-spun cloth]; and, therefore, we do not require mills. We should try to produce all the necessary cloth in the villages, and we need not be the slaves of machines. I am afraid, by working with machines we have become machines ourselves, having lost all sense of art of handwork." Quoted from *Mahatma*, vol. 4, pp. 238-39, by D.P. Mukerji, "Mahatma Gandhi's Views on Machines and Technology," *International Social Science Bulletin*, UNESCO, vol. VI, no. 3 (1954), pp. 418-19.

52 *First Five Year Plan*, 1952, Paragraph 60. These principles were earlier developed by a conference of labour and management representatives convened by the government in Delhi in February 1951. This became known as the "Delhi Agreement" and was a pattern for subsequent regional agreements, as in Ahmedabad. Industrial tribunals earlier established standards for retrenchment and compensation of workers affected by rationalization. See "Retrenchment," *Indian Labour Gazette*, vol. VIII, no. 3, September 1950, pp. 165-79.

53 *Second Five Year Plan: A Draft Outline*, Planning Commission, Government of India (February 1956), p. 43. In June 1956, the government sanctioned the installation of 14,600 automatic looms for production of cloth for export and 2.1 million spindles in an integrated programme for the expansion of the textile industry. According to T.T. Krishnamachari, then Indian Minister for Commerce and

Industry, the new installations were likely to be spread over a period of years and would not offset the "employment position" of weavers. *Times of India,* 19 June 1956. However, the emphasis on protection of the handloom sector is even evident in this permission for the importation of automatic looms. To assure that exports will be increased, and to protect village handloom interests, restrictions have been imposed on the use of the new automatic looms: each loom must produce a minimum of 2,400 square yards per year, and all production from the new looms is to be earmarked for export. If a mill fails either to meet its production quota or export its total output on these looms, a sizable penalty tax is to be imposed. *Times of India,* 24 June 1956, p. 3.

54 For a fuller discussion, see Charles A. Myers, "The Labour Problems of Rationalization: The Experience of India," *International Labour Review,* vol. LXXIII, no. 5 (May 1956), pp. 431-50. Also reprinted in *Indian Worker* (Independence Number), vol. 4, nos. 43 and 44 (15 August 1956), pp. 44-8, 54.

55 A recent study of increasing capital-output ratios in Indian industry explains these, in part, as a consequence of other government labour policies: "The effect of government policy has been both to raise labour costs directly in terms of higher wage and amenity costs, and to greatly reduce 'the area of manageability' of labour. The latter factor, especially, which operates, for example, in such a manner as to make the reduction of labour force difficult encourages management to build new plants with a minimum labour force and to attempt to reduce the permanent labour force in older plants by natural attrition. Where an industry is expanding rapidly, it is possible to introduce more automatic machinery in the newer or expanded plants without reducing labour force; where an industry is expanding only slowly (as in cotton textiles), the problem of introduction of new machinery raises serious difficulties between management and labour." George Rosen, "Capital-Output Ratios in Indian Industry," *Indian Economic Journal,* vol. III, no. 10 (October 1956).

56 See Richard S. Roberts, Jr., *Economic Development, Human Skills and Technical Assistance, A Study of I.L.O. Technical Assistance in the Field of Management Development,* Librarie E. Droz, Geneve, 1962, esp. Chapter 7, pp. 111-37.

CHAPTER X

CONCLUSIONS AND IMPLICATIONS

OUR analysis of labour problems in the industrialization of India has now brought us back to our starting point. We began with a statement of the goals of economic development as outlined by the government in the Five Year Plans, examined the growth of industry and entrepreneurship in India, then analyzed the development and commitment of an industrial labour force, the growth and development of labour organizations, the managerial response to labour problems and the nature of labour-management relations at the plant level. Finally, in the last chapter we have considered in detail the crucial role of government in structuring labour-management relations. Thus, in the Indian context, government is of critical importance. What the state does or does not do is vital in the development of any society; but its special role in an industrially underdeveloped country like India needs particular emphasis.

In this final chapter, we shall first note the distinctive features which help to explain the direction and character of Indian labour problems. Next, we shall outline the tasks facing management and labour, indicating some of the implications of the policy-making role of government, and make some recommendations.

Distinctive Features in the Indian Setting

Not all the following points are unique to the Indian experience, but they are distinctive enough to be singled out for special mention. Parallels and contrasts with other countries in similar stages of economic development will occur to readers familiar with the process of economic development in relation to labour problems elsewhere.

The Indian people, through their government, desire rapid economic development, and the ideas which were shaped during the struggle for independence from a colonial power are still powerful. The goal is the elimination of poverty and unemployment, and the attainment of higher standards of living, without surrendering individual freedoms to an all-powerful state. The initiative for the present economic development effort is with the government, and the resources are largely internal.

Rapid population growth, as economic development initially reduces death rates, is a central fact facing economic planners in India. More employment, therefore, becomes a goal in itself in a nation already confronted with millions of unemployed and underemployed adult citizens whose plight challenges the political stability of government.

Although numerically and relatively small, the industrial labour force in India today is growing in importance with industrialization and has been the special concern of leaders of the Indian Congress party and of the government. Nehru once served as president of a labour federation. Congress party officials played a leading role in the formation of the Indian National Trade Union Congress, and three former leading trade union officials have been ministers in the Central Cabinet.

The heritage of almost 200 years of British rule, ending in 1947, was not only a strong and successful nationalist movement, but also (*a*) a trained Indian elite represented by the Indian Civil Service which provides a quality of government administration unique in industrially underdeveloped countries; (*b*) an educational system which helped to produce this elite and has left a common core of knowledge and a language of the elite (English) in a subcontinent of many linguistic, religious, and racial groups; (*c*) an English legal system which has helped to preserve individual rights; and (*d*) a managing agency system of business entrepreneurship and management. All of these institutions have been faced with the need to change as independent India attempts to mould its institutions to the needs of economic development and active political participation in a democracy.

The institution of the managing agency is a case in point. Although widely adopted by the growing and now dominant Indian business groups, which found that it was suited to the particular conditions of an immature industrial economy, the freedom of managing agents has been restricted by post-Independence legislation and the further extension of the management agencies has been circumscribed. The excesses of Indian business in the past account, in part, for the anti-business sentiment among intellectuals and government officials; colonial and traditional values, which discounted the contribution of enterprise and competent business management, are also responsible. However the pressures of economic and industrial development have emphasized the importance of management. Progressive leadership in business is aware of the need for higher standards of responsibility and competent professional management. India's "socialistic pattern of society" is also not a dogmatic or doctrinaire programme, and the private sector has an important and increasing role in national development plans.

Mahatma Gandhi's emphasis on the values of a self-sufficient village economy and his condemnation of the evils of industrialism and urbanism have had some influence in causing government to protect handicraft and village industries at the expense of modern industry; but the present government has clearly chosen industrialization as the road to reducing the poverty and unemployment of India's millions. The Gandhian way of life, like the joint family, the caste system, and the other-worldly, ascetic aspects of Hindu religion, is being modified by the pressures of industrial development. The cultural setting is not an inflexible barrier; it bends and even accommodates to the new logics. Even India's villages, where 83 per cent of the population still lives, are changing age-old patterns of life.[1]

A stable labour force is developing in the major urban areas, particularly in those centres where adequate housing and other facilities are made available by employers. Group solidarities at the workplace have also tended increasingly to take the place of traditional ties of village and of kinship. Nevertheless, these ties continue to be important; the level of workforce commitment is also low in particular areas; and finally such factors as high absenteeism rates and disorganized protest patterns prevail. These attributes imply partial commitment, which in turn hinder the development of a disciplined and well-organised trade union movement. Worker indiscipline and even outbursts of violence are still not unusual.

Another factor impeding the growth of responsible trade unionism, with emphasis on the "give-and-take" spirit of bargaining and an active role in plant-level labour relations, is the centralization of authority in organizations, including business organizations. Superior-subordinate relations in Indian industry, as well as in many other facets of Indian life, are often characterized by authoritarian order-giving and subservience to superiors. There is very little challenge of constituted authority from below and poor communication upward. These tendencies were, if anything, fortified by the colonialist traditions of government. The lack of delegation of decision-making authority appears also to be a problem in the newly evolving public sector enterprises.

It was the struggle for national independence which gave initial direction and character to the Indian labour movement, which at first was simply an arm of the nationalist movement. Many of the "outsiders" who came to positions of trade union leadership were nationalist leaders. Perhaps some of the non-violent tactics of Indian unions and workers today are a carry-over from this period of nationalist agitation. The hunger-strike is peculiarly an Indian device.

The influence of Gandhi on the formation and direction of the Ahmedabad Textile Labour Association was very great, and this union, in turn, has influenced the formation and character of the Indian National Trade Union Congress. The acceptance of compulsory adjudication by the TLA and INTUC grows out of the Gandhian philosophy that, if two parties cannot agree, an impartial third party should decide what is right and just, rather than deciding the issue by a test of strength. This philosophy happens also to fit the needs of a central government seeking to prevent industrial disputes from impeding economic development plans and goals.

Despite the TLA's leadership, its experience of stable and harmonious bipartite industrial relations is still an exception to the general Indian practice. Developing political pressures and aspirations since Independence have also dictated an increasing intervention by the government in the structuring of the labour-management relationship. The overriding importance of economic development objectives, the concern for left-wing and Communist capture of labour protest, and the shortcomings of managerial attitudes and policies towards utilization of labour have all combined to bring government into the control of labour-management relations to a degree unthinkable in most Western countries today.

Government has assumed the rule-making function often left to labour and management in the West, although there are some interesting and growing examples of direct collective bargaining without government intervention.

Government has also been under pressure in India to provide a measure of social and economic gains early in the industrialization process, and, therefore, to adopt many of the standards of the more advanced industrial countries. Continued mass political support in a democracy demands these concessions of the governing party, but the conflict between this objective and that of rapid economic development through capital formation at the expense of present consumption is evident. The Indian government thus has an exceedingly difficult choice of achieving a balance among competing objectives and the degree of control that is consistent with the functioning of autonomous units in the Indian industrial relations system. The increasing emphasis on the "moral" requirements of an industrial relations policy, the efforts to formulate national policy in consultation with organized labour and management, and the efforts to secure their cooperation in the implementation of these policies, are thus representative of efforts to resolve the industrial relations dilemma in Indian development.

Tasks Facing Management and Labour

In the following comments directed to management, we shall proceed on the assumption that employers in every industrial country have the primary opportunity and responsibility for developing a stable industrial labour force, utilizing human resources effectively, and structuring initially the nature of the labour-management relationship. Labour organizations have a similar opportunity; but, to the extent that the recruitment and direction of the labour force are the essence of the managerial responsibility, private or public, the initiative rests with management.

The approach of many managements in India in utilizing human resources and in dealing with labour problems is still characterized by authoritarianism and paternalism. Changes are occurring under the impact of an increasingly articulate labour movement and a government which supports (as governments in most democratic countries have) the aspirations of industrial labour. But general labour shortages, which have put the most effective pressures on managements in the other countries, will be long in coming to India, where underemployment and unemployment still persist in significant magnitudes.

There are important exceptions to this prevailing pattern of management ideology and approaches in utilizing labour. In almost every industrial region in India, firms can be found which have in common a top management that believes in the importance of building an effective managerial organization and in developing workable relationships with employees and trade union representatives. Among these exceptions are a number of foreign firms whose leadership in these respects deserves to be noted and to be emulated when appropriate. The significant thing is that Indian managements have also demonstrated the advantages to be gained from building an effective managerial organization to utilize human resources at all levels. This approach is badly needed in private and public enterprise management as Indian industrialization proceeds, and failure of management to keep pace in this respect will impede industrial development.

One of the most important steps in building an effective managerial organization in Indian enterprises is to provide greater opportunities for middle management to participate in important managerial decisions and have access to higher managerial positions. Too many enterprises are highly centralized, with even minor decisions made by the managing agents or by highly placed officials. If these top managers would delegate more responsibility to junior executives, they would find this an effective method of management training and development. A policy providing for greater opportunities for advancement would blunt trade union demands, prevalent even among managerial ranks, based only on seniority and add to the supply of experienced talent for higher positions.

Nepotism in promotions to higher managerial positions is all too frequent. It may be argued that this is relatively "costless" in an industrially underdeveloped economy, where managerial skills are scarce and sons and relatives of the wealthy get most of the advanced training. But this overlooks the loss of managerial talent which may have developed under other conditions among those with comparable educational training, who do not happen to be related to the top managers or members of their caste or business community. Recognition of the value of professionally trained management (regardless of family and other connections) is growing, but not fast enough.

The role of foreign firms deserves special mention. National pride and aspirations put pressures on foreign firms in India for rapid "Indianization" of their staffs, including managerial staff. Foreign firms (as well as the larger Indian firms) are also under special pressure to adopt more generous personnel policies. These firms undoubtedly have a special responsibility, for they are often among the few major and indispensable sources of the supply of management talent. The success with which several of the forward-looking firms have expanded their operations with increasing employment of Indians at higher management levels would suggest that they were perhaps too cautious in the past. Foreign firms need constantly to increase the opportunities for Indians to take managerial responsibilities and to innovate in personnel and industrial relations practices, beyond the requirements suggested by government. Apart from the obvious investment in goodwill, such policies command increasing merit as it becomes difficult to recruit qualified personnel from abroad and as the supply of trained talent from within India increases.

At this point, note should be made of the many new programmes in management as well as the extension or modification of existing university programmes in commerce or labour and welfare to suit the requirements of industry. The new Institutes of Management in Ahmedabad and Calcutta deserve special mention for training graduates whose services are obviously in high demand. These programmes deserve greater top management interest and support and, indeed, more managements show evidence of doing so in their recruitment, training, and promotion policies. Successful managers have also displayed a willingness to share their experience with younger managers by serving as conference and discussion leaders and otherwise by encouraging a growth of management consciousness. In-plant supervisory training schemes, such as the training-within-industry programmes, have also been widely adopted. Unfortunately, rigid or inflexible top management approaches continue in many cases to limit the extent to which formal training can be successfully applied in industry or new managers developed. The anticipated future needs for managers require a considerable modification in these traditions.

The increasing importance attached to management is evident in the growth of professional management associations in the principal industrial centres. These also merit greater support from the leaders of Indian industry. Junior managerial officials may benefit greatly from the exchange of experiences with their associates in other companies, or from the more formal training programmes initiated by local associations; but they need to be encouraged and supported in these efforts by company managing directors and managing agents.

Indian employers are required by law as well as by the necessity of developing a stable, committed industrial labour force to undertake welfare activities. Many Indian and foreign employers are justly proud of the housing, child-care centres, employee canteens and stores which they provide for their workers, but these employers are probably in the minority. Conscious employer efforts to enlist worker participation in the administration of welfare activities, through works committees or union representatives, may also be helpful in tempering any eventual worker resentment of paternalism. Also, much more needs to be done to provide the "social overhead" of housing and other urban amenities which are needed as villagers come to the cities for industrial employment. Employers can do a good deal more than they have done, particularly by greater initiative in using public funds committed for this purpose, assistance to workers interested in house ownership, cooperation with workers' cooperative societies, and so on.

But the commitment of an industrial labour force requires more than providing material benefits. It means building an employer-employee relationship in which employees find that work helps them achieve some of their aspirations as individual human beings. The work environment which offers these opportunities includes many of the ingredients of a modern personnel administration programme. These may not wholly apply to an industrially underdeveloped country, but the successful experience of a number of foreign companies in India with personnel approaches and policies similar to those used in more advanced industrial countries suggests that the amount of transferability is substantial. The supervisor-employee relationship is crucial here. People at work tend to respond to fair, consistent treatment in the same way in most industrial societies, and Indian workers are no exception, despite all the differences in culture and social structure. Employers in India who justify authoritarian and inadequate personnel policies on the grounds that "Indian workers are different" fly in the face of contrary experience elsewhere in the country. Research studies which emphasize the importance of the "employee-centred" supervisor in Indian industry should not be ignored by Indian employers.

The appointment of a Labour Officer, or the Labour Welfare Officer, required by law, is no substitute for developing the ability of the line management to deal with employer-employee relations. Furthermore, the status of the Labour Officer needs clarification in Indian industry. The legal requirement tends to put him in an anomalous position—a sort of third force between management and labour, often trusted by neither. Some firms have appointed Personnel or Labour Officers, comparable with those in Western industrial nations, who advise and assist the line management in handling labour problems but do not attempt to relieve them of the entire responsibility for getting results through people. When managements treat Labour Officers solely as agents for administering discipline, handling grievances and performing other "unpleasant tasks," they have failed to understand their own responsibilities as managers.

While Indian labour is still plentiful in numbers, it is not always cheap. Indiscipline and poor performance, partly the consequence of inadequate managerial policies and legal requirements which limit managerial flexibility.in utilizing labour, make labour costs higher than hourly or monthly wage comparisons with other countries would indicate. Labour market tightness is also evident for several categories of labour as Indian industrial development proceeds rapidly along more diversified lines. This is a growing economic pressure on management to utilize labour more effectively as is the growing strength of organised labour. Furthermore, management policies which may have been politically adequate in the nineteenth century are explosive in the mid-twentieth. Industrial labour is now more articulate, has powerful political friends competing for its allegiance, and is ready to protest short-sighted and selfish managerial practices.

Management in India, nevertheless, is faced with more difficulties in utilizing labour and dealing with labour organizations than is management in most Western industrial nations. In addition to the problems posed by a partially stabilized industrial labour force, and the legal requirements imposed by the state, management is confronted with rival unions claiming to represent various groups of employees in a particular firm or industry. Some managements have developed direct negotiations with a works committee, or with a union confined to the particular plant and headed by the firm's employees. Their approach is designed to nurture and strengthen this type of labour-management relationship. Even in some firms with rival unions, managements have succeeded in establishing workable collective bargaining relationships by insisting on dealing with the most representative union and then negotiating a labour agreement directly. This small but growing number of examples deserves careful study and more experimentation by Indian employers—at least if they seek an alternative to state intervention and regulation of labour-management relations.

In addition to the Textile Labour Association in Ahmedabad, a remarkable union which has responsible relationships with an employers' association, there are a number of strong, effective regional and plant-wide unions. In each case, attention is given to effective processing of workers' grievances and to various union welfare activities which help to build membership loyalty to the union and real union strength. Many of these unions are found in companies where the management consciously attempts to develop good labour-management relations, and their experience deserves greater study and emulation by other unions.

The majority of Indian unions, however, are relatively weak in terms of a stable, dues-paying membership, and are confronted with rival unions whose leaders may promise greater gains to workers in the attempt to draw them away from another union. The tendency of Indian workers to switch union affiliations is notorious, but with one or two exceptions union leaders do not see the advantages to stable unionism of arriving at jurisdictional agreements or of a system of dues check-off, maintenance of membership or union shop clauses.

Trade unions in India suffer from the lack of capable "insiders" in the movement, that is, men and women who have worked in the firm or industry, know its problems and understand the workers in it. Until these develop—and this will take considerable time—"outsiders" will clearly be necessary to give leadership direction and support. Employer policies in both the private and public sectors also tend to strengthen reliance on outsiders. Responsible trade union leadership as at the TLA in Ahmedabad attempts to offset these tendencies by enabling insiders to acquire trade union experience in a climate of labour-management harmony. A number of trade unions have also availed of the facilities provided by the government workers' education programme and some have taken the initiative to develop their own. These tendencies deserve encouragement, although much will depend on how employers adapt their policies to the requirement of stable industrial relations.

The dominant Indian labour federation (INTUC) is confronted with the dilemma of being so closely identified with the Congress party and with Indian economic planning goals that it may lose membership support to rival federations which are often critical of the present government. INTUC unions need to pay increasing attention to problems of workers at the plant level, as the Textile Labour Association in Ahmedabad has done, rather than to depend on compulsory adjudication and labour legislation for the satisfaction of workers' needs. Possibly the existence of rival labour federations, which complicate the employers' problems in dealing with unions, serves to keep the INTUC more independent and critical of government than it otherwise would be.[2]

This dilemma, however, illustrates the role which a labour movement plays in an industrially underdeveloped country seeking to achieve fairly rapid industrialization. When economic development proceeded more slowly under private enterprise initiative, as in many Western countries during the nineteenth and early twentieth centuries, the labour movement developed as a response to industrialization and as a protest movement with varying degrees of freedom to use direct economic action to achieve its goals. But, when government is forced to take more of the initiative for economic development in underdeveloped countries today, the labour movement tends to be regarded (by government officials and by some trade union leaders) as an instrument of economic development in the interests of the whole nation, rather than as a class group. The danger here, of course, is that the labour movement may become a "labour front," as in totalitarian countries. So long as India remains dedicated to economic development by democratic means, such an outcome is unlikely in India. However, India faces a graver danger that the government, committed to economic development, and autonomous units, pursuing their own goals, may work at cross purposes and fail to develop an industrial relations system appropriate to Indian conditions. It is in this light that one should view with favour the increasing emphasis on developing national labour relations policies by voluntary and tripartite means embracing all affected parties. One of the major purposes of such procedures is to provide a forum for the resolution of worker pressures and aspirations.

A desire for a more democratic system of plant-level authority underlies much worker protest which crystallized in the demand for "worker participation in management." Apart from workplace frustrations, such a demand also grew out of a belief that it will lead towards the goal of a "socialist pattern of society." If "participation in management" means joint sharing of decision-making at all levels, the consequences of such a system on effective management have not been understood, and clearly Indian union leaders and workers will not be prepared for this type of responsibility for a long time. Furthermore, even in advanced industrial countries in the West, this type of joint responsibility has not developed, apart from nationalized industries—and possibly those affected by codetermination—and nationalization is even losing its attraction as a goal.[3] But if "participation" means greater consultation between management and labour, then unions and workers will clearly benefit, as well as management. The importance of adequate preparation for joint consultation of this type cannot be overstressed: unions need to develop training programmes for members of these committees, as unions in Sweden, for example, have done so effectively. "Worker participation in management" in this sense is not achieved by directive or by legislation. If Indian unions and workers believe that it is, disillusionment is inevitable. And if management wishes to avoid the consequences of legislation and this disillusionment, it should take the initiative in demonstrating that joint consultation is possible.

Trade unions in India, as in most industrial countries, continue to press for a "fair wage" or a "living wage," and oppose the introduction of labour-saving machinery where this will immediately add to the existing unemployment. In achieving these objectives, however, the unions rely heavily upon government, for direct collective bargaining with employers on these matters is still fairly infrequent. This is another indication of the importance of the role of government in structuring labour-management relations in India.

The Role of Government: Some Policy Implications

Before World War II and Independence in 1947, government was primarily a passive regulator of labour-management relations. To be sure, important labour legislation was passed under British rule, and two government investigating commissions suggested needed changes. But, for the most part, the labour problems of industrialization had not become so acute that direct intervention was considered necessary on the scale that subsequently developed.

The emergency resulting from World War II and Independence brought government directly into the settlement of labour disputes and the necessity of structuring of labour-management relations. The post-war wave of strikes and the overriding goals of the First Five Year Plan forced the new government of India to seek an "Industrial Truce Resolution" and to implement this with compulsory adjudication through the Industrial Disputes Act of 1947. Several states, notably Bombay, increased the intervention of government at the state level. Other national laws provided for the establishment of "standing orders" (terms of employment approved by government), appointment of labour welfare officers, regulation of other conditions of employment, provision of medical and sickness benefits, and old-age pensions. The labour sections of the several Plans have spelled out government's concern with labour and labour problems *in the context of* economic planning and development.

Compulsory adjudication remains the corner-stone of labour dispute settlement in India, and is likely to continue for the near future, at least. During 1952–53, under Labour Minister Giri, an attempt was made to reduce and limit its applicability so that stronger, independent unions and collective bargaining would be encouraged. This attempt failed because it was opposed by important elements in the Central and state governments which wanted to retain some measure of control over labour relations, by most of the labour federations, and by some employers and employer groups. Compulsory adjudication remains a "way out" of serious labour strife for the latter two groups, in the face of rival unionism, including Communist unions. For government, it provides a measure of control consistent with overall objectives and with the belief that it is better to let an impartial third party decide what is right, if two parties cannot agree, than to permit them to fight it out.

Compulsory adjudication will continue to be unavoidable in India for some time to come. The alternative in many cases will be near chaos, for neither managements nor unions have yet developed the ability to reconcile and bargain out conflicting claims. Even in advanced industrial countries, with a tradition of collective bargaining, collective bargaining is not completely free, nor are "private" labour-management relations and contracts without substantial "external" consequences. In India, the immaturity of labour and management, and the overriding importance of development goals further circumscribe the freedom of the parties immediately involved in industrial relations.

It ought to be realized, however, that, once a country adopts compulsory adjudication, it is not easy to reverse the pattern and move to freer collective bargaining. Compulsory adjudication also commands the time of much scarce talent in government and has the further danger of aggravating the political tension surrounding labour disputes. It is thus necessary to work towards a progressive relaxation of government control. This involves encouragement to labour and management to settle their differences directly as well as a more realistic assessment of when government's actions hinder desired long-term developments. Government's efforts may also be more fruitfully directed towards the development of workable national consensus on important issues in industrial relations rather than to settle every difference or dispute between labour and management. As noted earlier, public policy has moved increasingly in this direction. There are still several shortcomings in practice which will need further attention.

There is a tendency in some Indian states to refer disputes too readily to adjudication, without carefully examining whether there has been a genuine effort to reach agreement. The conciliation process in many cases appears to be a "rubber stamp" for reference to adjudication. A common complaint of management, and to a lesser extent of union officials, is that conciliators are frequently inexperienced and inept. Much can be done to improve the quality of conciliators or of conciliation, by better selection, training, and conference programmes. There is room for more agreements between management and unions in India, and these could be encouraged by less ready reference to adjudication and by better conciliation. While the availability of compulsory adjudication does, of course, tend to discourage direct settlements, there is a growing number of managements and unions which prefer to settle their own differences in order to avoid the delays in the adjudication process. Where managements and unions want to bargain directly, there is still plenty of incentive to do so in order to avoid the litigious atmosphere of the tribunals.

In order to reduce further the load on the tribunals and to avoid delays, the parties might be more positively encouraged to use private voluntary arbitration, along the pattern adopted in Ahmedabad. There is, however, very little private voluntary arbitration of unsettled grievances, as there is in the United States, and the lower tribunals and state labour ministries will probably continue to handle these rather than refer them to private arbitrators.

Wage disputes, including those involving annual "bonuses," continue to be the most important single cause of work stoppages in India. The compulsory adjudication system has developed a formula for determining the amount of bonus, related to company profits, and, more recently, the Bonus Commission's recommendations, as modified by the government, provide the general formula which will be employed. These indicate that "social justice" to workers has been tempered with the realities of the economic condition of the firm or industry. Furthermore, the wage boards for setting minimum wages in particular industries are in line with the conflicting objectives of helping workers achieve a "living wage," not so fast that economic development is impeded, but fast enough so that the political allegiance of the growing industrial labour force is retained.

Except possibly in a few states, there are no adequate procedures for determining which union is "representative" or, in the American sense, which union is to be designated as the "exclusive bargaining agent" for employees in a particular unit. Rival unionism seems to perpetuate this condition, rather than to compel action to meet it. The secret ballot for selection of the bargaining representative is opposed by those in government and in unions who fear that easily misled Indian workers would vote for Communist-led unions which promise much and are often also more militant. The alternative is a membership list check, and yet this is open to charges of abuse, especially by non-INTUC unions. If government wants to provide the conditions under which collective bargaining can develop effectively, it must resolve the indecision with which it is now confronted and develop some India-wide method of determining the most representative union with which employers are expected to bargain. If, on the other hand, government prefers to perpetuate its present measure of control over the labour movement, perhaps rival and fragmented unionism is congenial to this objective. From another point of view, rival unionism, as we noted earlier, is not an unmixed evil, for it may keep a measure of freedom and vigour in the labour movement that would not otherwise exist. One united labour federation would be either more independent or less independent of government, and in either case would spell major political changes.

Government structuring of labour-management relations in India has not extended to specific protections of the right to organize and bargain collectively, as in the Wagner and Taft-Hartley Acts in the United States. The 1947 Amendment to the Trade Union Act of 1926 contained provisions almost identical with the "unfair labour practices" sections of the Wagner Act, but these were not implemented for reasons never made explicit. Section 33 of the Industrial Disputes Act, even with the 1956 amendments which give employers deserved freedom in disciplinary cases not connected with a pending dispute, does provide some protection to trade union leaders against "victimization" (discrimination for union activity). Other legislation restricts the number of "outsiders" on union executive committees. But, for the most part, it is difficult to conclude that a strong, independent trade union movement is among the top priorities in government's present labour policy.

The present role of government is further illustrated in the experience with labour protest over rationalization and labour's demand for greater "worker participation in management." In both cases, the Central government has stepped in to moderate and contain the course of events. Installation of new automatic machinery, particularly automatic looms, in the cotton textile industry was prohibited in the face of labour protests, and was relaxed only when it was apparent that the survival of export markets (an economic development objective) required some plant modernization (and sacrifice of the employment objective). Protection of the handloom industry was similarly motivated by the objective of providing increased employment and was also a factor in the initial decision to slow down mill rationalization. Disillusion with works committees required by law led to government sponsorship of "worker participation in management" under its overall guidance.

As the importance of the public sector in the economy grows, government's obligation as "model employer" becomes even more apparent than it has been in the past. While there are notable exceptions, government enterprises are not regarded widely by trade union officials as more enlightened in their labour-management relationships than the leading private employers. Government needs to give more specific attention to management training and development for public enterprises, better personnel policies, and more workable relationships with trade unions and works committees. If government is serious about promoting "worker participation in management," it might well begin with its own enterprises and establishments. Further, if compulsory adjudication is likely to face severe strains when any and every dispute is referred to adjudication, there is no less serious a danger when government fails to act quickly and amicably in disputes with its own employees. Progress in these respects is contingent on decentralized and effective management of the individual enterprises and the development of bipartite machinery to resolve pending disputes. The larger national enterprises like railways may consider in addition some form of arbitration, and an improved overall coordination of policy among the ministries concerned, including finance and possibly the entire cabinet, with a view to defining the budgetary limits within which wage claims may be settled.

The need for better management training programmes and for the development of professional management associations was recognized early by the Central government. As a result, India has now made an impressive, although by no means adequate, beginning in the field of postgraduate management education. Vigorous local management associations developed without government support, and the interest and initiative among private and public enterprise managements in a number of industrial centres have aided the development greatly. By way of contrast, however, the trade union education programmes are likely to be significantly dependent on government direction as there appears to be no corresponding enthusiasm and initiative among the leading trade unionists. In both cases, the government can serve best as a catalyst, without imposing rigid restrictions on the experimentation which must necessarily take place in the various centres of instruction. The universities, too, can do much by revamping their curriculum and by encouraging a more creative approach among their faculty and students to the study of labour and management problems in India.

The government's role is and will continue to be crucial, as innovator or catalyst in the entire field of management and industrial relations education. Nowhere is this more apparent than in its assumption of responsibility to secure skills and technical assistance from abroad. The government will have thus continuing problems of better utilization of technical assistance made available by other countries on a bilateral basis and by international agencies. These problems require in turn a more careful and continuing assessment of India's manpower needs and determination of methods of meeting them. A beginning was made in 1956 with the establishment of a Manpower Committee of the Cabinet, to be chaired by the Prime Minister, a Manpower Committee of Secretaries to assist the Cabinet Committee, and a Directorate of Manpower Coordination in the Ministry of Home Affairs. Since then, a more inclusive approach to manpower planning has developed, and more recently a National Council of Manpower Research has been established. All these are highly desirable steps as they give promise of better integration of technical assistance programmes with the government's own activities in the manpower field as broadly defined. Not only are trained technical personnel in short supply in India, but the need for administrative, managerial and supervisory skills in private and public industry is great. There are encouraging signs that government, as well as private industry, is increasingly aware of the overriding priority that should be given to meeting these high-level manpower needs.

NOTES

1 An example of striking and rapid changes is provided by V. Nath, "The New Village-III," *Economic Weekly*, 1 May 1965.

2 For a similar interpretation, see Oscar A. Ornati in "Current Issues in International Labour Relations: Problems of Indian Trade Unionism," *The Annals of American Academy of Political and Social Science*, vol. 310, March 1957, p. 161.

3 See George B. Baldwin, "Nationalization in Britain: A Sobering Decade," *The Annals*, pp. 39-54; *Beyond Nationalization* (Cambridge, Mass., 1955).

INDEX

ABSENTEEISM,
factors encouraging to, 106, 107, 122, 124, 125, 129n, 130n
in industries, 104–7
Abul Kalam Azad, Maulana, 67, 72
Acharya, H.G., 381n
Adjudication,
its abandonment, 371
wage disputes under, 349–57
Administrative Staff College (Hyderabad),
formation, 240, 241, 246, 340, 377, 378
Advanced Management Programme (Kashmir), 246
Advisory Committee, Central, 278, 279
Agarwala, A.N., 161n, 309n, 342n
Agreements,
collective bargaining of labour, 266, 299–302n
on labour-management relations, 265–9
Agricultural Labour Enquiry (Second), 28, 88, 89, 126n–128n
Ahmedabad,
agreement with labour, 197
Delhi Agreement, 189, 190
Electricity, joint stock co., 52
industrial dispute (1918), 137, 138
labour unions, 137, 138
Institute of Management, 394
Millowners' Association, 189, 262
relations with labour, 218
productivity of labour, survey, 115
Textile Industrial Research Association, 189, 218, 231, 241, 248n, 340n, 378
Textile Labour Association, 137, 145, 167, 168
and AITUC, 138

annual report (1953-54), 296n
and Bombay Industrial Relations Act, 248n
on bonus issue, 352, 353
on compulsory adjudication, 391, 398
formation with the assistance of Gandhi, 218, 391
Gandhi Labour Memorial Trust, fund for, 205
on 'grievance procedure,' 276, 281, 282
and INTUC, 151
on labour-management relations, 262
on leadership of trade unions, 369
and Millowners' Association Agreement (1955), 247n
as model of trade unions, 159n, 172, 173, 199
on public ownership of industry, 193
social justice in, 207n
AICC, see All-India Congress Committee
Air India International, 63
AIRMF, see All-India Railwaymen's Federation
Alfred, Theodore M., 247n
All-India Conference of Labour and Welfare Officers (1955), 291n, 328
All-India Congress Committee, 159n
Avadi session, on ... 'economic policy resolution,' 66, 71, 82n, 84n
Congress handbook, 205n
Karachi session, on 'fundamental rights,' 306
labour and capital, resolution on, 306
its official organ *Economic Review*, 81n

Potewalean 214, 215, 167